The three laws of robotics set forth by Issac Asimov, my inspiration, in his fiction books.

*A **robot** may not injure a human being or, through inaction, allow a human being to come to harm. A **robot** must obey orders given to it by human beings except where such orders would conflict with the First **Law**. A **robot** must protect its own existence as long as such protection does not conflict with the First or Second **Law**.*

—ISSAC ASIMOV

CONTENTS

Cover designed by Advait Marathe

Advait Marathe
Visit my website at www.AdvaitMarathe.com

Printed in the United States of America

First Printing: Aug 2018

ISBN-978-1-7327998-1-3

Library of Congress Control Number: 2018959456

ABOUT THIS BOOK

My name is Advait Marathe and I am a high school student at Mission San Jose High School. Robotics has been my greatest passion since seventh grade, but I am also passionate about karate, computer science, and educational community service. I have participated and won countless FIRST® LEGO® League (FLL®) and FIRST® Tech Challenge (FTC®) tournaments and I wanted to share the experience I have gained to help all of you excel in your competition. A little more about me, I have created robotics curriculum for classes all around the San Francisco Bay Area. I have coached over 100 students and have had over 3 years of experience in teaching robotics to K-8 students. Many of my students have went on to form teams, have won competitions, and have even developed a passion for robotics.

This book is unique in the fact that it is the only book that shows you exactly how to build competition robots from scratch with design recommendations from winning teams. There are comprehensive instruction manuals included to help you create modular robots (Basebot and attachments). In addition to excellent design tips this book helps you learn how to create your own advanced programs using Myblocks and algorithms. Thirdly, this book is a holistic guide to all three aspects of the FLL Competition (Robot Game, Project, and Core Values). Finally, the last portion of the book provides a brief introduction to the FTC competition. **Have Fun Building and Programming Robots for FLL and FTC** covers everything from building your first robot to everything you may encounter on competition day.

Robot Game:

You will learn about how to build and program winning robots through sturdy robot design and advanced programming. This book provides the instructions and concepts needed to build two sophisticated robots that are tournament ready. In addition, you will also learn about how to create your own program blocks, use sensors to their fullest capabilities, and create attachments to accomplish multiple missions. Finally, you will learn winning game strategy and how to create your own strategy based on points, difficulty, and variability.

Project:

You will learn how to effectively come up with a project solution, present to Judges, and share your solution with others. This book also includes helpful tips and a list of practice questions that Judges might ask for the competition

Core Values:

You will learn about team bonding exercises that help strengthen teams, and how judges look for Core Values. This book also provides helpful tips and practice questions that Judges might ask for the Core Value sessions.

The idea for this book was born during a community outreach session in the summer of 2016. I found that I was only limited to the Bay Area and wanted to find a way to help everyone everywhere. I have always loved helping others and providing others with resources to learn and knew that a book would be accessible to everyone around the world.

This book wouldn't be possible without the support of my friends and family. I would like to thank a few individuals that have supported and motivated me in creating this book. First, I would like to thank my family. Thank you, Mom, Dad, Aba (Grandpa), and Shardul (my younger brother) for supporting my passion for robotics and helping me whenever I needed help. Without your help and support this book wouldn't have been possible. Next, I would like to thank all the mentors I have had: Professor Susan Fox, Santosh Neyyar, Eric Klementis, Prakalpa Bhide-Bastianapillai and Moksh Jawa who have guided and helped me with various aspects of the book. Thirdly, thank you to all the robotics teams that have come before me. Their insight and findings have helped shape my knowledge on robotics and robotics competitions.

Finally, thank you to all my FLL and FTC teams who have been through thick and thin with me. The experiences I have gained from my teammates and competitions have been invaluable and will always be a part of my life.

BUILD AND PROGRAM WINNING ROBOTS FOR FLL

Using LEGO EV3

LOOK THE ROBOT IS WALKING

Motion

Robotics is the study of robots. Robots are machines that can be used to do jobs. Some robots can do work by themselves. Other robots must always have a person telling them what to do.

—NASA

I Was holding my first robot, realizing that it was so much better than any toy I had had before. This EV3 Robot turned out to be the one toy that I could do anything with: move it just like an RC Car, make it speak, and much more. Most importantly though was the fact that I could break it apart into pieces and rebuild it into something completely new. When I first got the robot kit, I quickly followed the instructions and built the various models that came in the LEGO EV3 set but soon realized that wasn't enough. I wanted to be tested, I wanted to learn even more about the subject. When I was younger I always used to play any game, I could get my hands on and loved competing with my friends. So, when one of our family friends told me about this great competition in Robotics – FLL® I wanted to join it as soon as possible. That started my journey into learning robotics, resolving community issues, and working as a team.

I hope this book will help you get started with your own robotics journey. In this chapter I will cover **what to buy to get started, how to set up the programming software, and how to build our first robot.**

WHAT TO BUY? (IDEAL)

Note: If you already own an EV3 set and if it is not the core set mentioned below, you should check the 'What to buy? (Minimum)' section.

If you are entering a robotics competition you should ideally buy the "LEGO MINDSTORMS Education EV3 Core Set" (or equivalent) - Part – 5003400 or 45544 and the "LEGO MINDSTORMS Education EV3

Expansion Set" (or equivalent) – Part – 45560. **LEGO allows you to buy these sets for a slightly discounted price as part of the FLL team registration process**

LEGO core Set - Part – 5003400 or 45544 as shown in next picture.

45544

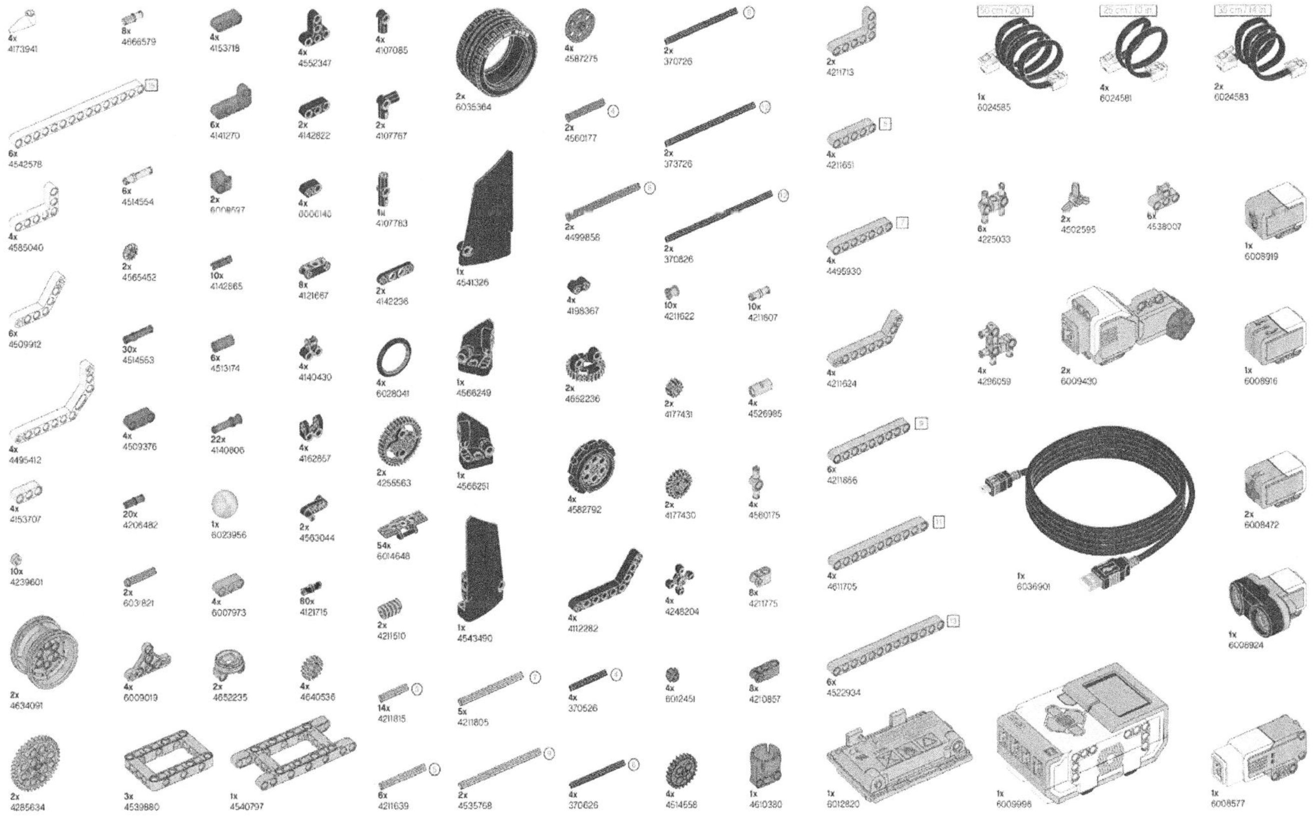

LEGO Expansion Set- Part – 45560 – as shown in the next pictures.

45560

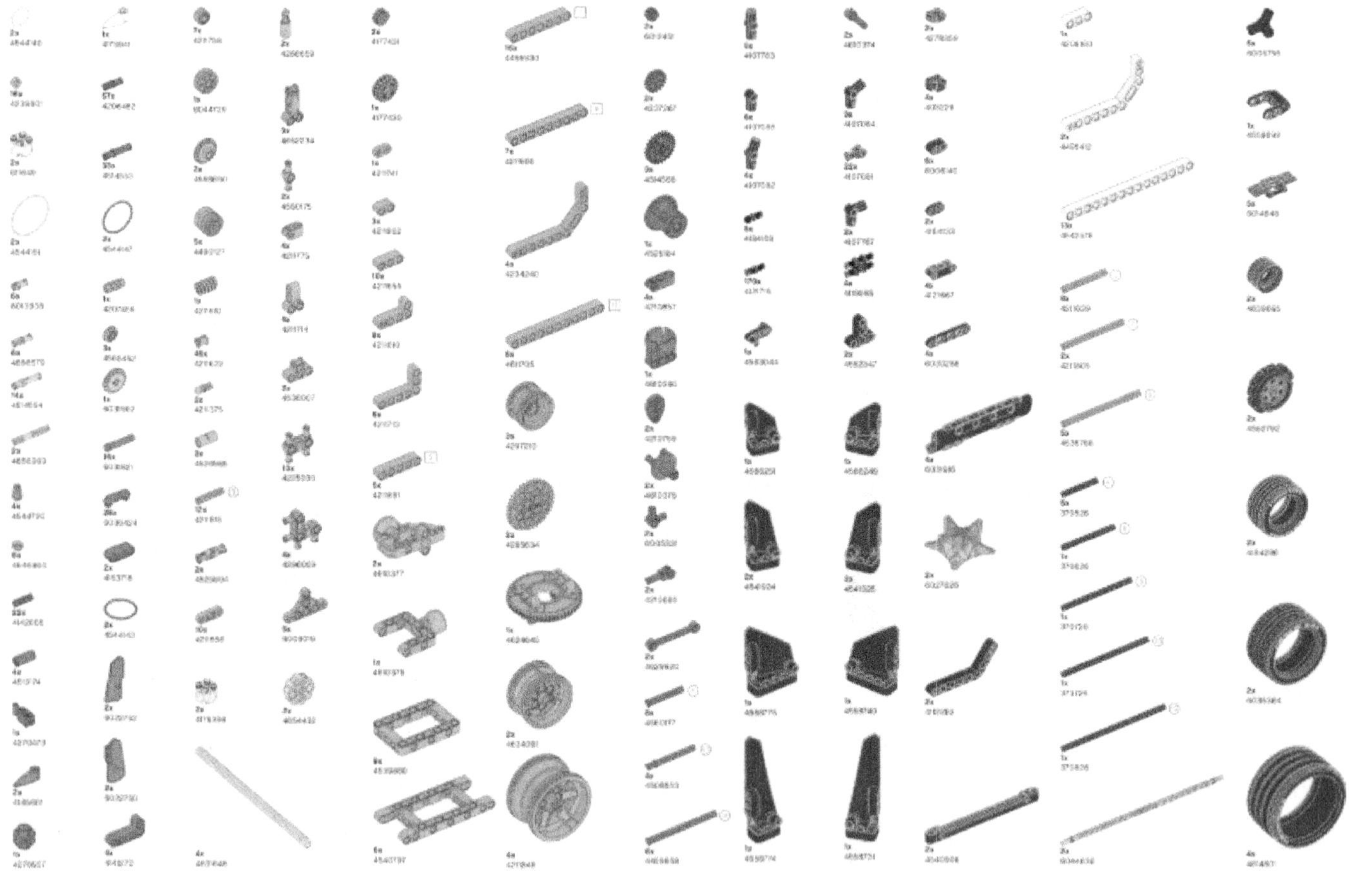

In addition, you should also buy **2 EV3 Large Servo Motors -Part – 45502.**
Many robotics competitions allow a maximum of 4 motors in the competition. The standard kit only comes with 2 large Servo Motors- so 1 or 2 additional Large Servo Motors are required for the competition. An alternative is to use the medium Servo motor in the Kit and only buy 1 additional large or medium Servo motor.

For the competition, you should also **buy 1 EV3 -Color Sensor-Part – 45506 in addition to the one obtained in the core set.**
Typically, 2 color sensors are required for the competition for accuracy and backup purposes.
You should try to buy these parts from the LEGO Education shop to get the latest versions of the robot hardware.

WHAT TO BUY? (MINIMUM)

If you have already bought the LEGO MINDSTORMS EV3 set – Part-31313 and are planning to participate in FLL then you should buy the "LEGO MINDSTORMS Education EV3 Expansion Set" (or equivalent) – Part – 45560(Shown previously in the book)

In addition, you should also buy
2 EV3 Large Servo Motors -Part – 45502.
1 EV3 -Color Sensor-Part – 45506.
1 Ultrasonic Sensor- Part- 6008924
1 Gyro Sensor -Part – 6008916
and any other parts that are in the core set but do not come in the LEGO MINDSTORMS EV3 set.

LEGO MINDSTORMS EV3 set – Part-31313– as shown in the next picture.

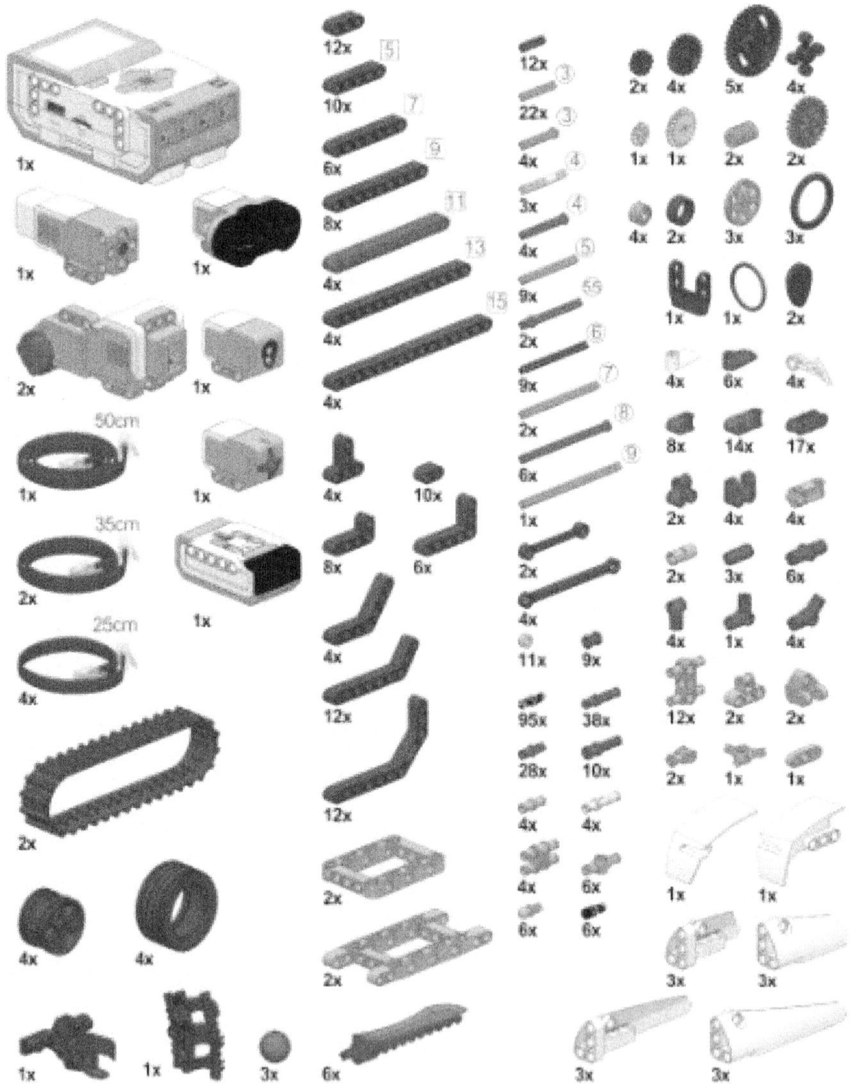

Once you have gotten the kit you need, open your LEGO MINDSTORMS set and install the LEGO MINDSTORMS EV3 Education software on your laptop. (Check 'EV3 Software' section in this chapter) Take help from parents, where required.

We will now be moving on to the structure of EV3 robots:
Ev3 Robots are made up of 3 main parts that are very similar to humans. First and most important is the **Brain** or the computational brick of the robot. The second is the arms and legs or **actuators** of the robot (example: Motors) – that move objects. The last one is the eyes and ears or **sensors** of the robot.

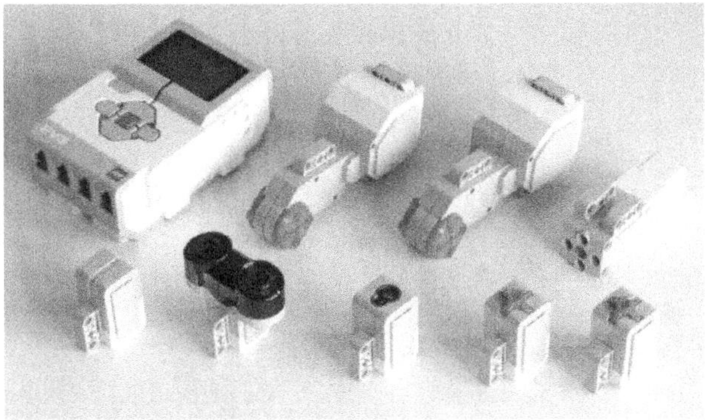

This picture shows the hardware that you will be using to build your competition Robot.

The Brick is the intelligence center and the power source of the Robot. It houses the batteries and holds all your programs.
You can see Brick display functions in the next picture.

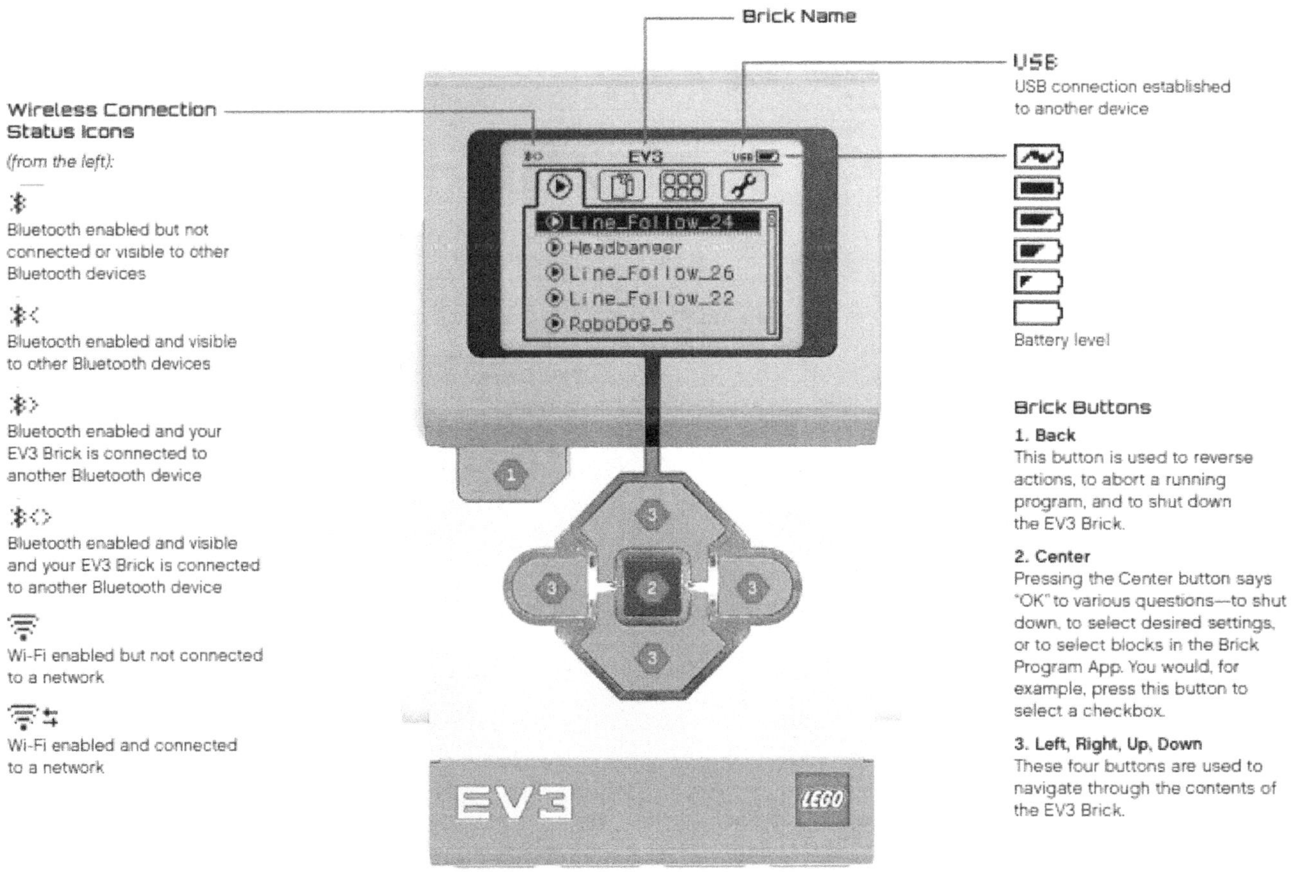

You can see Brick ports in the next picture.

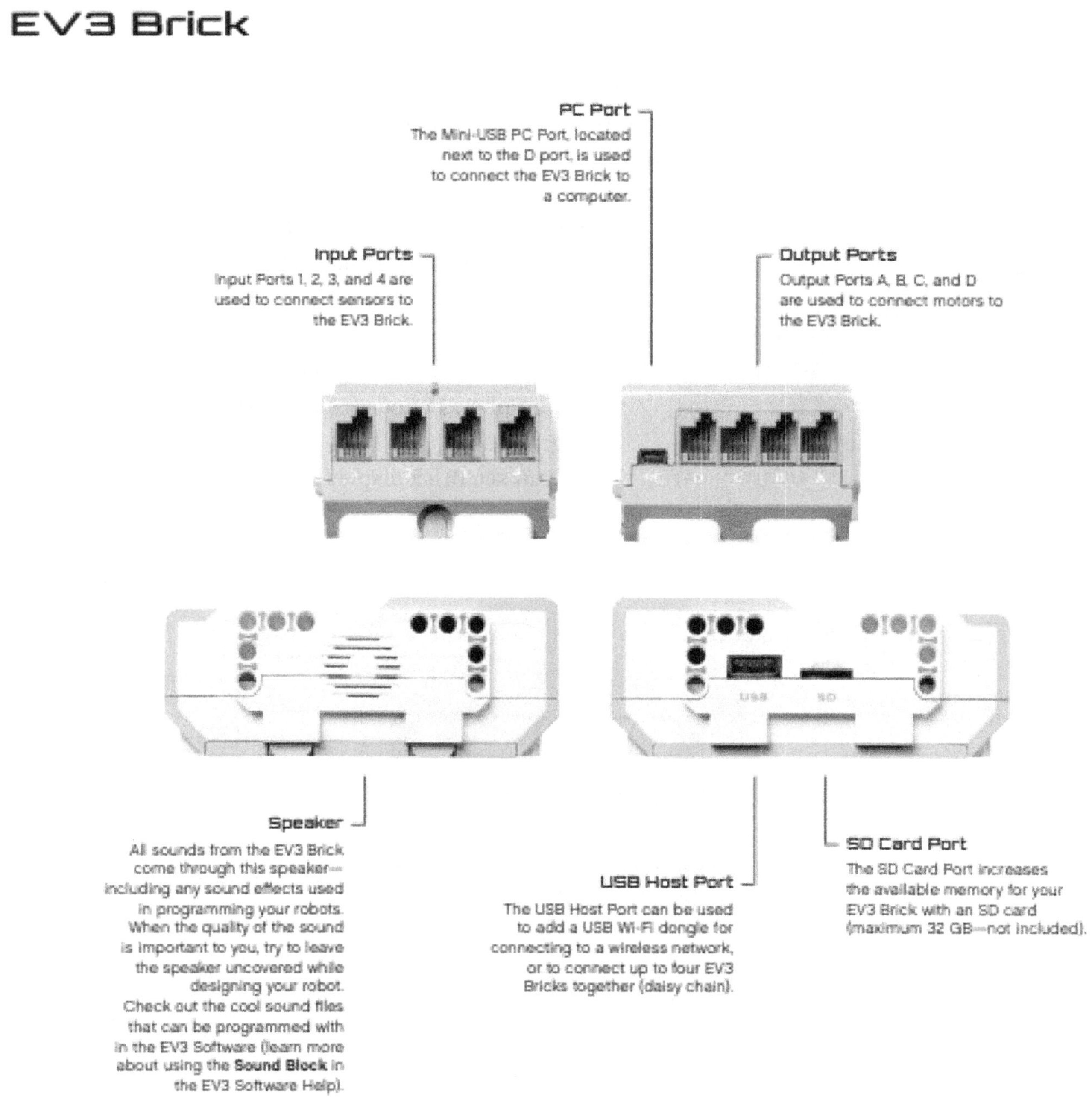

The next picture shows all the essential components connected together.

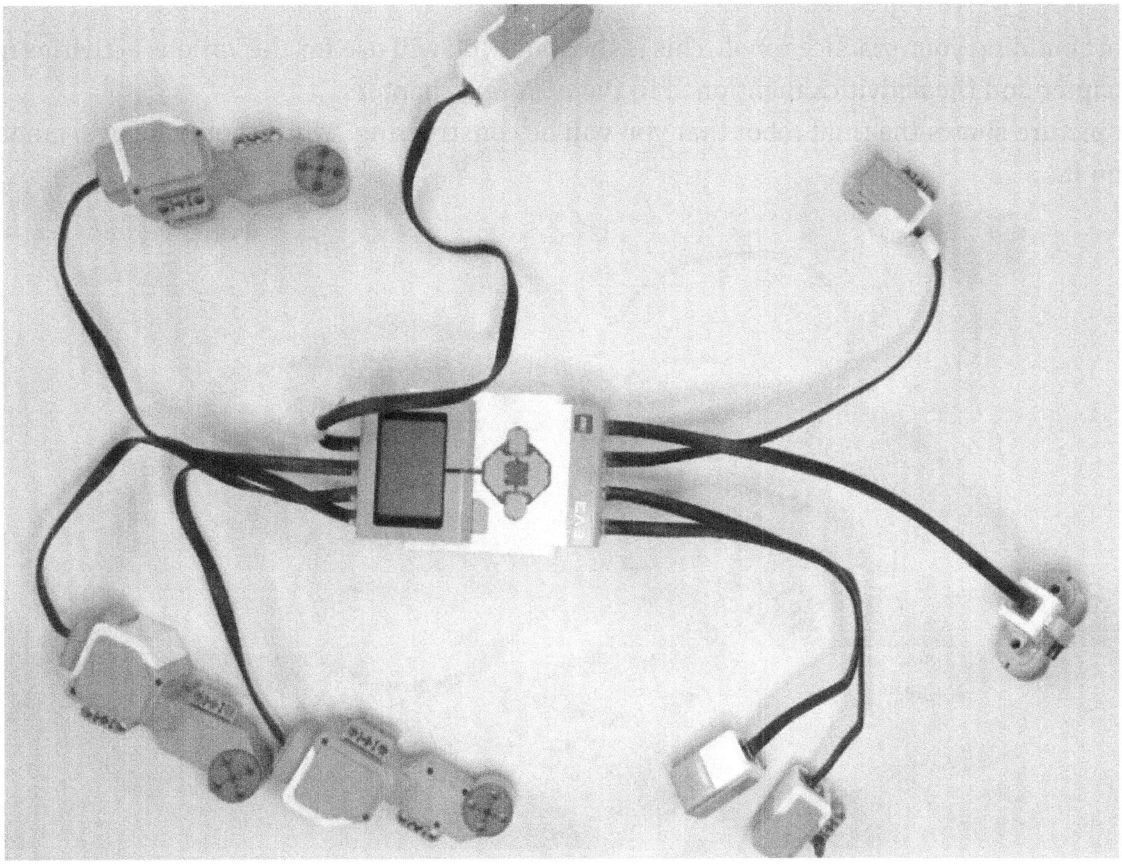

All motors should be connected to the alphabet ports and all sensors should be connected to the numeric ports as shown in the next picture.

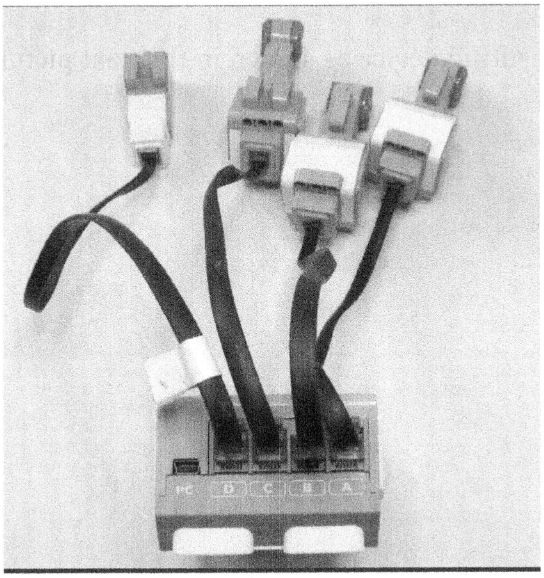

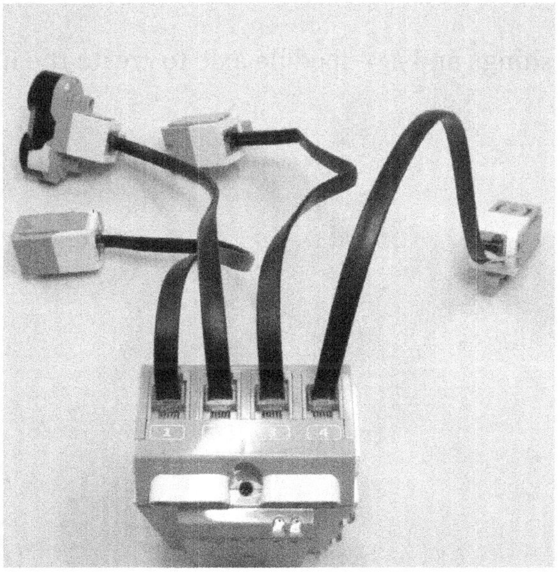

LET US BUILD

Let us start building your practice robot. This is the robot you will use for the various activities mentioned in this chapter and the activities mentioned in the next few chapters.
The next picture shows the final robot that you will be constructing. This robot will have 3 motors and 4 sensors on it.

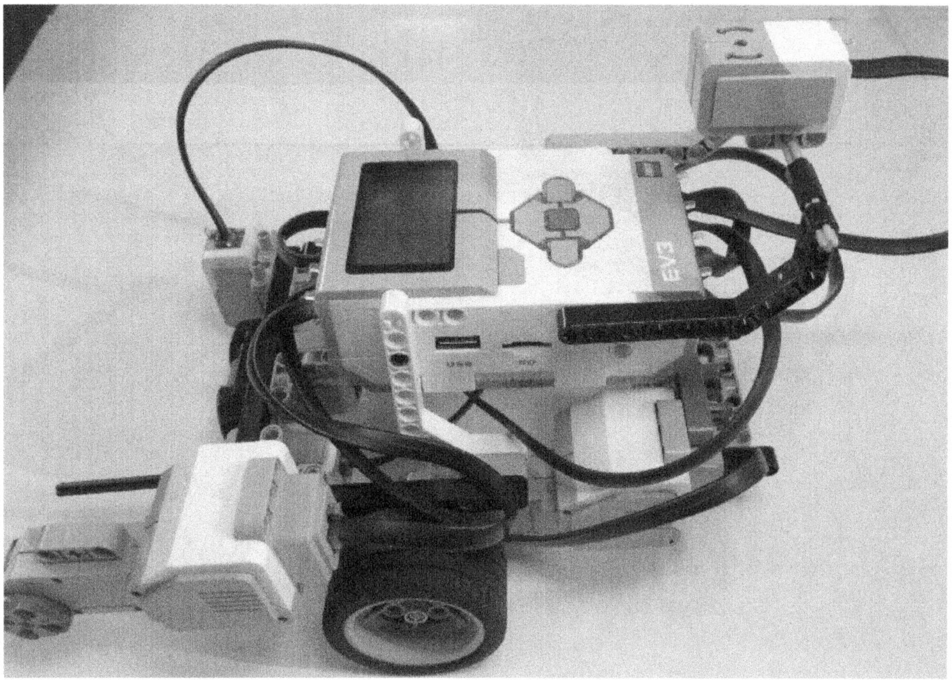

To create this robot, we will be using different sized pieces and will need a way to measure them.
You should create a measuring device for measuring various axles and beams. I have provided an example below.
Use 2 bushings and a 9-module axle to create the measuring device as shown in the next picture.

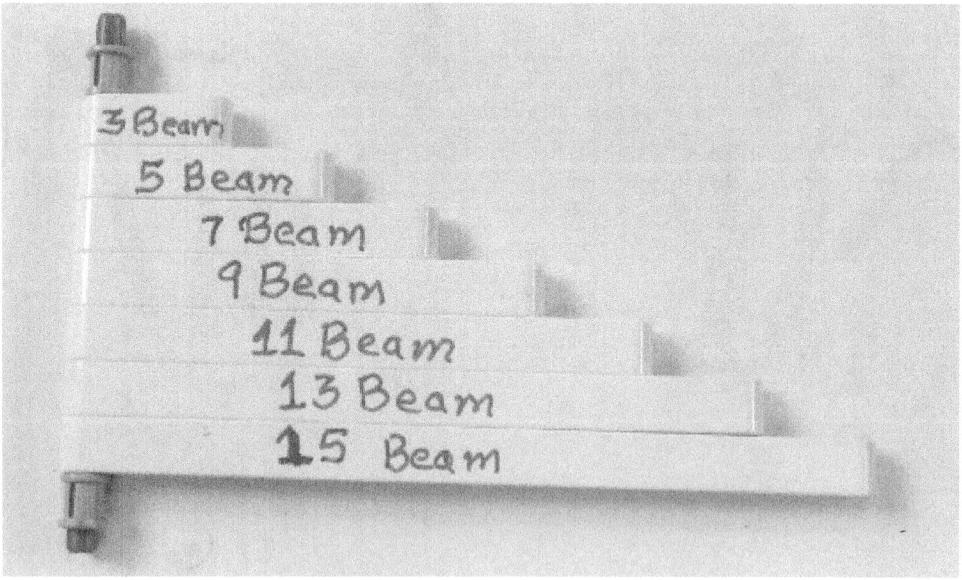

There are 3 main assemblies involved in constructing your first robot.

1. The Chassis
2. The Brick
3. The Sensor and Arm assembly

The next picture shows the completed chassis assembly.

The completed brick assembly is shown in the next picture.

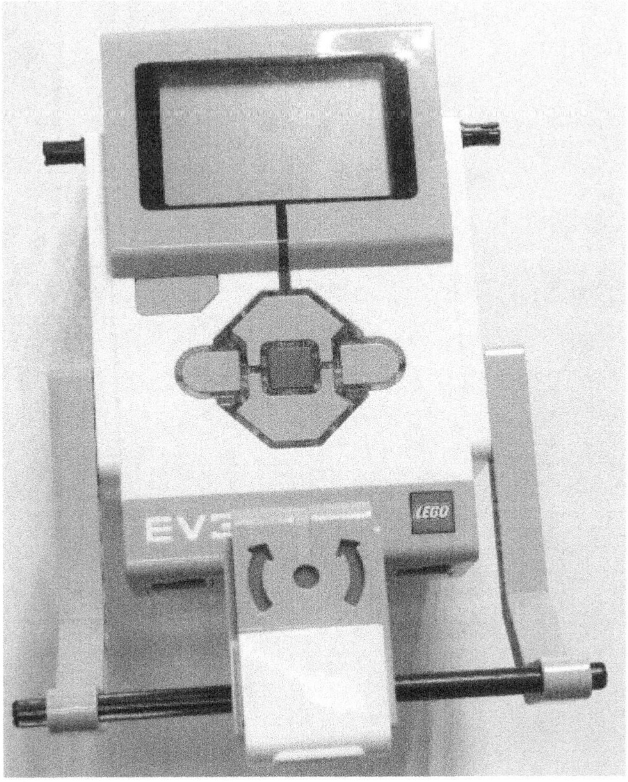

The completed sensor and arm assembly is shown in the next picture.

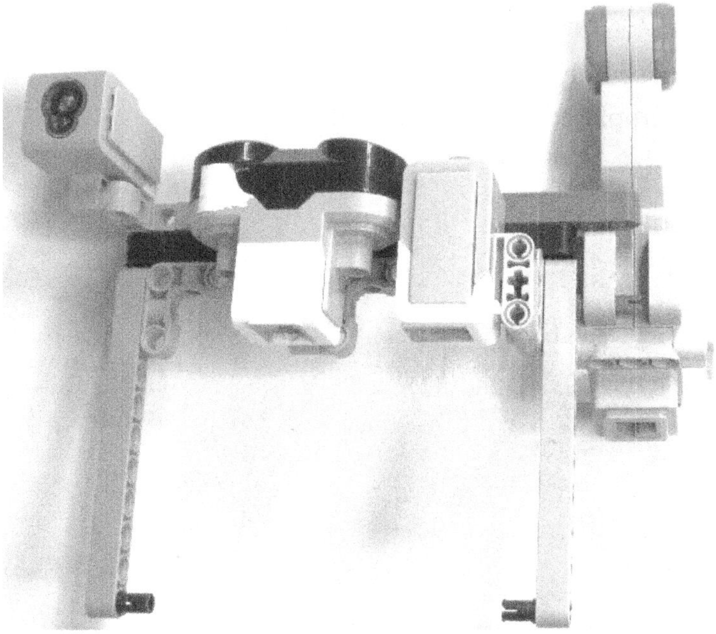

Now let us start constructing our first assembly, the chassis. Follow the series of steps in the next pictures to complete the chassis assembly.

Start by constructing the wheels using low-profile tires, 56x28 mm, black 6035364 and hubs, 43.2x26 mm, grey 4634091 from your core set or expansion set. (You can find the dimensions of the wheel on the side of the rubber of the tire.) Attach the wheel to a 7-module long axle and attach a full bushing on the axle. Create 2 of these wheel assemblies.

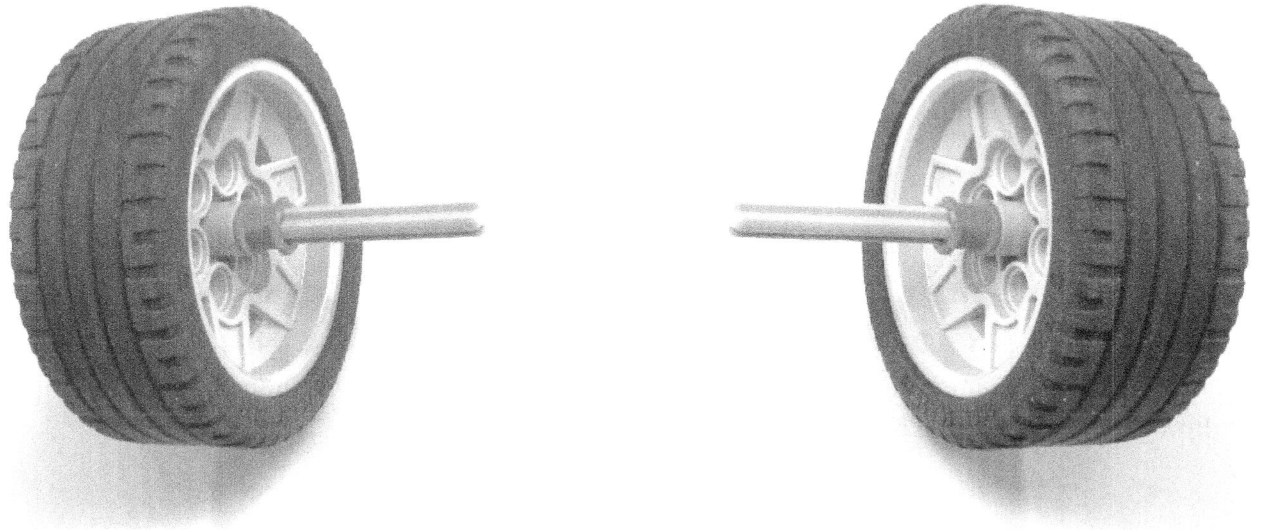

Use one 9-module Beam, 2 long blue friction pegs, and 2 black friction pegs to construct the following part. Construct 2 of these parts.

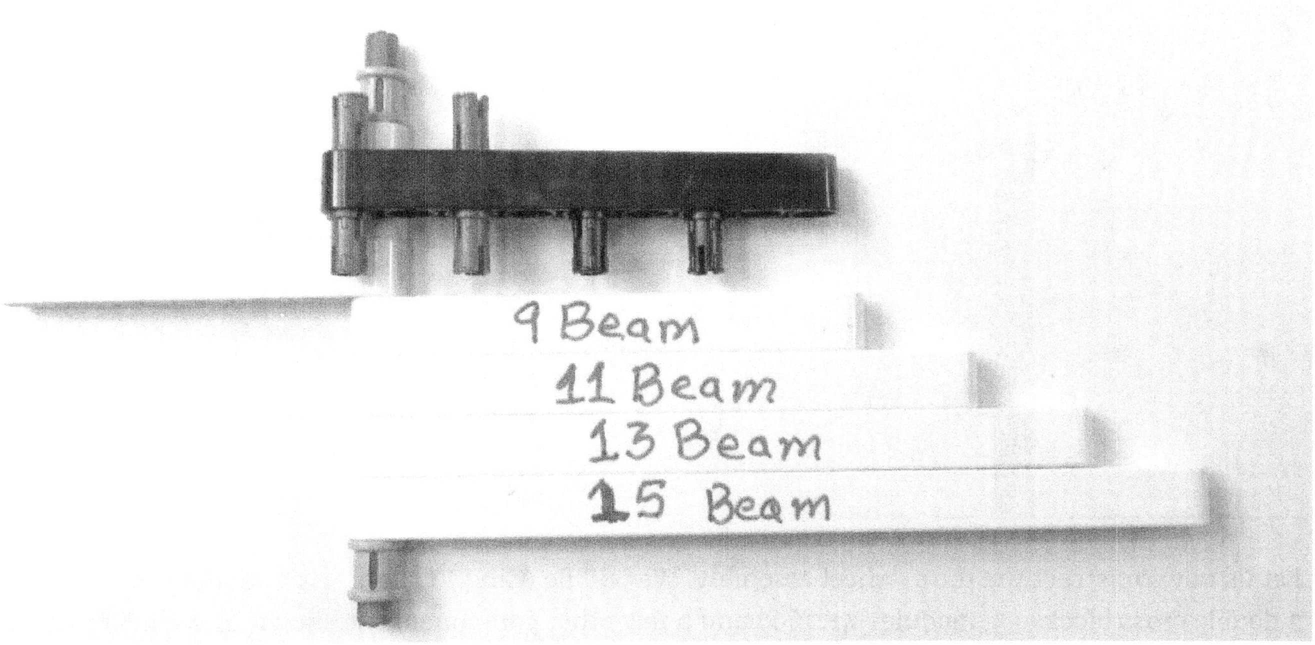

Use 1 double angular beam, 2 connector pegs with bushings, and a long blue connector peg to construct 2 assemblies as shown in next picture. Attach the angular beam to the motors exactly like how it is connected in the next picture.

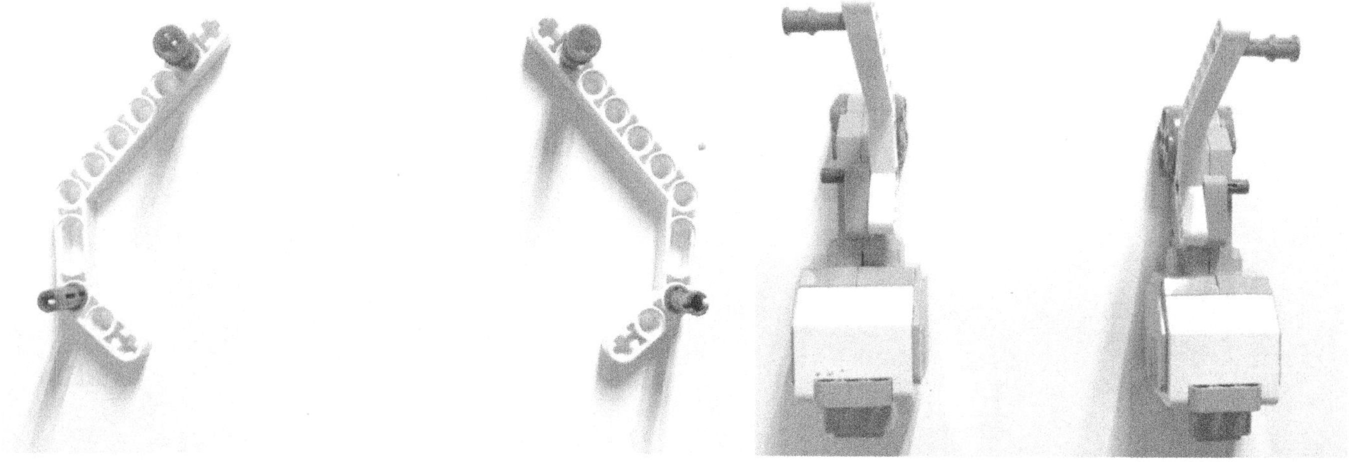

Attach the 9-module beam piece to the motor. Create a similar assembly with Motor 2. The next picture shows how they will look side by side.

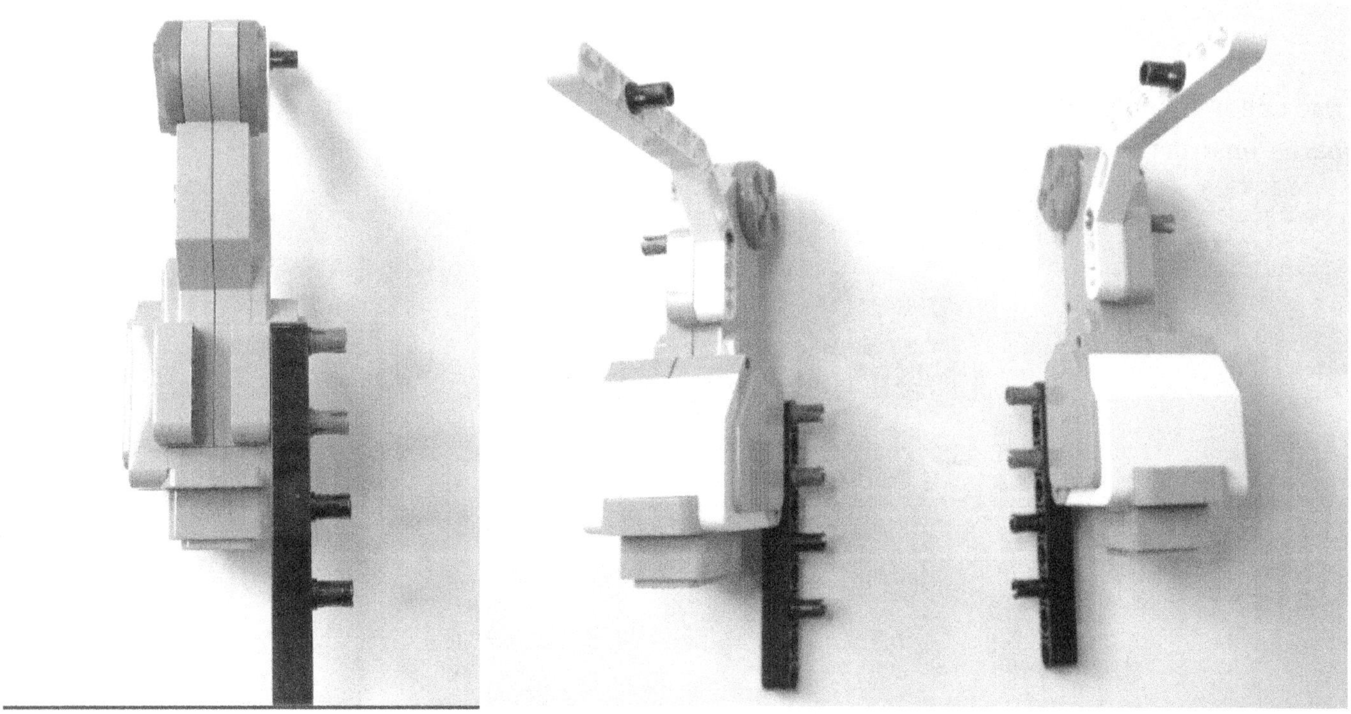

Let us now construct the third-wheel assembly. We will be using 1 frame - 5x7-module- grey 4539880, 2 double cross blocks- 3-module- 4121667 and a few other components as shown in the next picture.

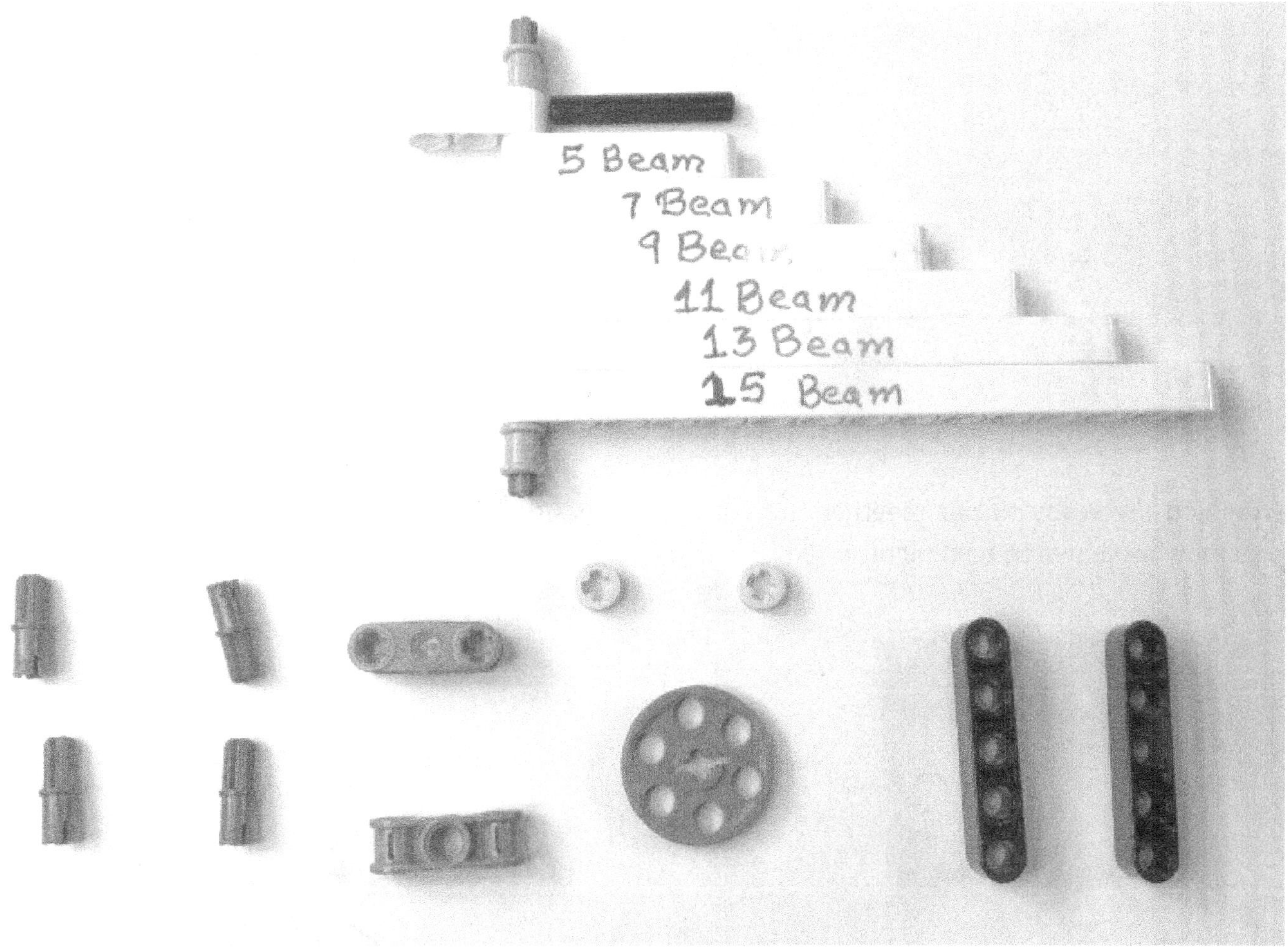

Start by putting together the axle and the wheel, and the axle pegs with the double cross blocks. Attach the double cross blocks to the 5-module beams as shown in next pictures.

Attach the wheel by inserting the axle in the middle hole of the double cross block. Attach the wheel assembly to the frame using 4 black pegs as shown in next picture.

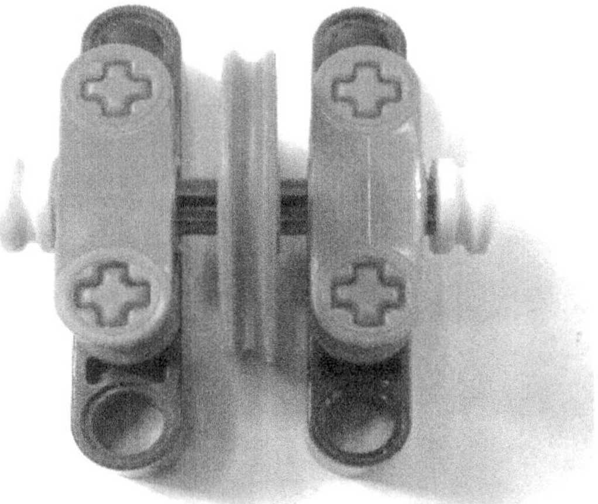

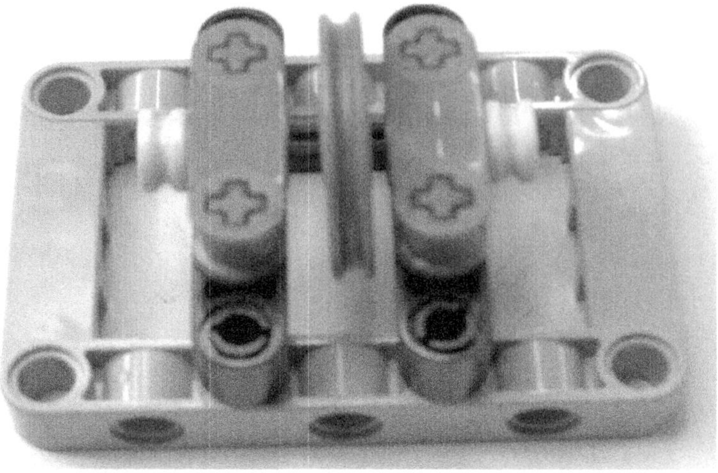

Now you are ready to put together the entire chassis. Attach the 2 large motors to the third wheel assembly as shown in next picture.

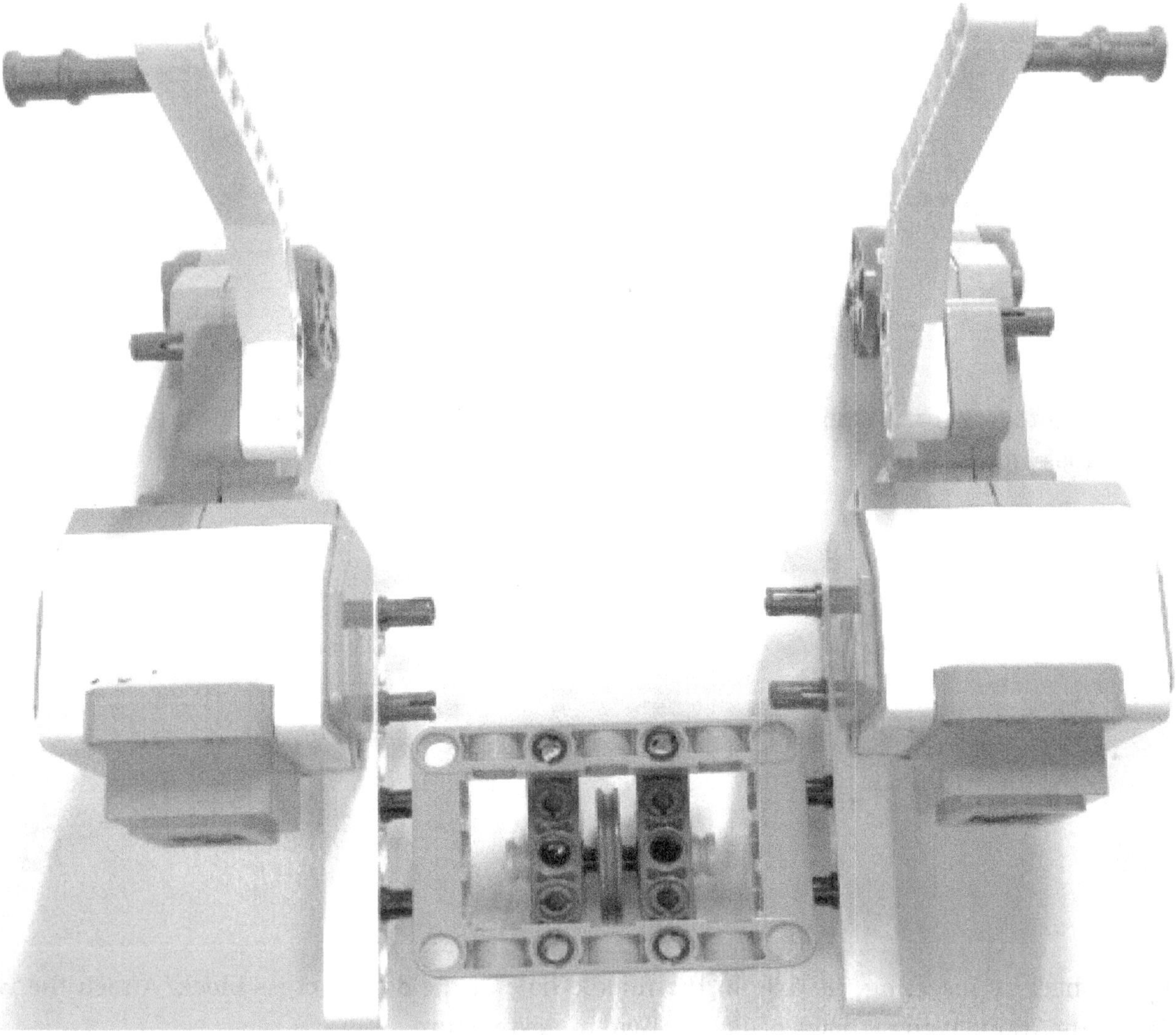

Use a 13-module beam and various pegs to create the following structure shown in the next picture. Attach the 13-module beam to the chassis as shown in the next picture.

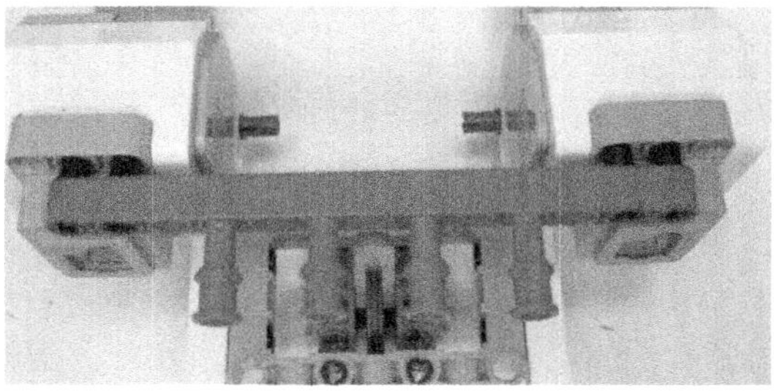

Your chassis assembly is now ready.

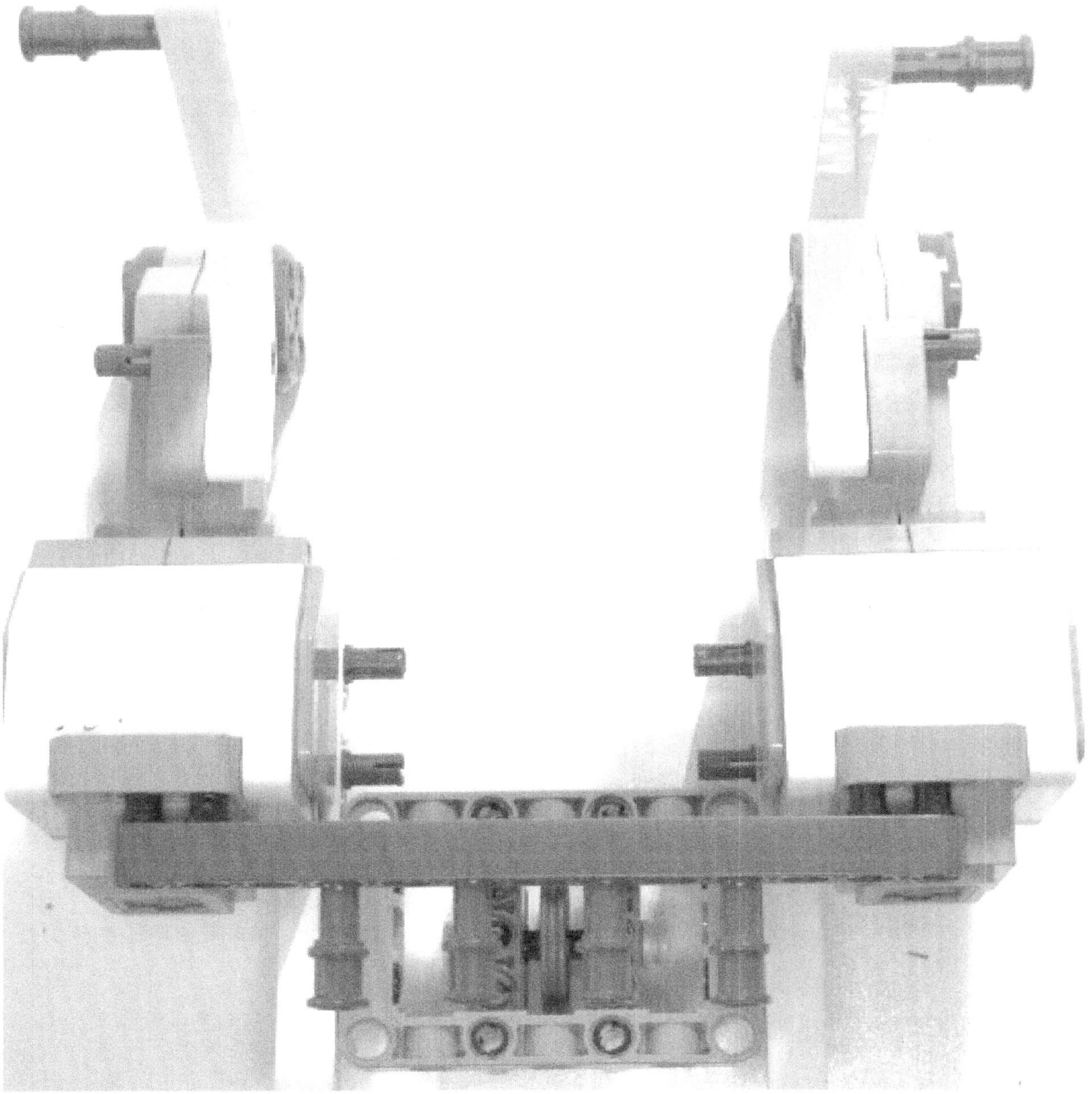

Let us now build the brick assembly by using the brick, 1 gyro sensor, 2 double angular beams, 2 6-module long axles, 6 black pegs, and 2 double connector pegs -4225033.

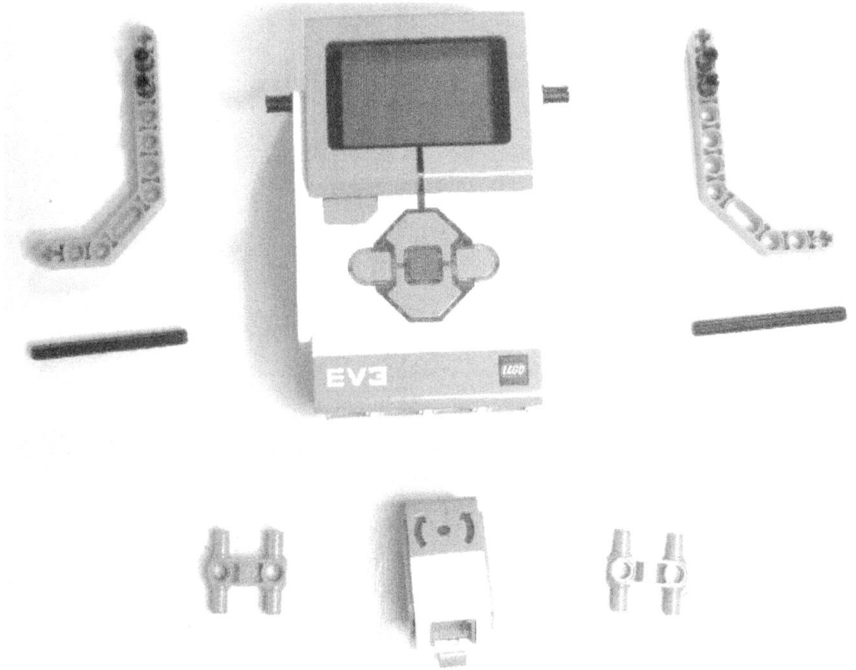

Attach the 'H' connectors on the sensor side of the brick.

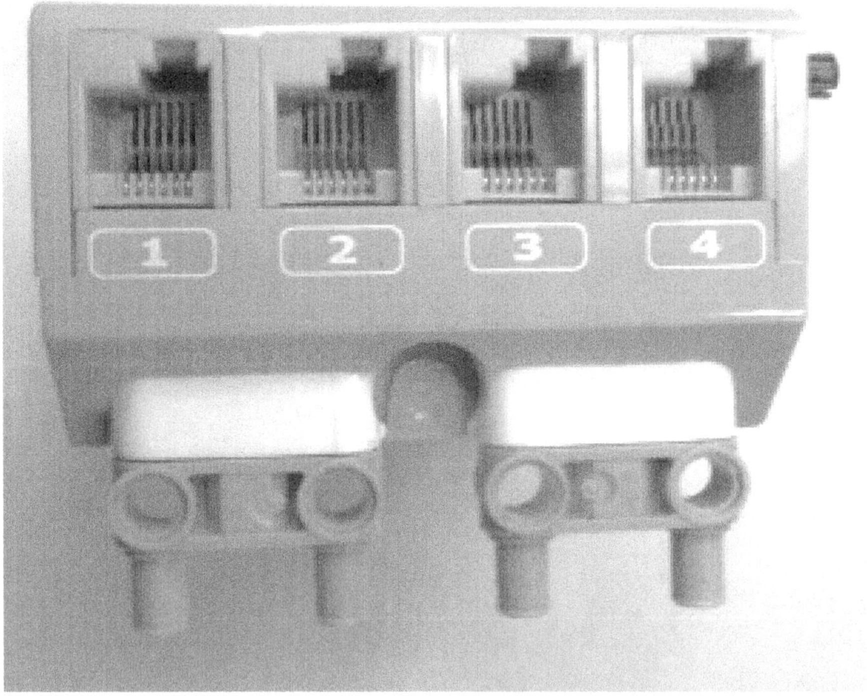

Connect the 2 angular beams using 4 black pegs as shown in the next picture. Insert 6-module axles through both angular beams or use a 12-beam axle and insert it into the gyro axle hole. Insert the gyro sensor with the axle attached into the angular beams to complete the assembly. If using two axles, make sure both axles are connected, and the gyro sensor is sturdy.

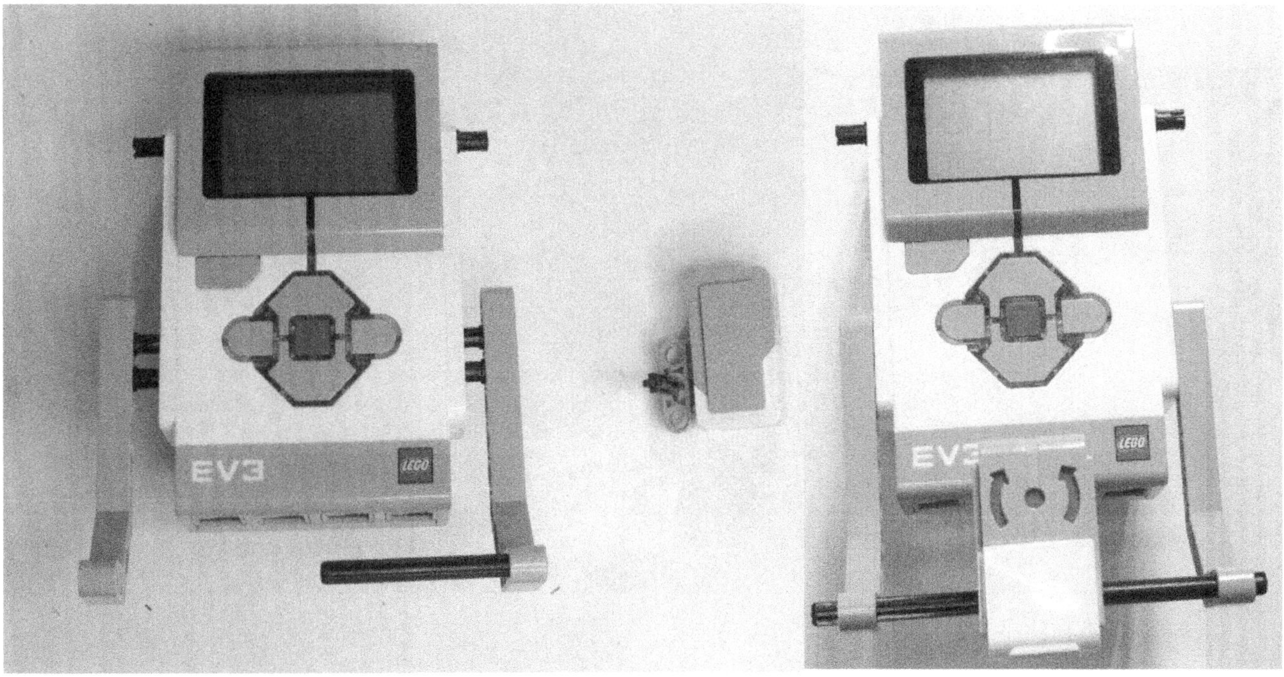

Attach the brick to the chassis as shown in the next few pictures.

Picture -1

Picture -2

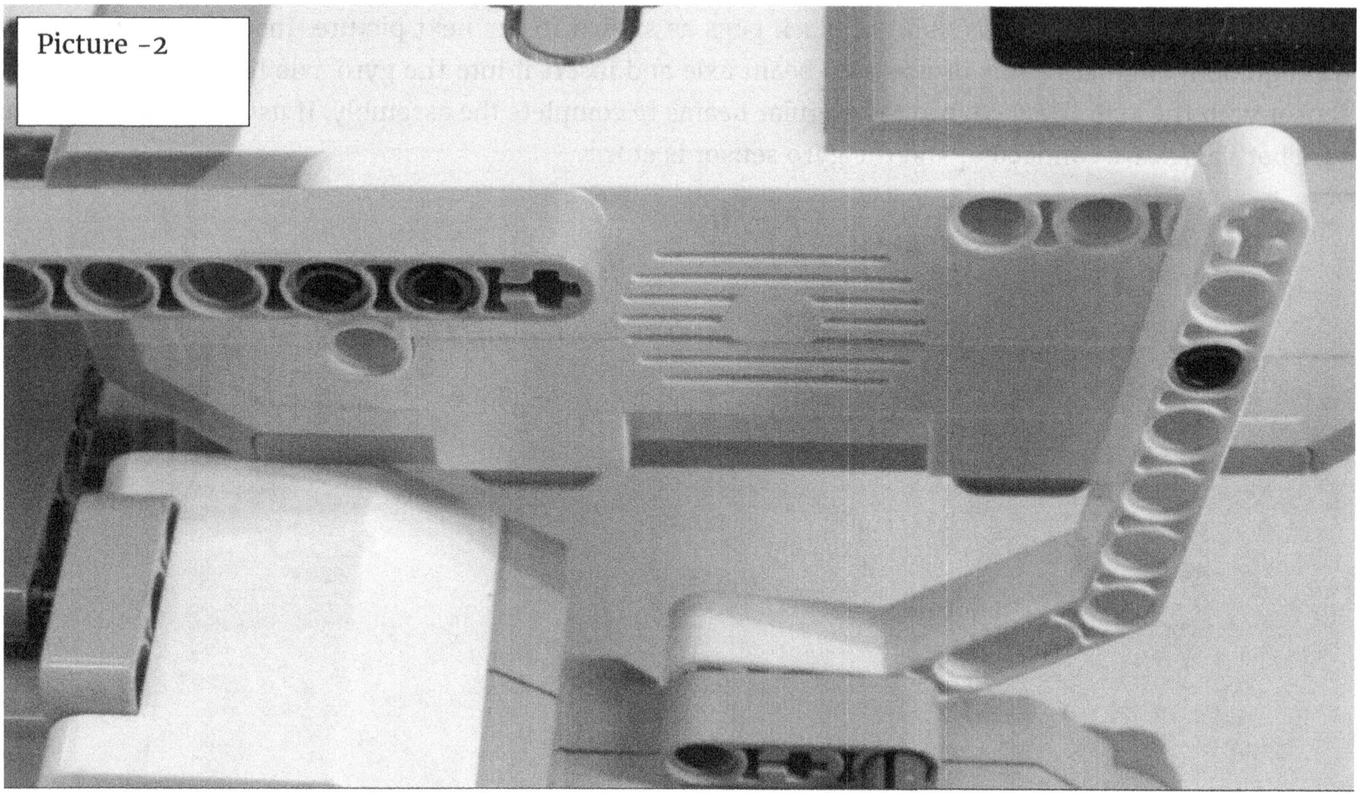

Picture -3

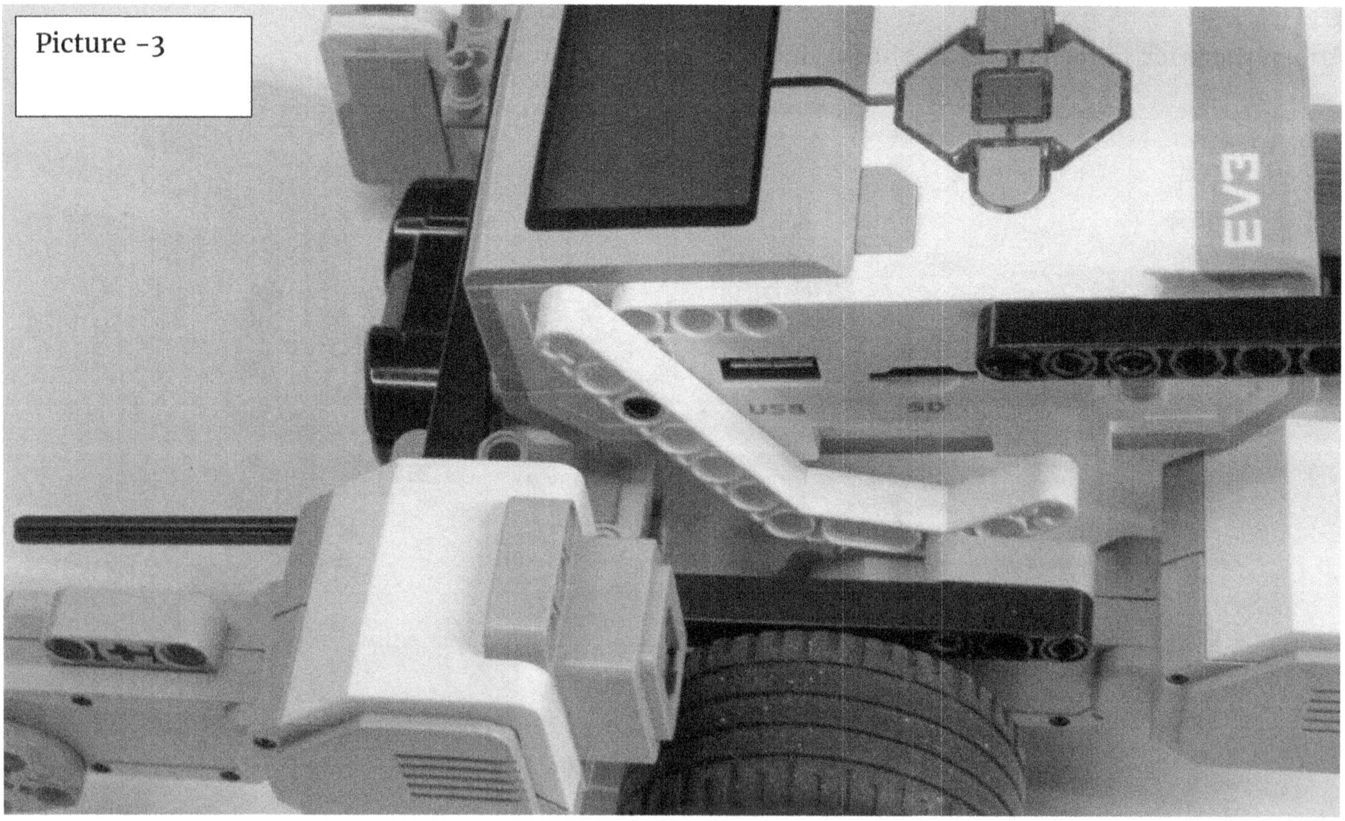

Attach the back of the brick as shown in the next picture.

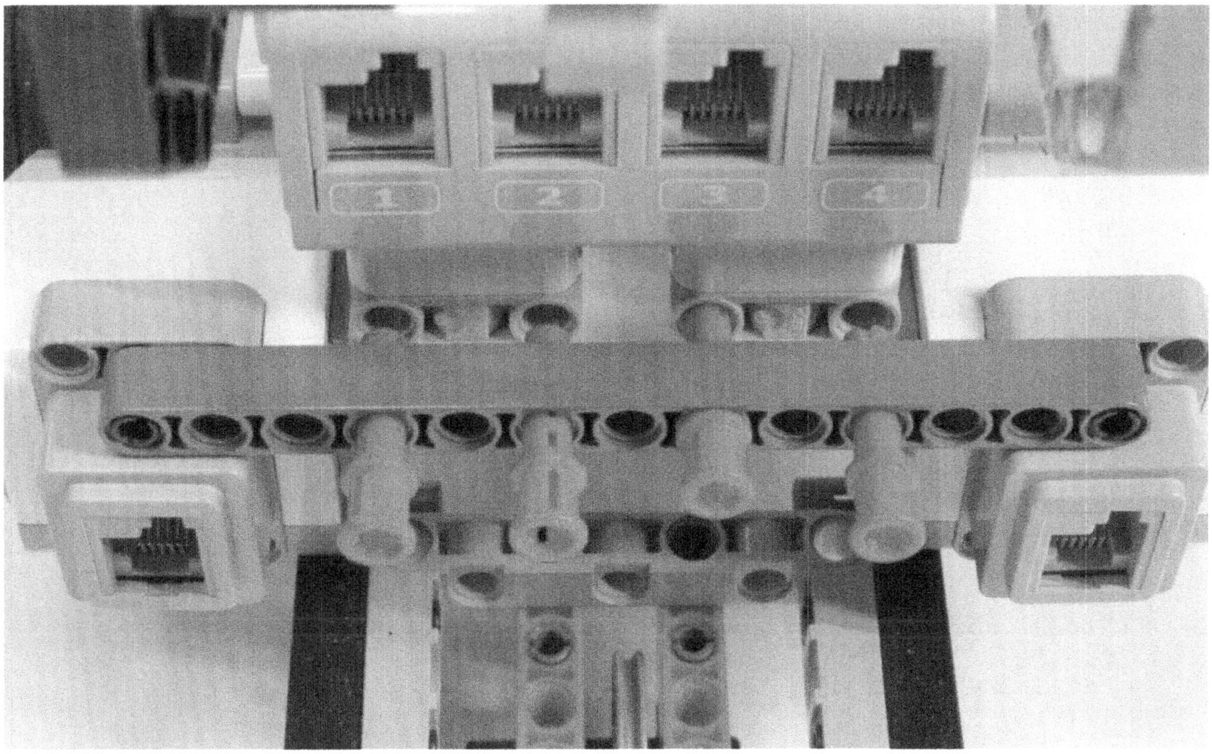

You have now finished the chassis and the brick assemblies.

Now it is time to build the final component: the sensor and arm assembly.

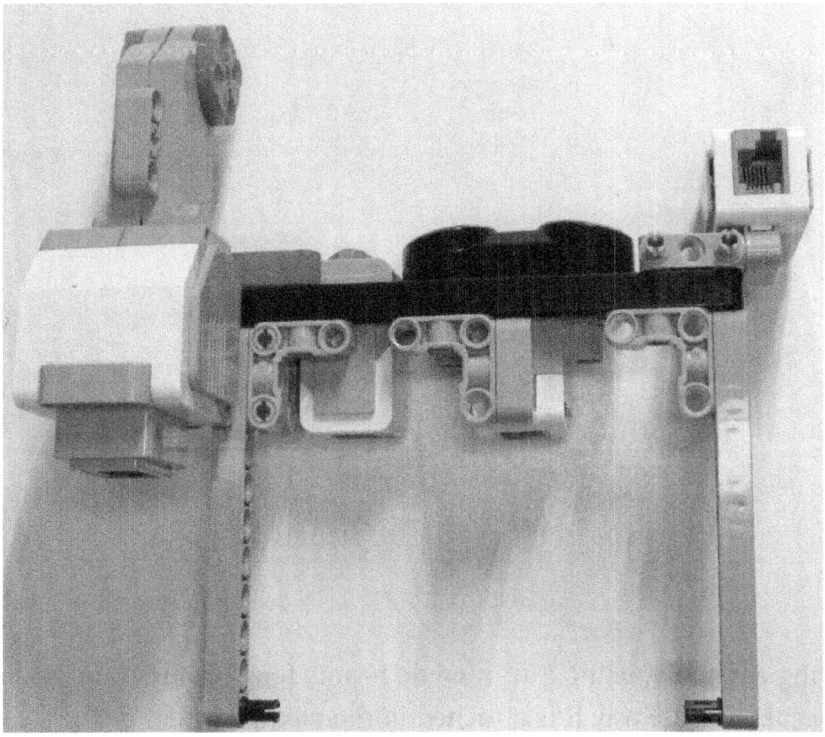

The parts that will be used are shown in the next picture. The new part is the angular connector peg – 4296059. You will be using use 4 of these new pieces.

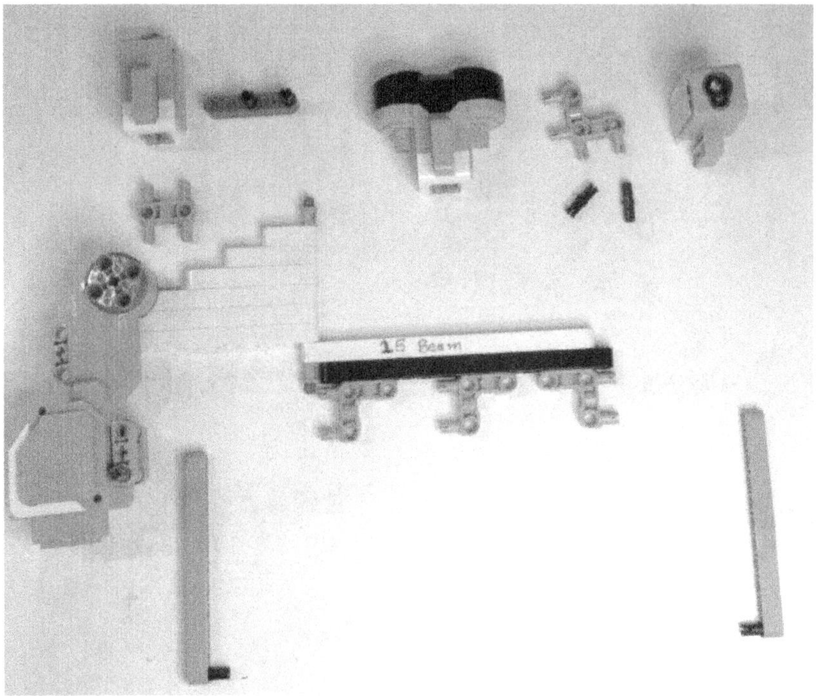

Take a 15-module beam and attach the angular connector pegs as shown in the next picture.

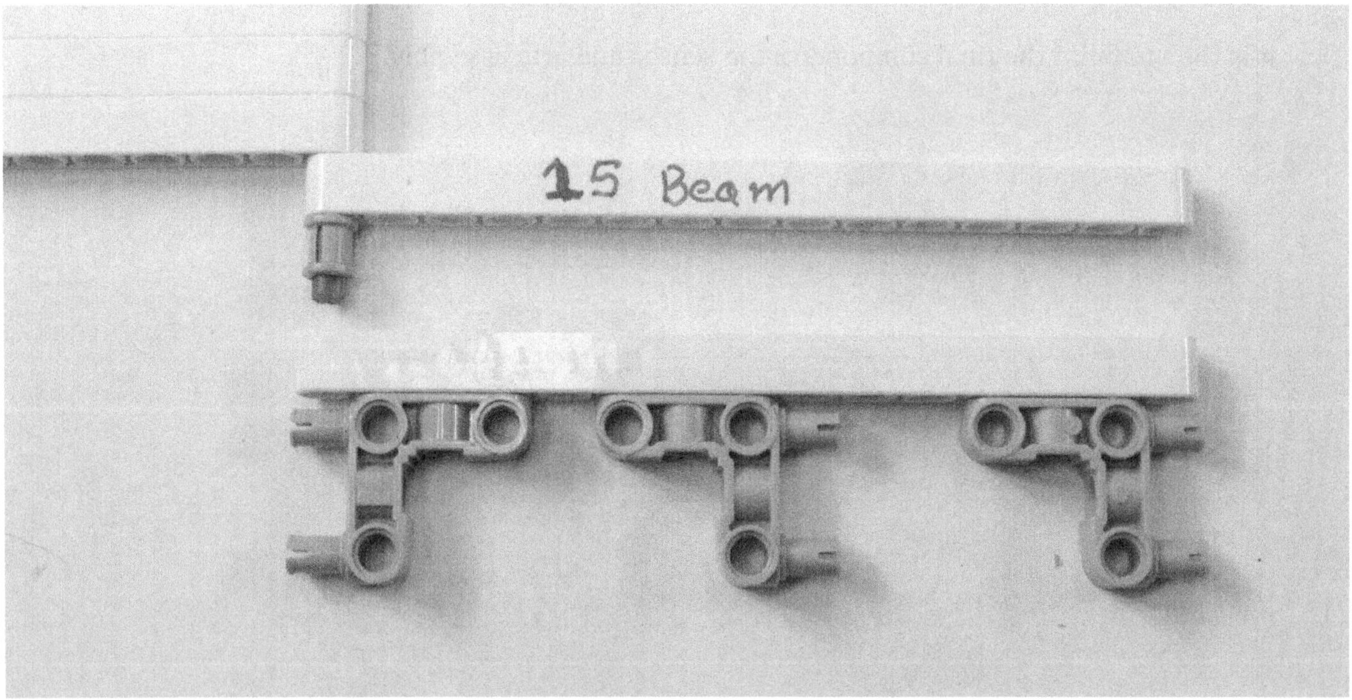

Complete the following assembly, using 2 11-module beams for the sides, and a 5-module beam. Attach the ultrasonic sensor just like the way it is attached in the next picture.

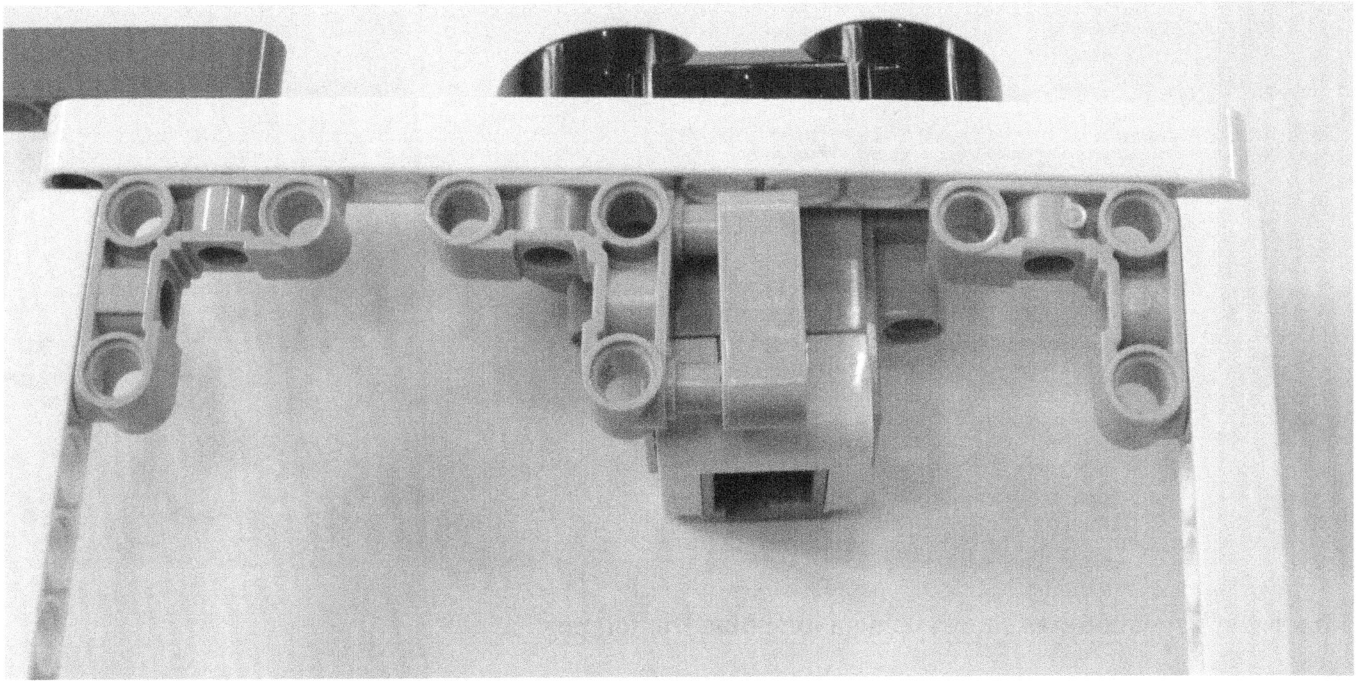

Attach the angular connector peg to the color sensor and attach 2 black pegs. Attach the color sensor next to the ultrasonic sensor as shown in the next picture.

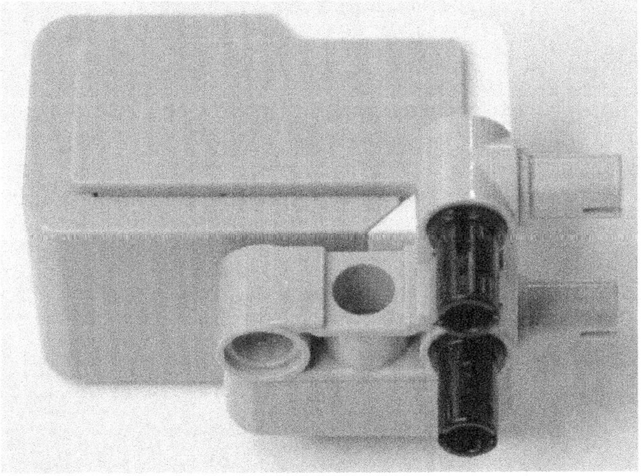

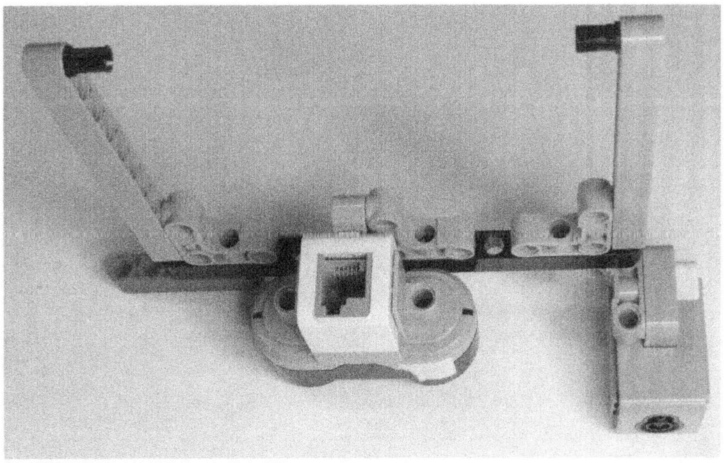

Attach an 'H' beam to the touch sensor. Attach the touch sensor to the left of the ultrasonic sensor as shown in next picture.

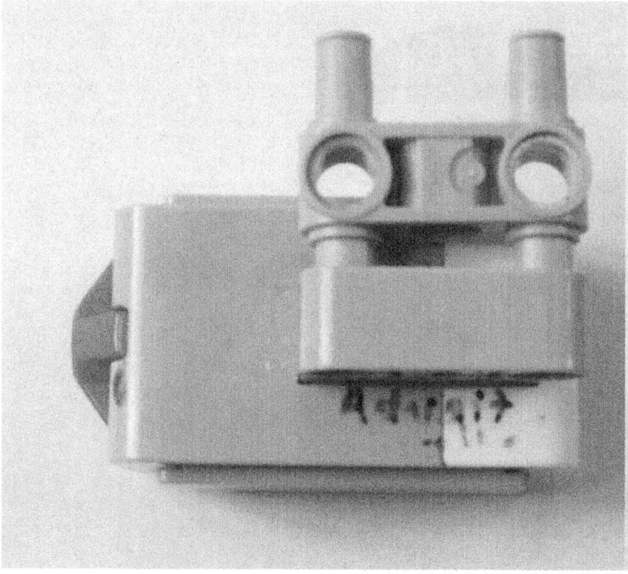

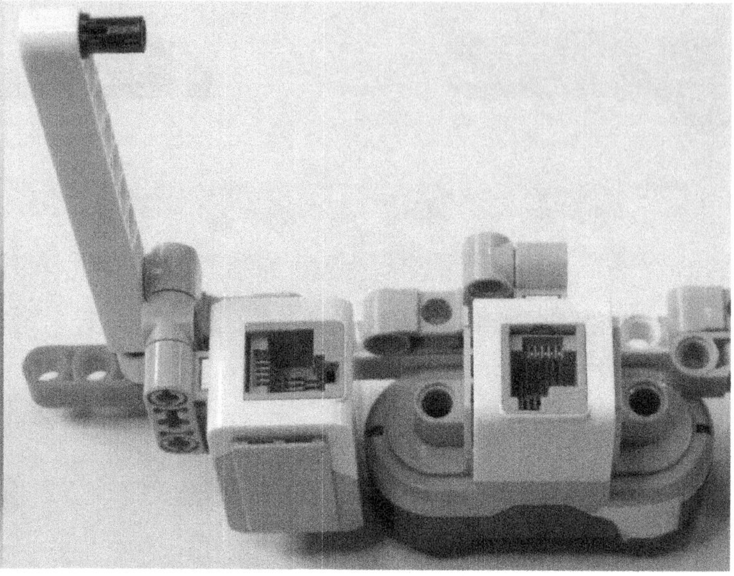

Attach the large motor as shown using a long blue friction peg.

Your arm and sensor assembly is now finished and should look like one shown in next picture.

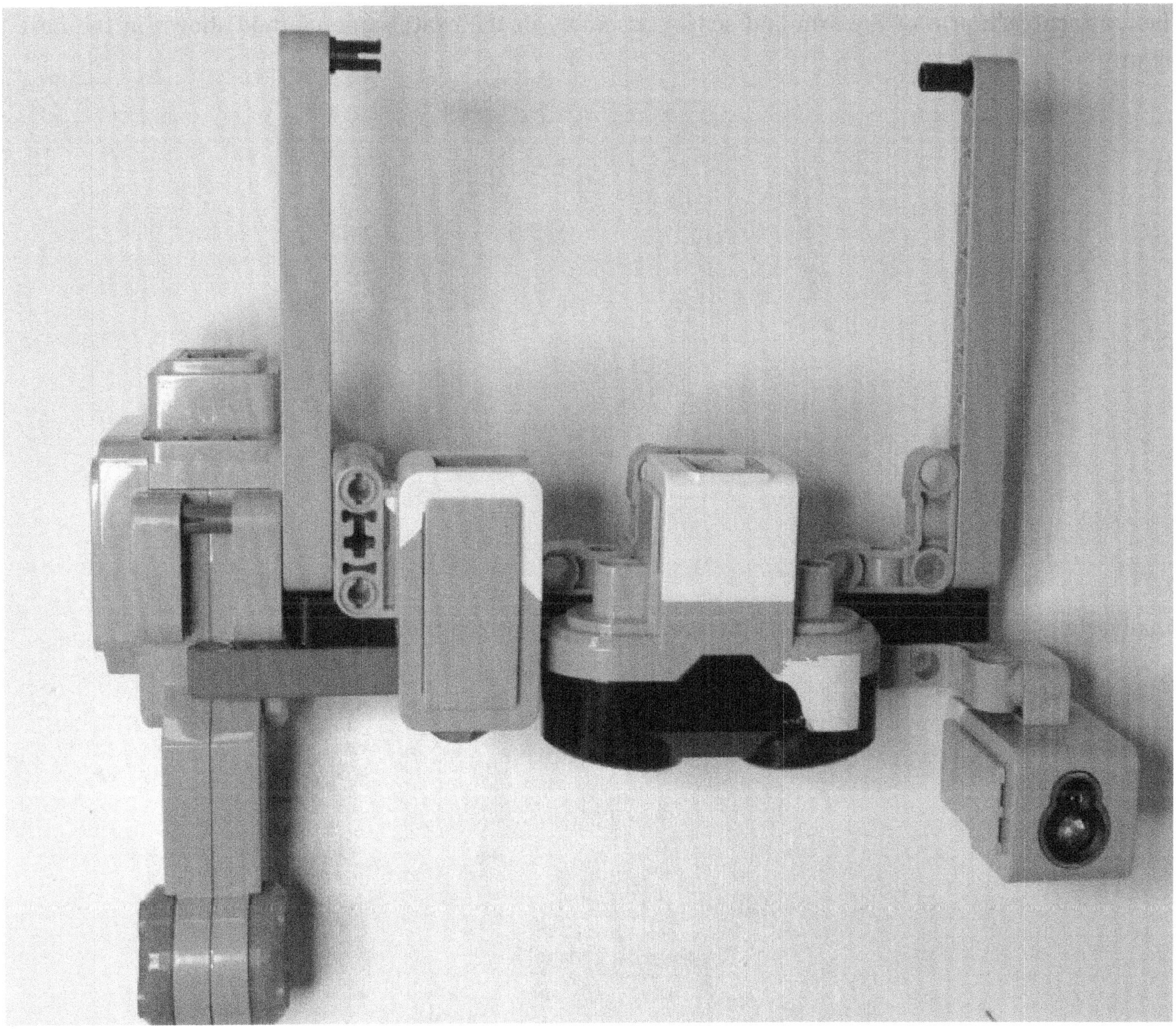

Now let us attach it to the robot. First, remove both the wheels from the motors as shown in the next picture.

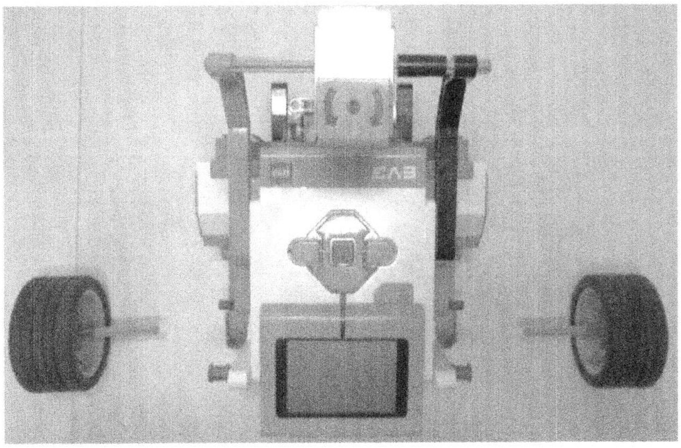

Then, attach each arm of the arm and sensor assembly in the exact same method shown in the next picture.

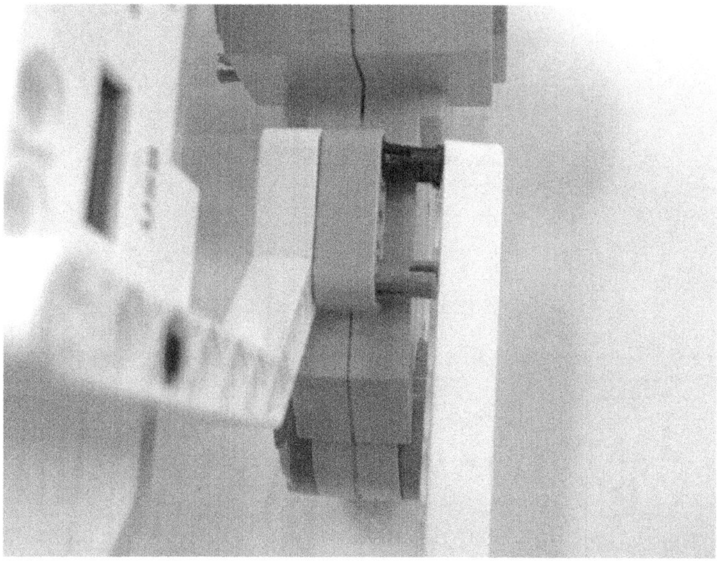

Finally, the robot should look like next picture once you re-attach the wheels.

Wiring:

The wires should not touch any wheels or the ground when connected. Make sure that the wires will still allow you to flip the brick to change batteries. (Shown in the picture below)

Connect Port A to the Arm Motor.

Connect Port B to the Drive Wheel Motor on the Arm Motor side.

Connect Port C to the Drive Wheel Motor on the other side.

Connect Port 1 to the Touch Sensor.

Connect Port 2 to the Ultrasonic Sensor.

Connect Port 3 to the Color Sensor.

Connect Port 4 to the Gyro Sensor.

Make sure the connections are done properly as the programming referred to in this book depends on the sensors and motors being connected to the correct ports.

The next picture shows how the robot looks after proper wiring.

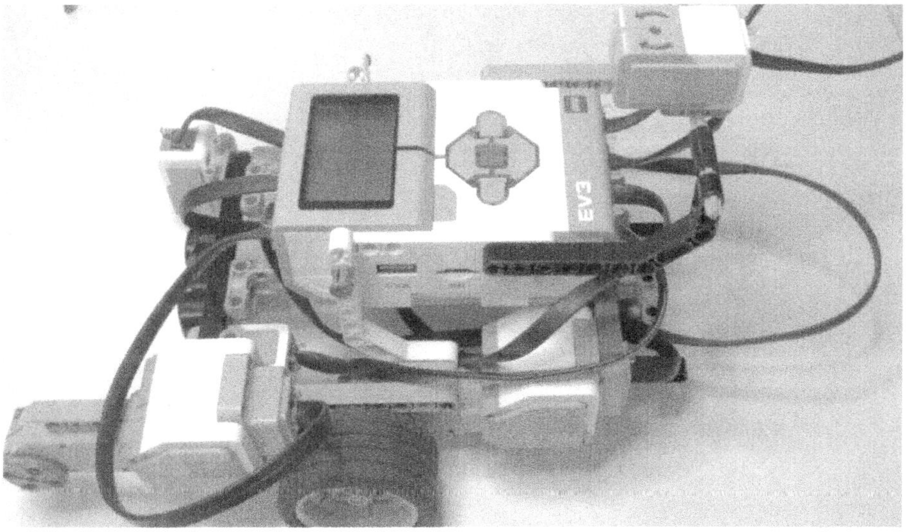

Next picture shows how the robot should look when you are changing the battery.

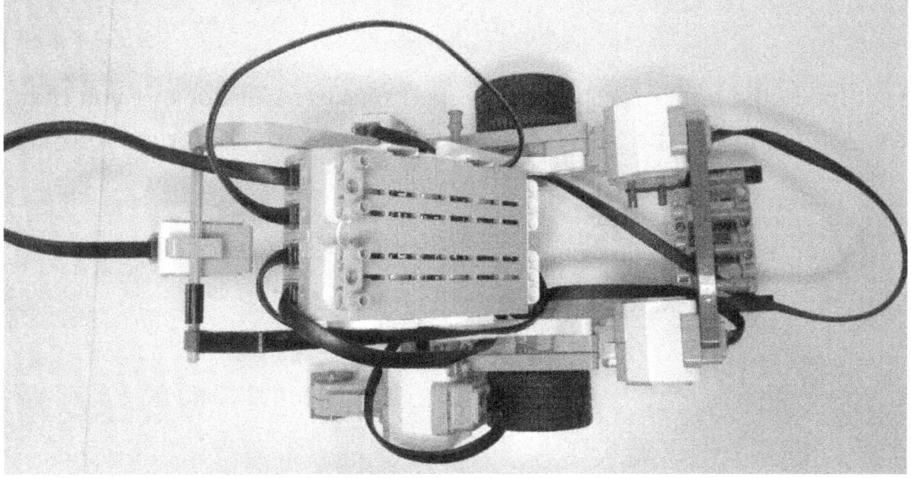

EV3 SOFTWARE

Downloading and installing the EV3 software:
First, search "Ev3 software download" on any search engine. Next, download the free Ev3 software (this shows up as one of the first search results and should be on the education.lego.com website).
Once you download the file, open it and install the software.

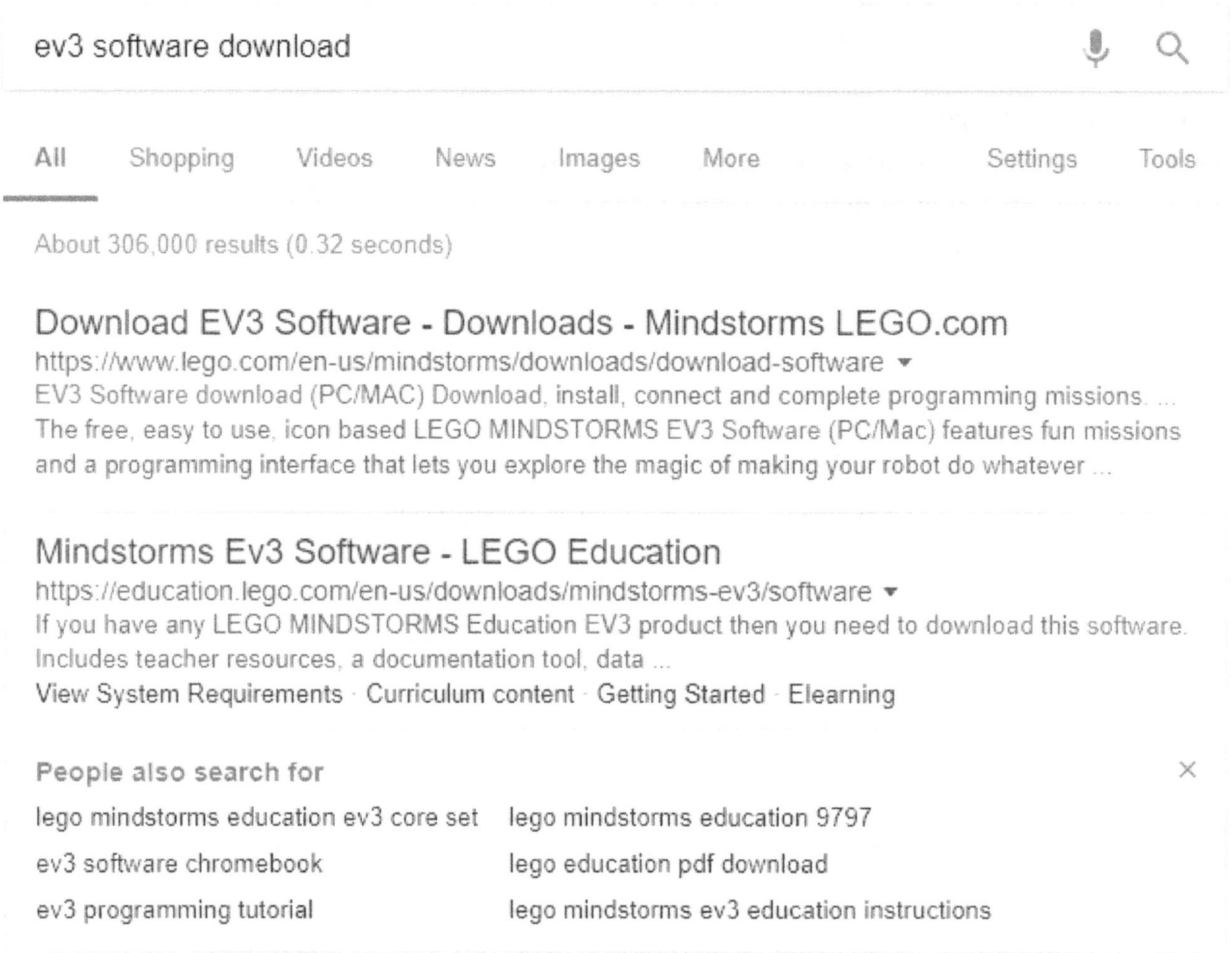

The Ev3 Software setup should look exactly like the next picture. If it doesn't you may have downloaded the wrong software. After running the installer, you can choose any folder on your laptop to install the software.

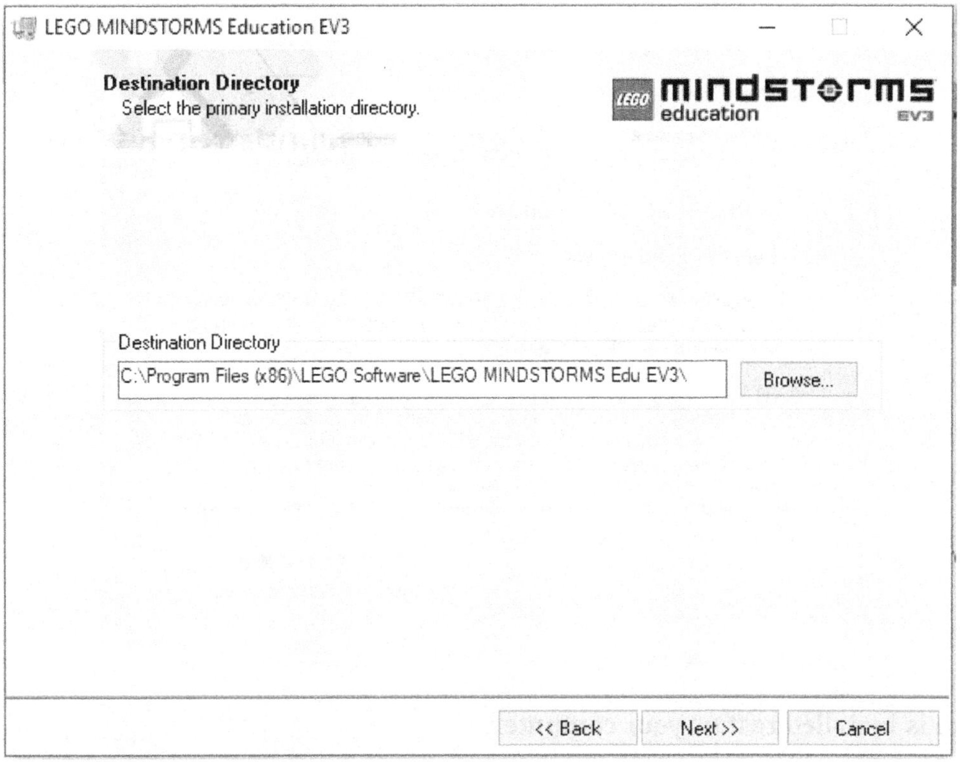

Select the 'Student Edition' Option.

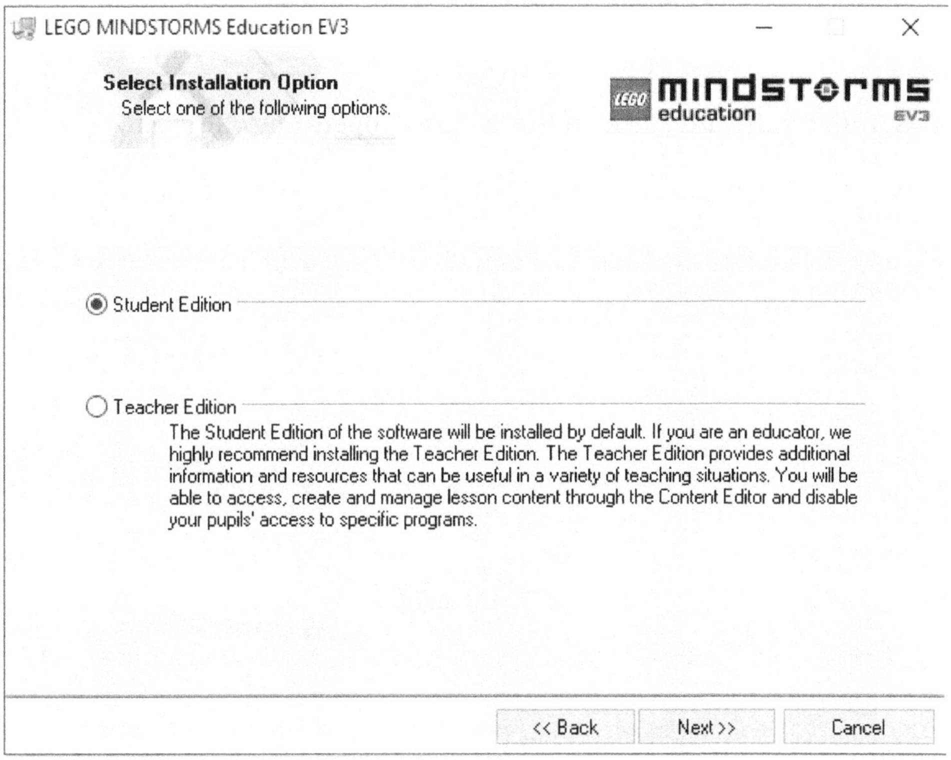

Make sure to accept the 2 license agreements.

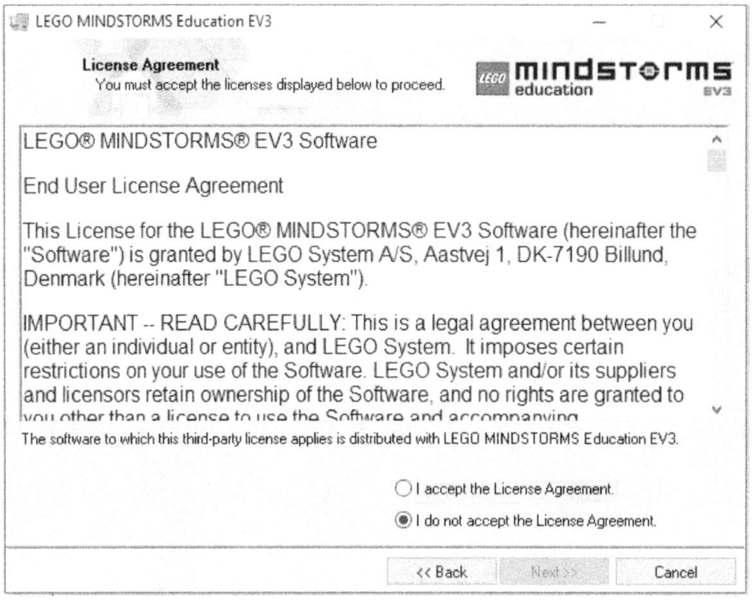

Once the program is installed restart your computer.

PROGRAMMING

Open the EV3 MINDSTORMS software. Click on the '+' tab to open a new Project.

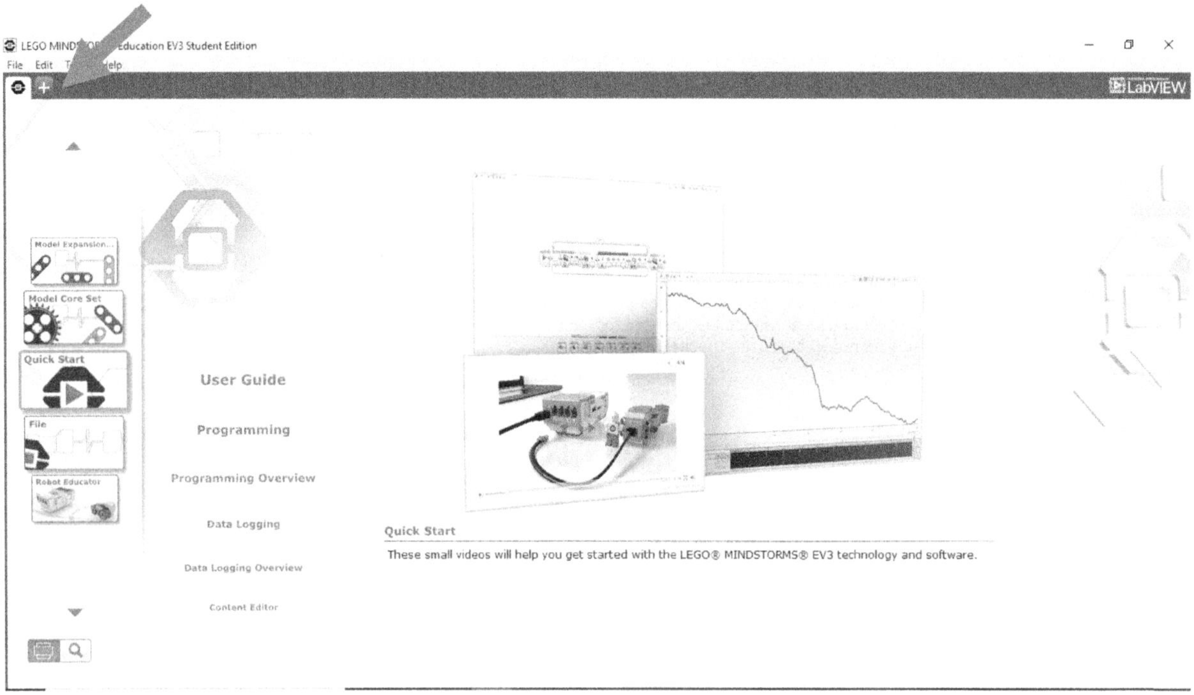

Clicking on the '+' button will start a new project and will allow you to start programming.

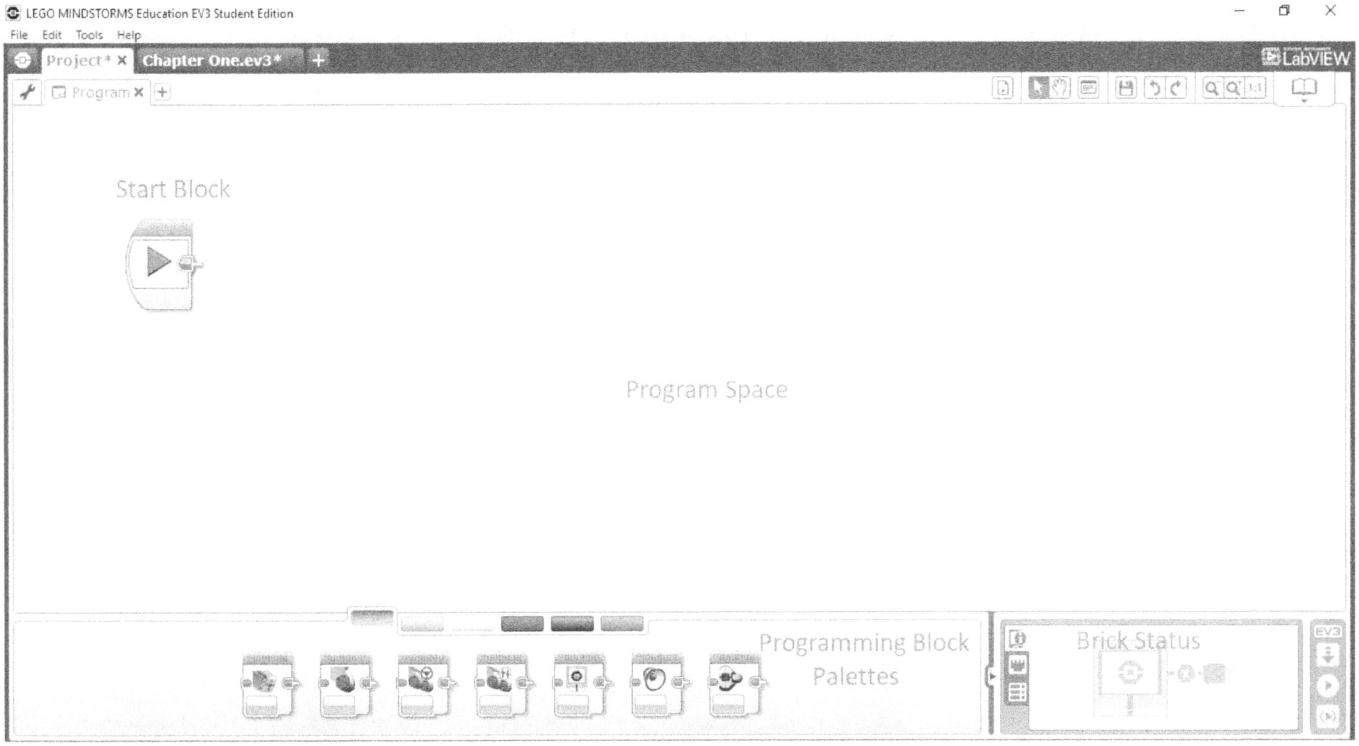

Before we begin our first program, familiarize yourself with the various programming blocks in the action pallette. (Green tab at the bottom)

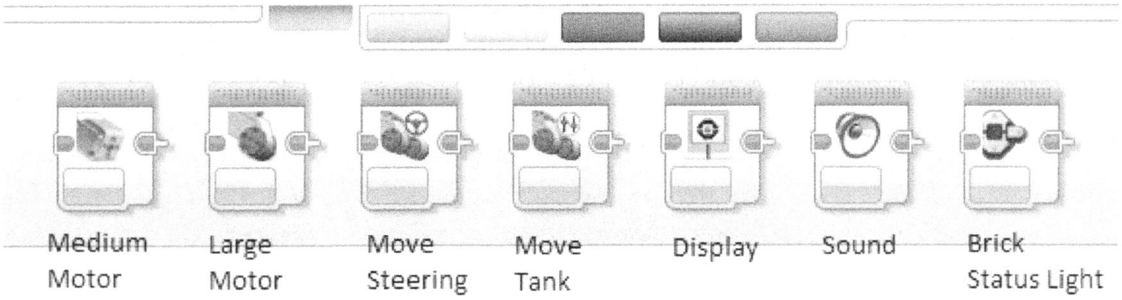

The Medium Motor block is used to program any connected medium motor.
The Large Motor block is used to program a single connected large motor.
The Move Steering block is used to turn the robot and controls 2 connected motors.
The Move Tank block is used to move the robot in a straight line or turn it and controls 2 connected motors.
The Display block is used to display various figures and text on the brick display.
The Sound block is used to play sound.
The Brick Status Light block allows you to program the backlighting of the buttons on the brick.

We will now create our first program. Our first program will be on motion and will focus moving the robot forward and backward.

First, drag the move tank block and attach it to the start block. If the block is not attached, it will show as a greyed-out block. There are various programming options included in the move tank block to program your drive motors (Ports B and C). We will be selecting the 'On for Rotations' option for this program. The 'On for Degrees' option allows you to program the robot for very small movements. The 'On for Seconds' option makes your robot move forward for a certain number of seconds but is not typically used. Finally, the 'On' option keeps the motor running once the program enters this block. Conversely, the 'Off' option stops the motors.

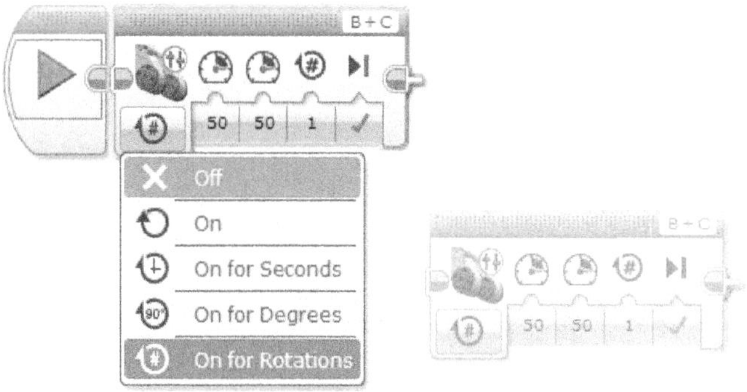

After choosing the 'On for Rotations' option, you will see four other boxes. The first two boxes are to tell the motor it's power(speed) and the last box tells the robot how many rotations to move forward. Set the power for both motors to 50 and set the rotation box to 1 rotation.

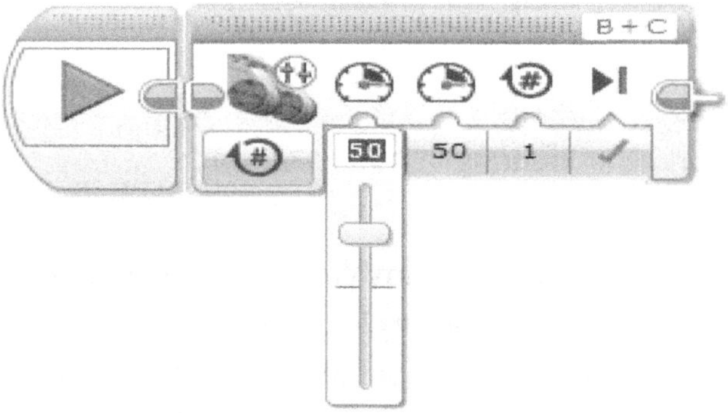

Complete the program shown in next picture using a combination of move tank blocks and single motor blocks. Once it is completed you can run your first program.

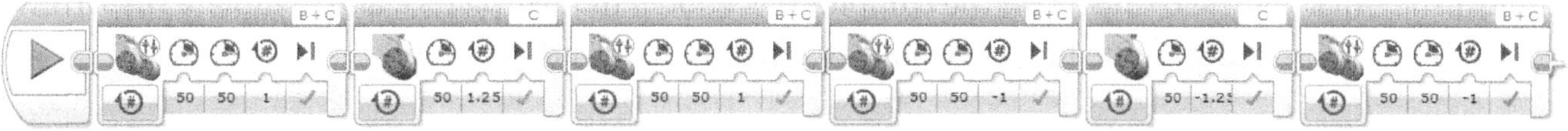

Now, save the project as ‘Chapter one’ and rename the program to ‘single wheel turn’- It’s easy to rename it: just double click on the program name. **Make sure to save your programs frequently and every time before you close out of the programming session. There is no autosave feature currently available in the EV3 software.**

Make sure the batteries have been added to the brick or the rechargeable battery that comes with the core set has been charged and attached on the brick.

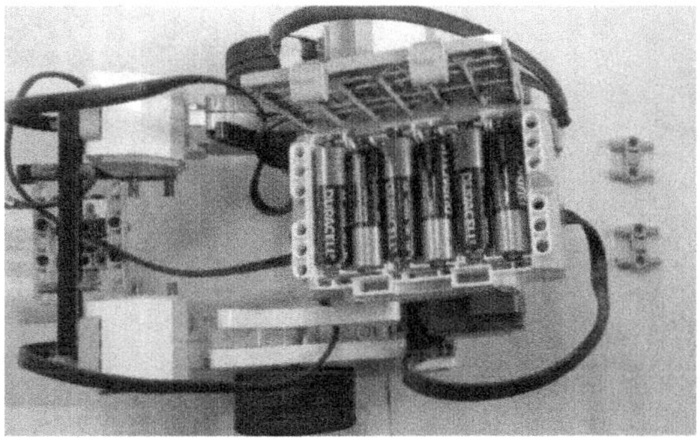

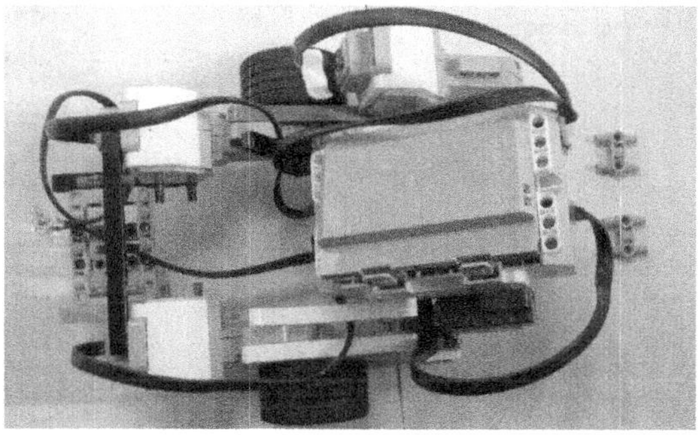

Once the batteries have been added, let us power on the robot. Press the middle button for a couple of seconds till the red status light turns on.

Connect the brick via the USB port on the computer as shown in next picture and complete the firmware update. During this process, the brick can stay attached to the robot assembly.

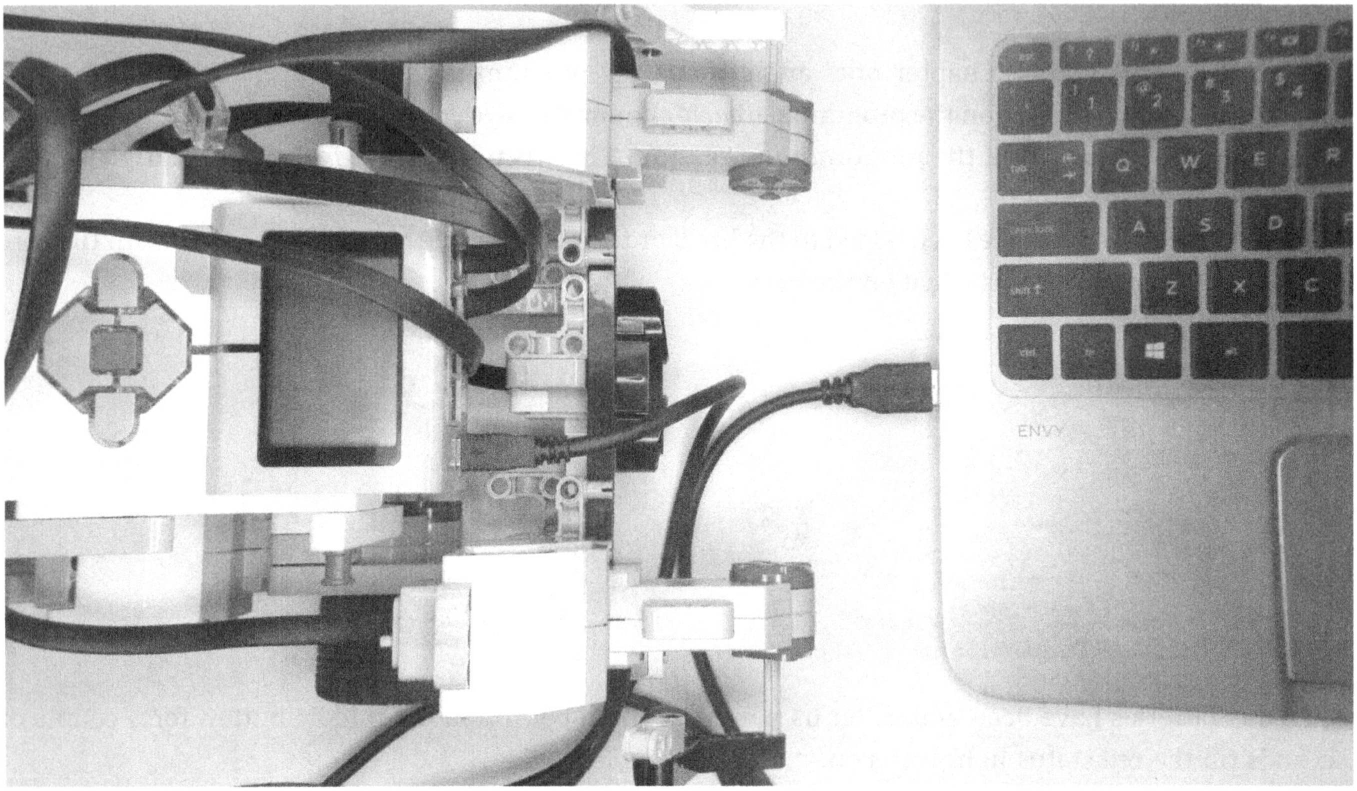

Go to the 'Tool' Menu option and click on the 'Firmware Update' option. Click the check button that will take you to browser where you can download the latest firmware (button to download is all the way at the bottom of the page). Typically, this will download in the Downloads folder on your computer.

Click the browse button and go to the Downloads folder and select the Firmware file (.bin) which you want to use for the update- the one that you just downloaded. Click on the Download button to download and install the firmware on the Brick.

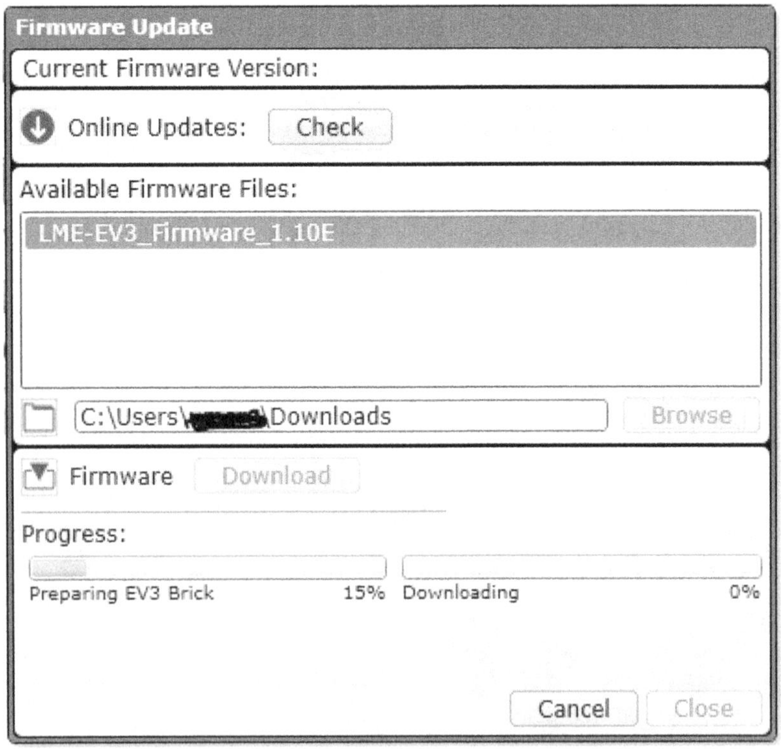

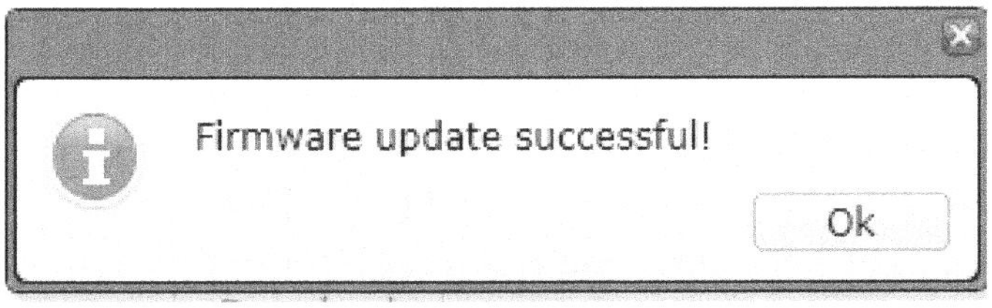

Once completed, you will get a firmware update message.

Now we will connect the Brick to the Computer via Bluetooth

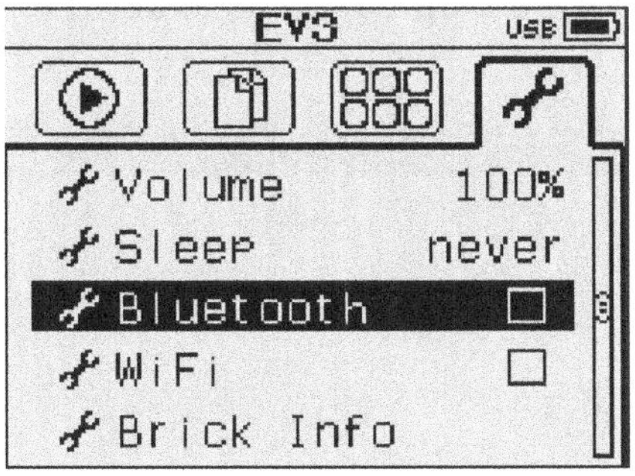

Go to the wrench icon in the brick using the brick buttons and select the 'Bluetooth' option and press the middle button. Make sure that the visibility box is checked, and the Bluetooth box is checked, and the iPhone/iPad/iPod box is unchecked.

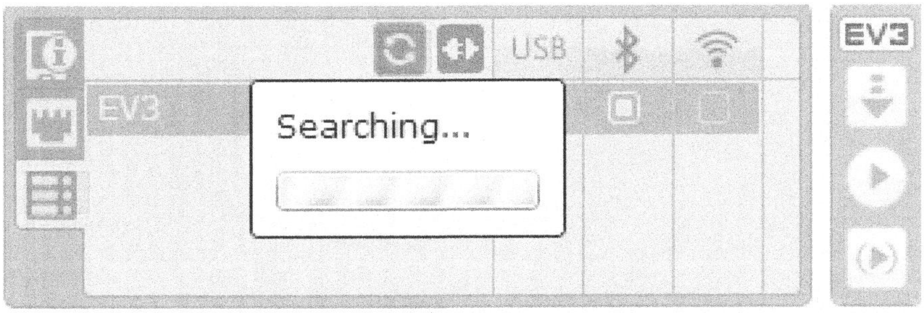

Now go to the EV3 software. Go to the 'Available Bricks Tab' and click on the refresh button.

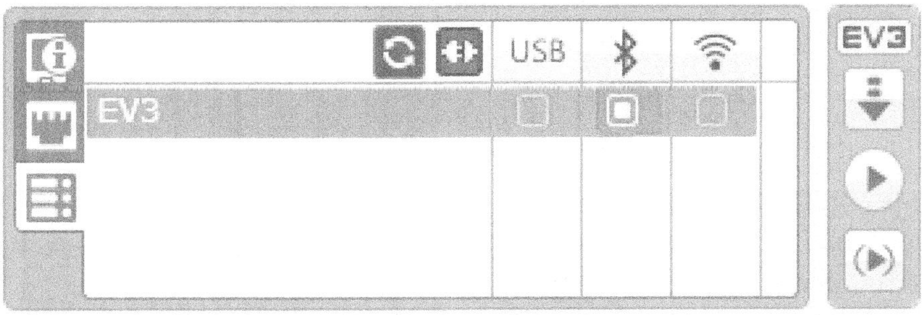

Once you see the Brick you are trying to connect to, click on the Bluetooth connect box.

Acknowledge the message and move back to the brick and you should see a code entry screen. Navigate to the Select Button and accept the Default 1234 code.

Then, check for the same code on the computer. You may have to do these 2 times before the connection is established.

Note: If you are not able to establish Bluetooth connection, there can be multiple reasons. One is that your computer does not have inbuilt Bluetooth. In case of Bluetooth connectivity failures, continue to use the USB wire for transferring the program and then running it using the Play Tab on the Brick. In this method you will need to connect the Brick every time with the USB cable to download the program (as you develop new ones or make changes) and then disconnect the USB from the robot to run it.

Once connected, go to the 'Chapter one' project and the 'single wheel turn' program in the EV3 software and click the play button. Make sure to place the robot on a flat surface with enough space around it.

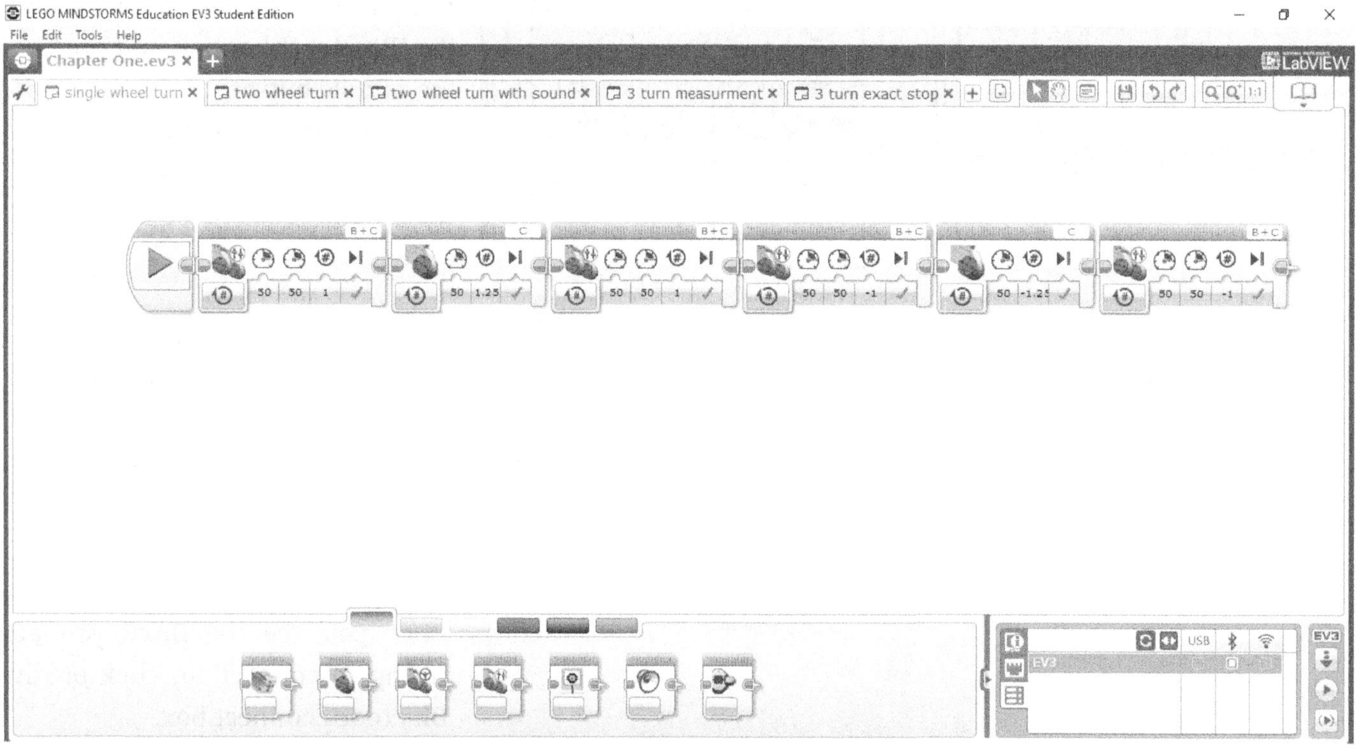

You have 3 options to run the program on the robot. You can click the play button in the 'Start Block', click the Download Button on the right-hand side bottom corner of the 'EV3' block and download the program, or you can click the play button in the same EV3 block.

Robot's Expected Behavior:

1. Travel straight due to the 1st move tank block in the program
2. Turn left due to the 2nd Single Motor block
3. Travel Straight due to the 3rd block: move tank block
4. Blocks 4,5,6 will reverse those motions and have it return to the place where it started, as shown in next picture.

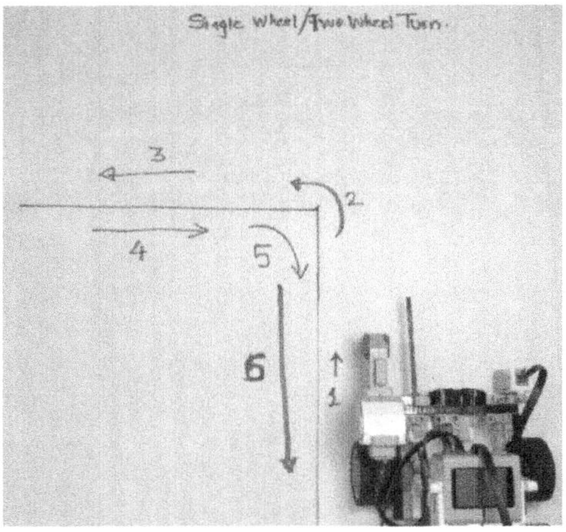

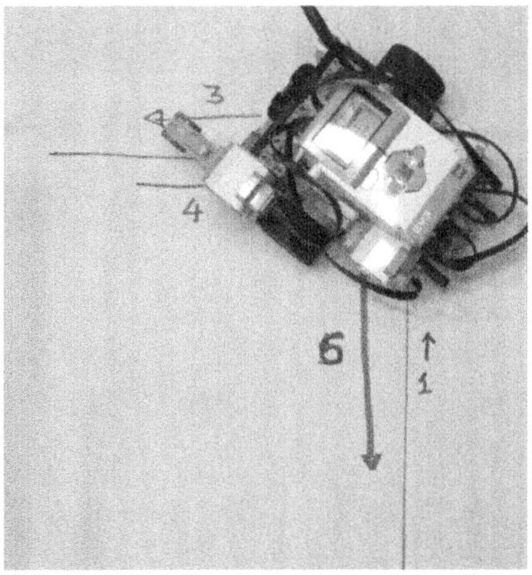

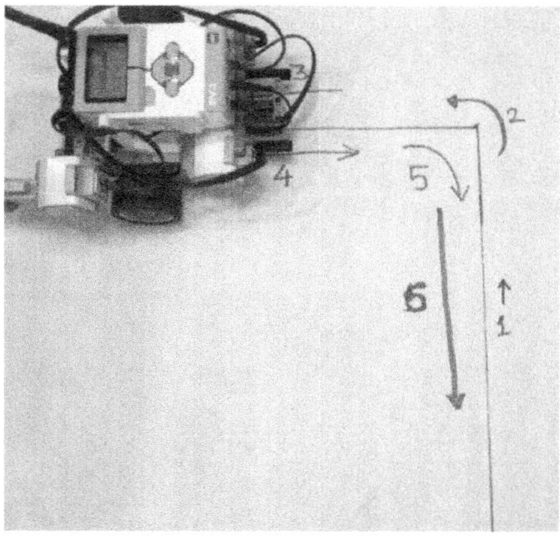

If you are using the USB download cable or if you are only downloading the program to the Brick using Bluetooth, then you should run the program from the Run Tab in the Brick or the Programs tab in the Brick.

Using the Run Tab in the Brick to Run the program:

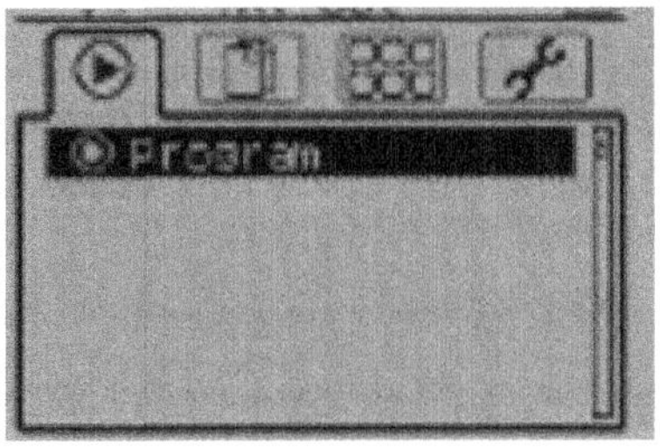

The run tab only shows recently run programs and is very useful in sequencing programs if you are planning to run multiple programs in the competition. OR using the Program Tab in the Brick to run the program.

This is how you will be running programs in competitions.

FLL or other Robotics competitions do not allow the use of Bluetooth in the competition venue. Therefore, you should know how to download the program using the USB cable and run it from the Brick.

Second Program:

Let us create our second program. In this program you will have the robot perform a 2-wheel turn and also format the program to appear on 2 different lines.

Add a second program in the **'Chapter one'** Project and name it **'two-wheel turn'**. Create this program using the move tank blocks as shown in next picture. If you click the top yellow highlighted point you can extend a connector by dragging it out and connecting it to the blocks below.

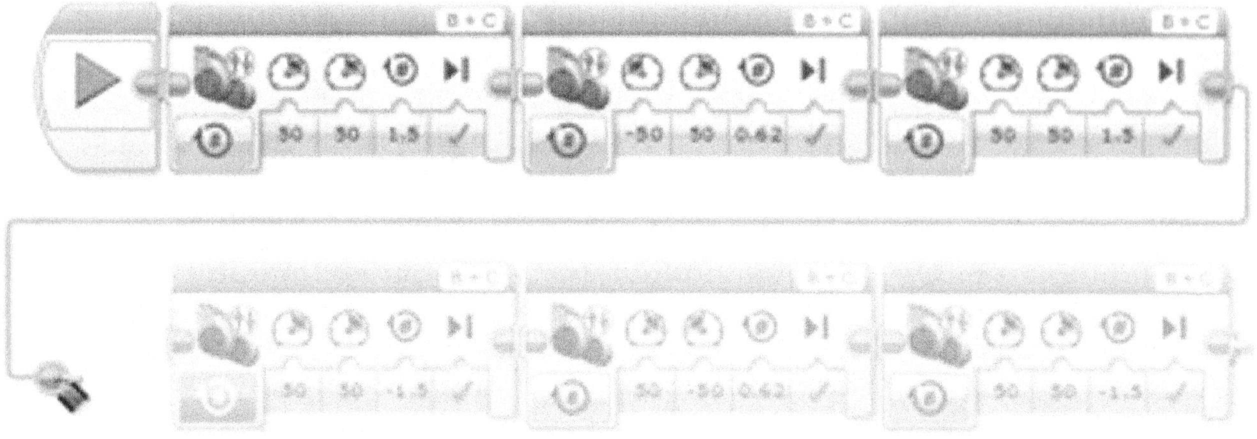

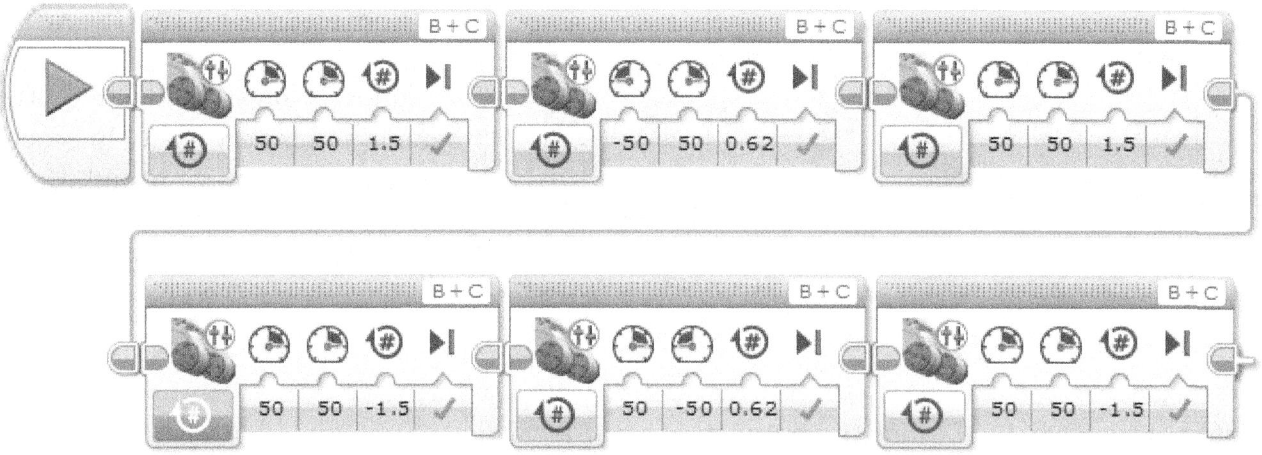

This program should make the robot move the same way as in the 'single wheel turn' program. The difference here is that the robot will now be turning with two wheels instead of one wheel.

The advantage of a two-wheel turn is that the robot can turn the same direction in a smaller amount of space.

See the next pictures for a single-wheel V.S. two-wheel turn.

In next 'two-wheel turn' picture the robot is turning one wheel in one direction, and the other wheel in the opposite direction. The area covered by the robot for the turn is less. (two-wheel turn) Also in next 'one-wheel turn' picture the robot is turning by keeping one-wheel stationary while the other wheel is moving. The area required for single-wheel turn is more than the area required by the two-wheel turn.

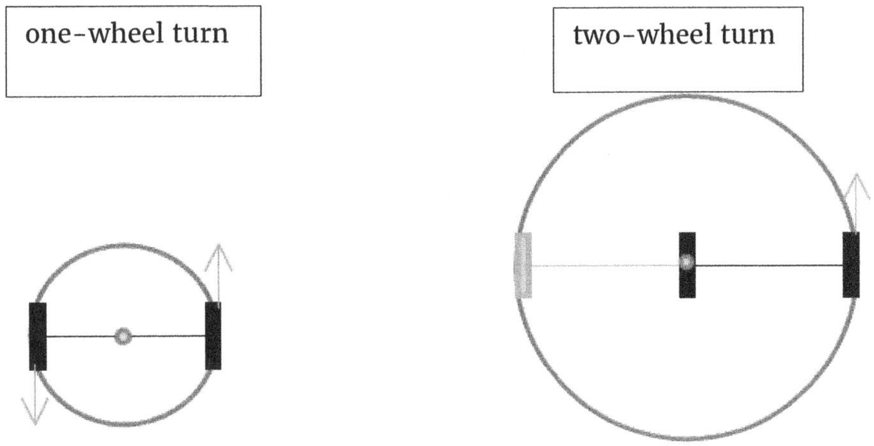

Now, let us create our third program in the **'chapter one'** project and name this program: **'turn using move steering'**. The move steering block drives 2 motors but takes angle, power, and rotations as its input. The angle you put in the move steering block will not always make the robot turn to that angle, as the turn depends on how big the wheels are and the distance between the 2 turning wheels of the robot. Typically, we solve this using trial and error.

There is a way to calculate the turn and program it, which we will learn as part of 'My blocks' in later chapters.

Complete the program below in the new program you have just created.

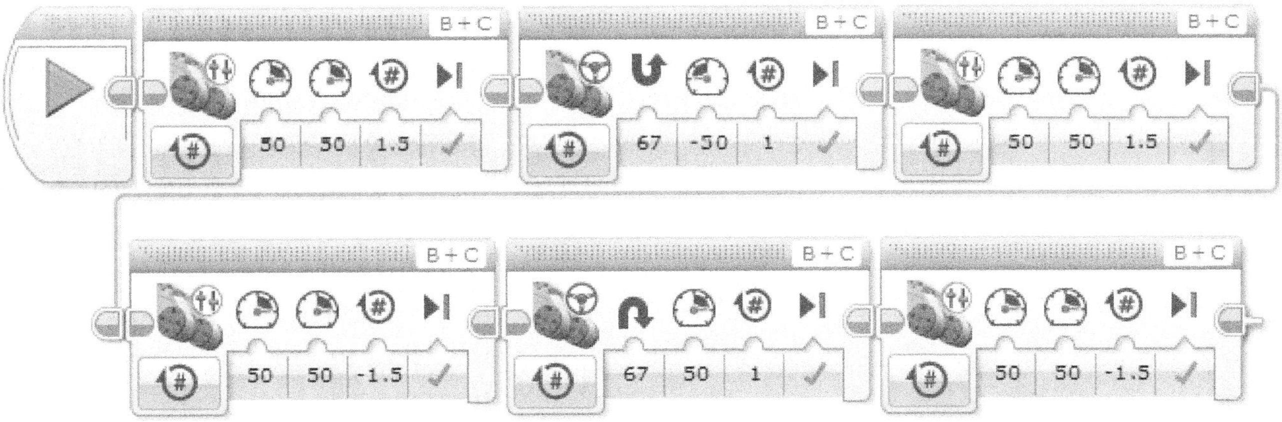

This program should also make the robot move the same way as it did in the first program.

How much distance does the robot travel in one rotation of the move tank block? How do we calculate the distance travelled?

Let us find the answers to these questions using our fourth program.

Let us create this simple program and measure the distance travelled by the robot. Name this program as '3 turn measurement' in the **'chapter one'** project.

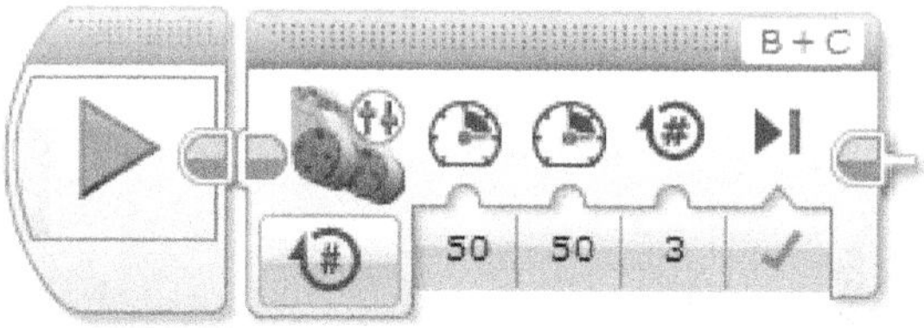

Measure the distance as shown in the picture. This should give you some idea on how to calculate the rotations to make the robot go a certain distance.

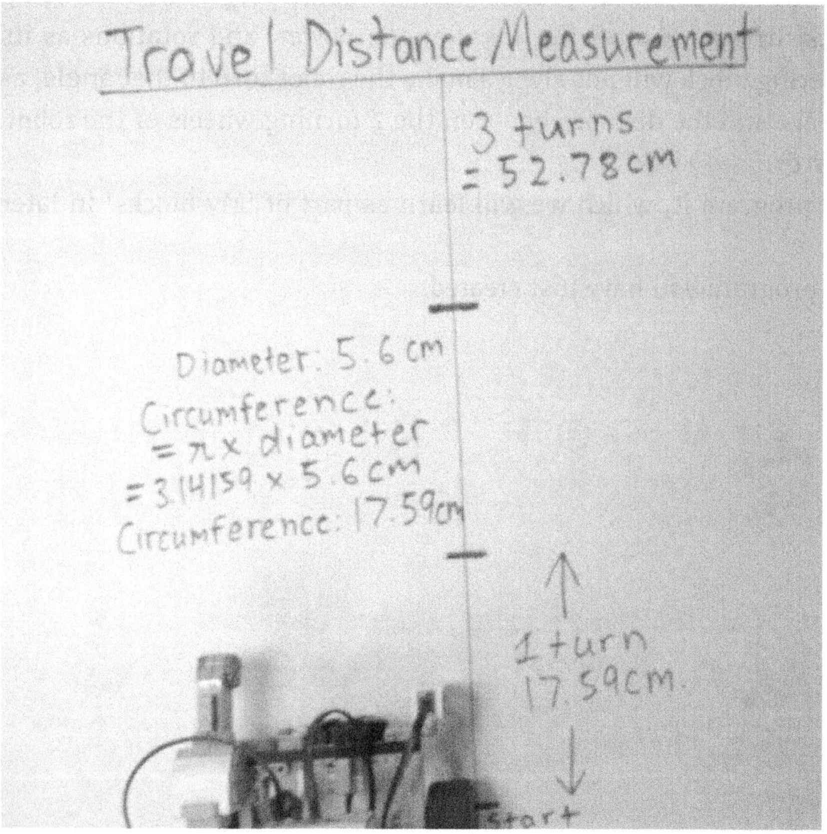

For the wheels we currently have on the robot, the robot travels 17.6 cm for one rotation.

This can be calculated using the diameter which can be found on the rim of the tires and a special value called pi (pi = 3.14159). The equation for finding the circumference or one rotation is

Pi x Diameter = 3.14159 x 5.6 cm x 1 rotation = 17.6 cm per rotation

So, if you wanted to travel 35.2 cm you should put two rotations. If you wanted to travel 30 cm then you should do slightly less than 2 turns or 1.704 rotations to be exact. You can find the exact rotations for any distance by rewriting the formula above to solve for rotations.

Finally, let us create one last fun program called 'chase the tail'. In this program the robot will turn round and round – as if it is chasing its tail.

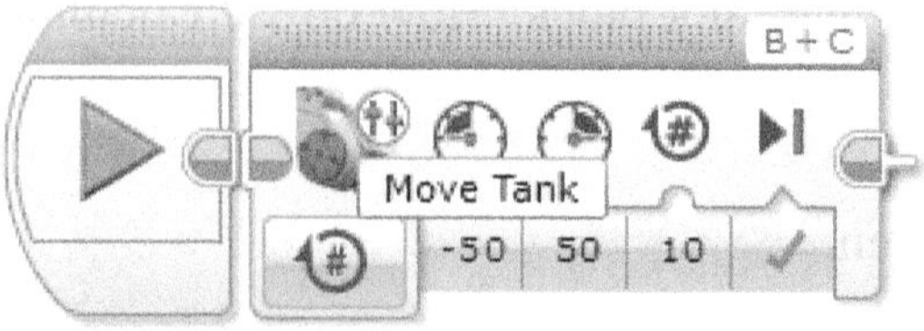

In this chapter you have learnt a lot about the different actions in the action pallet. I will be using the next few chapters to teach you about sensors and more complex programming techniques, before I start specifically talking about building robots and programing for the FLL competition.

MY ROBOT CAN SEE AND FEEL

Using Sensors

Robotic sensors are used to estimate a robot's condition and environment. These signals are passed to a controller to enable appropriate behaviour. Sensors in robots are based on the functions of human sensory organs.
— Wikipedia

Having ears, eyes and the ability to touch allows everybody to walk straight, do daily chores, enjoy playing and learn. Just like our senses, the robot has its sensors for this job.

Let us look at the various sensors which are allowed in competitions. There several sensors that are offered by LEGO but only select few are allowed in the robotics competitions. The 4 sensors allowed in FLL competition are Color, Gyro, Ultrasonic, and Touch.

SENSORS

EV3 Color Sensor –

- **Detects up to seven colors**
- **Can detect absence of color**

- **Detects light**
- **Can be used for measuring the intensity of light.**

Using the color sensor, you can build applications for sorting objects based on a color or line-following robot applications based on advanced features of the sensor. In robotics competitions we use color sensors for detecting color, for sorting, for stopping the robot at black lines, and for allowing the robot to follow lines.

EV3 Ultrasonic Sensor –

- **Can measure distance up to 250 cm (~100-inch)**
- **Has +/- 1 cm (+/- 0.394-inch) accuracy**
- **Can recognize other ultrasonic sounds**

An ultrasonic sensor works with sound waves and is often used in applications for measuring the distance between a robot and its surrounding objects. The sensor emits sound waves and receives their echoes to detect and measure the distance from one or more objects. The EV3 Ultrasonic Sensor can be used in competitions for measuring the distance to stop the robot at precise points, detecting hurdles, or allowing the robot to travel along a wall at a precise distance.

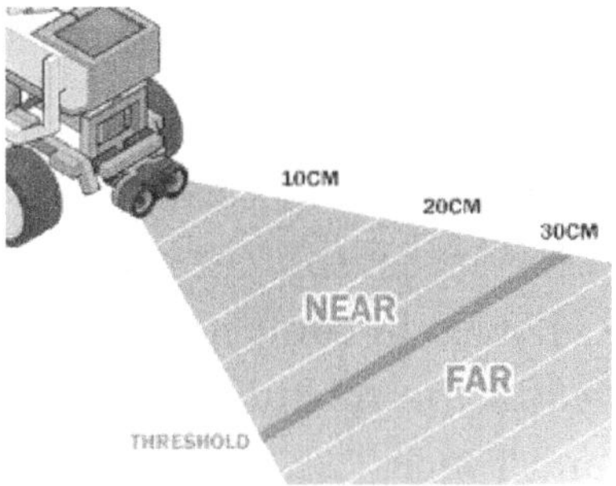

EV3 Gyro Sensor –

- **Can Measure rotational motion and changes in its orientation**
- **Has +/- 3 degrees accuracy**
- **Can detect maximum output of 440 degrees/second (Large movements are detected)**
- **Detect changes in Angle at 1 kHz (It detects fast changes in Angle)**

Gyro sensors can determine the rotation orientation of a robot on several axes giving the possibility for users to measure angles and design robots with proper navigation systems. The gyro sensor is used in competitions to allow the robot to travel straight and make precise turns without calculating the rotations (for single and multi-wheel turns) or turn angles.

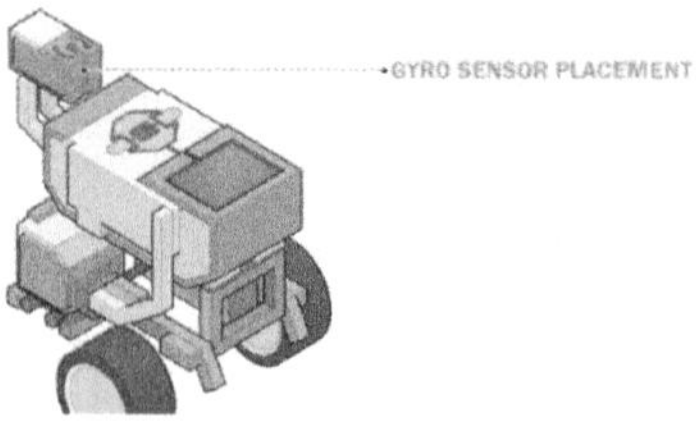

EV3 Touch Sensor –

- **Can sense touch**

The EV3 Touch Sensor is a simple sensor with a button located in the front which allows detection of press/release actions of the button. This sensor is usually used for start/stop control of the robot in competitions at a specific point.

USING SENSORS

To complete the programs below and test them you will need a plain white paper which is 25 inches by 30 inches. You can buy a standard easel pad from your local office supply store. Additionally, you will need a thick book for creating obstructions and of course EV3 parts.

Now, let us take a look at the flow control palette in the programming blocks.

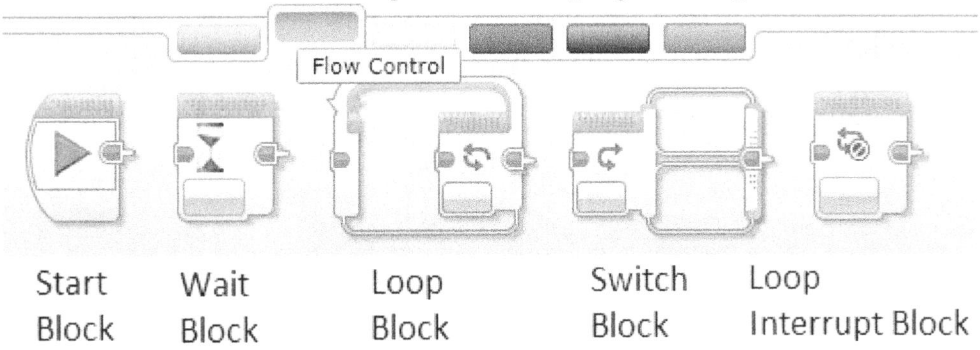

We will use the Wait block extensively in the programming included in this chapter. We will be learning about the Loop, Switch, and Loop Interrupt blocks in the next chapter.
Create a new Project called **'Chapter two'** and create the first program **'Color sensor with Sound'**. Program steps shown in next picture using the wait, sound, and move tank blocks.

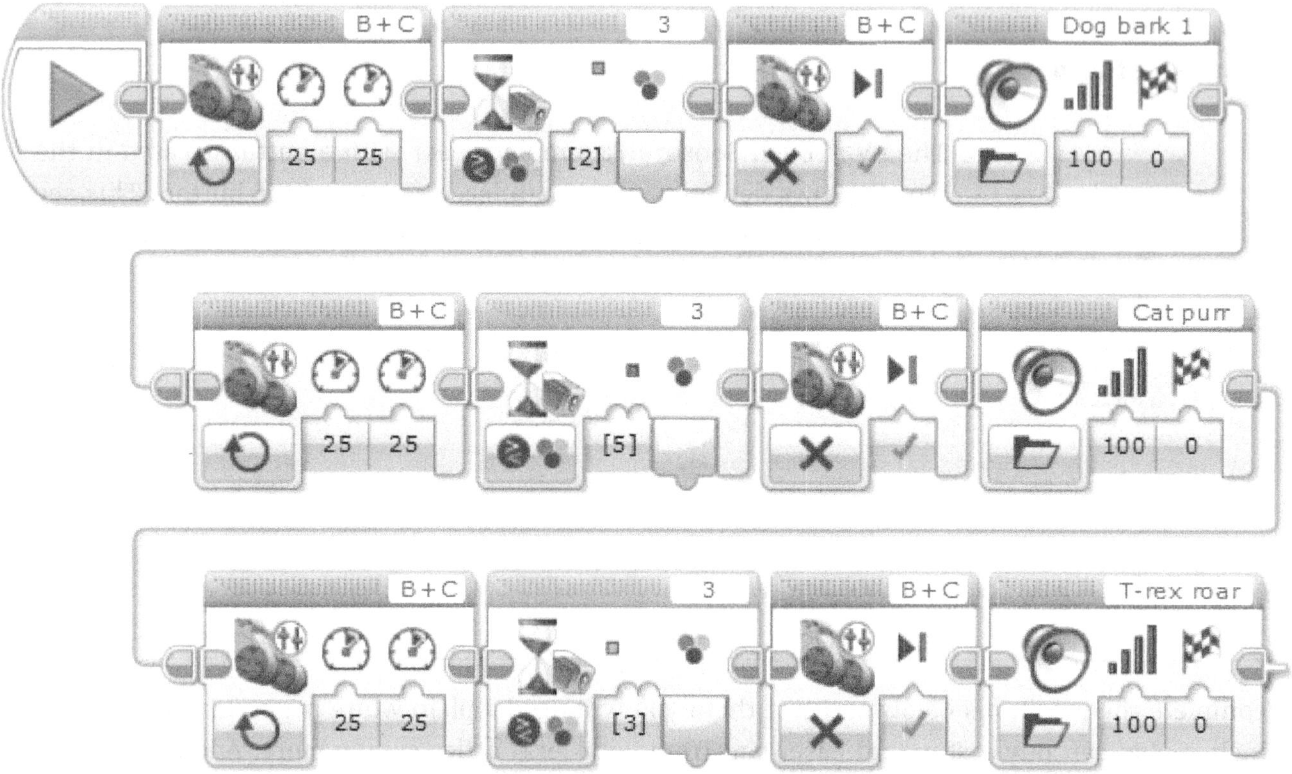

The first programming block is the continuous 'ON' Move Tank. The second block is the wait block which will stop the continuous rotations of the first block when the color sensor detects a particular color. (for the second block it is 'Blue', which corresponds to the number '2').

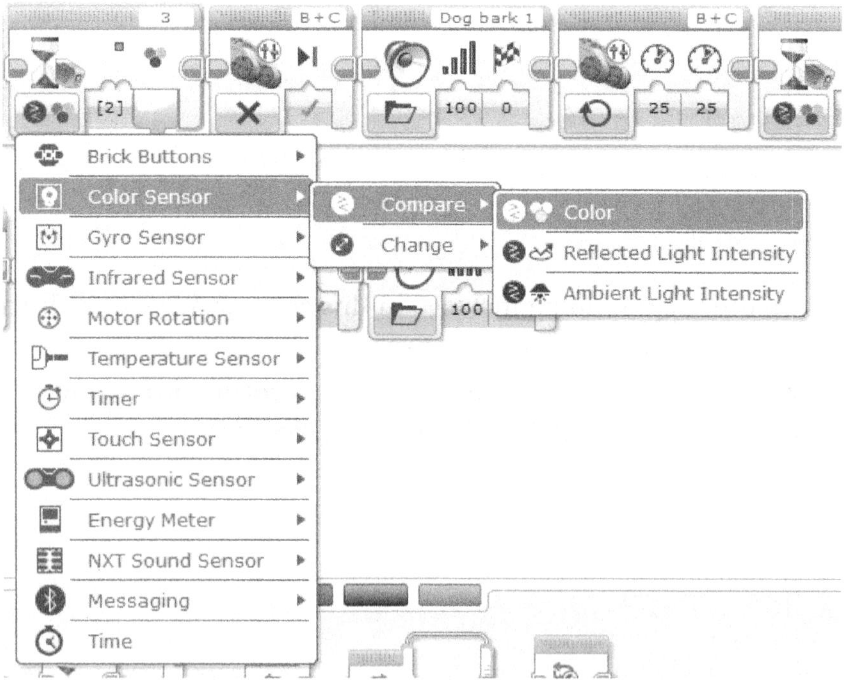

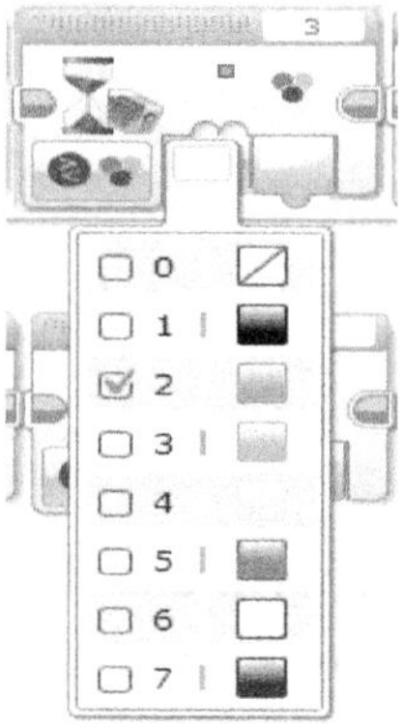

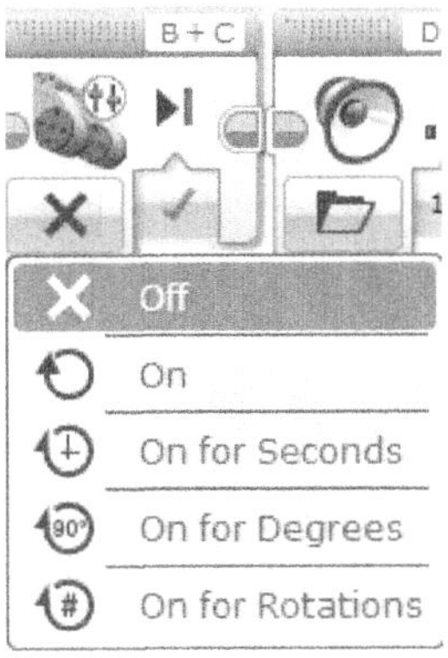

You should always add a Move Tank stop block after a wait block.

Drag a sound block and choose 'Play File'. Then click on the top box and select 'Dog Bark 1'. Select the volume as 100 and the sound type as 'Wait for Completion'.

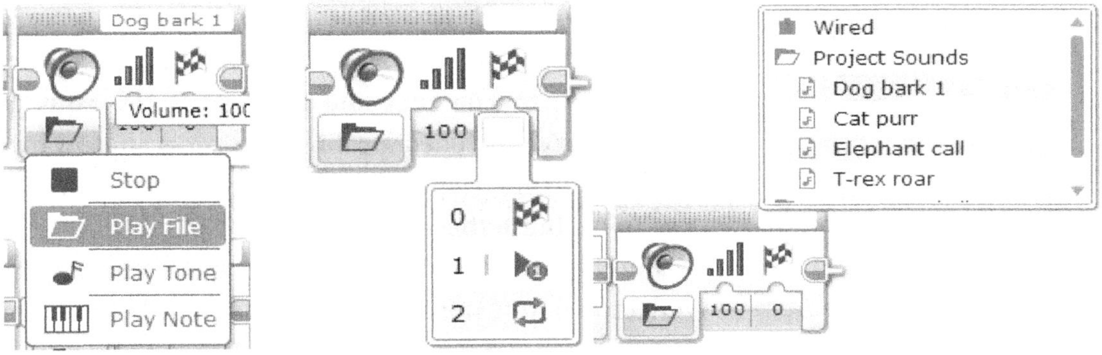

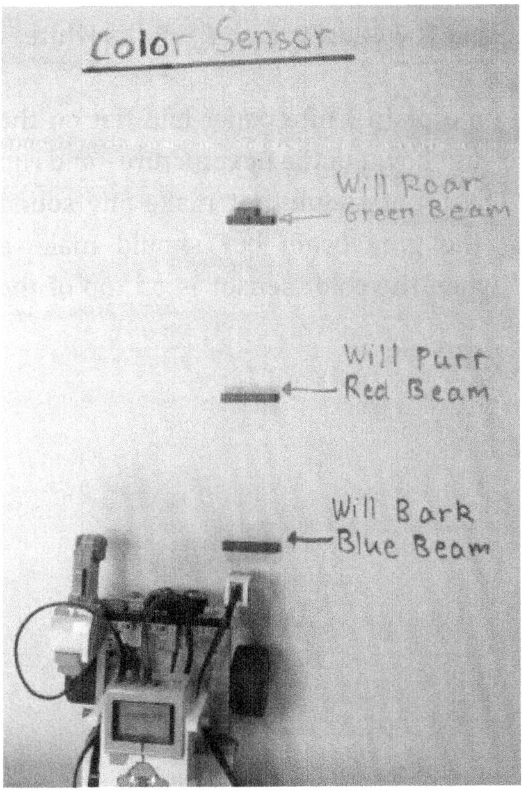

Complete the full program and setup 3 beams (Red, Blue, Green) on plain white paper, just like one shown in the next picture.
Make sure the color sensor will travel over the colored beams while the robot is moving forward.

Run the program. The robot should stop at the blue beam and make a barking sound, then it should continue and stop at the red beam and make a cat purr sound and then finally stop at the green beam and make a roaring sound.

Create a second program in the **'Chapter Two'** project and name it **'light intensity detection'**. Create the following program.

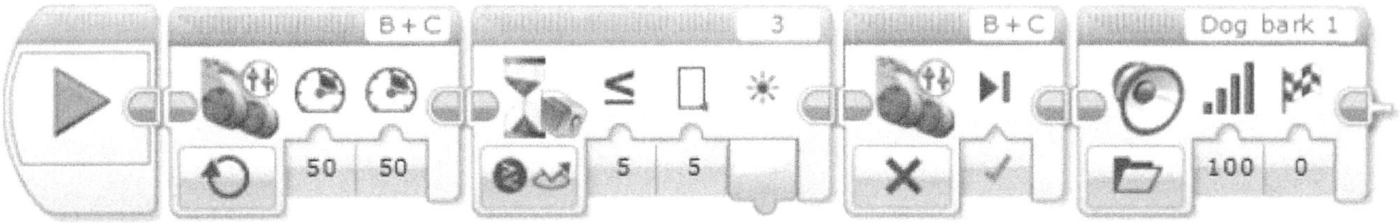

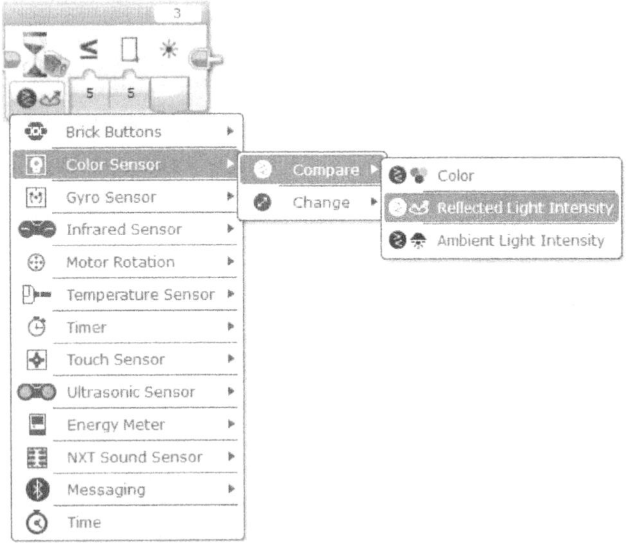

Here you are going to choose the reflected light intensity detection feature of the color sensor. This method is used to detect black lines. It is very important to calibrate the Light and Gyro sensors during the tournament and during practice runs at home. I have included a calibration program towards the end of this chapter which you can create and can use to calibrate these two sensors.

Using this programming block, you are comparing the reflected light intensity with a value '5'. If the Light intensity goes below '5' then the Robot will make a barking sound. In the light intensity detection feature a value of '0' is black while a value of '100' is white.

For running this program, setup a black beam and a grey beam on a plain white paper laid flat on the ground surface -as shown in the next picture- and run the program. The robot should not make any sound when crossing the grey beam but should make a barking sound when the color sensor is on top of the black beam.

You can always check the light intensity that is being detected by placing the color sensor over the black beam and checking the port view in the EV3 Brick or in the EV3 program software.

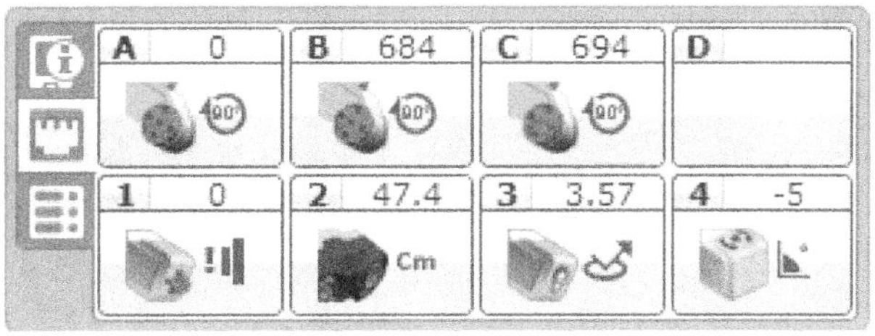

Create the third program in the **'Chapter Two'** project and name it **'ultrasonic sensor'**. Create the following program.

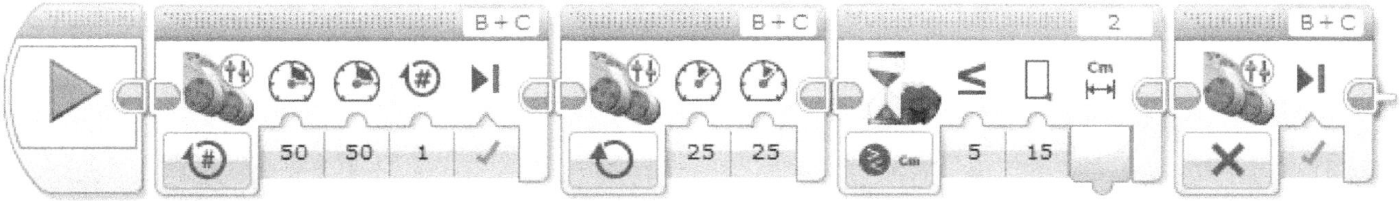

Program the wait block for the ultrasonic sensor as shown in the adjacent picture. Select the distance as less than or equal to 15 cm. Ultrasonic sensors detect distance by sending sound waves and detecting the time it takes for those waves to reflect back from a surface that is in front of the ultrasonic sensor.

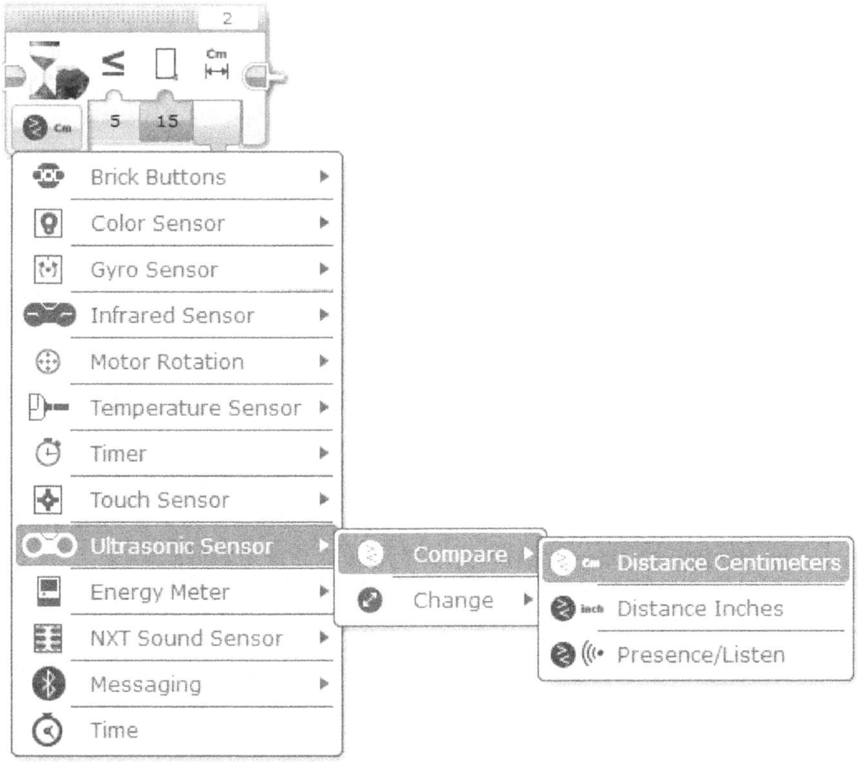

To run this program set it up as shown in the next picture. Place a thick book on the plain white paper and lay it flat on the ground. Make sure that the ultrasonic sensor is facing the flat surface of the book.

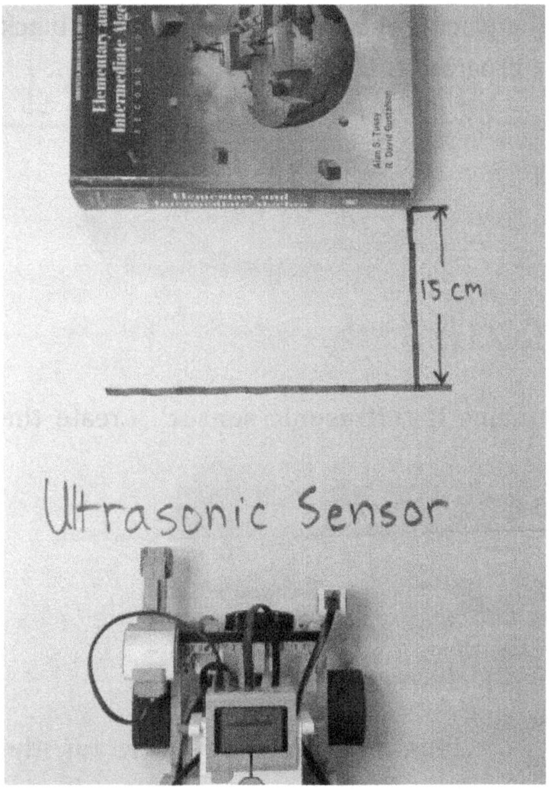

Run the program. The robot should stop 15 centimeters away from the book. The actual distance is measured from the point indicated in the picture below.

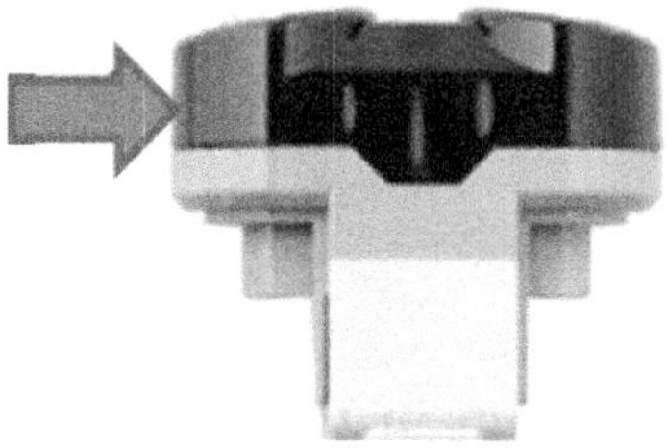

Create a fourth program in the **'Chapter Two'** project and name it **'touch sensor'**. Create the following program.

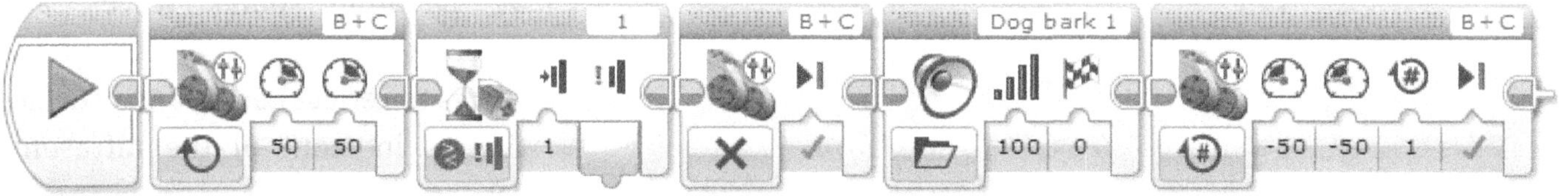

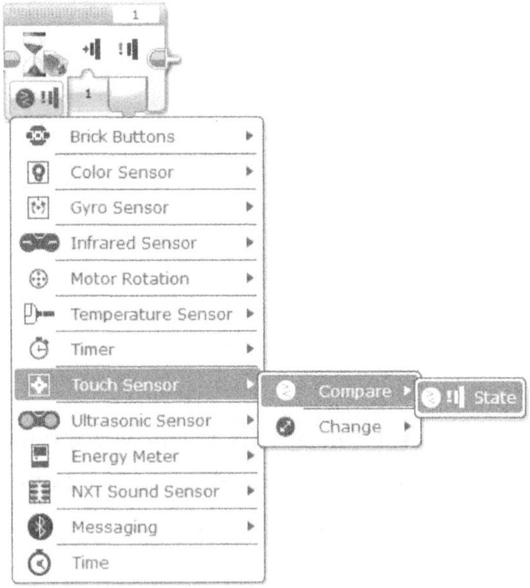

Program the wait block for the touch sensor as shown in the next picture. Select the state as '1 – pressed'.
The touch sensor has a button, that detects touch whenever the button is pressed.

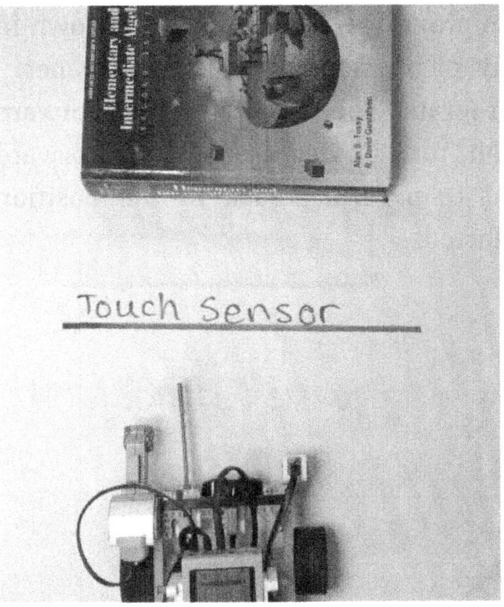

For running this program follow the setup in the next picture. Place a thick book on the plain white paper to serve as the obstruction. Make sure that the touch sensor has an axle and is facing the flat surface of the book.

Run the program. The robot should stop when the axle attached to the touch sensor makes contact with the book. Immediately after touching the book, the robot should make a barking sound and return back.

Create the fifth program in the **'Chapter Two'** project and name it **'gyro sensor'**. Create the following program.

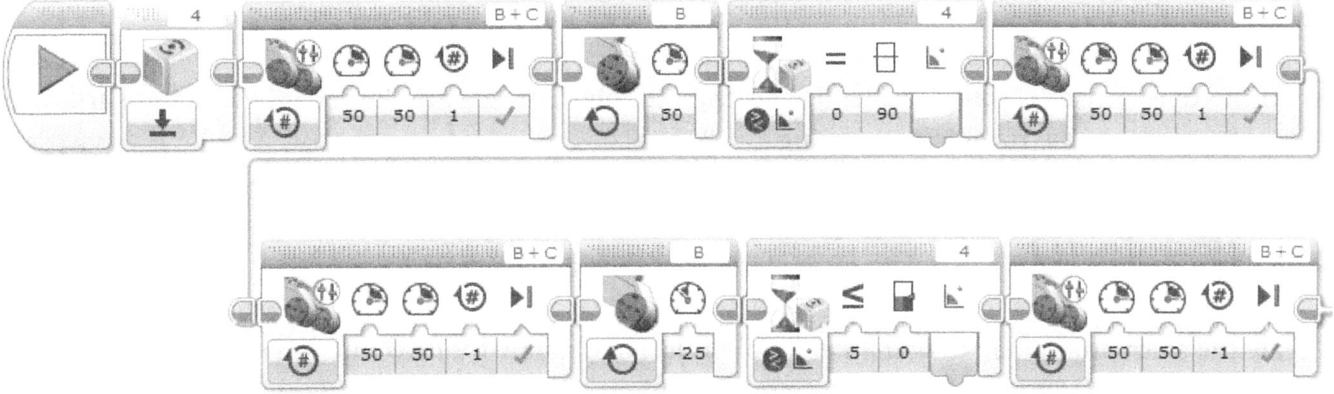

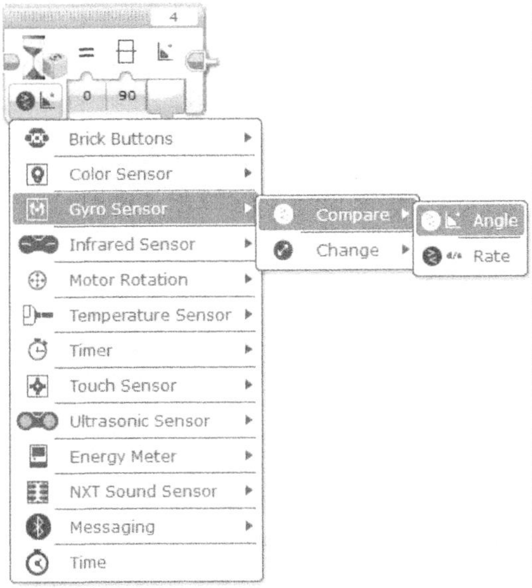

Program the wait block for the gyro sensor as shown in the picture. Select the angle as 90 degrees

The gyro sensor detects angles and allows the robot to turn precisely based on the angle provided in the programming block. Since the gyro sensor is very delicate, you must restart the brick before the program.

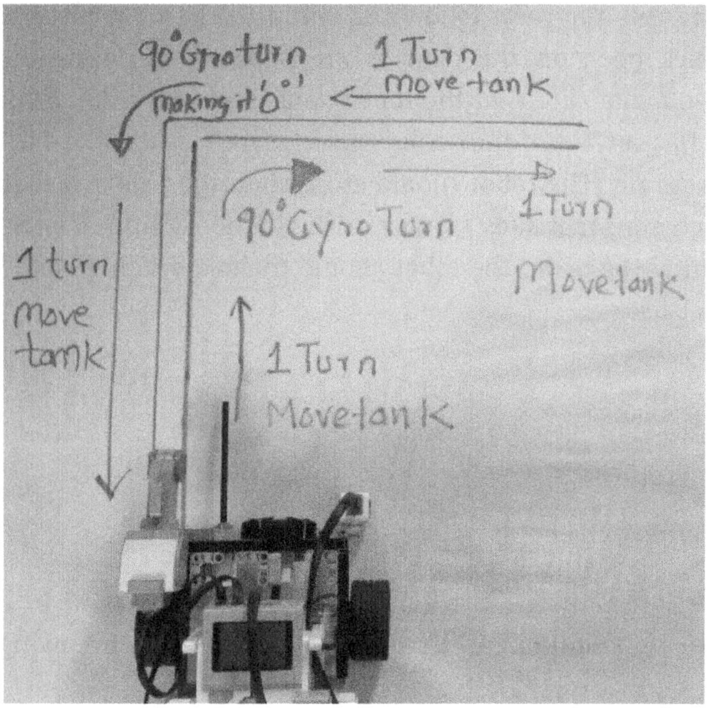

To run this program, create the setup shown in the adjacent picture using a plain white paper. Run the program. The robot should go forward one rotation, turn 90 degrees right, go forward again, and then return back to the position where it started.

To achieve reliable behavior from the Gyro sensor, make sure you follow these tips:

- If the Gyro sensor is connected while starting the robot, make sure the robot is on a flat surface and make sure that the robot is not moving.
- Disconnect and reconnect the gyro sensor while the robot is on only if you are seeing significant issues with the angle constantly changing, while the robot is at rest.
- Always calibrate the gyro sensor after starting. - see Calibration.

Create the sixth program in the **'Chapter Two'** project and name it **'ultrasonic sensor precise'**. Create the following program. **This is the programming technique you should use in competitions for ultrasonic sensor programs that are used to stop the robot at a specific point.**

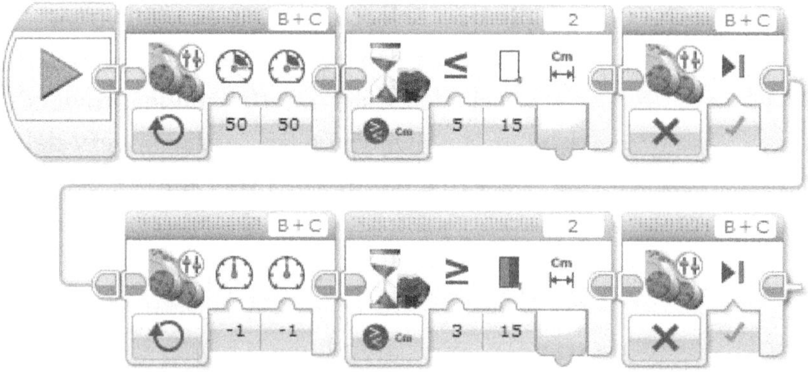

To run this program, follow the setup shown in the next picture. Place a thick book to serve as the obstruction. Make sure that the ultrasonic sensor is facing the flat surface of the book.

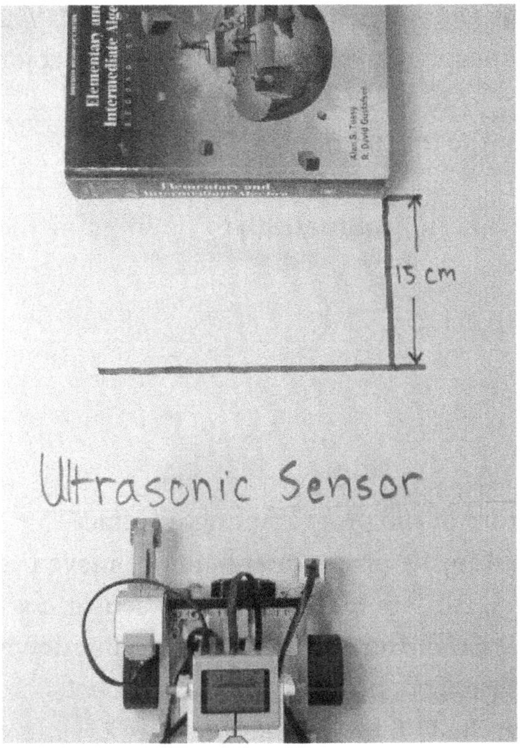

Run the program. The robot should stop 15 centimeters away from the book. This program actually accounts for the fact that the robot can move a little closer than 15 centimeters away from the book during the first stop. Therefore, it slowly backs the robot up to ensure the distance is exactly 15 centimeters.

Again, the actual distance is measured from the point indicated in the picture below.

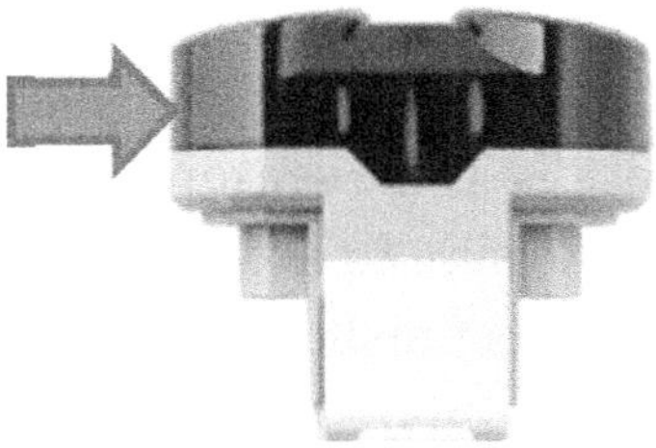

CALIBRATION

Running Calibration programs – Visit my website to download both programs.
Create the seventh program in the project **'Chapter Two'** and name it **'calibrate color'**. Program the following.

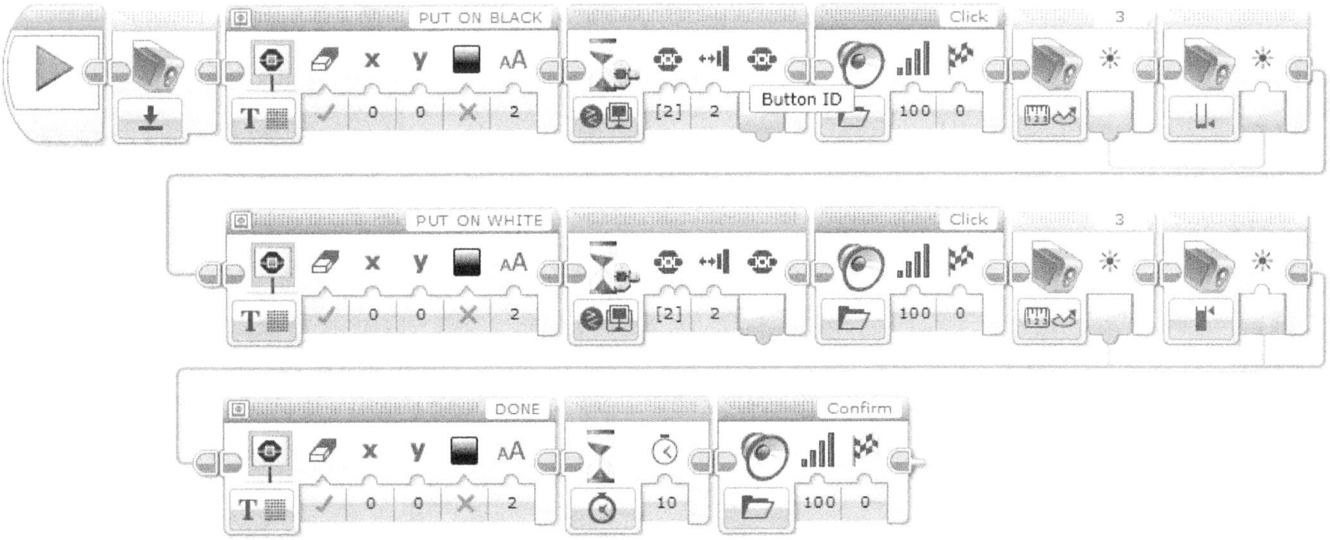

Run the program and place the color sensor exactly on top of the black beam and then press the center button. Wait for 5 seconds and place the color sensor on top of a white background (the paper we have been using for our previous programs) and press the center button. Once done wait for 10 seconds till you hear the confirmation beep. Once you hear the confirmation beep, you will know that your color calibration is finished.

I have always performed this color calibration for every match in the tournament.

Create the eighth program in the project **'Chapter Two'** and name it **'calibrate Gyro'**. Program the following.

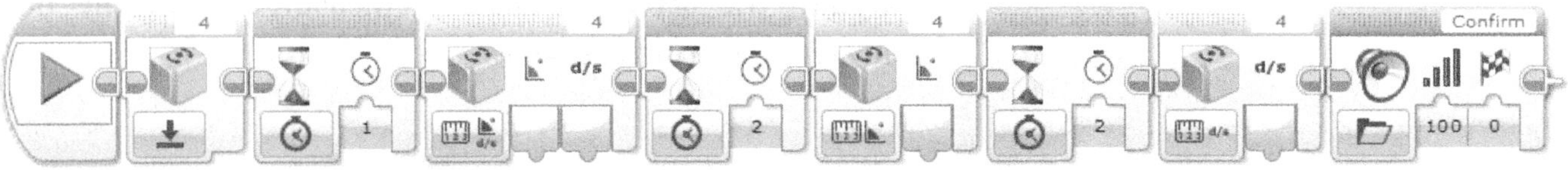

The Gyro Sensor Block is in the sensor palette(yellow) at the bottom of the programming interface. When calibrating, make sure to keep the robot on a flat surface. Run the program and do not move the robot till the program has finished running. Based on my data analysis, sometimes the gyro sensor does not respond to calibration and angle drift occurs. The best calibration of the gyro sensor is to shut down the robot, disconnect the gyro sensor wire, reconnect it after 10 seconds, and then restart the robot.

I have always calibrated the gyro sensor before every match in the FLL tournament.

ROBOT HAS INTELLIGENCE

Programming

Logic will get you from A to B. Imagination will take you everywhere
—Albert Einstein

The most discerning aspect of human beings is their intelligence. You can make decisions based on your environment. A simple example of this is that you will always walk through an open door but will open the door first if its closed. Furthermore, think about how drivers will drive their car if the street signal is green, but stop if it is red. Finally, how do you open a bottle of juice or soda? If the lid does not open the first time you try, you will keep trying but in different ways and that is the bare bones of intelligence. Robots get this intelligence through programming. While programing the EV3 robots you are constantly making better programs by experimentation. Today scientists and engineers are writing programs (Machine Learning) that allow robots to learn and use those inputs to autocorrect and improve activities they do. This is called 'Artificial Intelligence'.

What is Artificial Intelligence?

AI was coined by John McCarthy and is the simulation of human intelligence processes by machines (computer systems and robots). These processes include learning (the acquisition of information and rules for using it), reasoning (using the rules to reach approximate and definite conclusions) and self-correction. Applications of AI include expert systems, speech recognition, and machine vision.

Now, let us build some programs that consists of logic blocks and learn about all the different programming palettes we can use. We will gradually build more and more complex programs in this chapter that will be very useful in competitions.
You have done a great job in understanding the building blocks of EV3 by building a simple robot and creating programs to use actuators(motors) and sensors. Let us learn about the other programming palettes.

LOGIC AND SENSOR PROGRAM BLOCKS

We have already looked at the flow programming palette and used the 'Start' and 'Wait' block in chapter-2. Let us take a look at other program blocks in this palette.

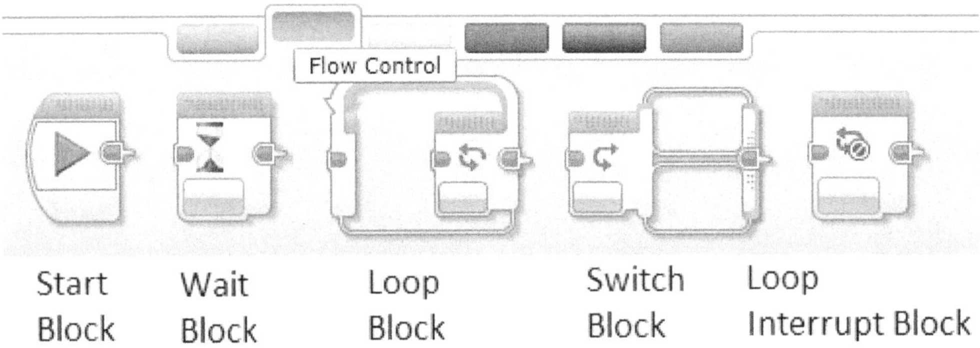

Loop Block – It is used to repetitively do actions you program and stop repeating the program steps in the loop when certain criteria are met.
Switch Block – Is the power of logic in your hands. It allows you to create conditional programming. Eg: if the color is red then move the robot but if the color detected is green then do nothing.
Loop Interrupt Block –The Loop Interrupt block makes a Loop block end. No more blocks in the loop sequence will execute, and the program will continue with any blocks that are after the loop. You can specify which loop block to interrupt by using its loop name.
You can use the Loop Interrupt block to make a loop exit sooner than it normally would, or in response to a different condition. You can interrupt a loop from inside the loop itself, or from another block sequence that is running at the same time.

Next, let us take a look at the 'Sensor' programming palette.

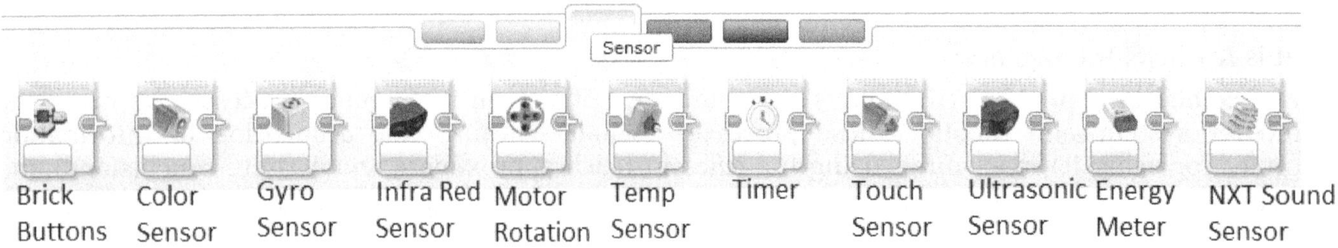

Brick Buttons: The Brick Buttons block gets data from the Brick Buttons, which are the five buttons on the face of the EV3 Brick. You can find out which button is pressed and obtain a numeric output. You can also test one or more buttons to check if one is Pressed, Released, or Bumped, and get a True or False output. We have used this block with limited success to start programs in competition by pressing brick buttons instead of going to the 'run Program' tab on the Brick.
Color Sensor: The Color Sensor block gets data from the Color Sensor. You can measure the color or intensity of light and get a numeric output. You can also compare sensor data to an input value and get a True or False output.
Gyro Sensor: The Gyro Sensor block gets data from the Gyro Sensor. You can measure the rotation rate or rotation angle and get a numeric output. You can also compare the sensor data to a threshold value to get a True or False output.
Touch Sensor: The Touch Sensor block gets data from the Touch Sensor. You can test whether the touch sensor is pressed, released, or bumped, and get a True or False output.
Ultrasonic Sensor: The Ultrasonic Sensor block gets data from the Ultrasonic Sensor. You can measure the distance in either inches or centimeters and get a numeric output. You can also compare the distance to a threshold value to get a True or False output.
Motor Rotation: The Motor Rotation block gets data from the Motor Rotation sensor that is built into the medium motor, and large motor. You can measure how far a motor has turned in degrees or rotations. You can also get the current power level that a motor is running at. The Motor Rotation block can also compare the rotation amount or power level to a threshold value to get a True or False output.
Infra-Red Sensor: Not used in competitions.
Temperature Sensor: Not used in competitions.
Timer: Not used in competitions.
Energy Meter: Not used in competitions.
NXT Sound Sensor: Not used in competitions.

Lastly let us look at Data Operations palette.

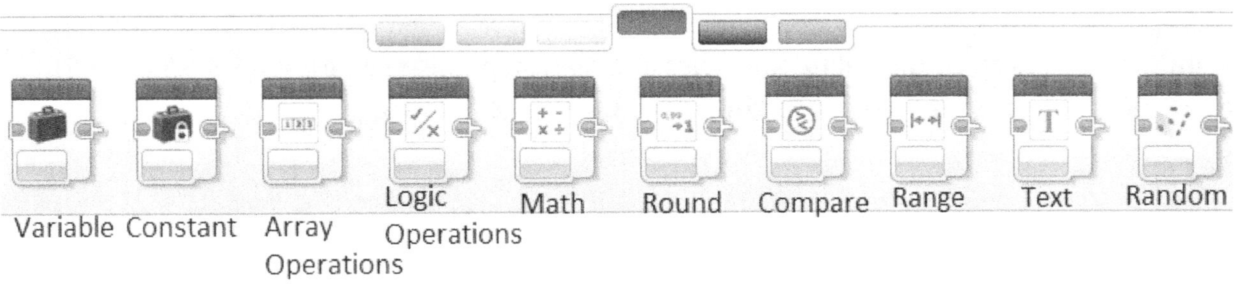

Variable: The Variable block lets you read or write a variable in your program. You can also create a new variable and name it.
Constant: The Constant block lets you enter a value that you can use in several different places in your program. If you change the value of the constant, all places where you use the constant will get the updated value.

Array Operations: The Array Operations block does operations on the Numeric Array and Logic Array data types. You can create an array, add elements, read and write individual elements, and get the length of an array. I have used this to store the color code for the various colors of the game elements in the FLL competition. Using this instead of individual variables is much more convenient but at the same time more complex.

Logic Operations: The Logic Operations block does a logic operation on its inputs, and outputs the result. A Logic operation takes inputs that are True or False and produces a True/False output. The Logic operations available are AND, OR, XOR, and NOT.

- AND returns True when both inputs A and B are True and False for all other cases
- OR returns True when either of the inputs A and B are True
- XOR returns True as result only when one of the inputs is False and another is True.
- NOT returns False as result when the input is True and True as a result when the input is False.

Math: The Math block does a math calculation on its inputs, and outputs the result. You can do a simple math operation with one or two inputs or enter a formula with up to four inputs.

Round: Rounds the number.

Compare: The Compare block compares two numbers to find out whether they are equal, or which number is greater. You can choose one of six different comparisons. The output result is True or False.

Range: The Range block tests whether a number is inside or outside a specified numerical range. The output result is True or False.

Text: Merges up to 3 text strings

Random: Not used in competitions

The Advanced block has program blocks that can be explored but I have found it of no specific use for competition programming except for data logging.

LOOP PROGRAMS

Let us start with a simple program of the robot chasing the tail.

You want the robot to chase the tail for 30 circles and then stop. Create a new Project 'Chapter Three' and create the first program **'chase the tail using loop'**. Create the following program

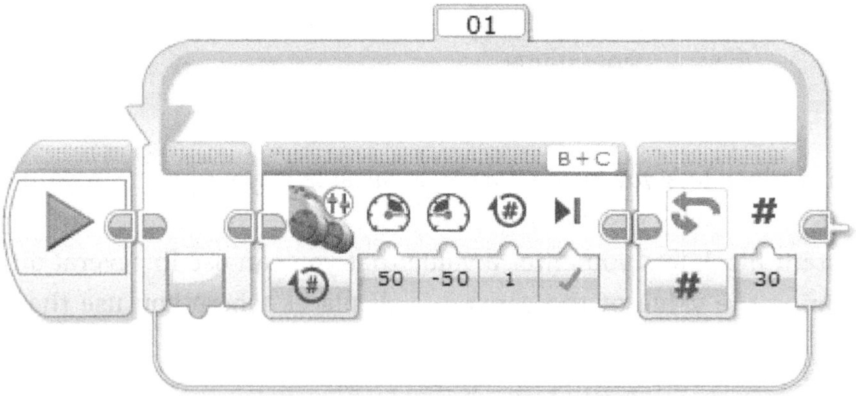

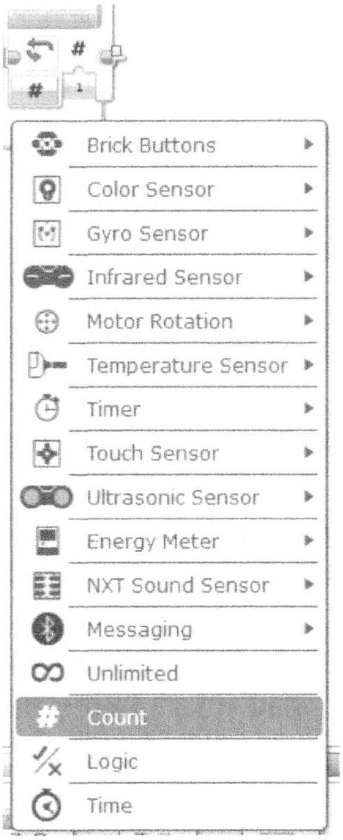

Here for the loop block, the exit condition is a count of 30.

When you run this program, the robot will turn around for 30 rotations and then stop. (The actual rotation will depend on how much the robot turns in a one-wheel rotation).

In this program the 'Loop Block' continues to perform actions (in this case: Move Tank) again and again till the count reaches 30.

The other options for the loop block are described below.

The 'Time' option specifies how many seconds the loop block should continue. This option is rarely used in competition programming.

The 'Brick Buttons' option can be used to make the robot wait till a particular brick button is pressed. This is very useful in competitions to make the robot wait in the 'Pit area' (Base Area) till you change the attachment.

Logic - The Logic mode, the loop will repeat until the input to this block is True at the end of the loop sequence.

Most of the times we will use the 'Logic', 'Color Sensor', 'Gyro Sensor', 'Ultrasonic Sensor' or 'Touch Sensor' options.

Create a second program in project **'Chapter Three'** and name it **'Ultrasonic Sensor Precise'.** In this program we will use the 'Loop Block' and 'Math Block' to program the robot.

Program the following:

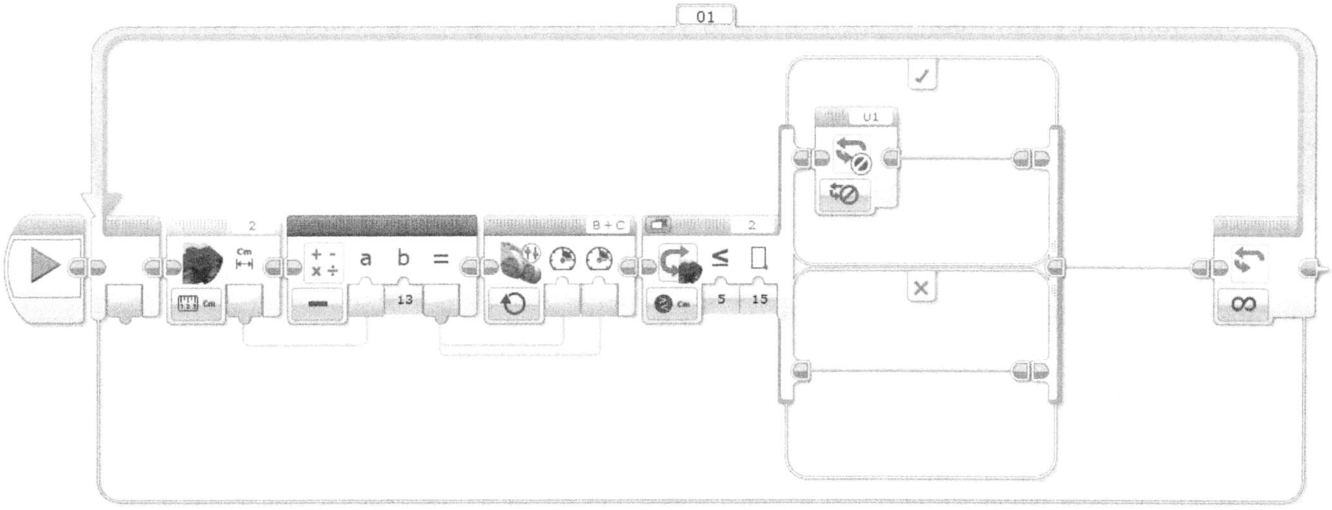

Before we understand how this program works, let us make sure we understand how to create it. Apart from the normal drag and drop of the blocks we will also be using 'Data Wires'.

Check the next picture to learn how to connect Data Wires.

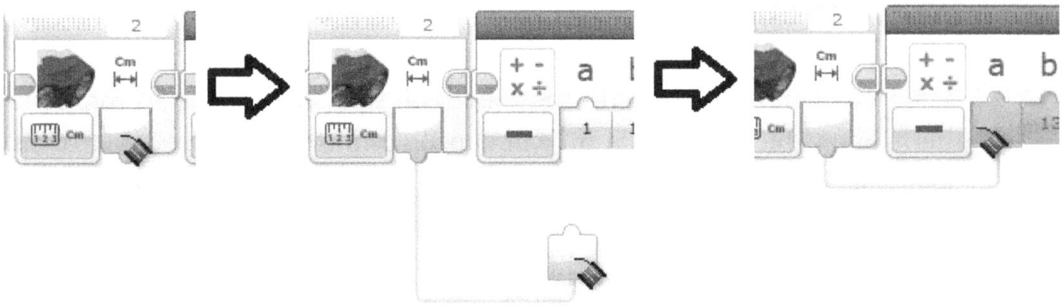

When you run this program, the robot will slow down as it approaches the obstacle and then will stop precisely 15 cm away from the obstacle.
We are using the ultrasonic sensor block to continuously measure the distance from the obstacle and that numeric value output is fed through the data wire to the 'Math' block. The Math block subtracts 13 from the value and feeds it as the power to the move tank through the data wires.
As the Robot approaches the obstacle the power to the motors decreases and the ROBOT slows down. **The reason why we do not bring the power to '0' is because at a power less than 2 the Robot stops completely, as the power is not enough to drive the weight of the Robot.**
The switch block checks for distance and if the distance is less than or equal to 15 cm then it interrupts the loop. The reason we use the 'less than or equal condition' is because the rate of detecting the distance is not fast enough to detect exactly 15 centimeters and if we only use the 'equal to' condition then the loop will never interrupt and the block right after the loop will never be executed
Coming out of the loop block is very important in the competition in order to perform actions that you have programmed after the loop block. Otherwise you will need to pick up your robot and incur a penalty

Create a third program in project **'Chapter Three'** and name it **'Unstoppable'.** This is a fun program where the robot will try to find its way and will avoid any obstacles that the ultrasonic sensor senses in front of the robot.

Program the following:

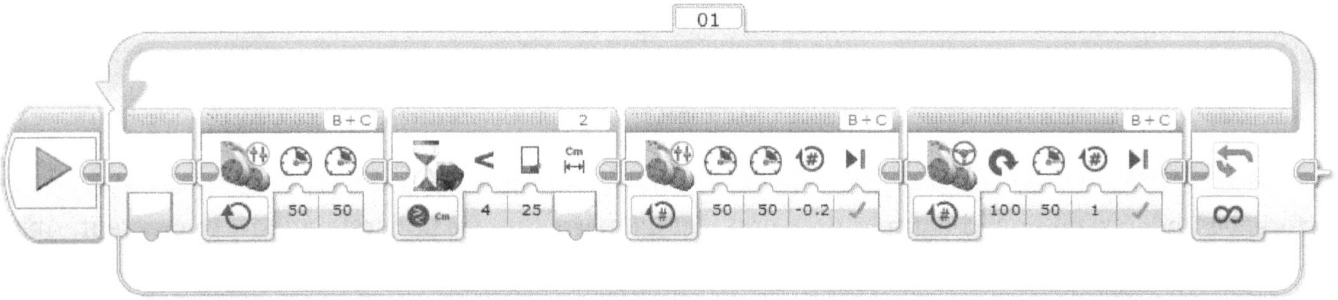

When you run this program, it will get within 25 centimeters of an obstacle, backup a little bit and then turn to avoid the obstacle. The robot will keep looping through this program, so ideally in a square room

with no furniture, this program will never let the robot stop. I think a similar but more sophisticated program exists in vacuum cleaning robots.
Create a fourth program in project **'Chapter Three'** and name it **'Unstoppable Random'.** This program can be used to play a game between the team members to guess where the robot will turn on the Game Table.

The Game Table is where the FLL robotics mat is laid out and the competition robot completes challenges. We will learn more about this in the next chapters.
Program the following:

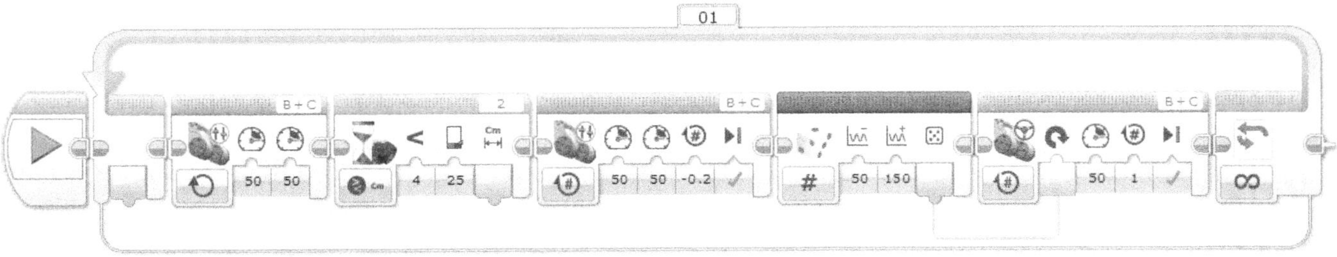

When you run this program, the robot will turn based on a random input between 50 and 150 provided by the 'Random' block to the move steering block. People in the team can try and predict the next turn of the Robot by placing hand in the anticipated path of the Robot.

Create a fifth program in project **'Chapter Three'** and name it **'random Color Sensor w sound'.**

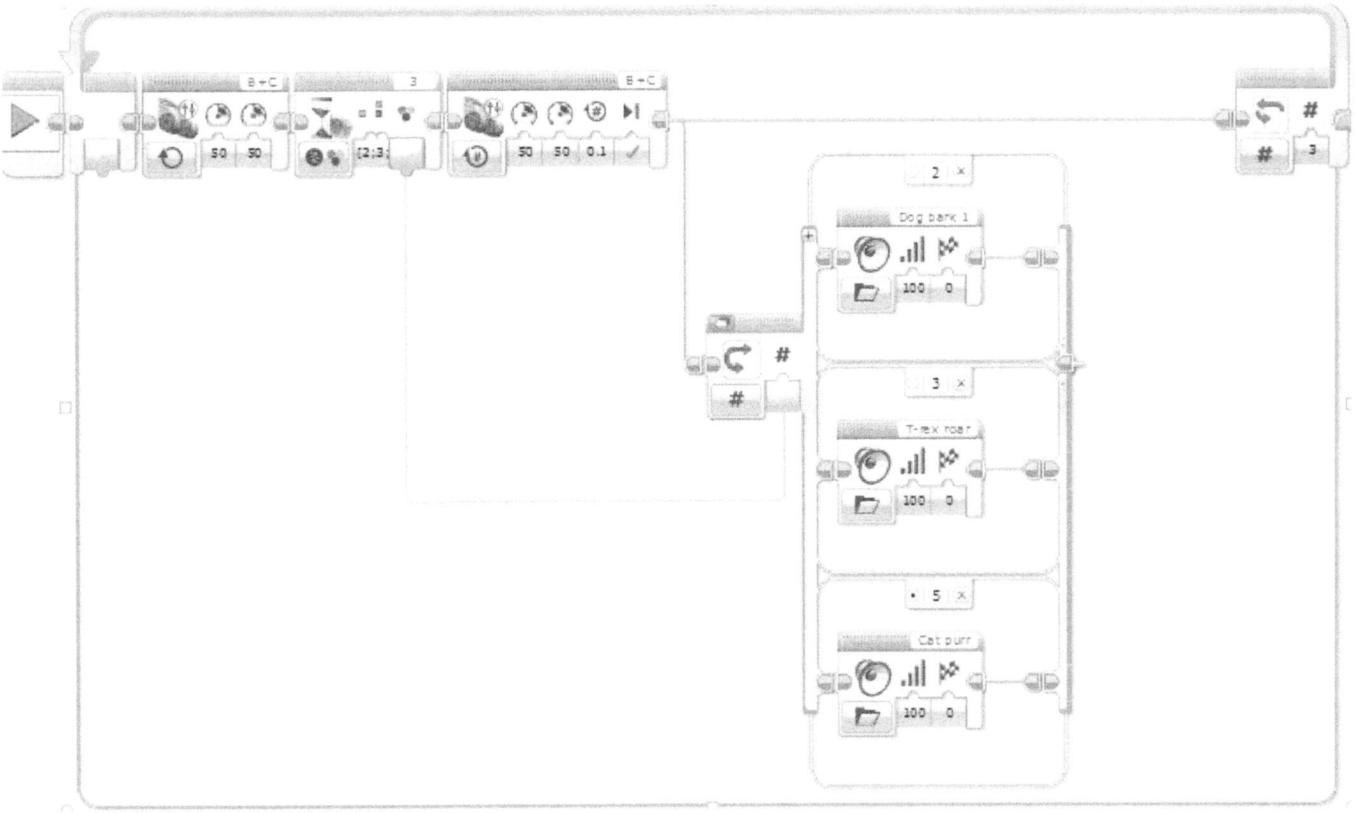

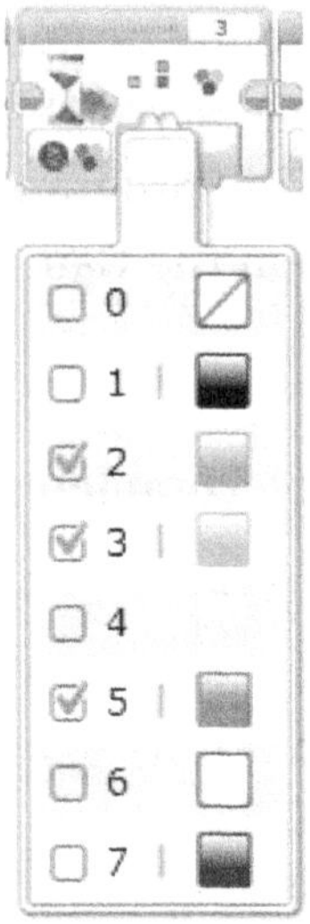

This program is similar to the program we created in Chapter-2 but you can order the colors red, blue and green in any order and the robot will make the dog barking sound for Blue, cat purr sound for red, and T-Rex roar sound for green.

Note that the 'Wait block' has 3 colors selected.

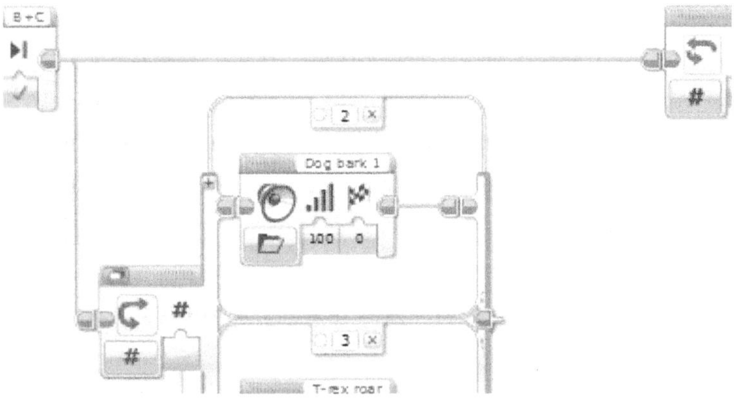

You must have noticed that from a single block you can draw lines to 2 different set of program blocks. This is called 'parallel processing' or 'multi-threading'. This allows the program to do 2 jobs at same time.

Setup the beams like the picture below, but now you can set the beams in any order. With the switch block you do not have to worry about the order of the colored beams The loop count is set to 3, so the program detects three beams in any order and then stops.

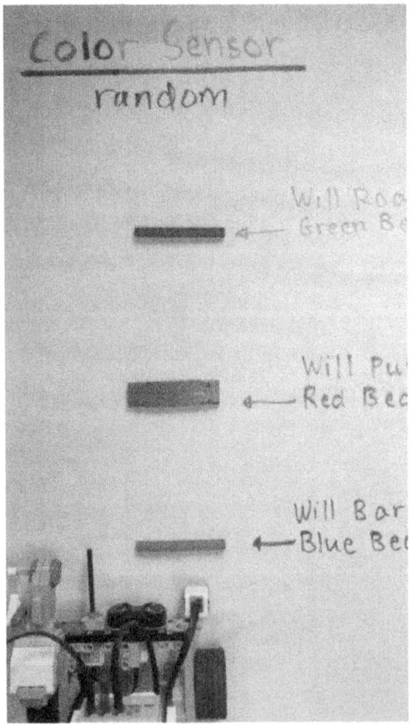

Typically, in the competition you have to detect a color and perform specific actions based on the color. Create the sixth program in the project 'Chapter Three' and name it 'black line detection and stop' Create a claw as shown in the picture and attach it to the arm motor as shown. Use the following parts.

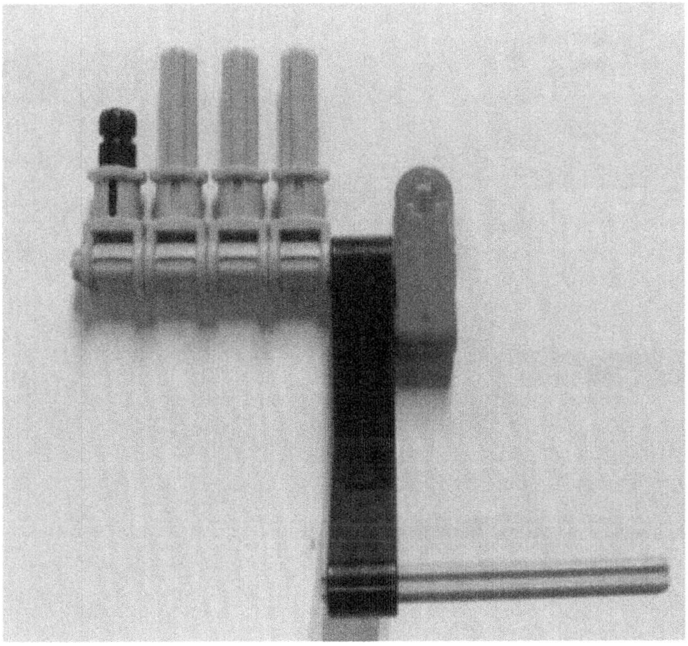

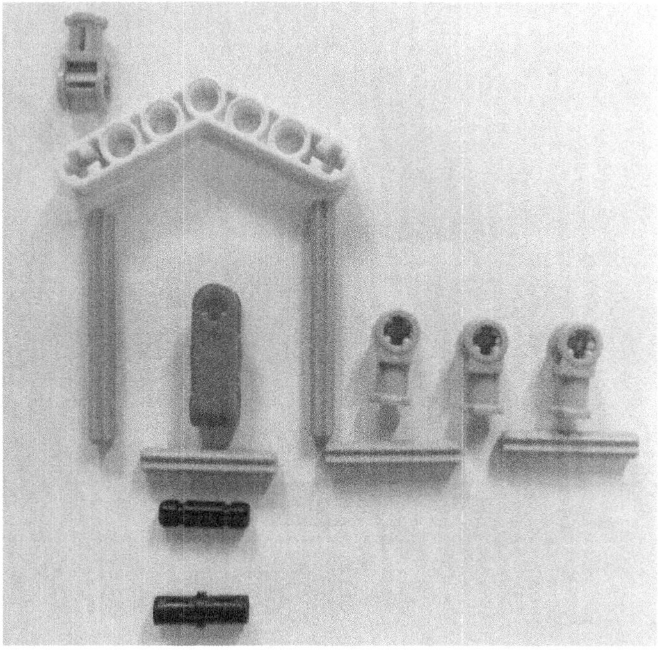

Construct it as shown in the picture. You don't have to be perfect as this is just for fun.

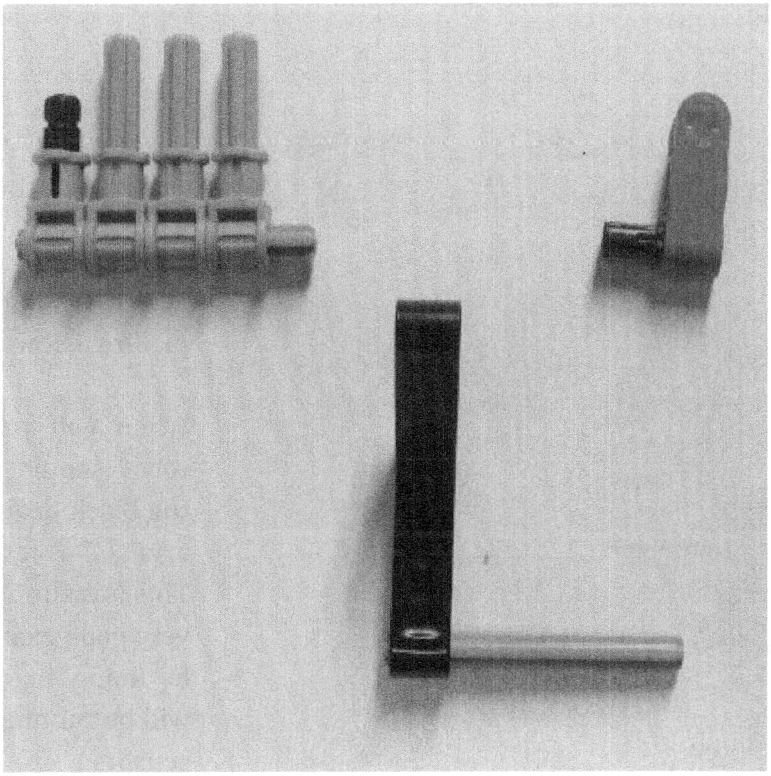

Attach it to the Robot as shown.

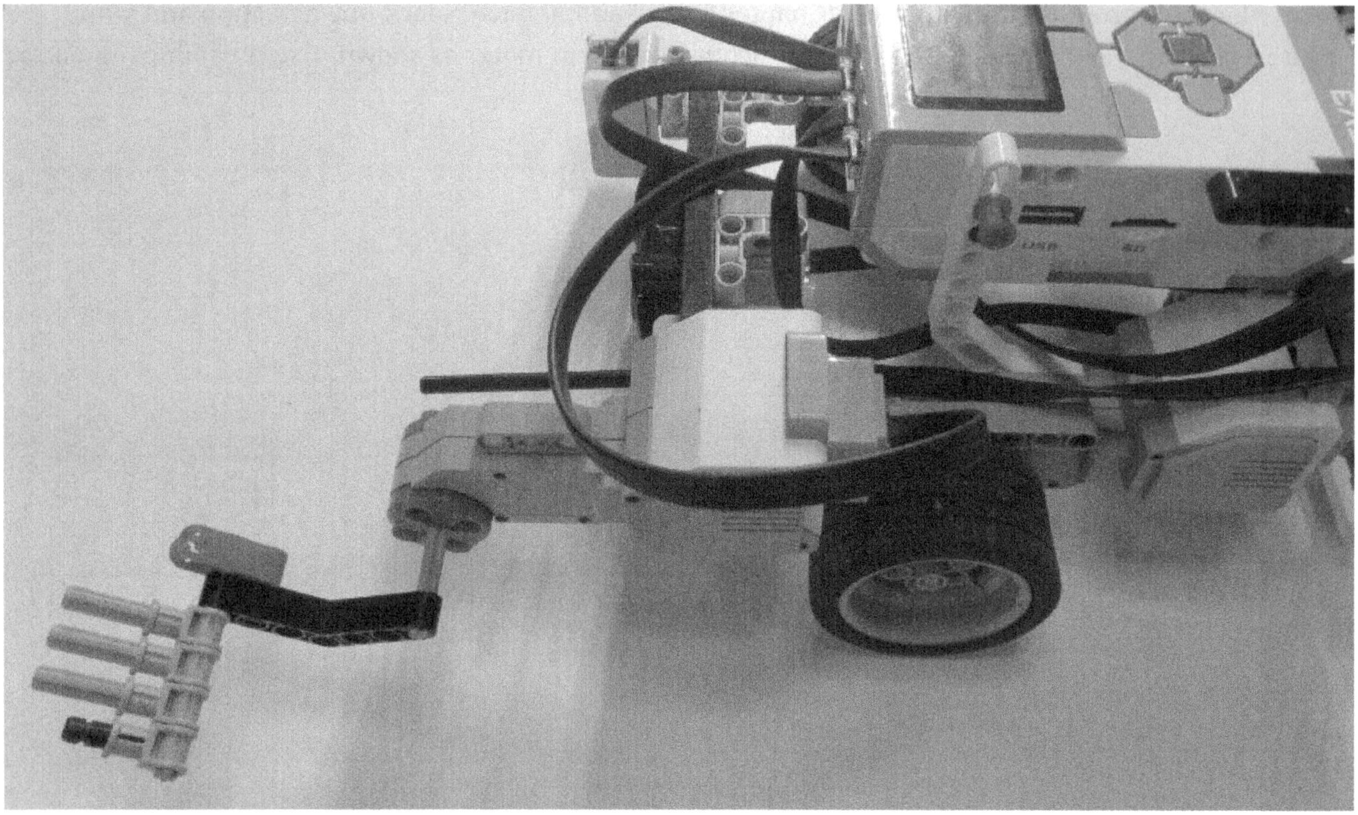

Modify the sixth program.

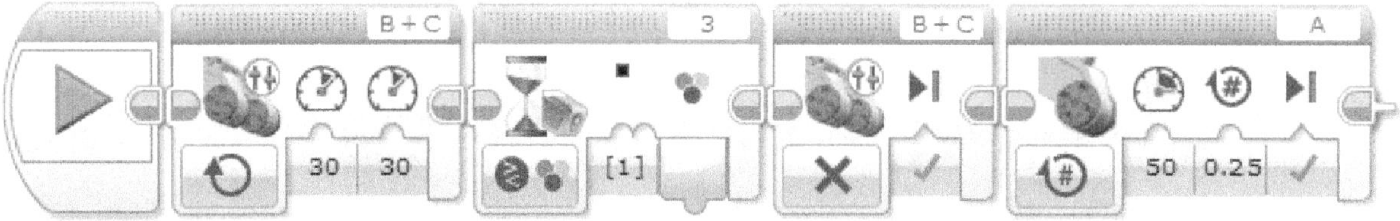

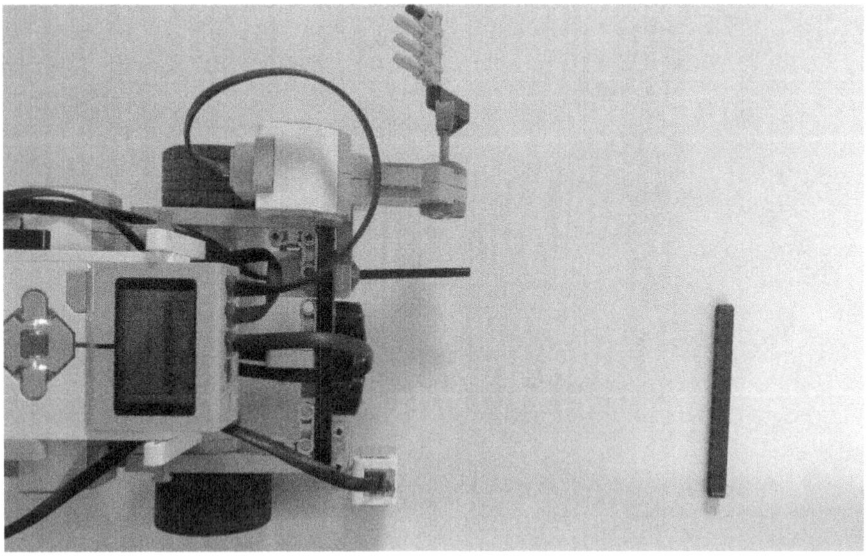

Setup the Robot as shown in the picture below and run the program.

When you run the program, the robot should stop after detecting the black beam and then move the arm 1/4th rotations.

This is a simple program, but it is a very good example of what you will be doing in the competition. You will be running the robot and using sensors to detect a certain condition. These certain conditions can be that a black line is crossed on the mat or the distance from the game table wall is 15 cm. Once the condition specified in the program is met, you will make robot act by running actuators to perform a task or complete a challenge.

PROGRAMS USEFUL FOR COMPETITION

Create a seventh program in the project **'Chapter Three'** and name it **'random Color Sensor w action'**. Continue to use the same claw.
Create the following program:

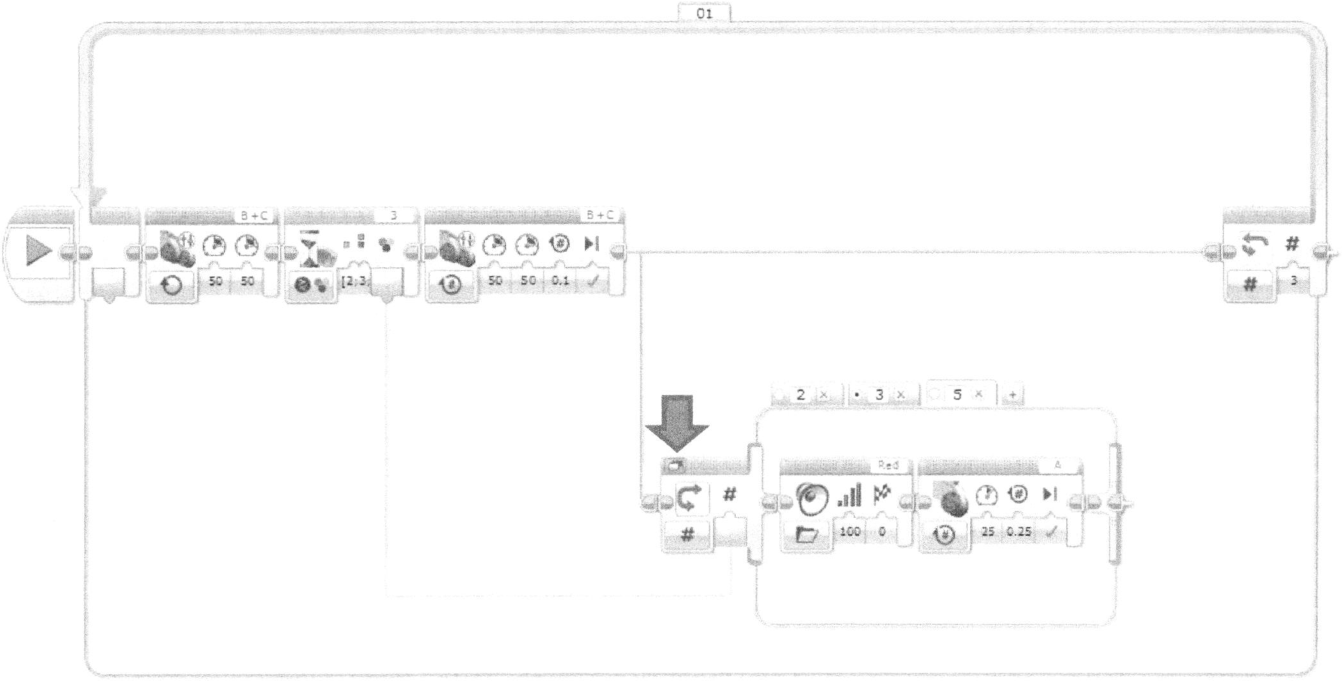

In this program I am showing the tabbed view of the switch block. This can be easily changed to flat view by clicking on the button shown by arrow at the leftmost corner of the switch block. The Tabs 2,3 and 5 when clicked, will show the programming under each tab.

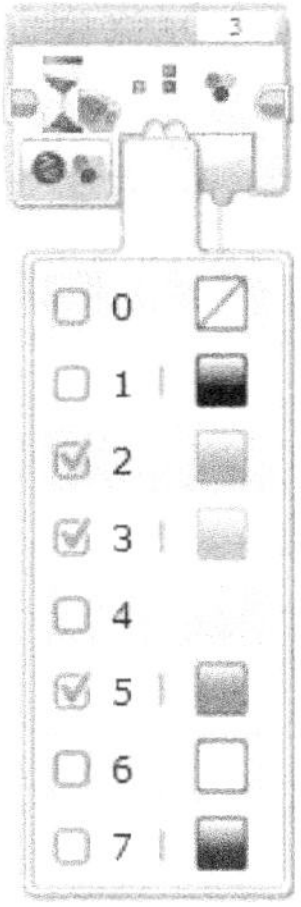

In this program, we are selecting 3 colors Blue, Green and Red for the color sensor wait block.

Here is the programming under each tab.
For the blue tab you move the arm anticlockwise.

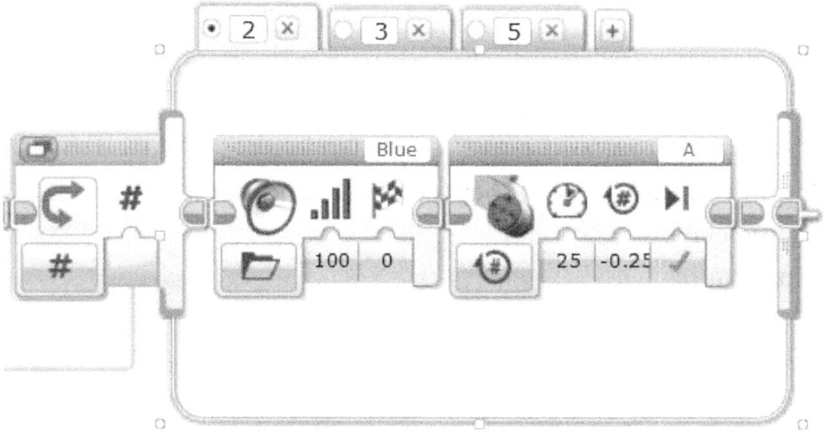

For the green tab you do not move the arm at all.

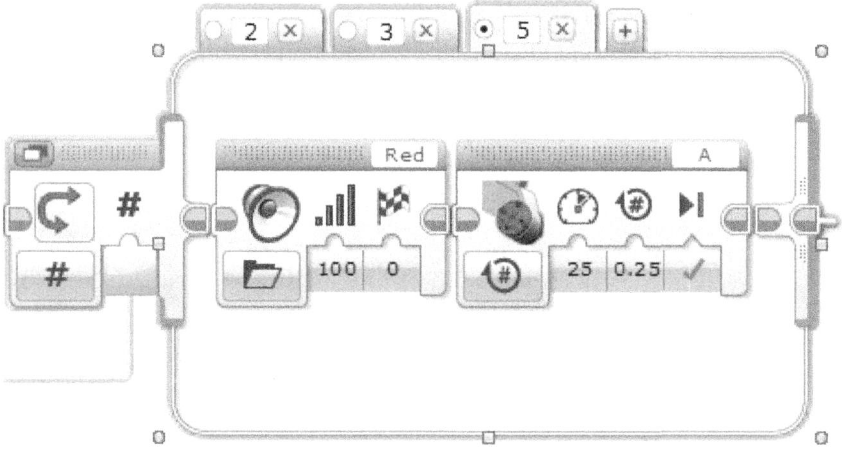

For the red tab you move the arm clockwise.

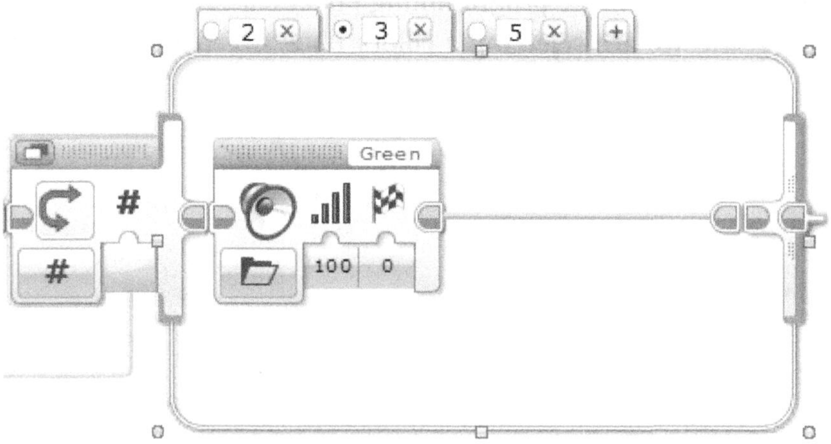

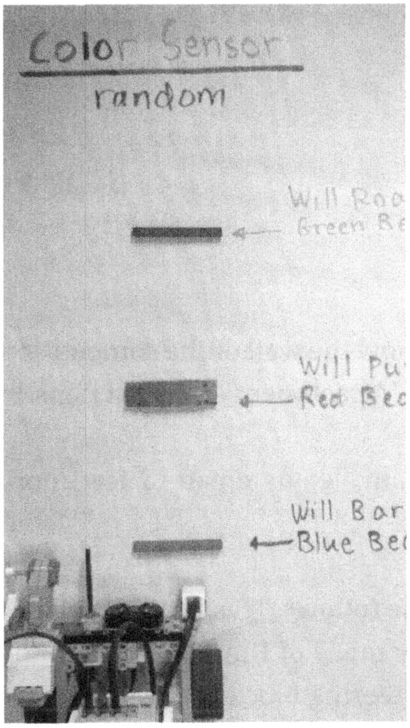

You can set up the beams in any order as shown in the picture below. Make sure that the robot arm is facing in front when you start the program. When you run the program, the robot will detect each color, declare the name of the color detected, and then move the arm based on which color is detected.

Create the eighth program in project **'Chapter Three'** and name it **'gyro straight'.** Typically, the construction of the robot and the slight differences between the wheels of the robot creates robot drift. You will notice this drift when the robot is running for long distances (8 to 9 rotations). This program will allow you to keep the robot running straight in competitions.

Create the following program.

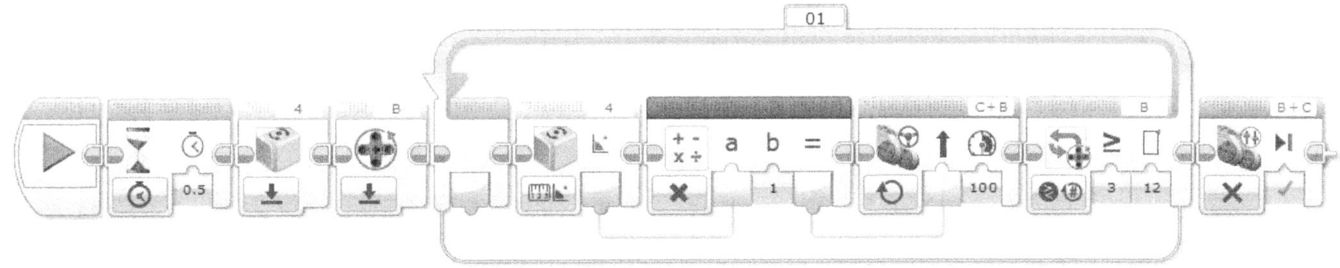

In this program you will be using the 'Motor Rotation' sensor block to check how many rotations the robot has completed and then exit the loop based on a certain number of rotations.

The gyro sensor is reset to '0' at the beginning of the program. If the robot drifts, the output of the gyro sensor, the angle value, is fed to the math block to decide the turn angle for the move steering block.

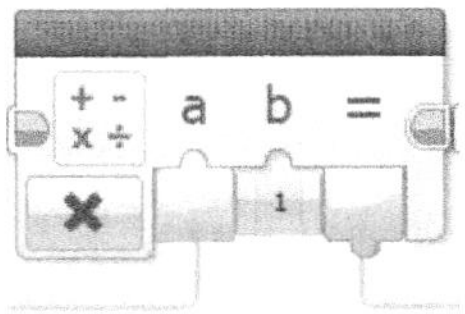

You will have to adjust the multiplying factor, highlighted in yellow, based on the drift you are noticing.

Run this program and you will notice that the robot is going relatively straight compared to the simple 12 rotations move tank program shown below.

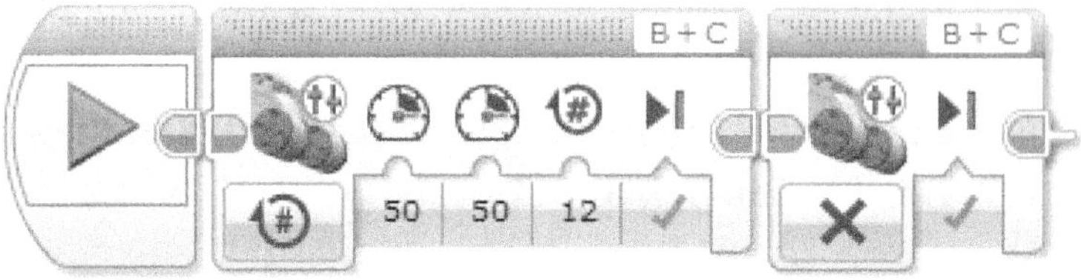

The best method to run the robot straight in competition is by making it follow the wall of the competition table using side wheels. We will discuss this method in the 'Basebot' and 'Attachment' constructions in the next chapter.
Now that we have used most of the programming blocks in our program, let us create a few more programs that are also frequently used in competition programming.

Create the ninth program in project **'Chapter Three'** and name it **'curve line follow'.** This program allows the robot to follow straight and curved black lines using the light intensity mode of the color sensor. Create the following program using the range, switch, sensor, and move steering blocks.

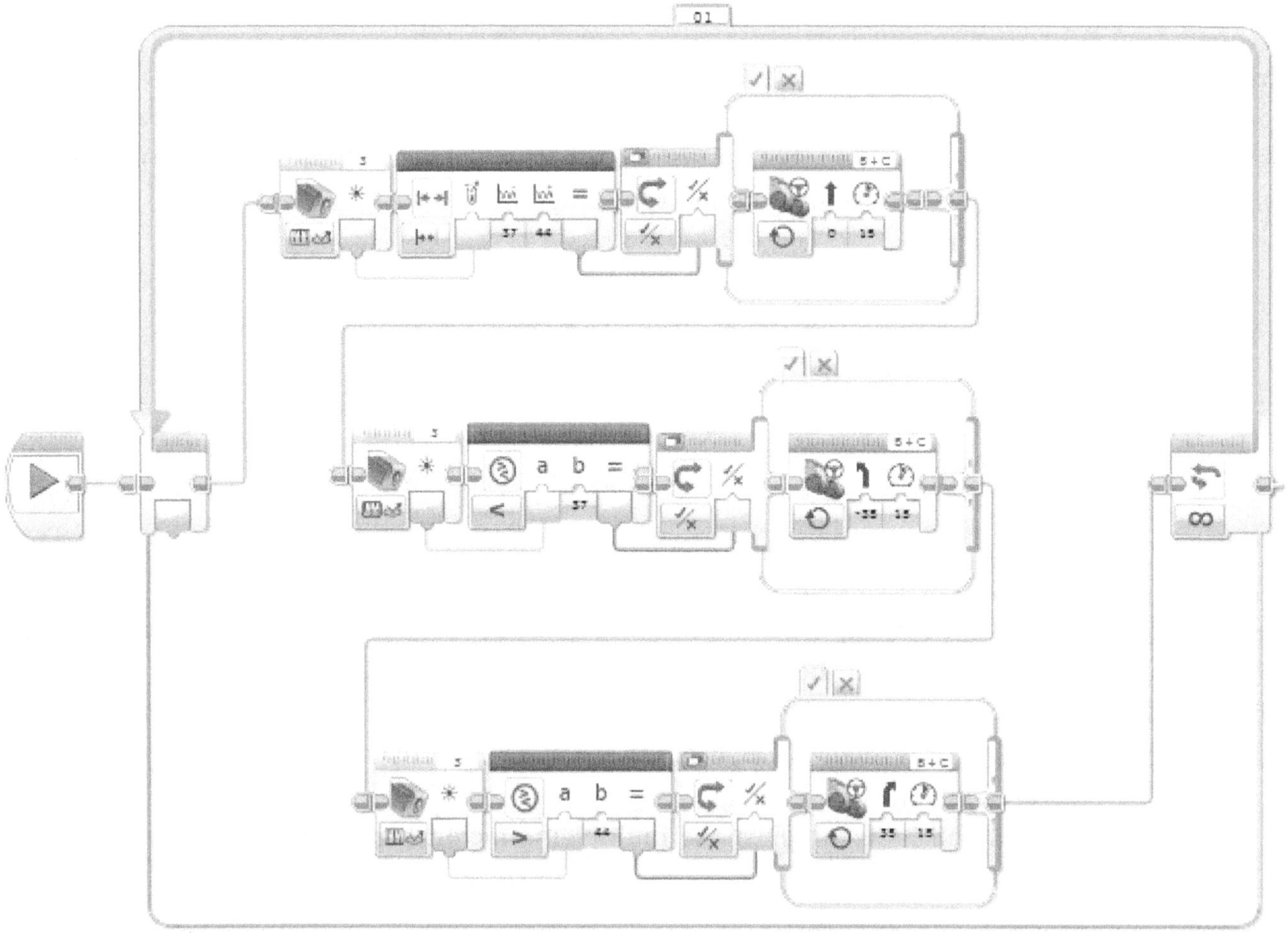

The switch blocks are in tabbed mode and the next picture will show you what is programmed in the 'False' condition of each switch block.

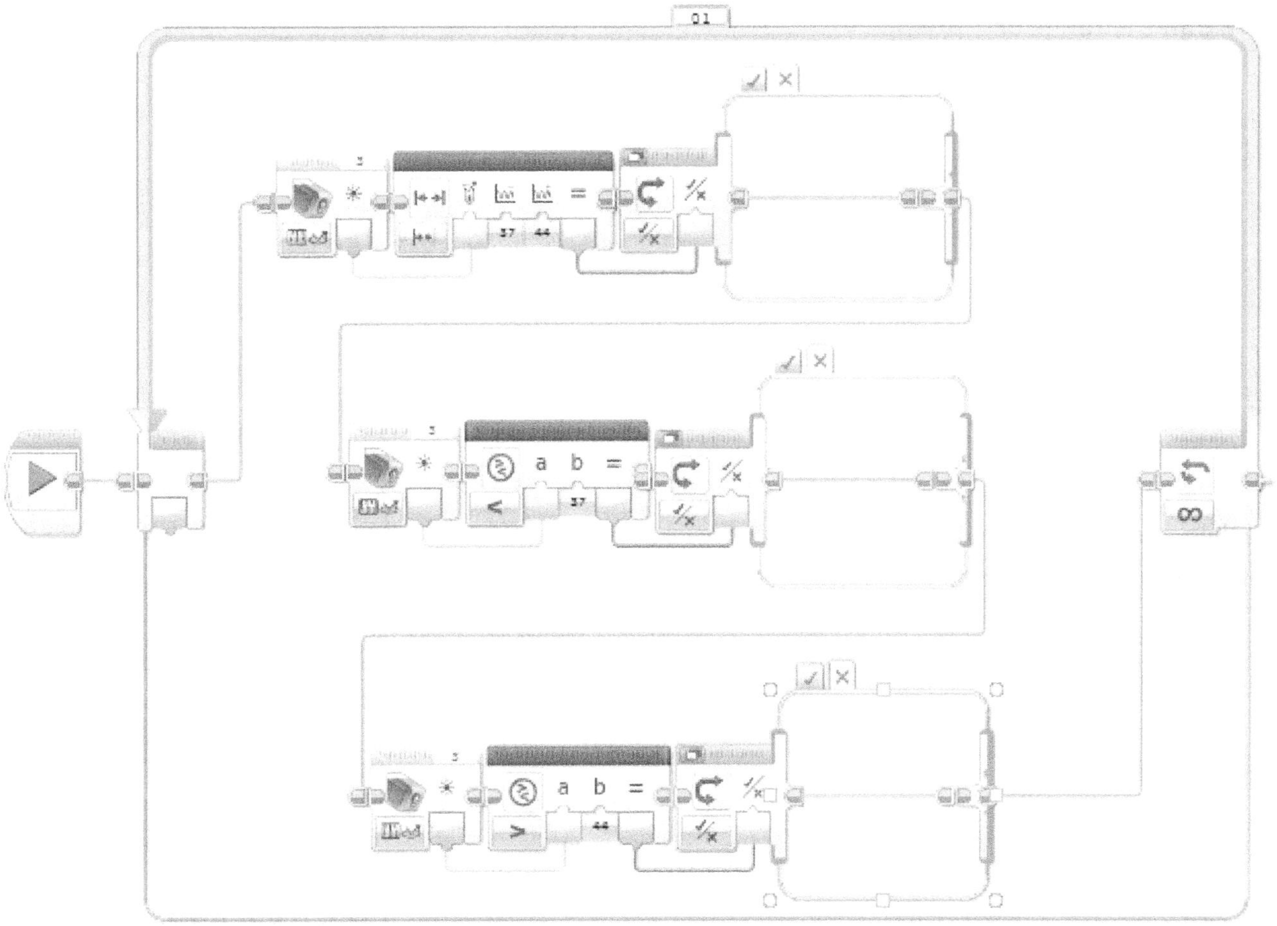

This program uses the range block to keep the reflected light intensity in the 37 to 44 range, which is the light intensity of the edge of a thick black line. The range block is found in the data operations tab.
The sets of blocks below will make the robot move forward till the reflected light intensity is between 37 and 44.

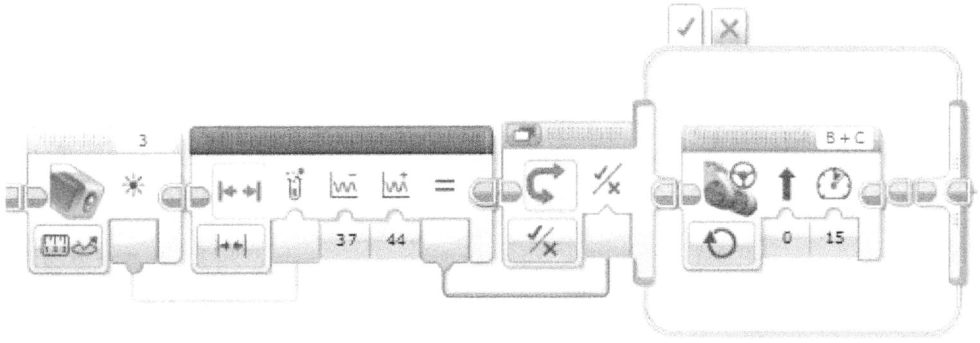

When the light intensity falls outside the range of 37 to 44, the program execution moves on to the next set of blocks.
These blocks below will check if the detected light intensity is below 37, and make the robot turn to get back within the range of 37 to 44.

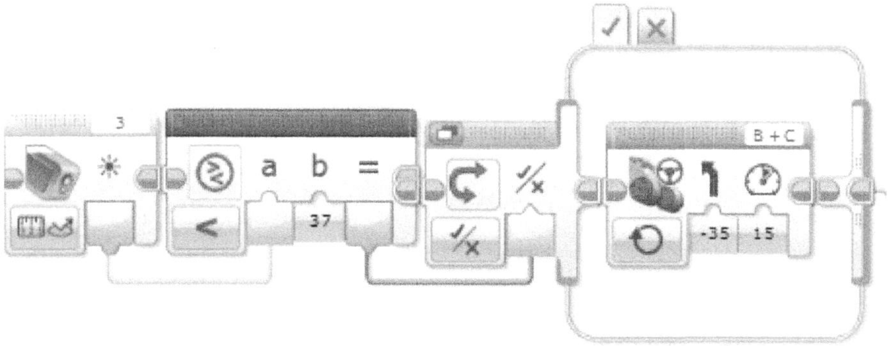

If the detected light intensity is above 44, the program execution turns the robot in the opposite direction to get it back in the range of 37 to 44.

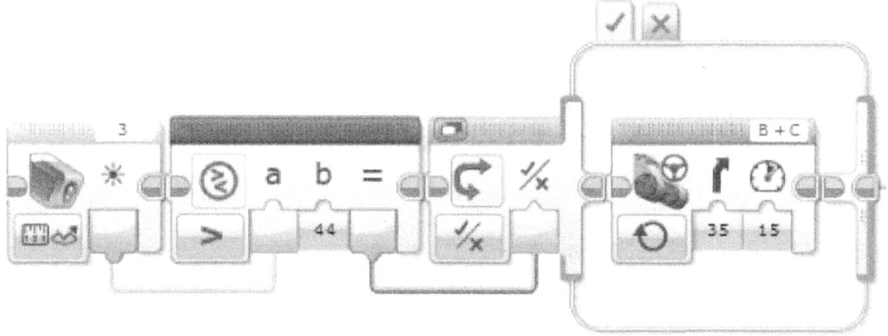

The loop around all these blocks will keep repeating these blocks and will keep the color sensor on the edge of the thick black line.
This program is built for lines on an FLL mat, but for home purposes you can draw a thick black line on a white piece of paper and try it out.

Create the tenth program in the project **'Chapter Three'** and name it **'curve line follow with interrupt'.** Create the program shown in next picture. This program is the same as the ninth program except the loop exit criteria is based on the detection of a red line.

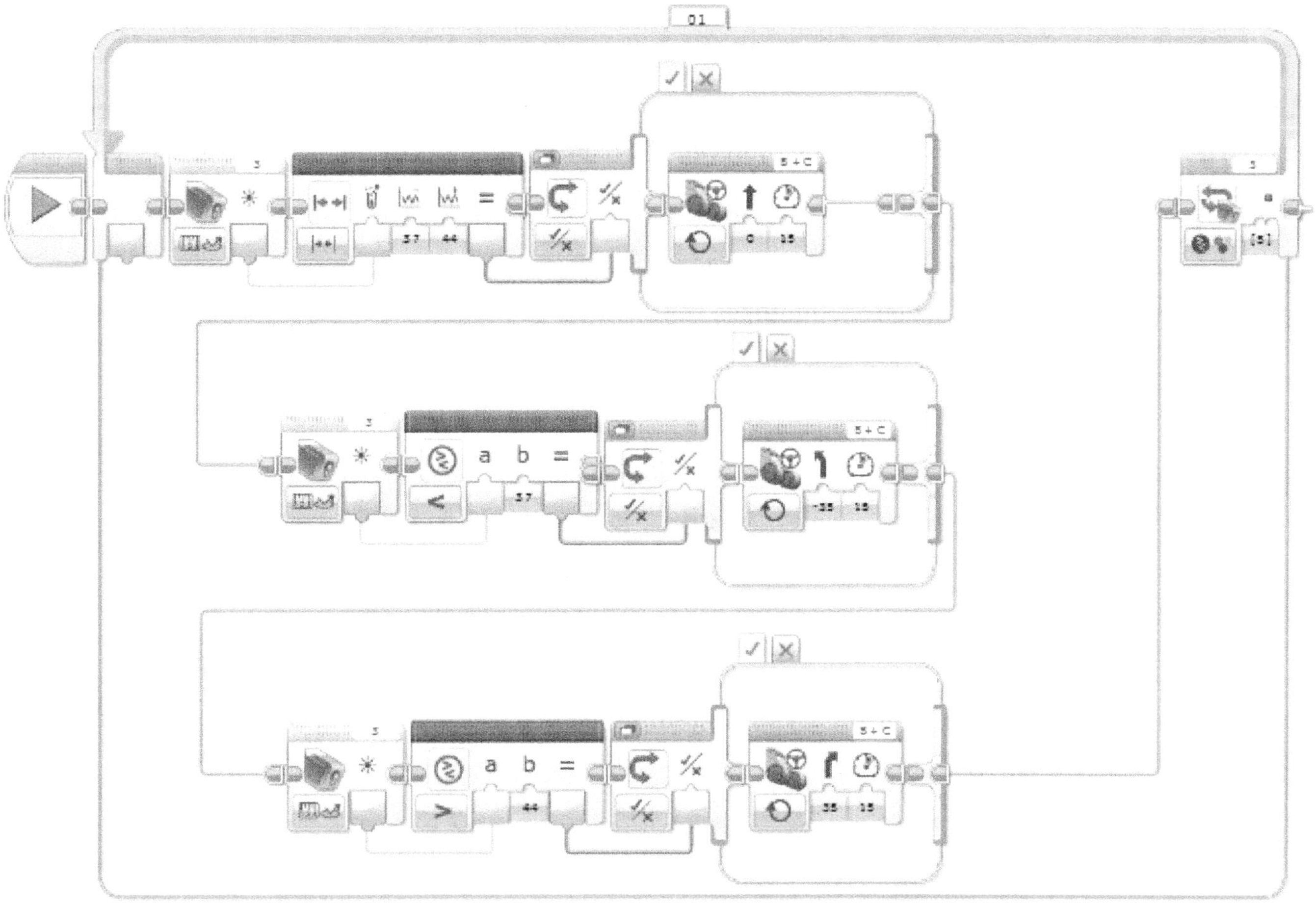

Create the eleventh program in project 'Chapter Three' and name it 'straight using encoders'.
This program uses the internal encoders in the motors and detects the difference between the rotations of the 2 motors allowing the robot to travel straight. It uses this difference to adjust the direction.

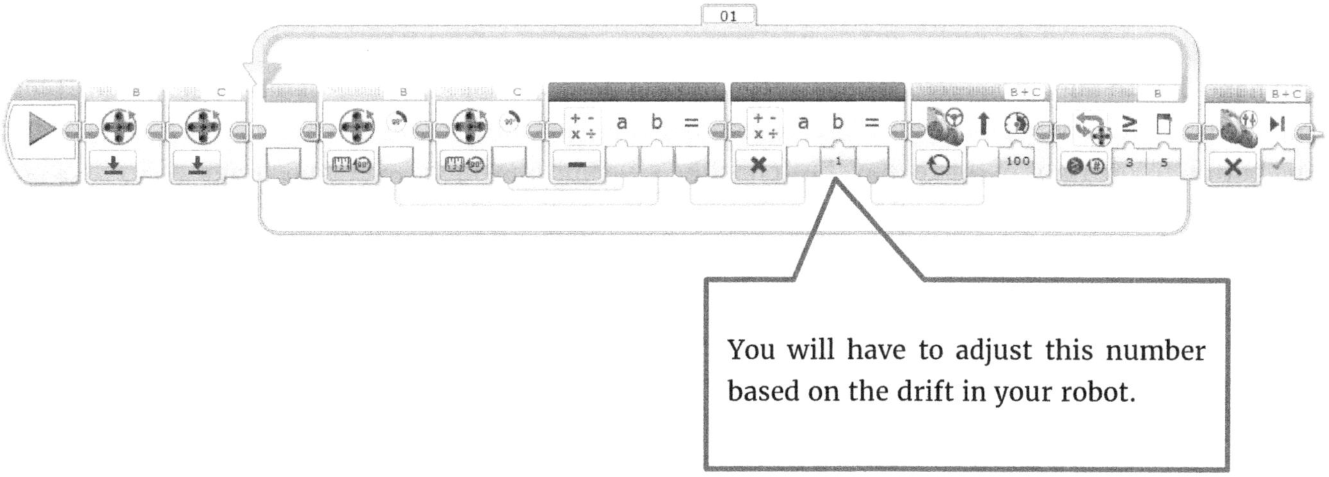

Create the twelfth program in project 'Chapter Three' and name it 'stall detection'
This program uses the internal encoders in the motors and detects the difference between motor positions separated by a 0.01 second time interval. If the program detects that the motor has not moved, it stops the motor. This program is very useful in avoiding stall situations which might unravel the gear train connected to the motor.
Sometimes the gears come off from the beams they are attached to, due to the excessive force on the gear train. This typically happens when the motor is running but is too weak to move the object on it.

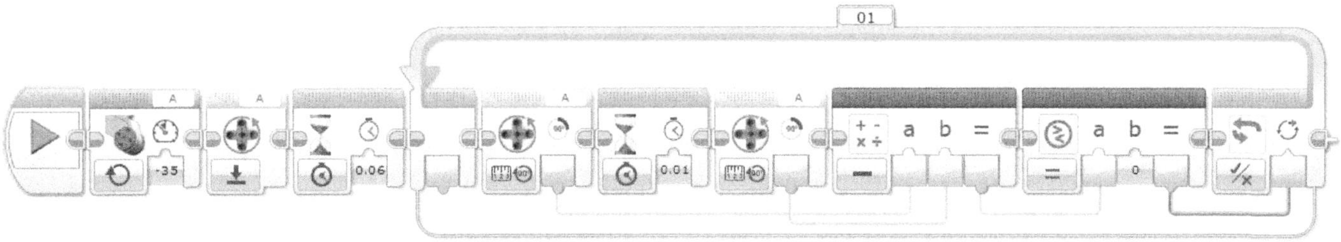

Finally let us understand some of the EV3 programming interface features. You must have noticed an action palette at the top right corner of the EV3 software. This is shown in the next picture.

The plus button at the left-hand side adds a new program.
The file button to the right of that shows you all the programs you have created.
The arrow button allows you to click and drag various programming blocks
The hand button allows you to drag the screen around and will not let you click on programming blocks
The textbox button will allow you to create comments in your program.
The button to the right of the textbox button is the save button which saves your program.
The arrow button that points to the left undoes your last action.
The arrow button that points to the right does the opposite of the undo button
The magnifying glass button with the – sign, decreases the magnification of the screen (zooms out)
The magnifying glass button with the + sign, increases the magnification of the screen (zooms in)
The final button (1:1) brings the screen back to its original magnification of 100%.
We will look at the project properties after the 'Myblocks' section.

MYBLOCKS

Now that you have learned how to program your robot, let us learn how to make the programming less time consuming and reusable. The way to achieve this is through Myblocks which are modular programming blocks.

Let us take an action that you use often, like turning the robot. In your previous programs you have had to use trial and error to check whether the robot had performed the proper turn. One way to fix this is to use a turning Myblock which I will be showing you how to make in this section.

The meaning of a 'Myblock' is a block like any other you have used before except you create the action it performs. When I learned how to create my first 'Myblock', I found it to be a very powerful tool and it has changed programming methods.

In the previous sections in this chapter, you have already learned about math blocks and data wires. Now, let us understand 'Variables' blocks which are used extensively in 'Myblocks'. Variables are small containers that store an object or value for a certain period of time in the program or for the entirety of the program. Their use will become very clear when we use variables to create your first 'Myblock'.

What's my favorite dessert in the world? ICE CREAM!

I will be using an analogy with ice cream to show how 'Myblocks' work. In this case the variables are like ice cream cones, they are able to take any type of ice cream (Vanilla, chocolate, etc.). You are the server who puts ice cream in the cone. This is called providing a value to the variable. The program running on the robot will then taste the ice cream on the cone. Let's say the robot loves the flavor of chocolate, finds strawberry OK, and doesn't like mint at all. Here the program will read what you have served it (an ice cream flavor) and will then process that information to tell us how it feels about that flavor.

Let us create a 'Tasting' Myblock that will display 'Love it', 'It is OK', and 'Don't like it' on the screen when a particular ice cream name is entered in the block's value field.

We will be using two new blocks in this program (The 'Constant' and 'Variables' block). The constant block will only be used in Myblocks when you want the value to stay the same. The next picture shown is not a Myblock yet, so we can still change the value of the constant. The variable block will take in this value from the constant and will go through the necessary steps for the output.

Let us create your first Myblock. Create a new project 'Chapter three – Myblock' and in this project create a new program and name it 'Tasting'.

Create the following program that will display what you think about an ice cream flavor.

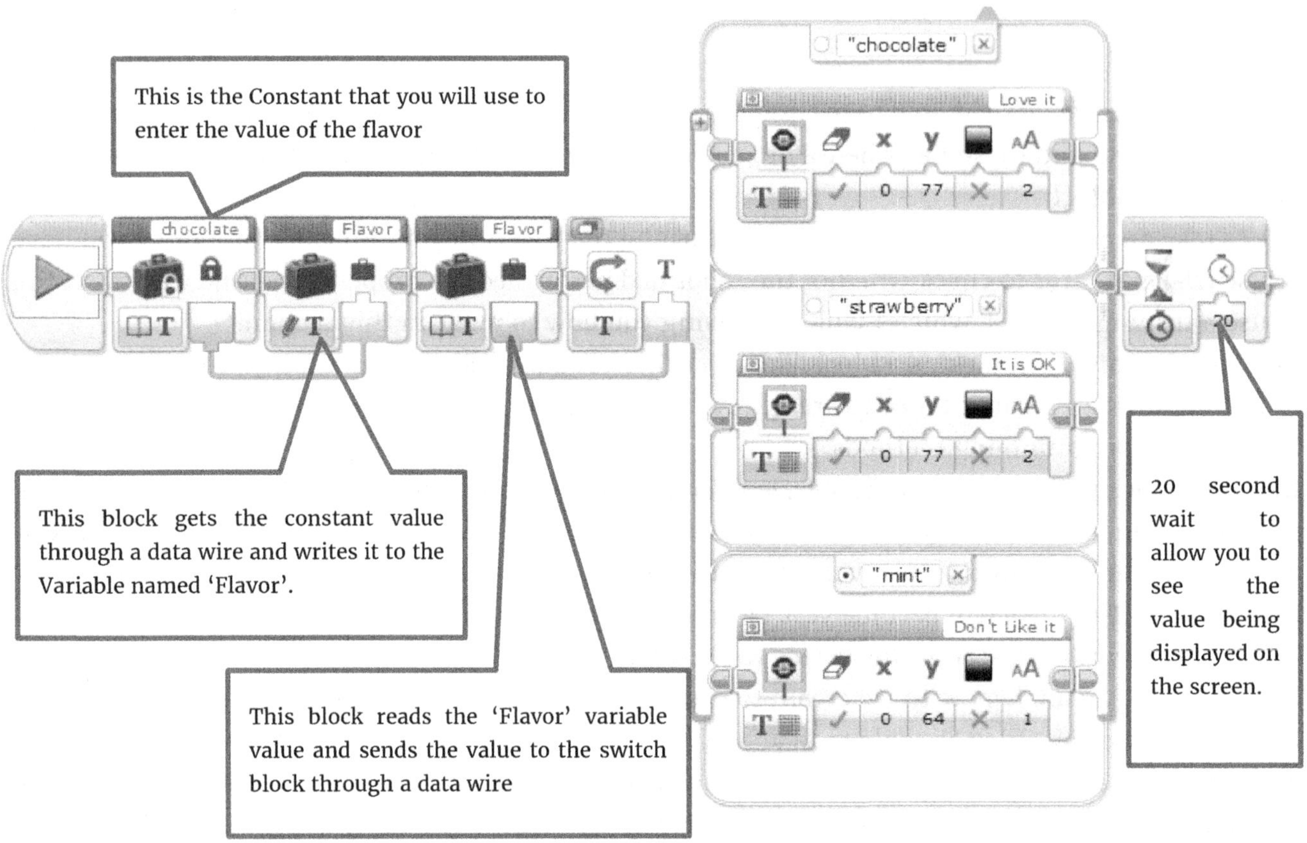

To run this program, enter the value of 'chocolate' in the constant block's field at the top and run the program. You should see 'Love it' on the brick screen. Now change the value in the constant to 'strawberry' and run the program again. You should see the sentence 'It is OK' on the brick screen. Now let us make the Myblock. Select the entire program but leave out the start block.

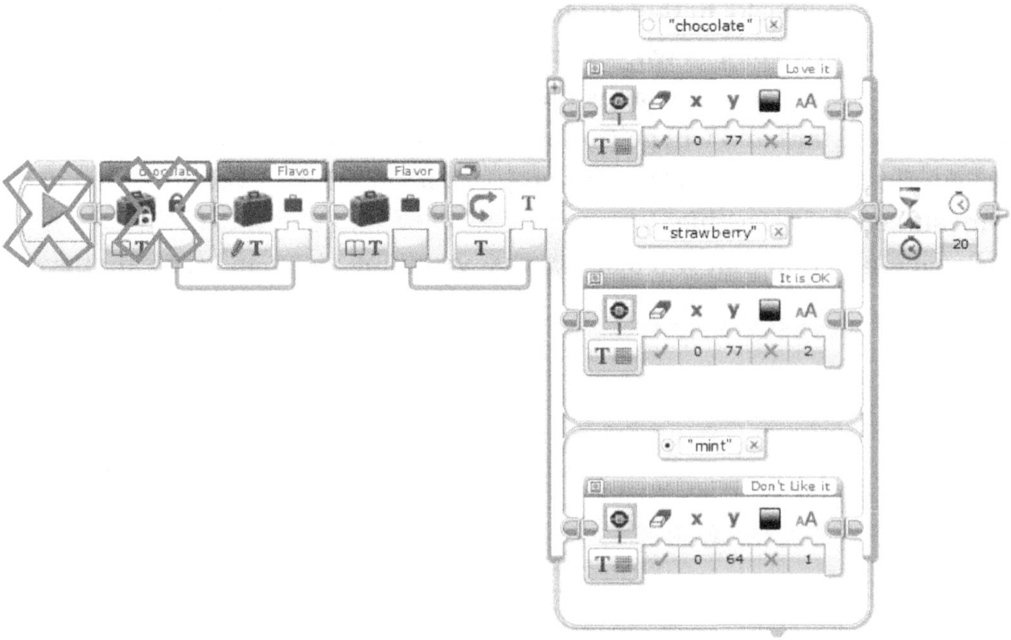

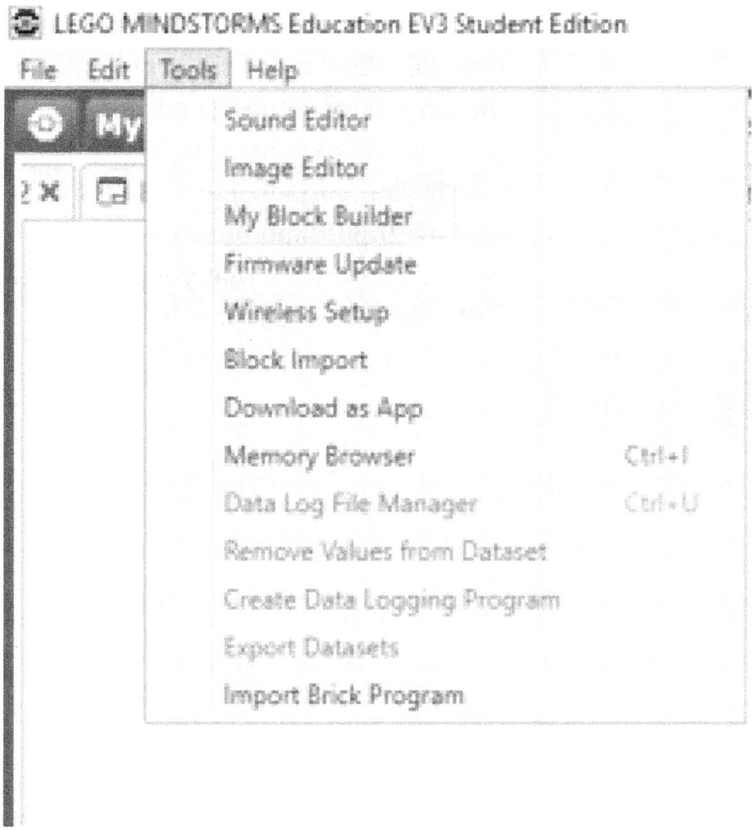

While these blocks are selected, you will have to navigate to the 'Tools' menu at the top of the screen choose 'Myblock builder'.

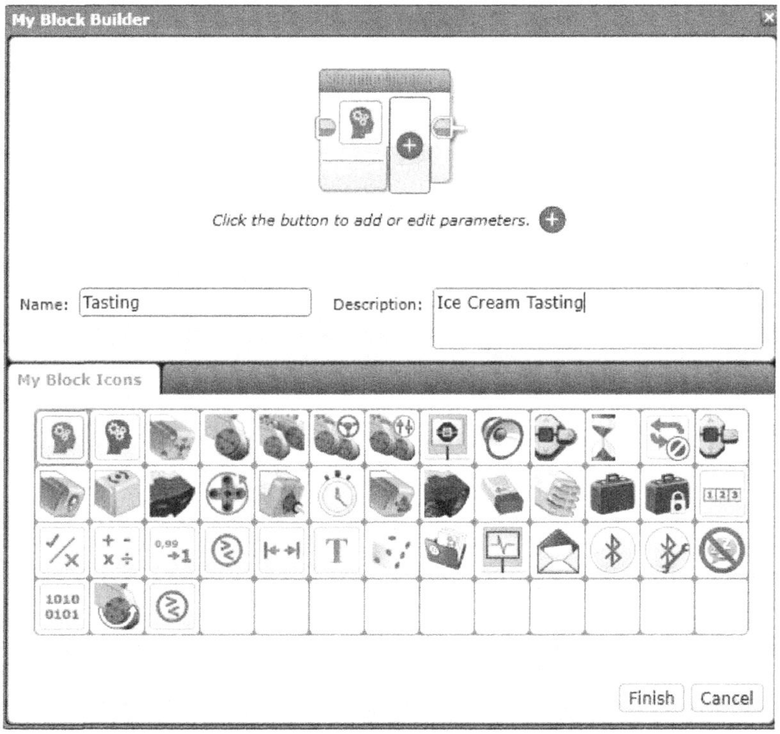

Set the name of the Myblock to 'Tasting' and enter a description for it. Next, select the block icon. This icon is the icon your Myblock will have every time you use it. Click the '+' sign to add or edit parameters. Parameters are exactly the same as variables but they only show up in Myblocks that you create. The name of the parameter and the variable can be different but for convention you should name them the same.

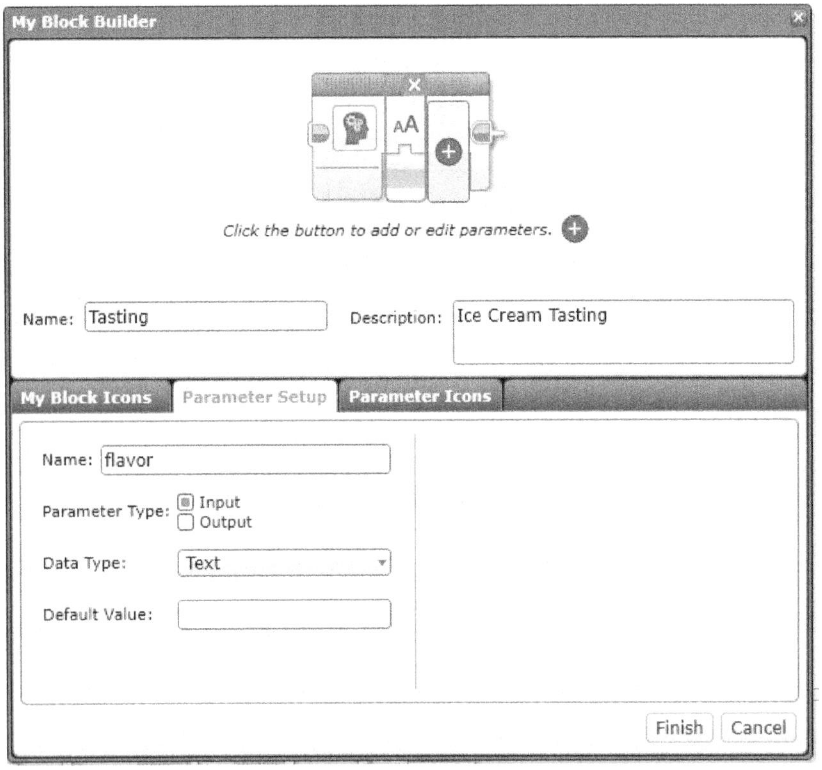

Once you click 'Add Parameters' 2 new tabs will show up on the screen. Go to the parameter setup tab and set the name of the parameter to 'flavor' as that is your variable name. Select the type as 'Input' and the data type as 'Text'. This means that your parameter will only take in a text value.

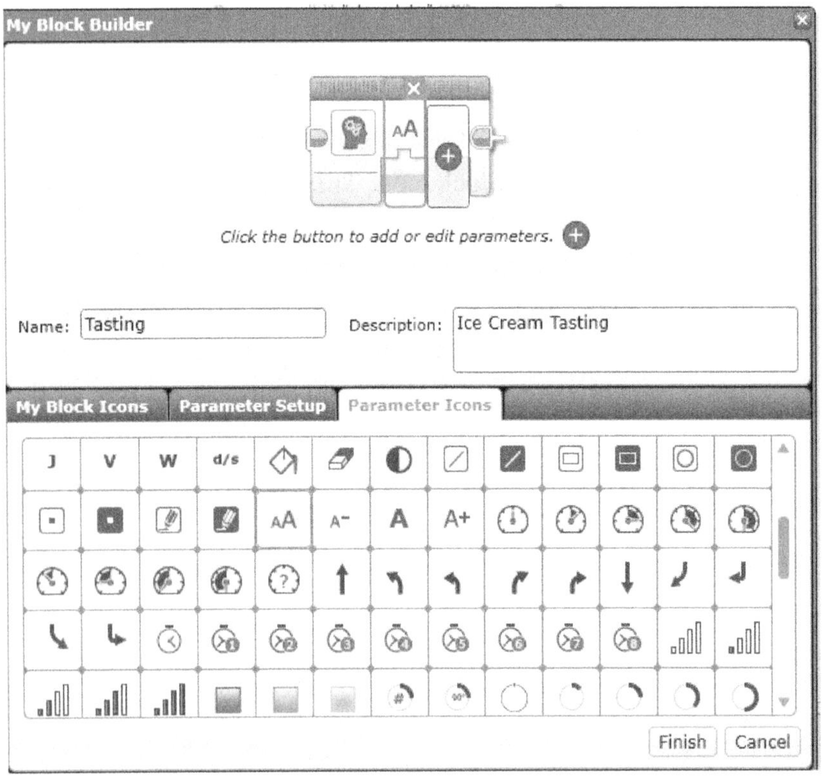

Navigate to the 'Parameter Icons' Tab and select the parameter icon. Then, click finish.

You will see the new parameter on the screen as shown in the next picture.

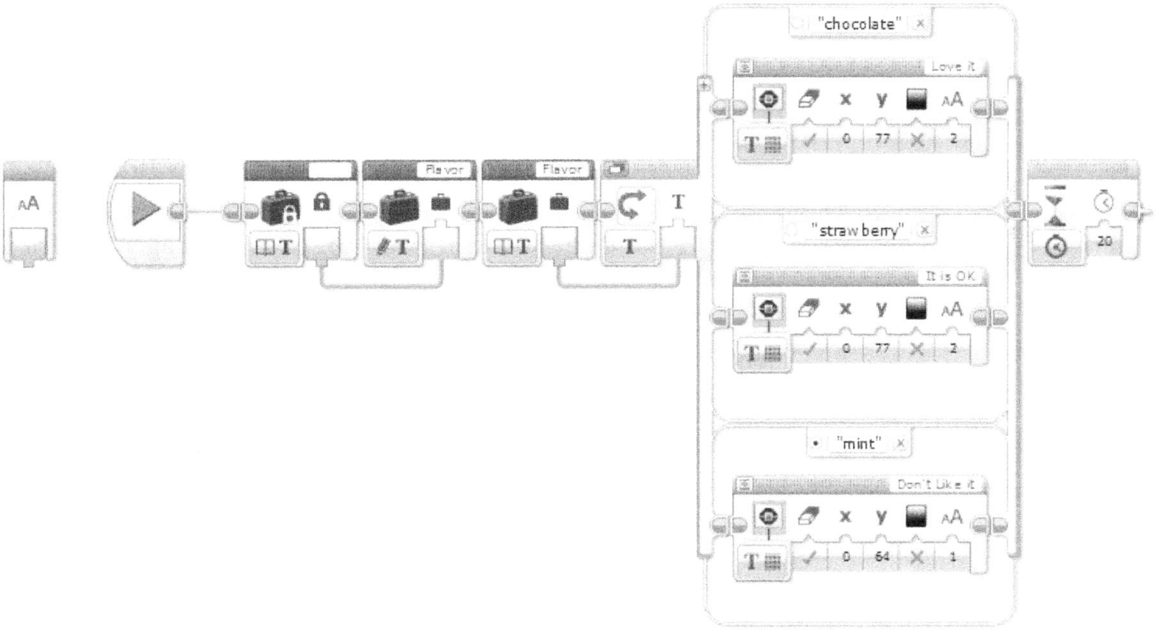

As you hover your mouse over the parameter, the parameter's name should be 'flavor'. First, remove the data wire from the constant. Then, connect the parameter to the 'flavor' variable input by a data wire as shown in the next picture.

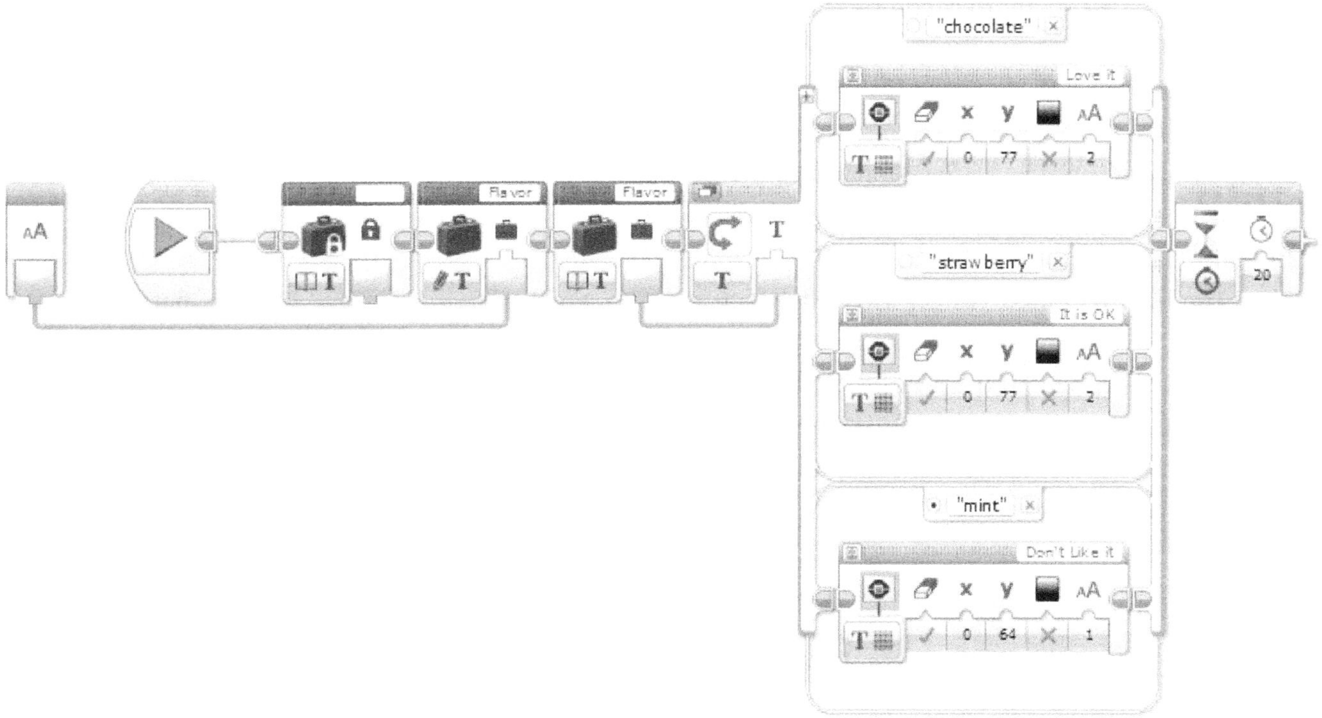

Save the project and now your 'tasting' Myblock is ready. You should be able to see it in the Myblock Palette.

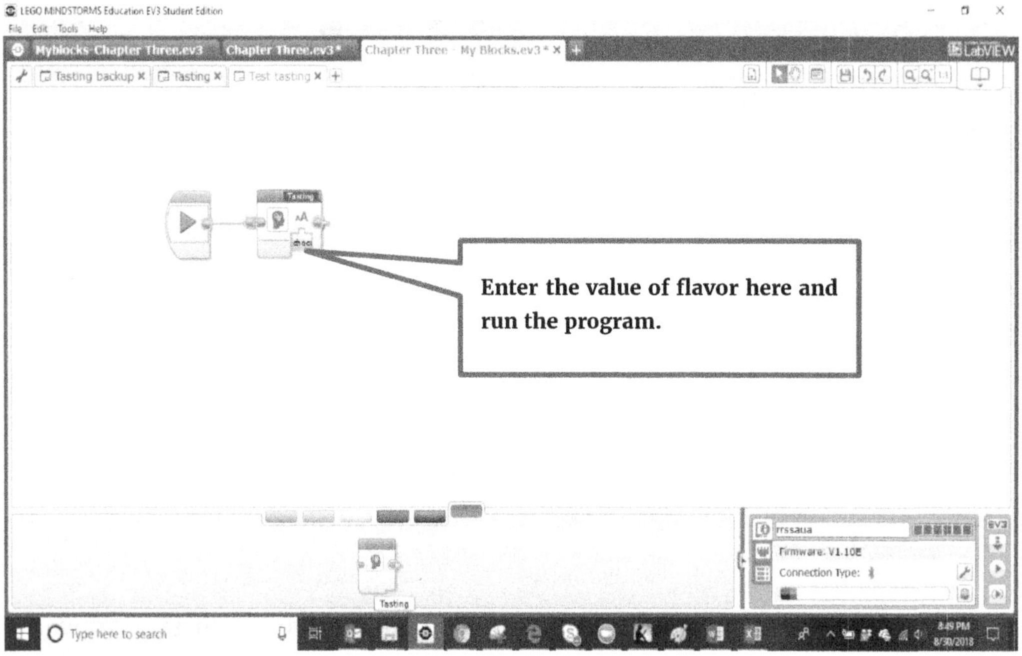

Create a new Program and name it 'Test Tasting'. Now go to the Myblock Palette and drag your Myblock to the start block. With this you have created your first Myblock and as you can see this one block takes the place of 7 blocks.

Congratulations you have created your first modular program (Myblock) and are now an expert software engineer for EV3

Now, let us create one more Myblock this time with multiple variables/parameters to allow you to create a proper 'turn' program

You can always turn the robot using the gyro sensor, but gyro sensors are not the most reliable, based on my experience. To create accurate turns, you will need to use a **2-wheel turn** and calculate the rotations for the robot to achieve a particular turn angle.

To get the specific turn angle you will need to know the distance between the 2 driving wheels and the diameter of each of those wheels.

Look at the next few pictures. In the first 2 pictures, the wheel size is the same but the distance between the wheels in the first picture is larger than the distance between the wheels in the second picture. So, the wheels in the second picture must turn a lower number of rotations to make the same angle turn compared to the wheels in the first picture. The wheels in the 3rd picture is small compared to the wheels in the first picture. Due to the small wheels, the third picture's wheel would have to rotate more to turn the same amount of degrees as compared to the wheels in the first picture.

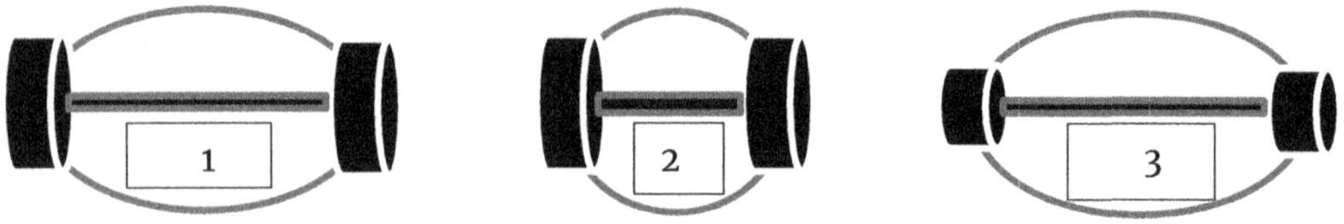

This means the turn is dependent on variables such as **the distance between the wheels and wheel diameter**. So, every time you have to make a precise turn with degrees, you will have to calculate the rotation using the following formula provided below. Then you will input the answer to the equation (the answer is in rotations) into the move tank block. Instead of that you can create a Myblock called 'turn' which will take in 4 variables: distance between wheels, wheel diameter, angle of turn and power.

The Formula: The circumference of the 2-wheel turn divided by the circumference of the wheel, will give you the number of rotations the wheel has to make to complete a 360-degree turn. Then you divide that answer by 360 to get the rotations required for a one-degree turn. Finally, you multiply that number with the degrees that you want the robot to turn.

The formula for the number of rotations to achieve a certain angle turn is shown in the following picture.

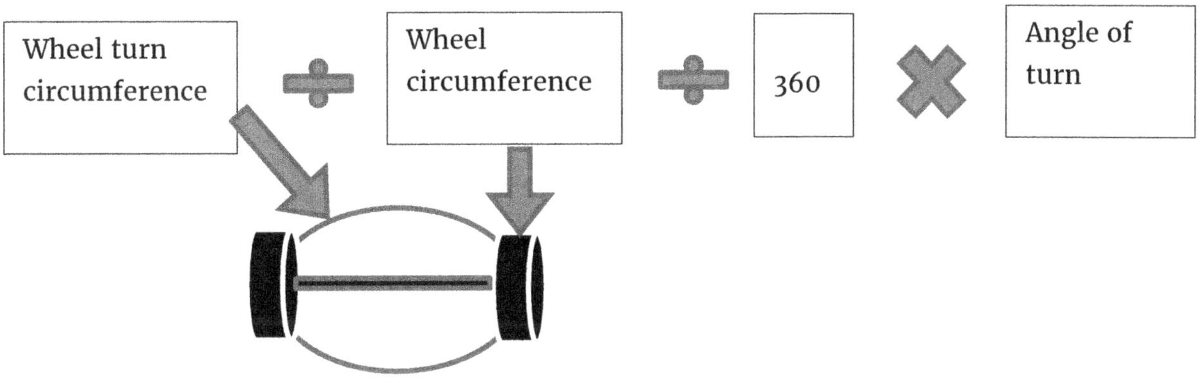

First, let us create the program to calculate the rotations and feed the rotations into the move tank block. Create a new program in 'Chapter three – Myblock' and name it as 'Turn'.

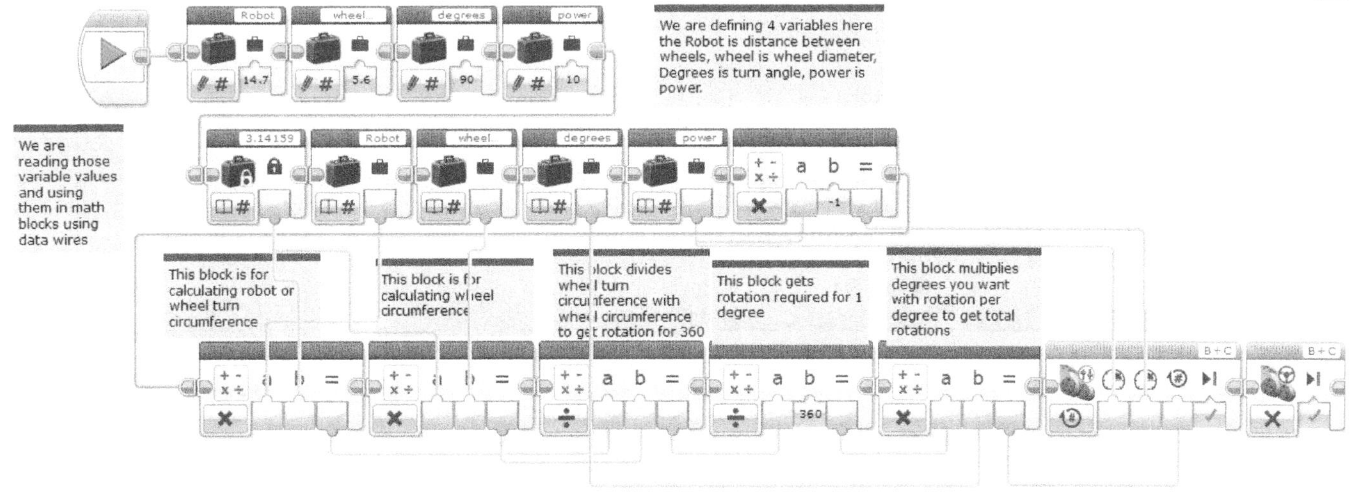

Let us break this program into 4 parts for better visibility.

Part-1

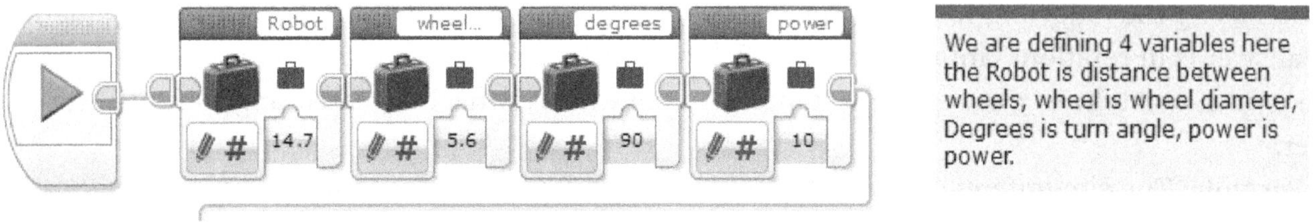

Part-2

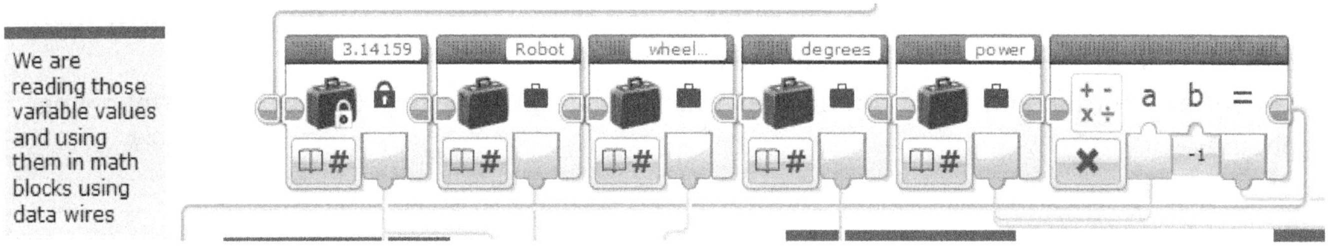

Part-3

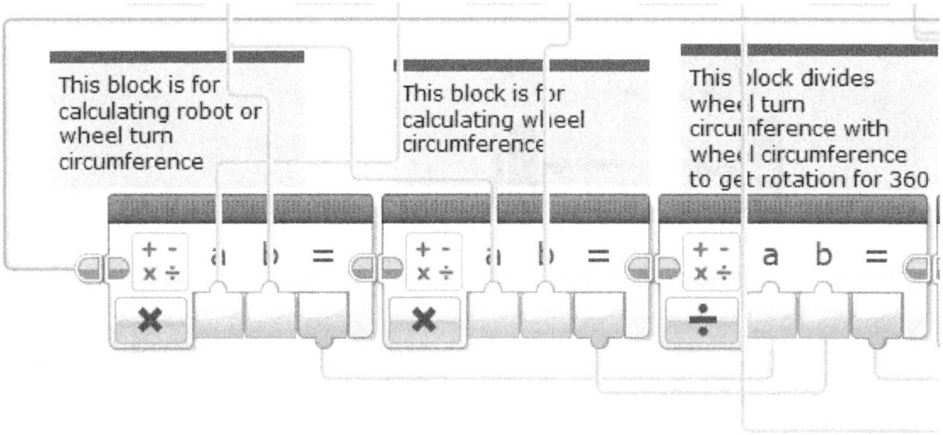

Part-4

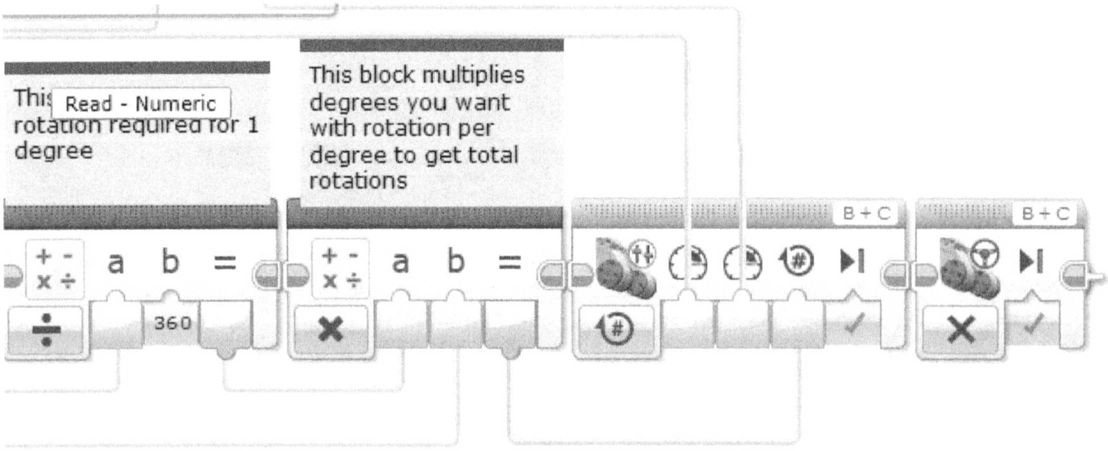

As you can see the program has comments on what each block is doing and I recommend you do that for every EV3 program you make to increase readability.
To run this program, enter the values of the wheel diameter and wheel turn diameter (distance between 2 wheels measured from the center of one-wheel rubber to the center of another wheel rubber). Input the angle as 90 degrees and the power as 20.
You will observe the robot turns 90 degrees. If there is a slight deviation from 90 degrees adjust the wheel turn diameter value.

Now, let us convert this 17-block program in to 1 single Myblock: 'turn'.
Again, select all the programming blocks except the 'start' block. You should also include the constant block as it used to calculate the diameters.

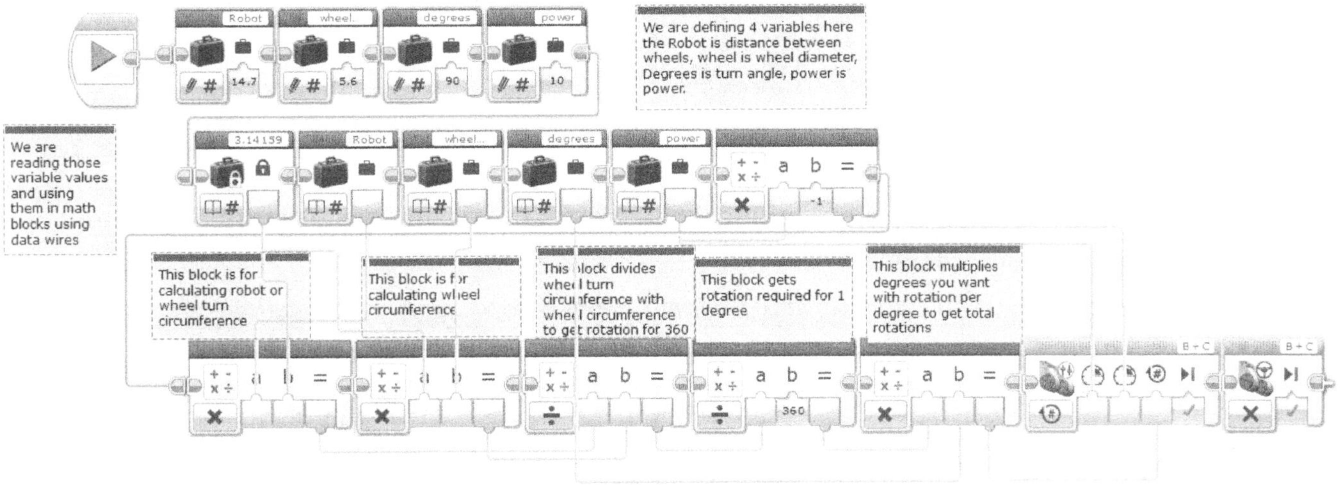

Now go to the 'Tools' menu and select 'My Block Builder'. Click 'Add Parameters' and name the block as 'turn'. Select the block icon as the motor turn icon.

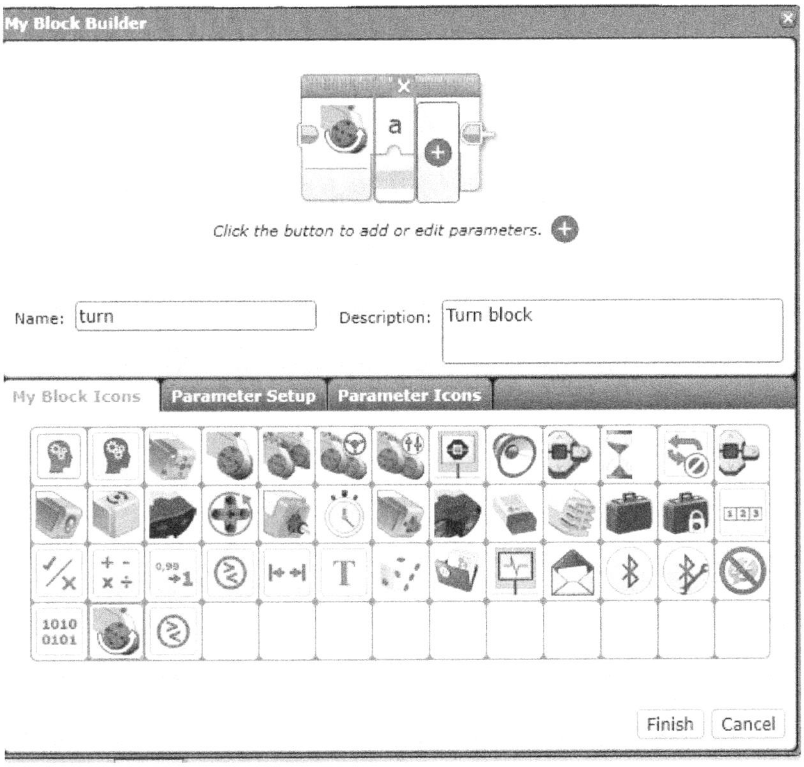

Create the first parameter and choose the parameter icon. Set the name to 'Robot Diameter'

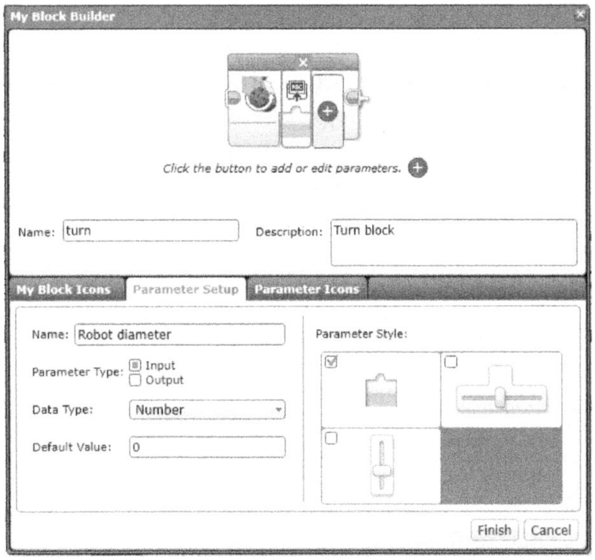

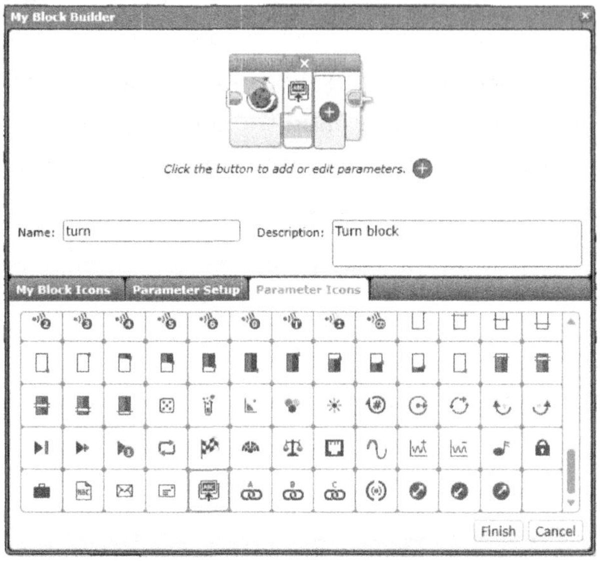

Add the second parameter. You can add additional parameters by clicking the '+' button at the top. Assign the icon to the Wheel Diameter.

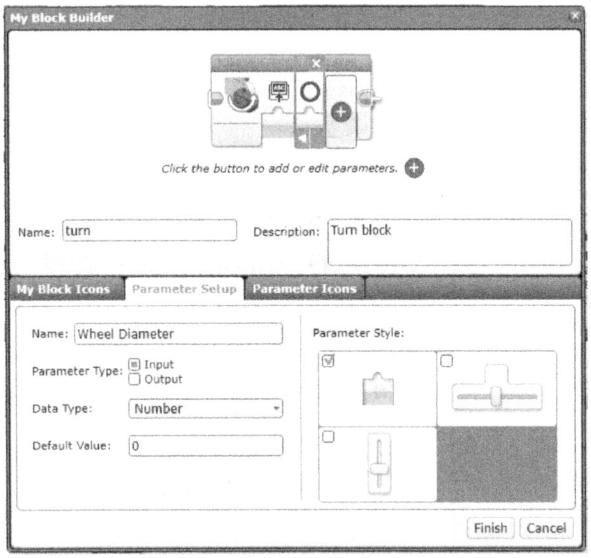

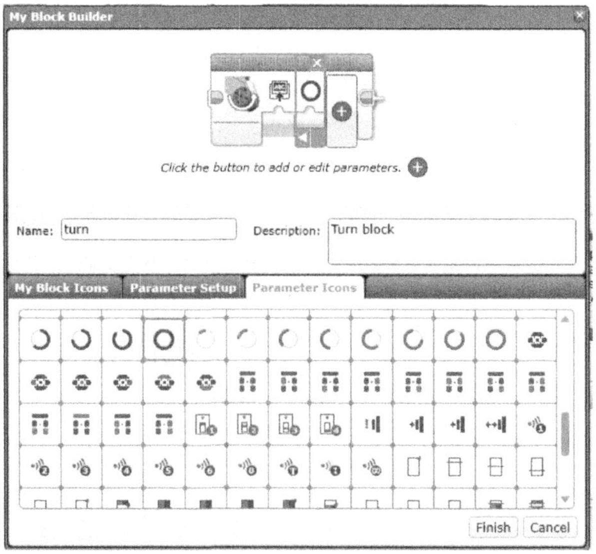

Add the third parameter as 'Degrees' and assign it the degrees icon

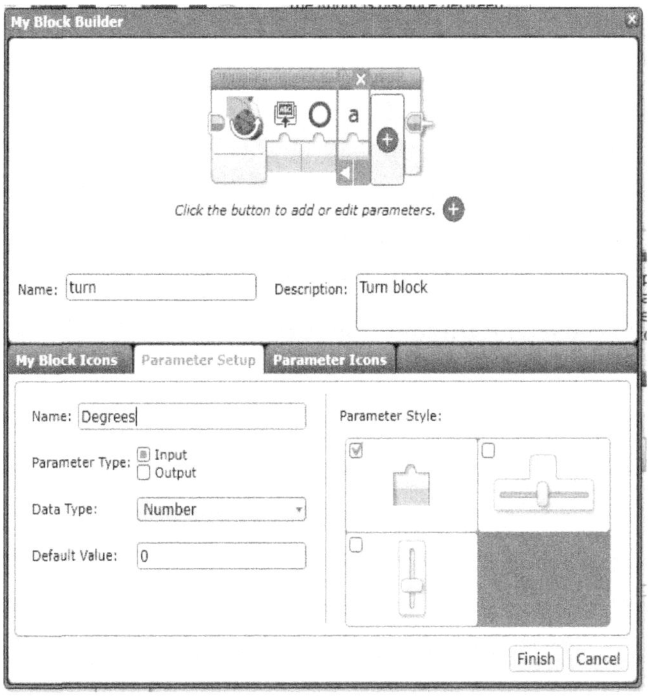

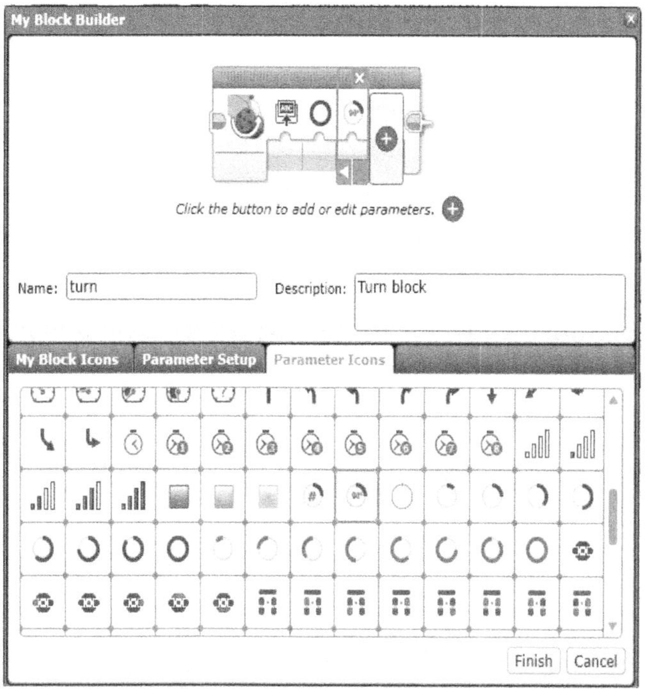

Add the fourth parameter as 'Power'. Select vertical slider for the parameter style.

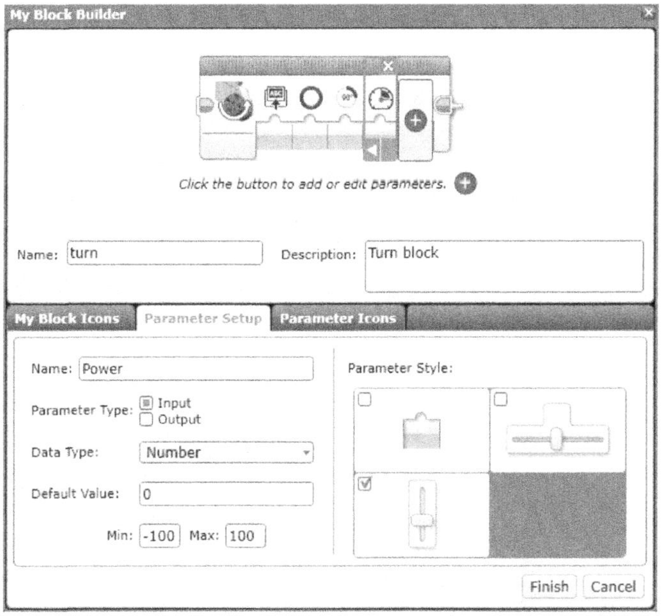

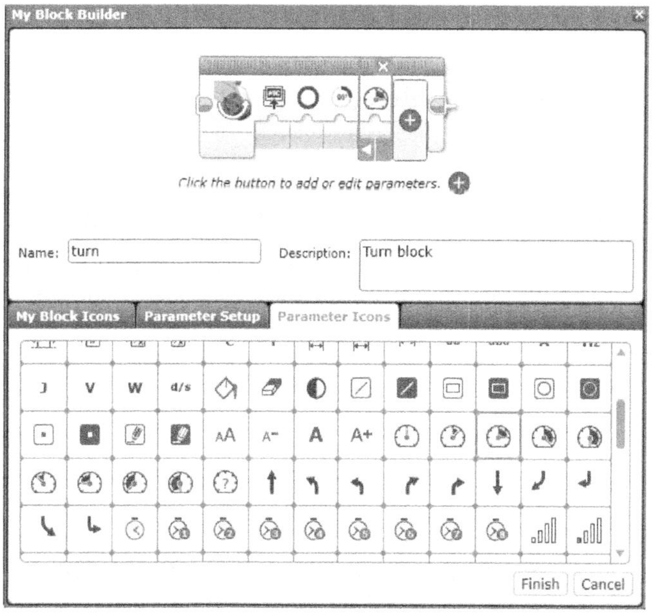

This is how the final Myblock preview will look.

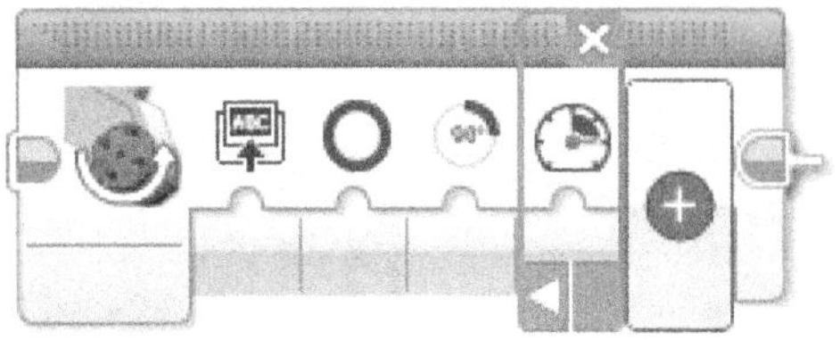

Click finish and your 'turn' block is ready. It should look just like the next picture.

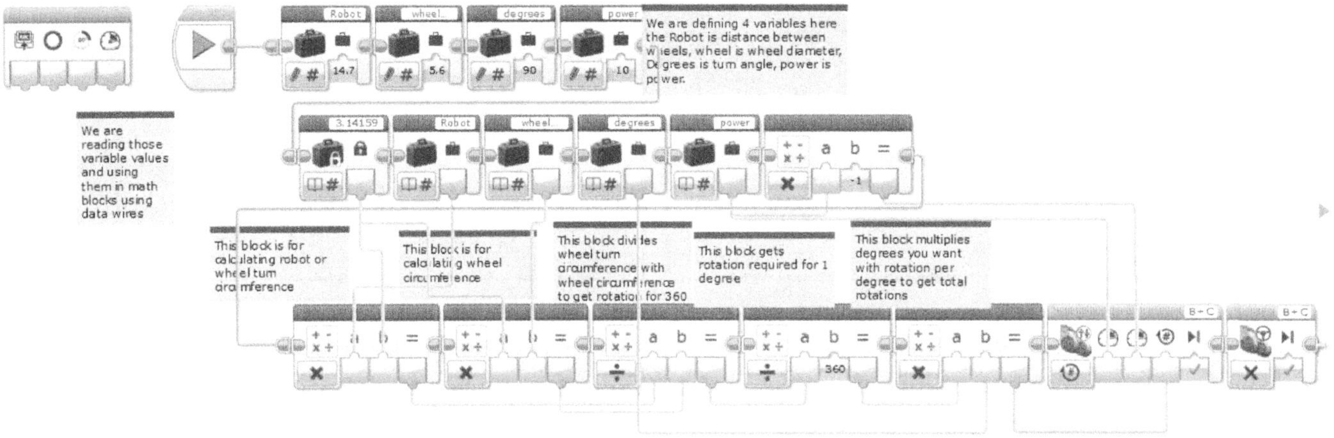

Connect the data wires from parameters to the corresponding variables and most importantly SAVE THE PROJECT.

To test your new 'turn' Myblock create a new program and add the 'turn' Myblock from the Myblock palette at the bottom. Input the necessary values and run the program. The following pictures show how the connection should look and how to test the program.

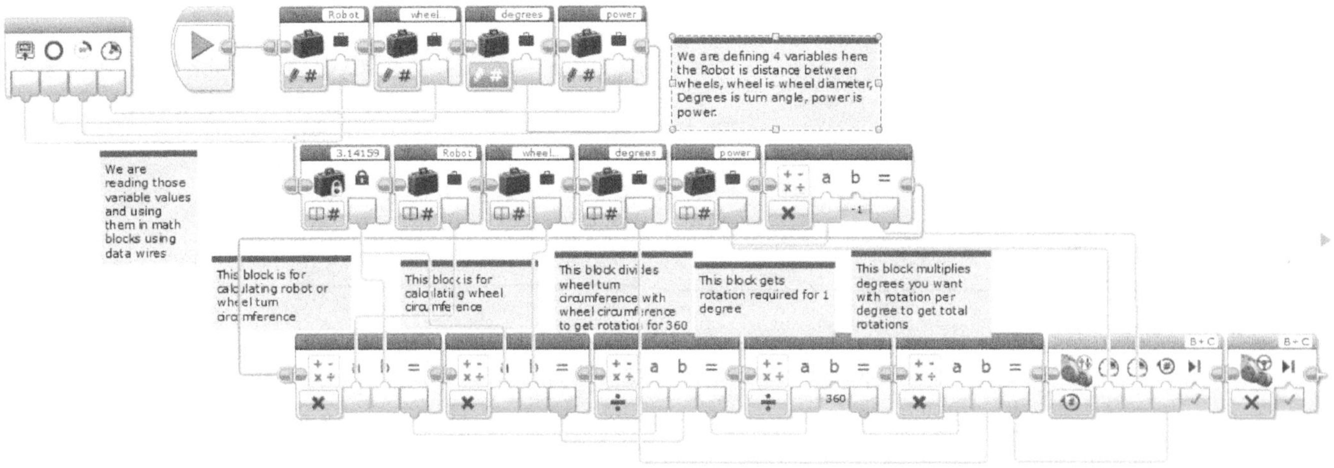

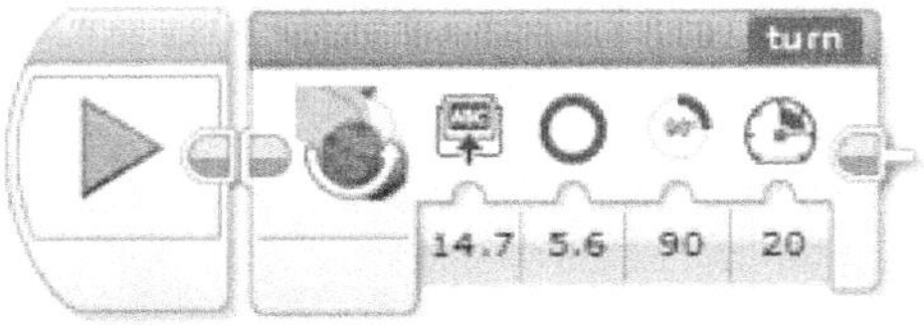

Now we will be creating a few more Myblocks called 'straight LF- LE' – straight line follow using left edge. Create a new program in 'Chapter three – Myblock' and name it as 'Straight Line follow - LE'. On competition mats the black lines are thick, and the black line surrounded by the white area can have 2 edges as shown in the next picture.

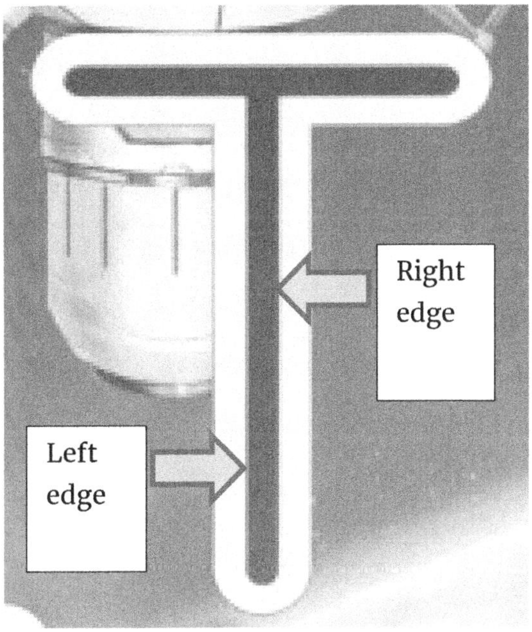

Create the program as shown in the next picture and convert it into Myblock. The explanation of the inner workings of the program are provided below.

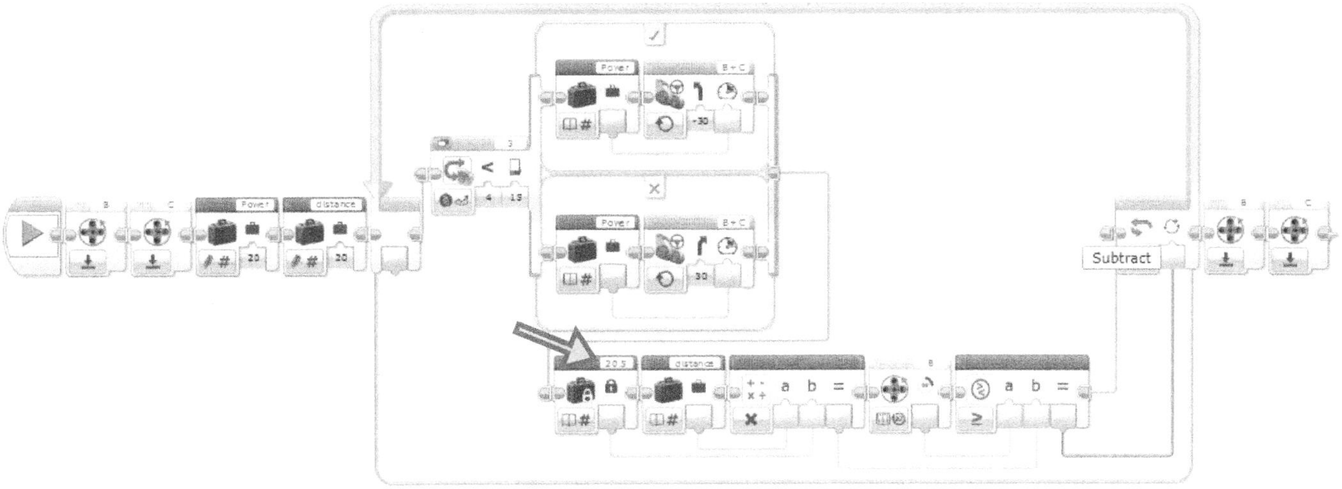

Let us break this program into 3 components for better visibility.

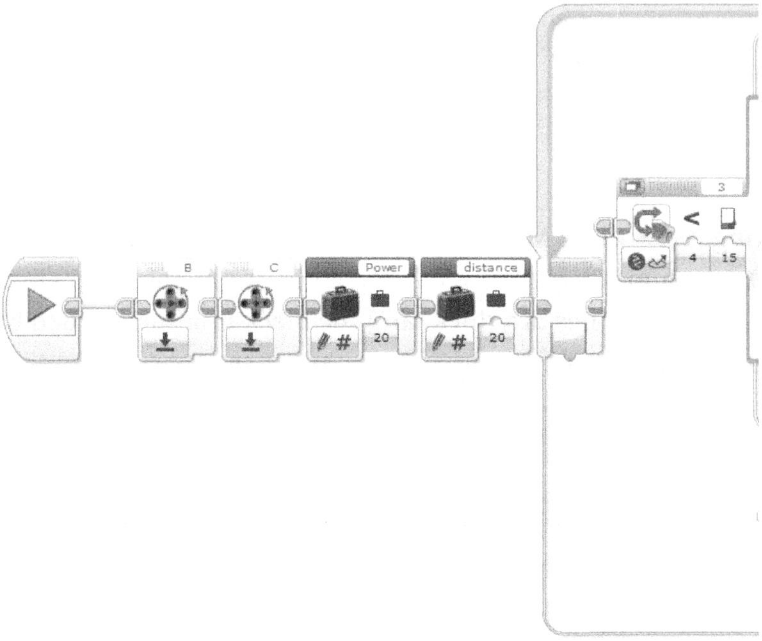

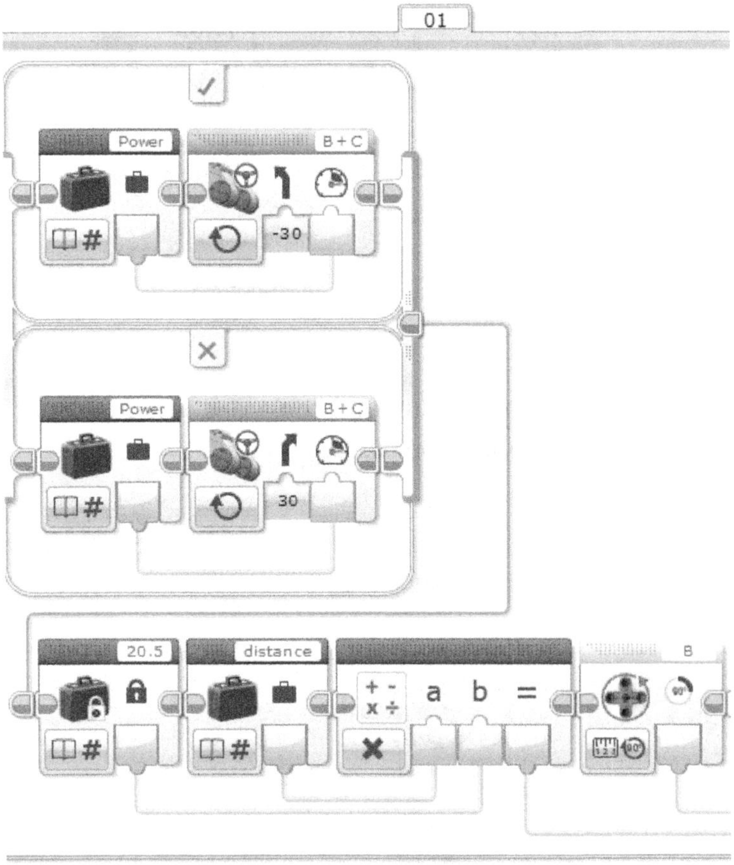

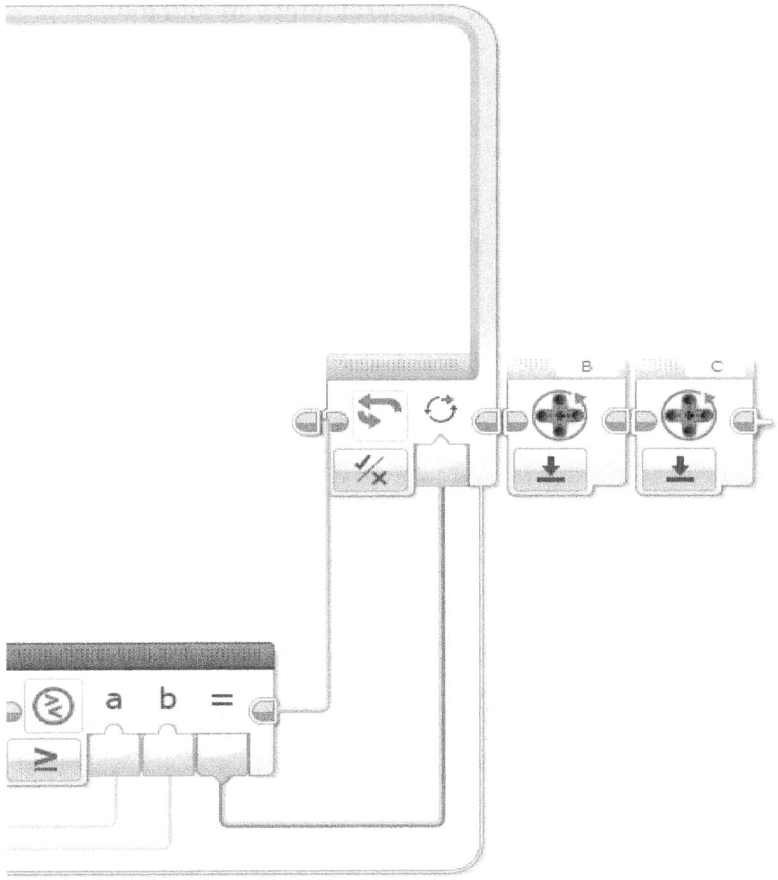

The constant with value 20.5 as indicated by the arrow in the previous picture is the amount of degrees the motor must turn for the robot to travel 1 cm. This program follows the line using light intensity and makes turns based on where it is on the line. The complexity of this program is the additional feature of telling the robot how far you want it to travel. If you want the robot to travel 5 centimeters on the line then you can specify that in this program. The program checks how many rotations 5 centimeters is and how many actual rotations the robot has traveled. Once the number of rotations the robot has traveled is greater than or equal to the calculated distance the program will stop.
The formula for degrees the wheel will travel in 1 centimeter is shown in the next picture.

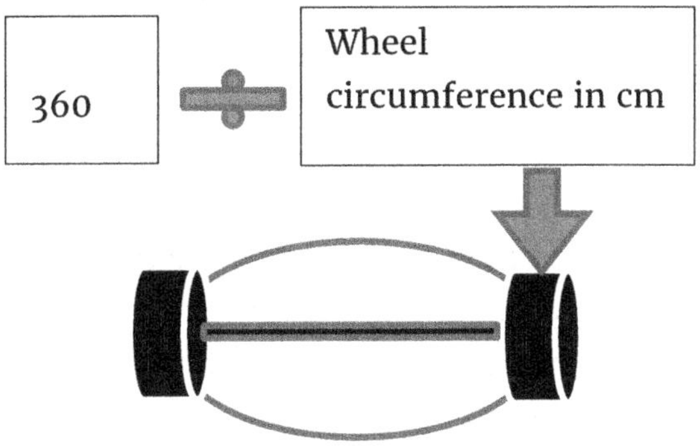

Once you convert it into a Myblock this is how the parameters should look.

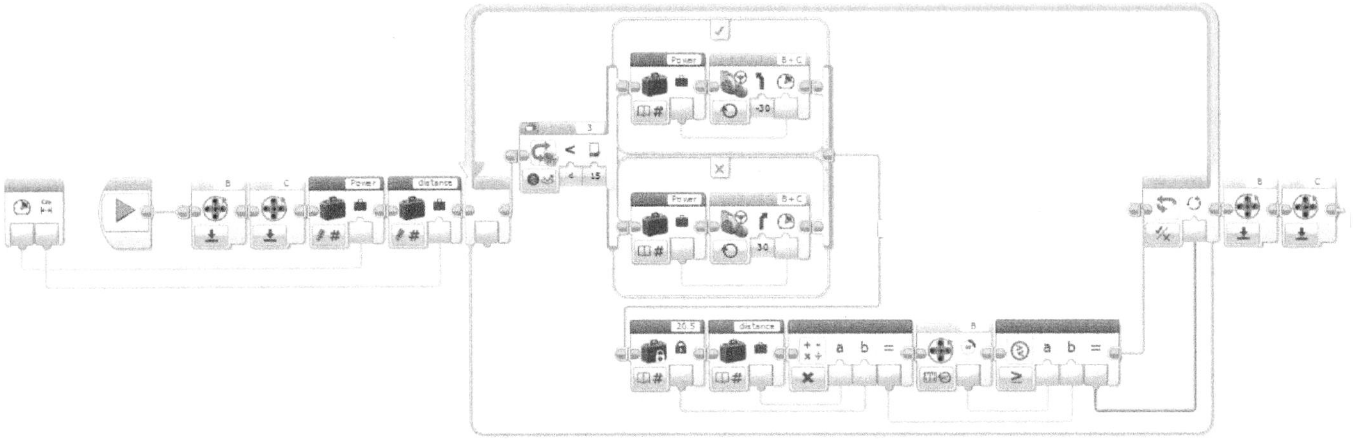

This is how you can test it

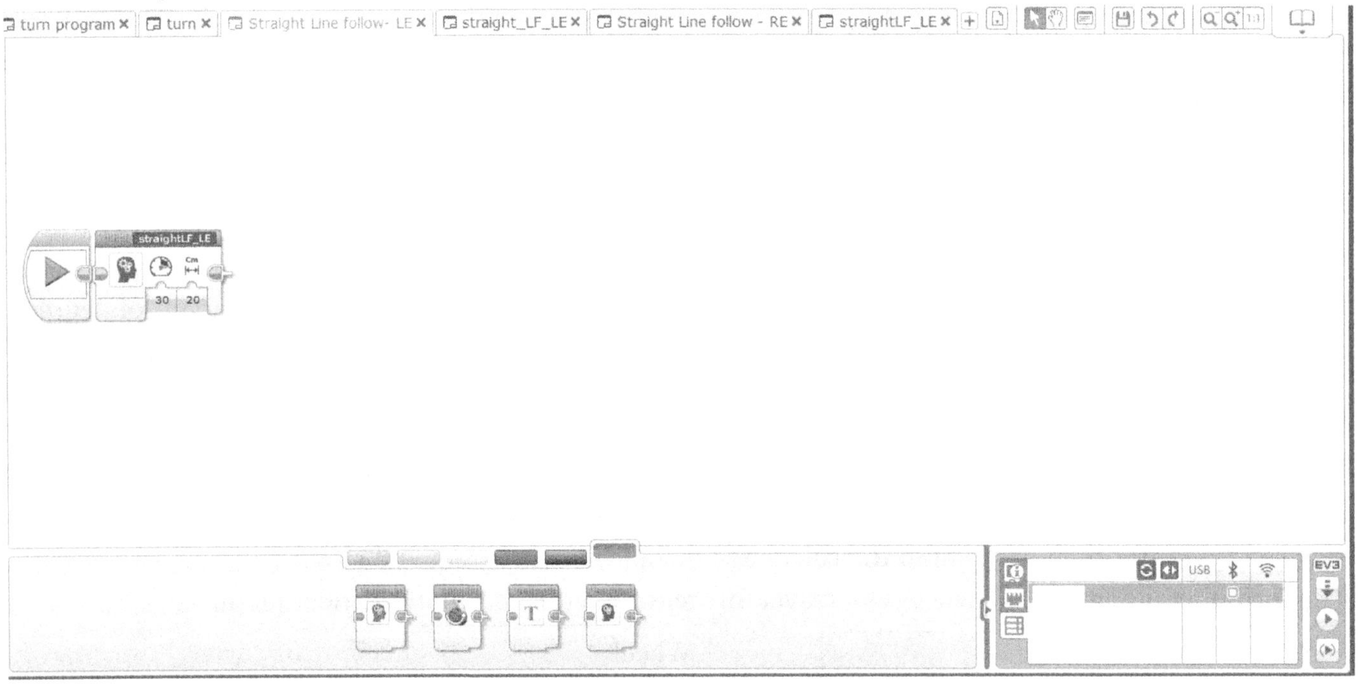

Create a new program in 'Chapter three – Myblock' and name it 'Straight Line follow- RE'. This program will allow the robot to follow a black line using the right edge.
Create the following program and convert it into a 'Myblock' with the name 'straightLF_RE'
This program is exactly like the previous program except it follows the other side of the line as shown in the differing direction of the 'Move Steering' blocks

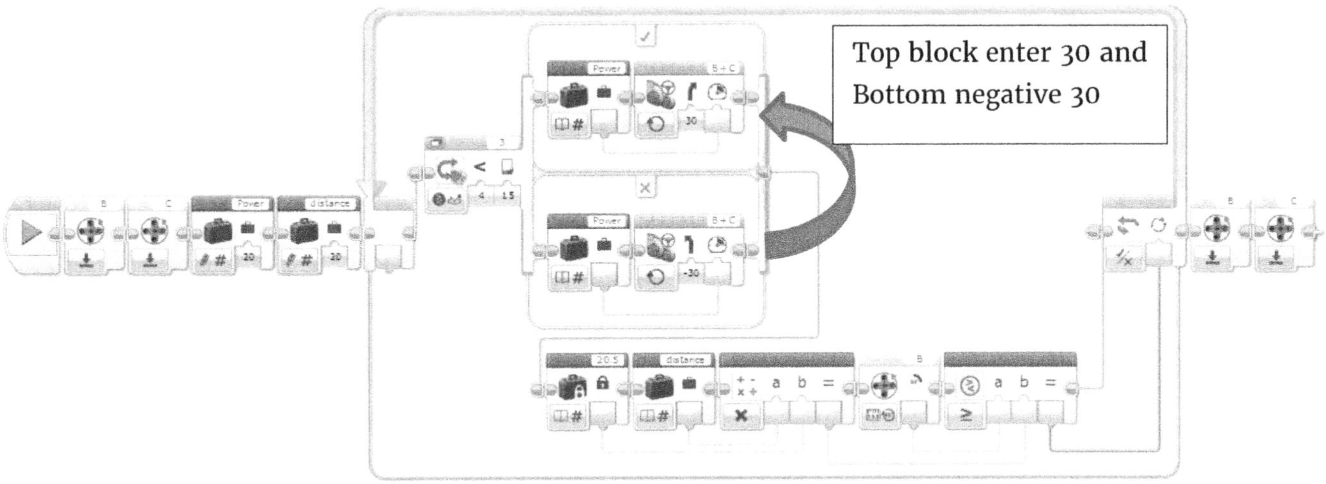

This is how the program should look after you convert it into a Myblock.

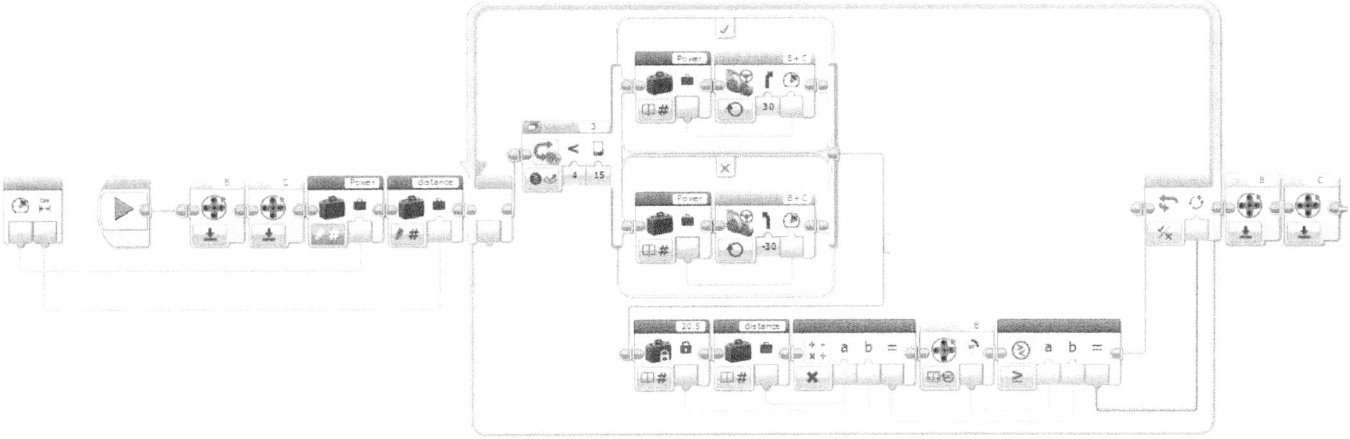

This is how you can test it.

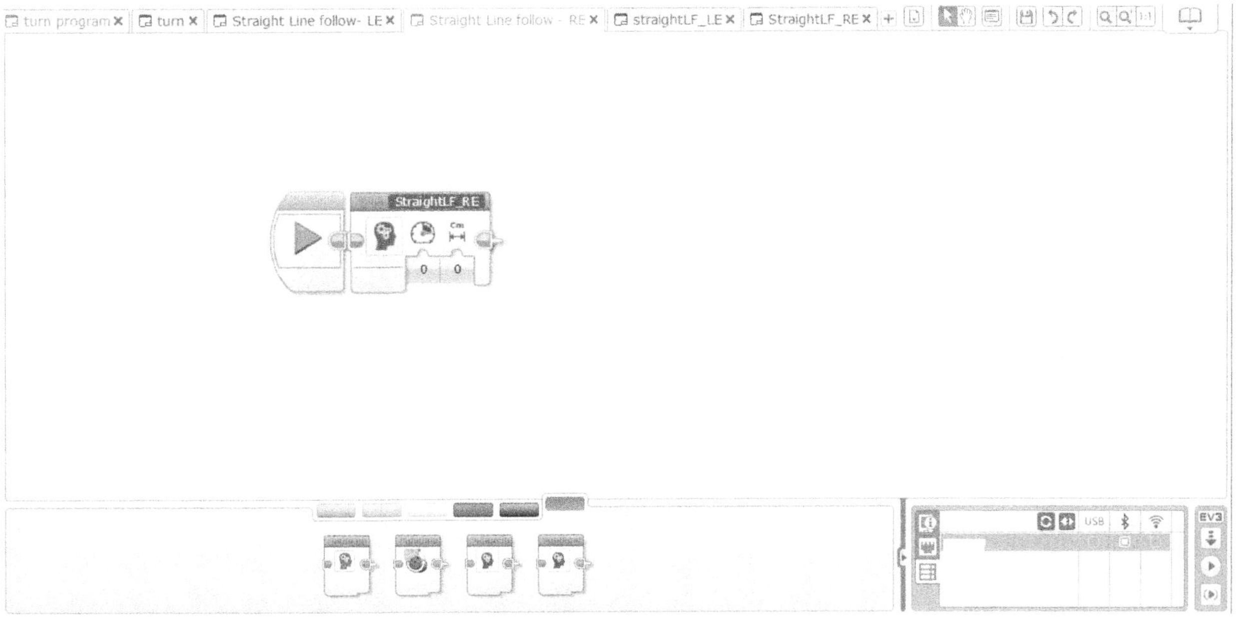

Create a new program in 'Chapter three – Myblock' and name it 'Curve Line follow- in'. This program will allow the robot to follow a line using the inner edge of the circle.
Create the following program and convert it into a 'Myblock' with the name 'CurveLF_in'. This program will use a lot of concepts covered in this section 'Myblocks' as well as information covered in the first few sections of the chapter.

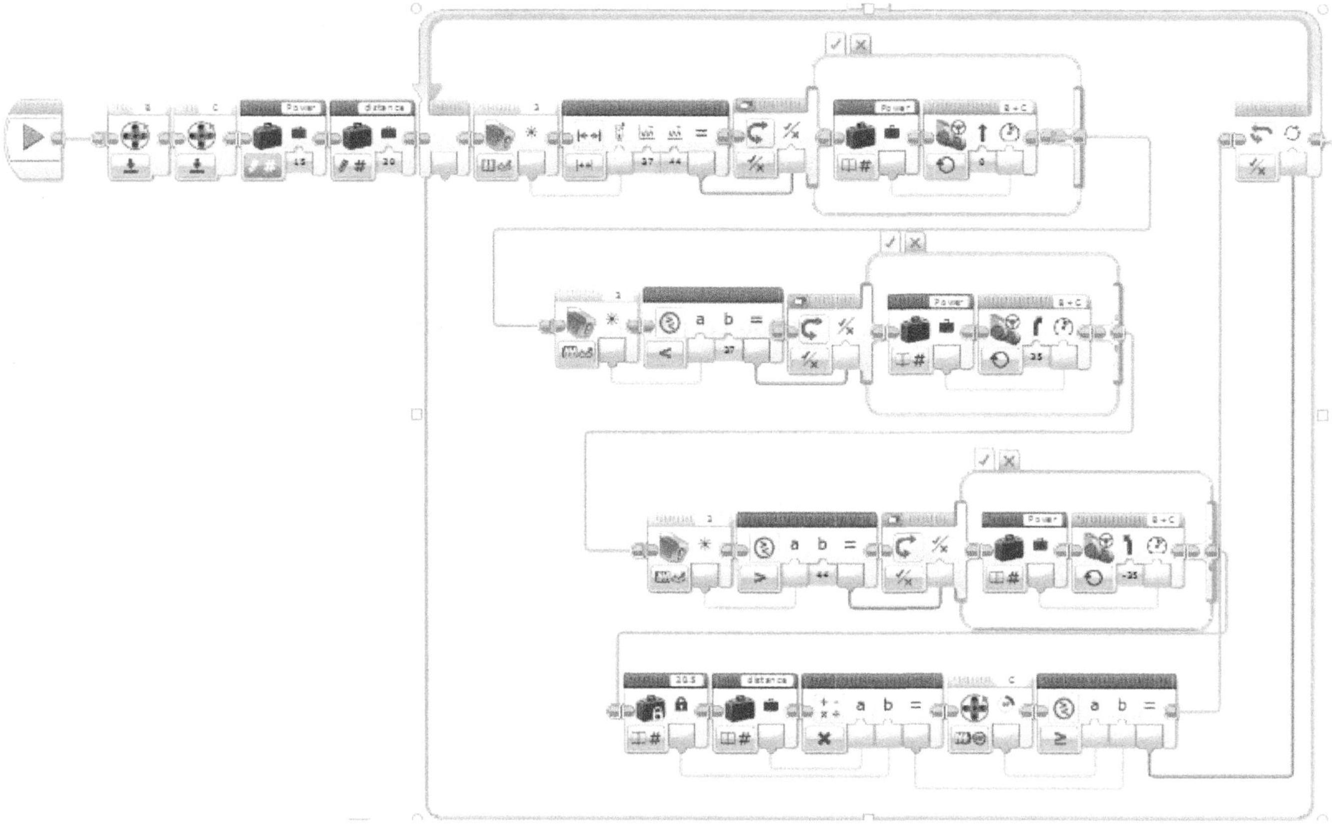

Let us divide this program into 2 parts for better visibility.
Part-1

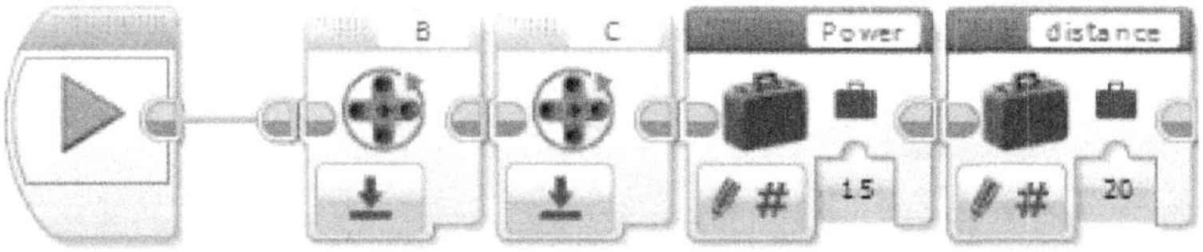

Part-2

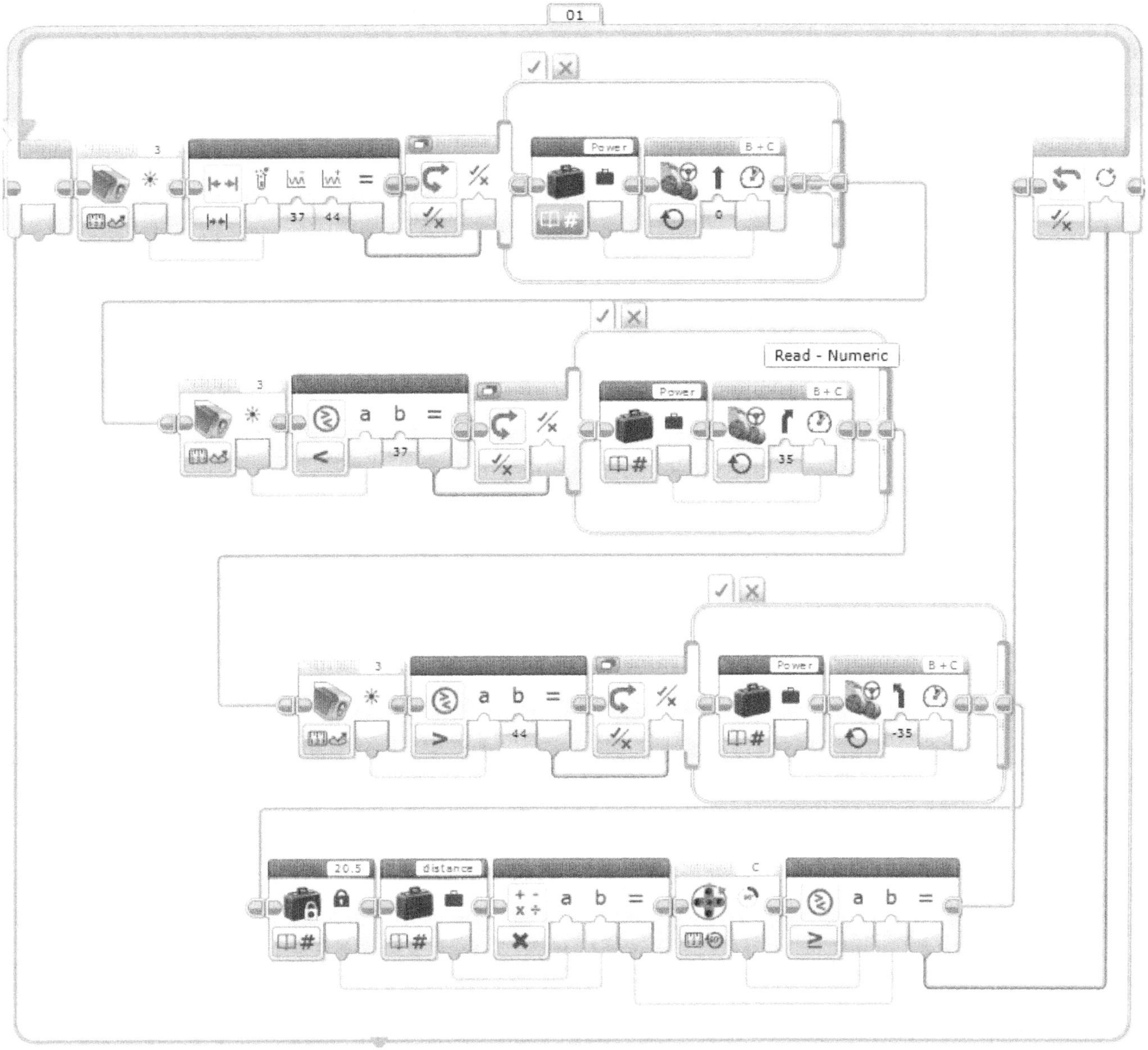

This is one example of a curved line follow that a robot needed to perform on an FLL mat.

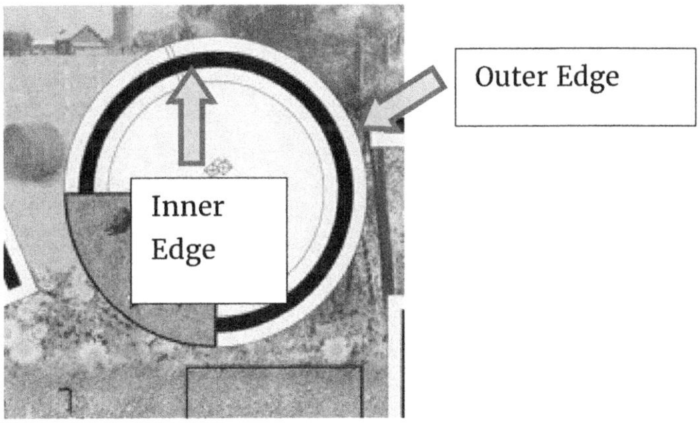

This is how the program will look after Myblock creation. This program also works for a straight line follow and is the recommended program to be used for any line follow requirements. Make sure to use the rotation measurement for the constant on the wheel that is on the side of the color sensor you are using.

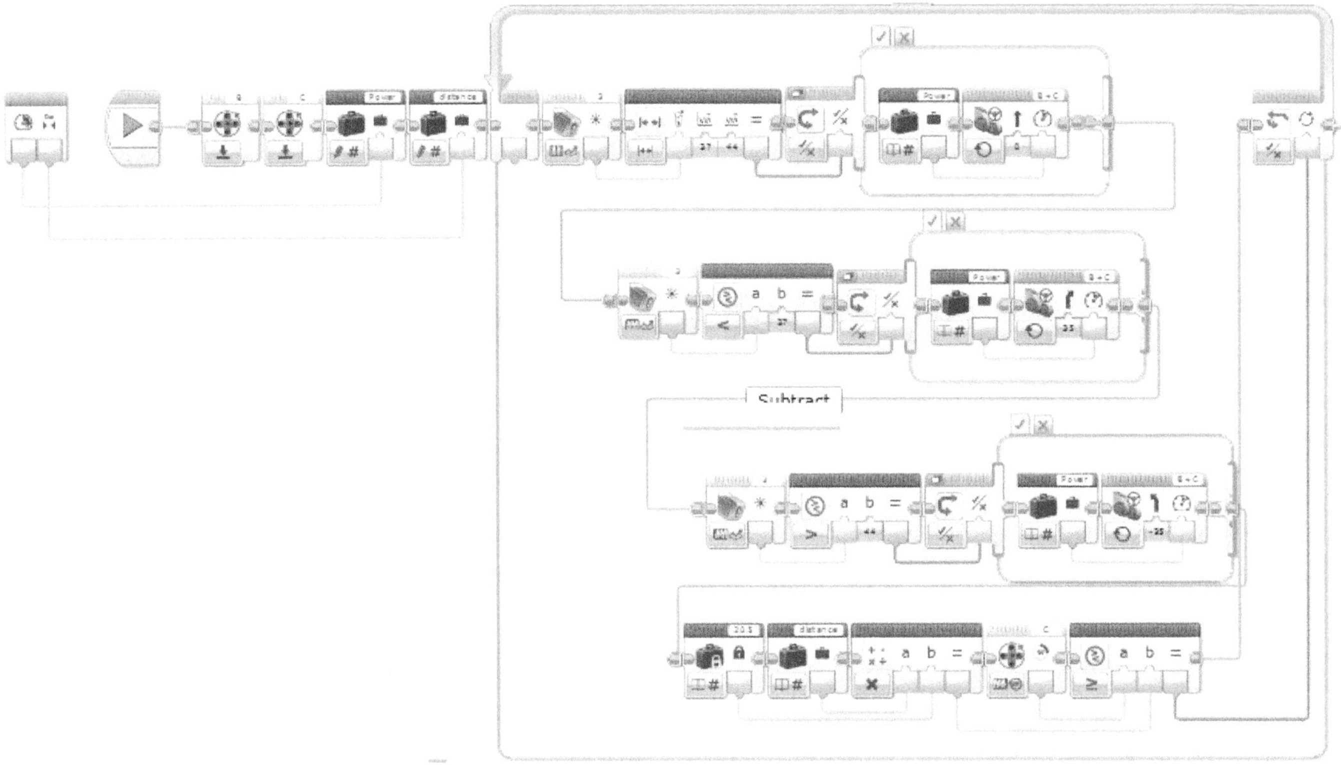

Create a new program in 'Chapter three – Myblock' and name it as 'Curve Line follow- out'. This program will allow the robot to line follow using the outer edge of the circle.
Create the following program and convert it into a 'Myblock' with the name 'CurveLF_out'

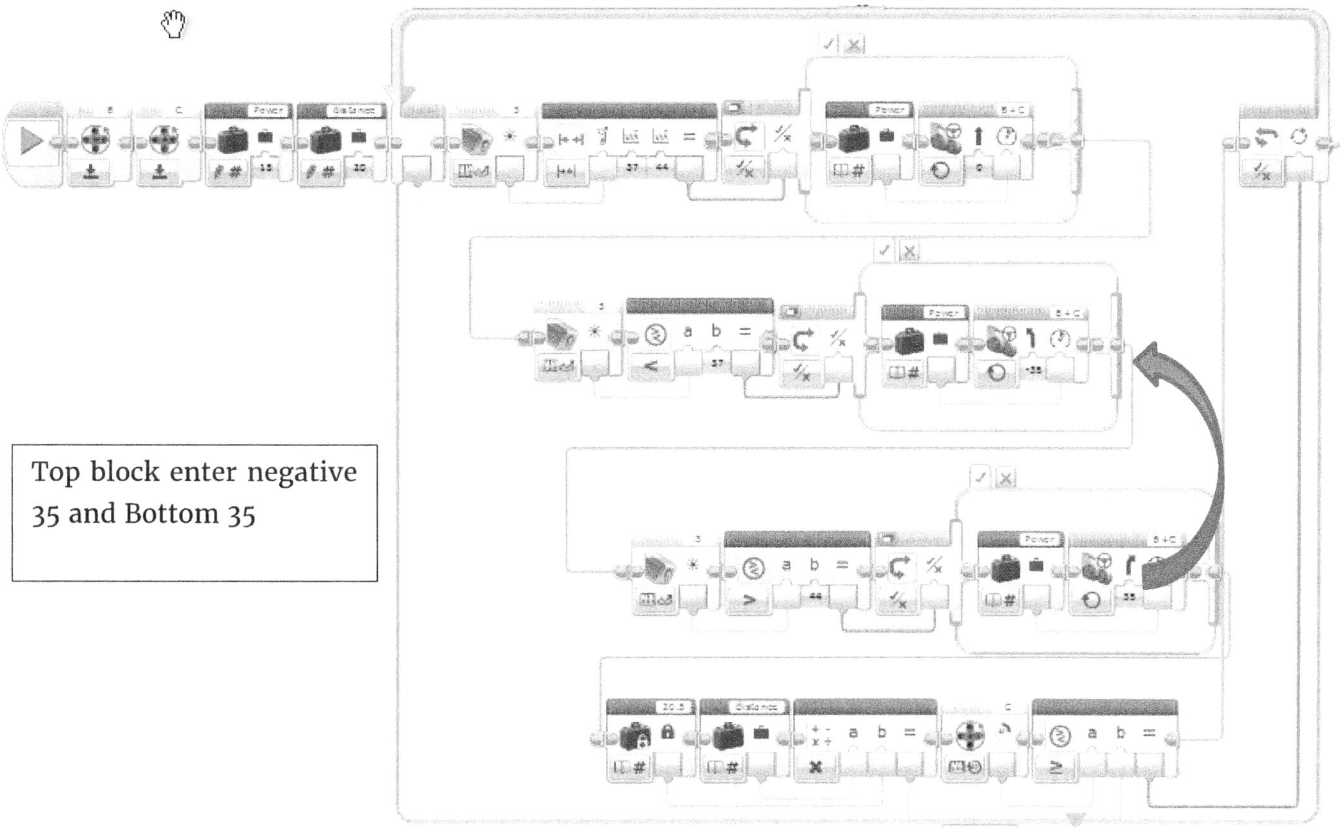

This is how the program will look after Myblock creation.

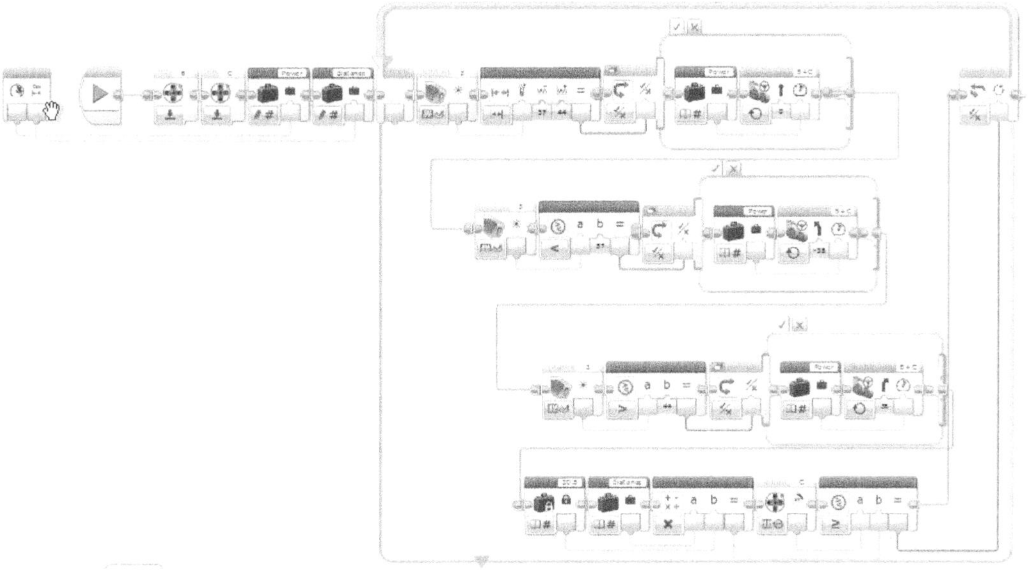

This program is recommended for straight as well as curved line follow. All the Above Programs are available for you to download on my website (advaitmarathe.com)

PROGRAM PROJECT PROPERTIES

The project properties allow you to get a full overview of the project and allows you to perform various operations like cleaning up your project, importing, exporting, and adding a picture to your project or custom sound.

Let us take a look at the various tabs that are available.

When you enter the properties window (tool symbol) you can add a project picture, project description and an image or video for more information. The default tab is the programs tab (shown below), where you will see all the programs in your project and this is where you can add or delete programs. You can import programs that you have exported out from other projects or export programs to a file.

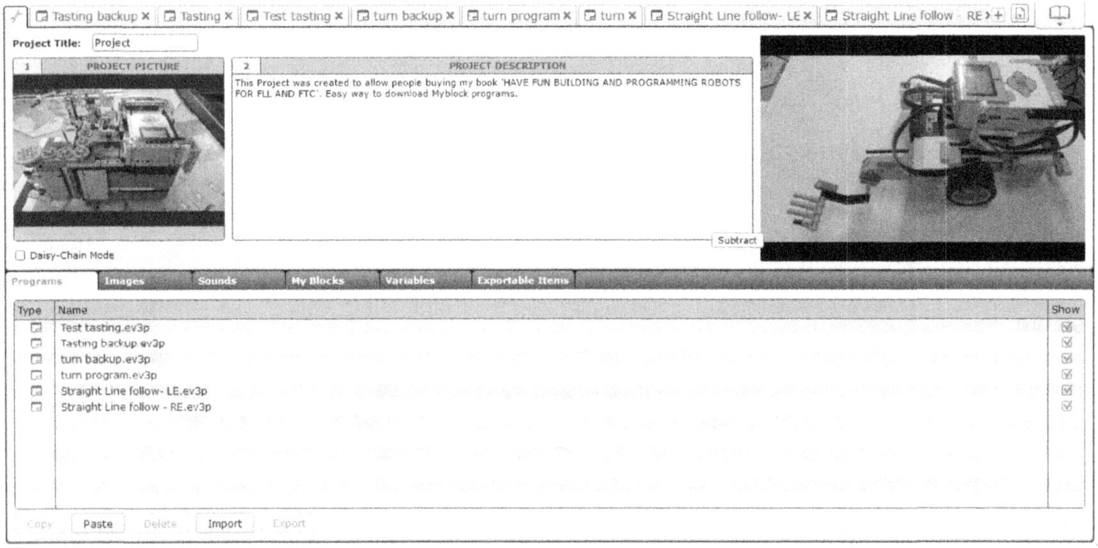

You can only 'Delete' programs from the properties tab. Closing the program tab at the top does not delete it. This tab is the only one that can do it and can be used for keeping the project clean by deleting unwanted programs.

The images tab allows you to load images that are of type RGF. The Tools menu has an 'Image Editor' that allows you to create images.

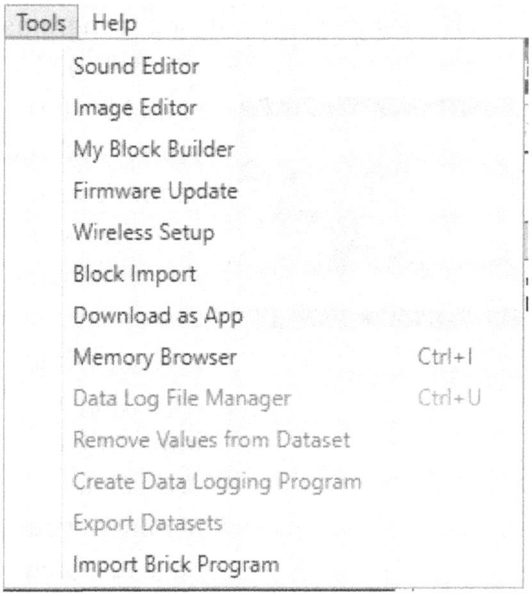

The Tools menu also allows you to create sound and image files that you can use on the Brick to display pictures and play sounds.

The sound tab is used to maintain the custom sound files you have created.

The 'My blocks' tab allows you manage the Myblocks you have created.

Myblocks you create in the project are only available in that project, so if you want to share a common set of Myblocks you should 'Export' it and 'Import' it into the new project. The cleanup of Myblocks can only be done from the properties screen.

The Variables tab allows you to manage the project variables. Any variables you create in your programs are centrally stored in the project and you cannot create 2 variables with the same name in a given project. While exporting and importing the programs or Myblocks you have to watch out for variables with the same name as a variable from the project you are importing into as this can issues. This might become a problem if the type of variable is different.

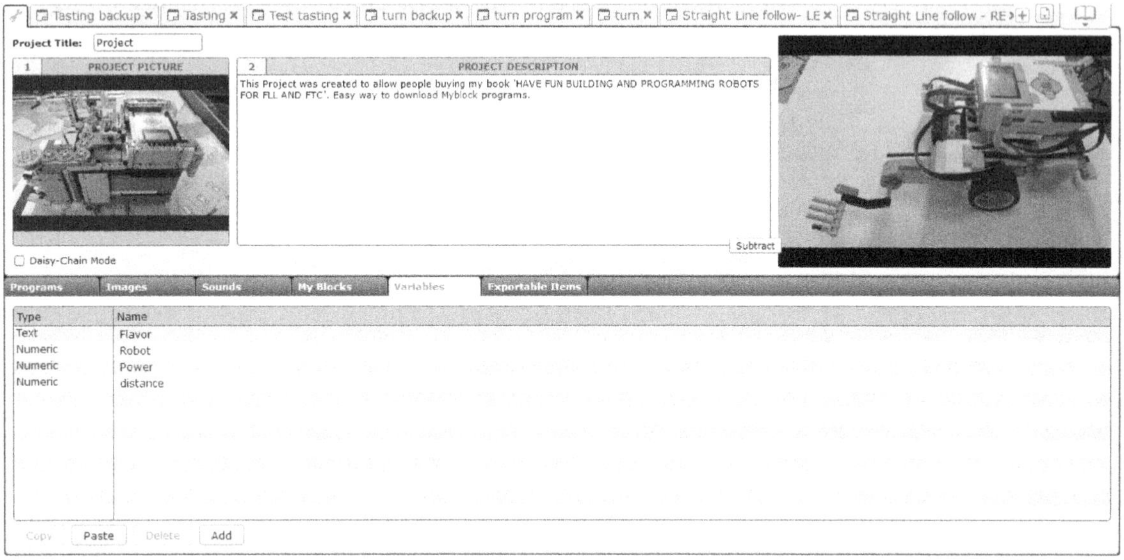

The last tab is the 'Exportable items' tab which gives you access to all the exportable items in the project.

BUGS AND DEBUGGING

When I visited Harvard university, I was able to see the very first computer. These computers were huge machines using electromechanical devices. There loops were performed by looping pieces of paper upon each other and had such a small amount of storage compared to our phones and computers. The computers were great but the most exciting learning experience was when I learned how the word bug came into computer science. Turns out that while someone was trying to operate the computer an actual bug got stuck in the computer.

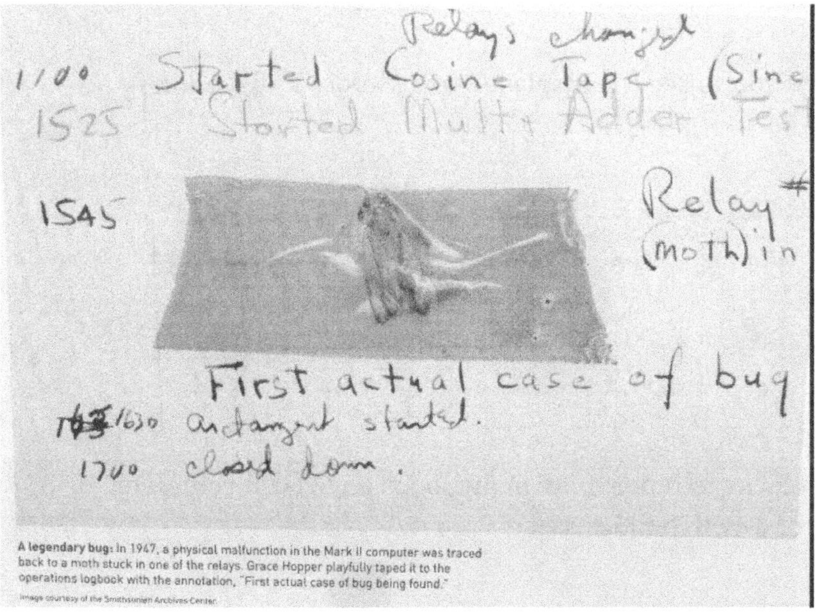

Most of the programs that you will make in your robotics journey will have a bug or two. This is not an anomaly but the norm for all types of programming. There are 2 types of bugs, one that is based on syntax (a bug that was created while typing) or one that is logical (one created because of incorrect understanding of the problem or incorrect solution logic).

1- Syntax related bugs are where you intended to enter '20' and instead entered '30'

2- Logical bugs are where you decided on logic that was not correct and the program is not doing what you want it to do.

In both cases you will have to debug the program and you should always follow this methodology.

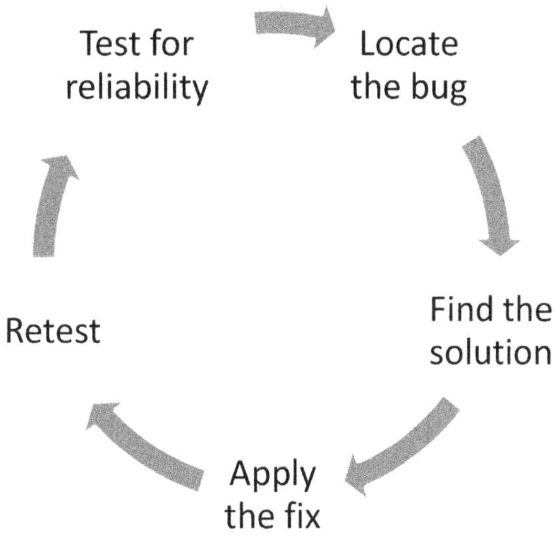

Locating the bug is the hardest task but programming blocks you have already learnt can be easily used for debugging.

1. Display block: You should use display blocks to display sensor readings or put text messages to understand which path the program took in a switch block

You may have to insert wait blocks to allow you to see the displayed text, before it disappears.

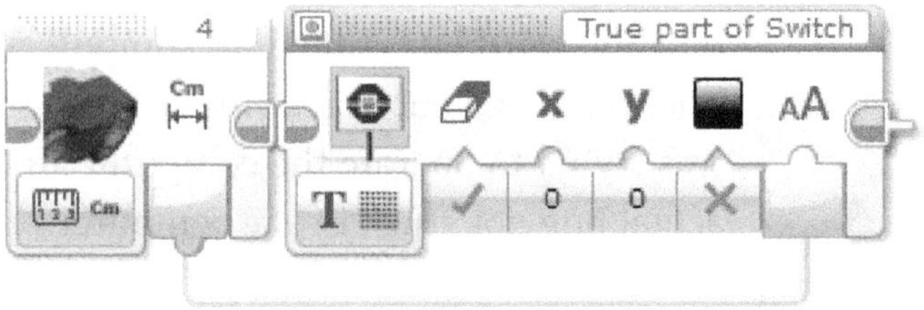

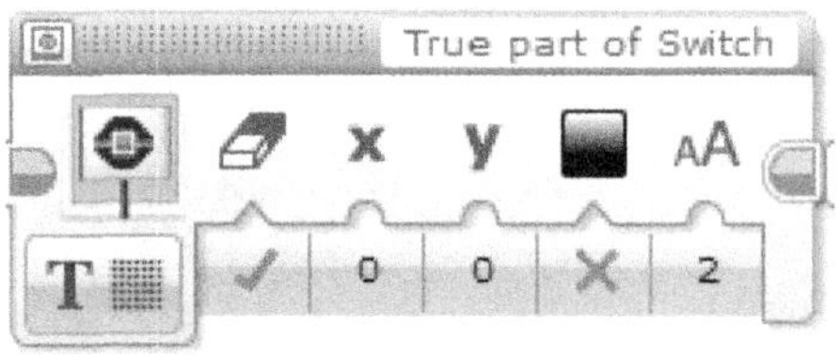

2. Use of sound alerts: You can use sound blocks to report how many loops have been completed or if the program has entered a particular part of a switch block.

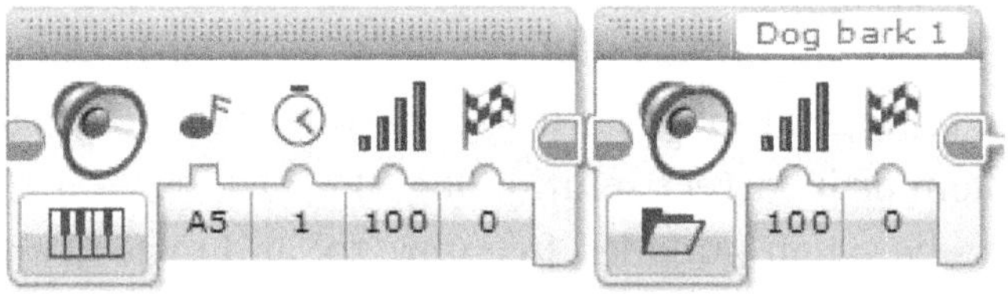

3. Visual alert through Brick status light: The Brick status light can provide visual cues on where the program is failing. This technique has limited use but can be used in conjunction with other techniques.

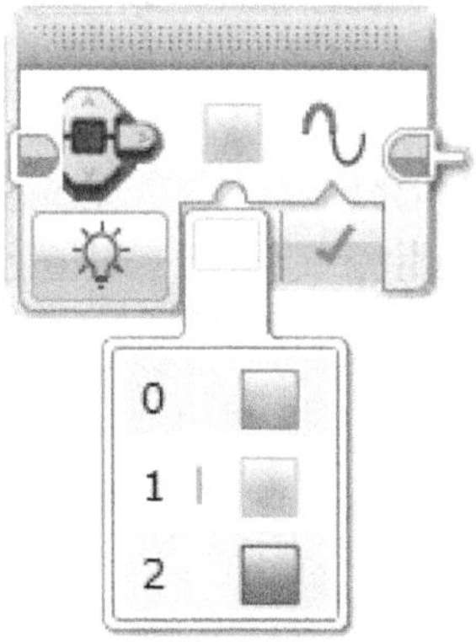

4. Run selected and wait for button press: This technique can be used to selectively run parts of your program, that you feel is creating problems. You highlight a piece of program that you want to run and press the run selected method. The Wait for Button technique allows you to add interruptions in the flow of the program to help you notice where the program is going awry.

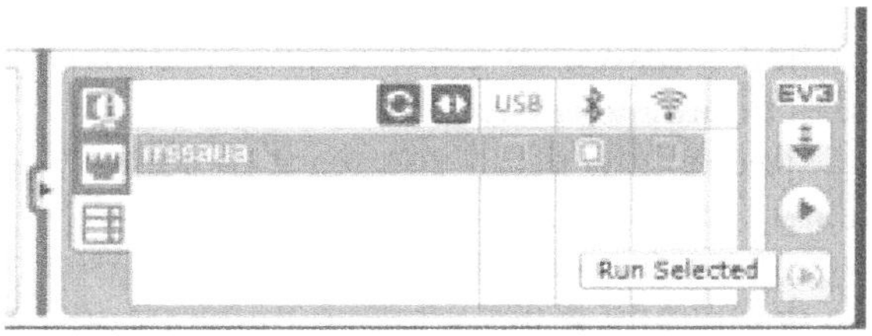

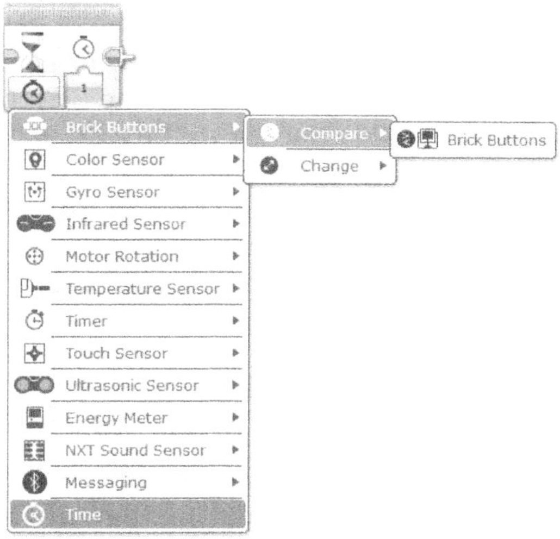

5. Visual cues on the programming interface: If you have selected the wrong port on the sensor block, the program will warn you.

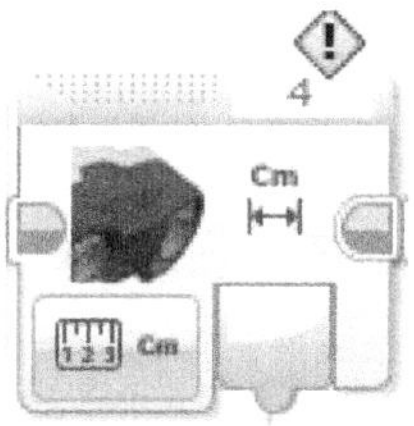

6. Video recording and slow-motion playback.
7. Forums to find answers to common problems.
8. Visual cues from the Robot- You can add additional move tank or motor blocks to the program to signify when an activity is finished. This will give you a visual cue from the robot to help you debug specific activities.
9. Advanced techniques like data logging.

ADVANCED TECHNIQUES - DATA LOGGING

The LEGO MINDSTORMS's beginning is deeply rooted in scientific experiments and data logging. Science is all about collecting information or data and using data and mathematics to prove (or disprove) theories. Without data we would never know how something is working the way that it is supposed to. LEGO has sold millions of their LEGO MINDSTORM robotics kits, but almost no one is using its most powerful tool- data logging. The interesting thing about the data logging feature of LEGO MINDSTORMS

EV3 is that it can help you analyze and organize your data as well as collect it. It is possible to read data while a program is running, and to use the EV3 Brick screen to display this information as well.

1. EV3 allows data logging from any of the attached sensors.
2. With data logging you can use the EV3 to collect data.
3. For each sensor attached to the EV3, you can specify how often you want to collect the data
4. Take data measurements(samples) as frequently as every 1/1000 of a second.
5. Sample time can be set to sample the data for few seconds or till the program has completed.

For competition programming data logging is useful in debugging programs and understanding why the robot behaved in certain ways during a robot run.

Let us take an example of a simple program you have written to move the robot forward until it is 10 centimeters away from the wall. In this program, you are using ultrasonic sensor. The problem is that the robot is stopping at the wrong location and you suspect that it is detecting another object. DATA LOGGING is your solution for analyzing that problem.

You have 2 options.

Option-1- Log data into a file using the 'File Access' Block and open that file on your computer.

Create the following program

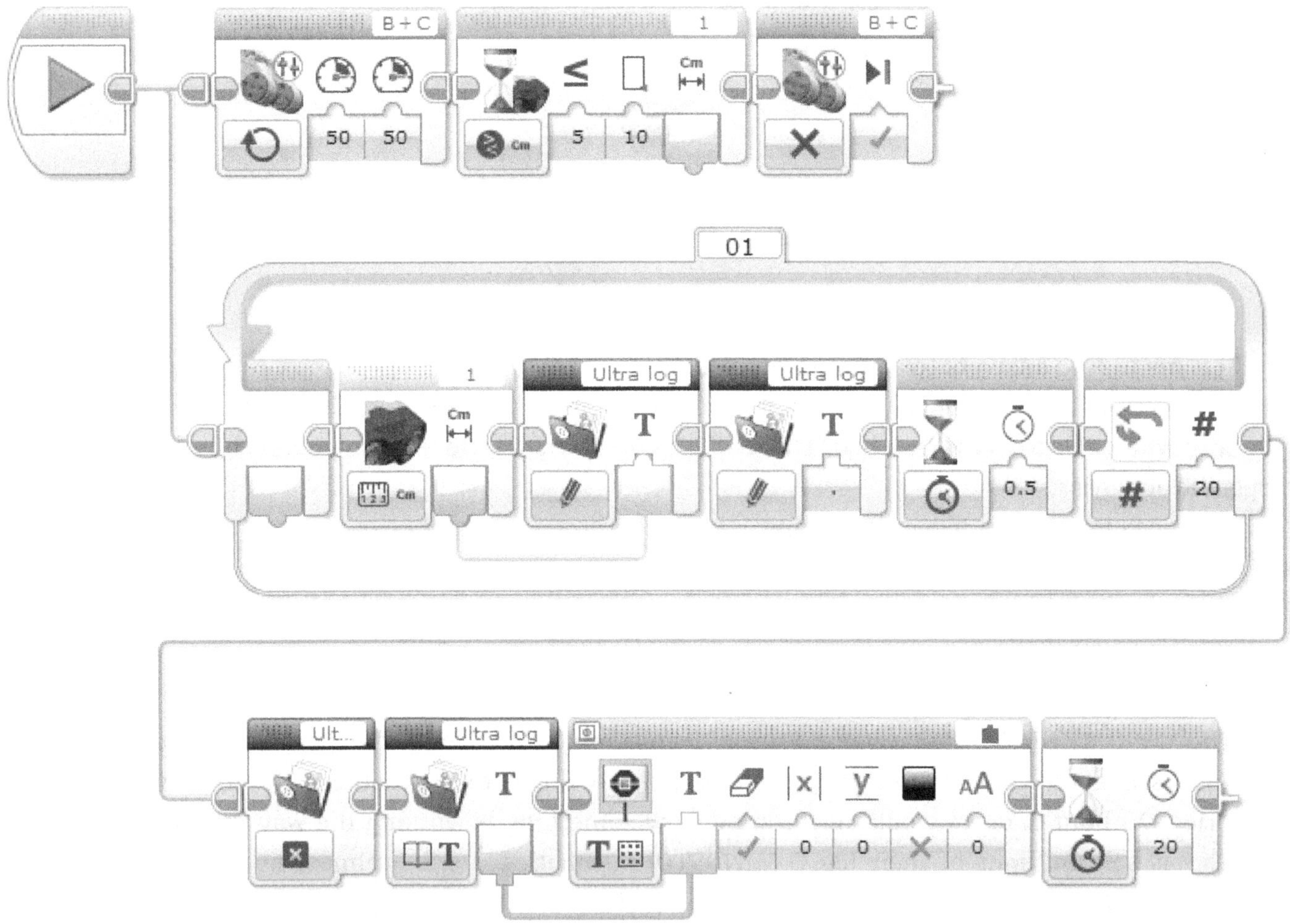

This program uses the ultrasonic sensor block to read the ultrasonic sensor reading every 0.5 seconds and then writes the information to the 'ultra log' file in the brick memory. After logging the data, this program closes the file (very important) and displays the information on the Brick Display by reading the file.

You can access this file by clicking on the 'Tools' Menu, going to the 'Memory Browser' option, and then uploading the .rtf file to your laptop.

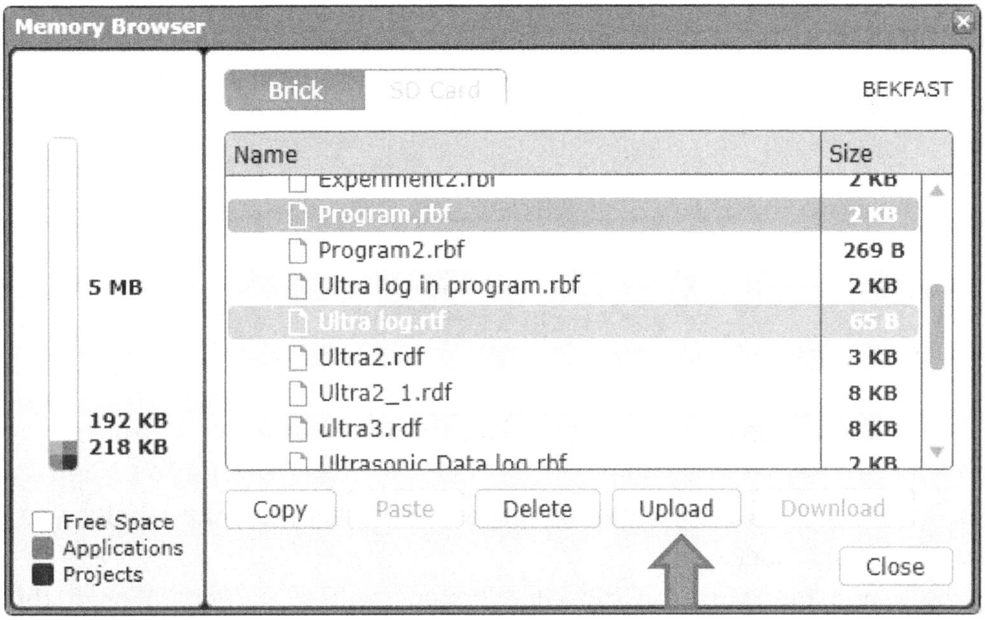

This is how the file will look once you open the .rtf file. (The .rtf file will open on any text editor)

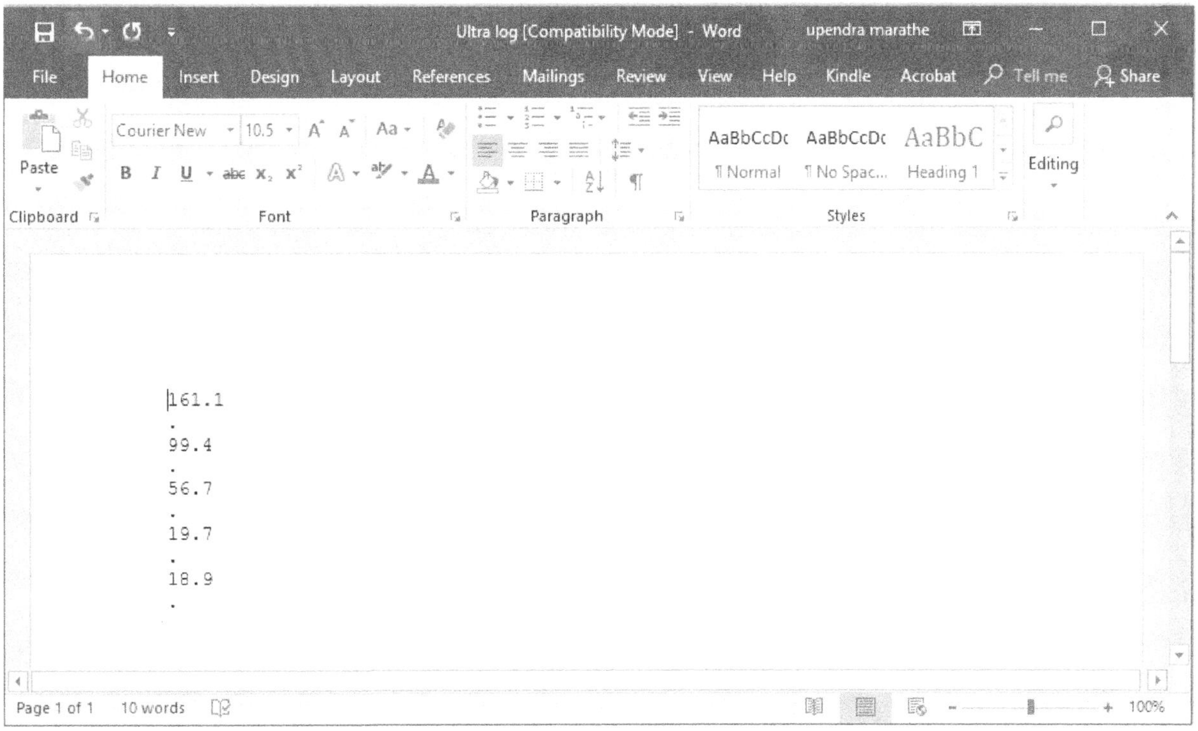

Option-2- Use the 'Data Logging' block to log the ultrasonic sensor data into the .RDF file and open it in an experiment.

Program the following:

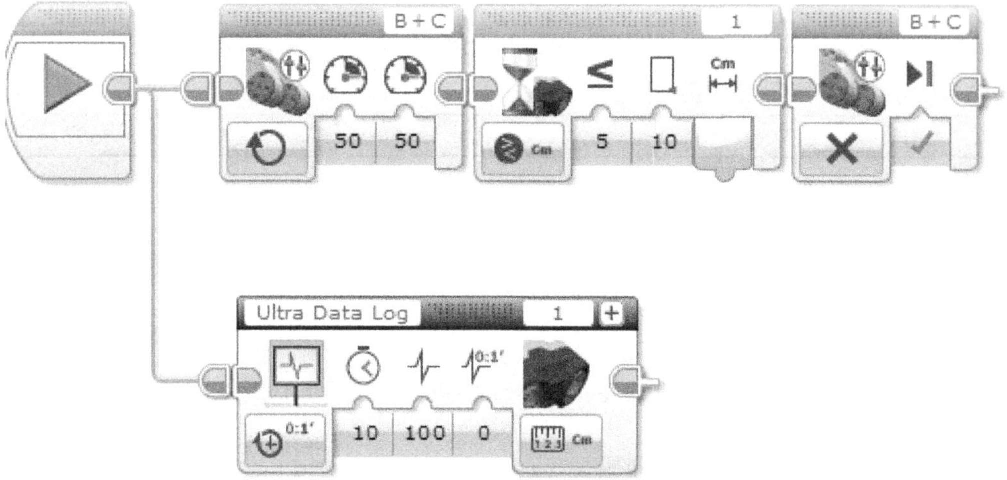

This program uses the 'Data Logging' Block to log data from the ultrasonic sensor to a .RDF file in the brick memory.

The time duration is 10 seconds and the sampling rate per second is 100. Additionally, you can add more sensors to the 'Data Logging' block.

Running the program and following the subsequent steps will allow you to open this RDF file in 'Experiment'.

Step-1 – Create a new Program of type 'Experiment'

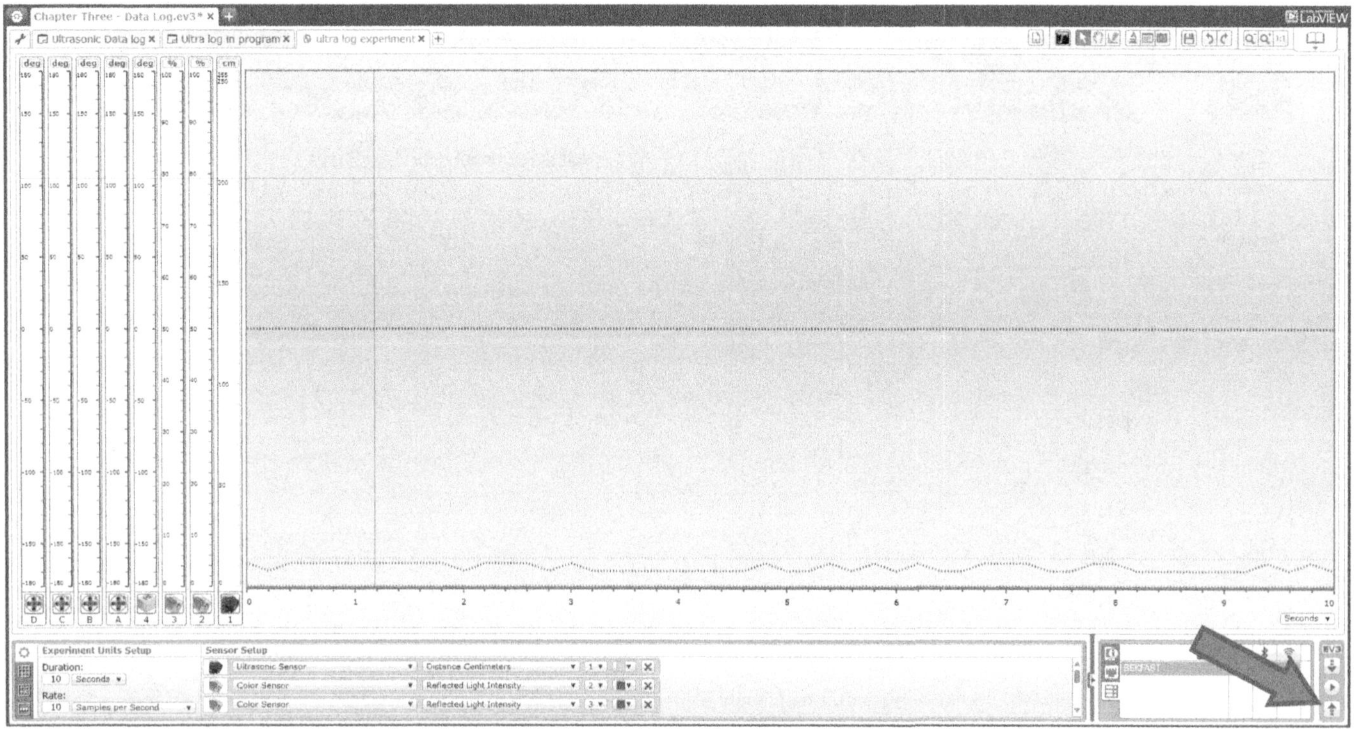

Step-2 – Upload the RDF file you created using the upload button indicated by the arrow in the previous picture. Once you have located the RDF file in the brick memory click on the import button shown.

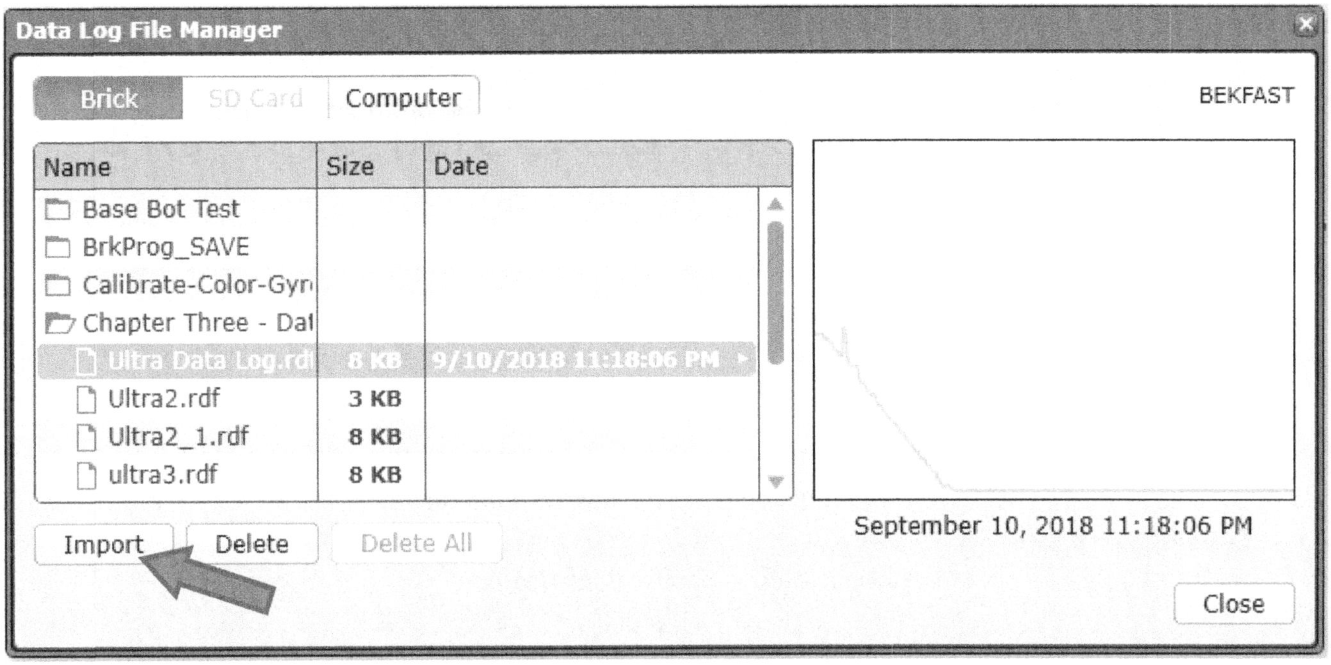

Step-3 – Explore the logged data in the experiment.

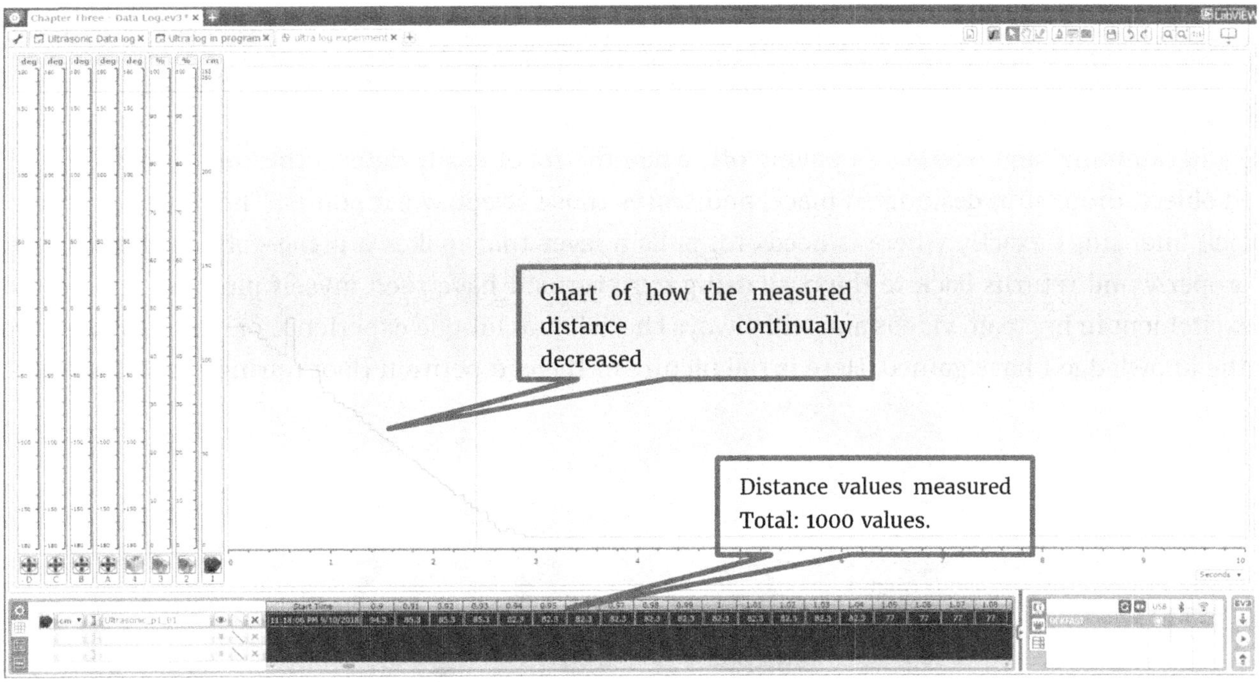

I AM GOING FOR FLL COMPETITION

Design and Game

A successful competition for me is always going out there and putting 100 percent into whatever I'm doing. It's not always winning.

—Simon Biles – Olympic Gold Medallist.

3-2-1 LEGO............ You send your team's robot out of the base to perform those impossible missions. There is clapping, cheering, 'oohs', 'ahhhs' from the spectators, but you are tuning everything out in the excitement you are experiencing. Finally, seeing your team's strategy, design, ideas, programming, and team work paying off, when the robot easily detects the colors, picks the right colored object, drops it in designated place, and scores those sweet sweet points. The robot then follows the black line, stops exactly where it needs to, pulls a lever that makes a plane- attached by a string- land properly and returns back to the base using gyro turns. I have seen myself jumping up and down with excitement in my team videos and will always cherish that unique experience of making things work from the knowledge I have gained. Here is the picture of the competition floor during the Robot Games.

FIRST is a non-profit organization established by Dean Kamen in 1989. In 1998, the very first FLL tournament was held to allow children to compete in a STEM competition with robots, technology, and more.

To participate in the FLL competition you have to form a team of 2 to 10 students (Region based age limits apply -Broad regions are North America, South America, Europe, Africa and Asia- including Australia - http://www.firstlegoleague.org/countries). Adult supervision is always required, and the FIRST youth protection policy should be followed. To compete, teams must be fully registered and must have paid all their dues for team participation (**Completing the Registration as soon as it opens up, helps in getting the Mat and Game elements faster- due to first come-first serve shipping**). All work presented at the competition should be work done by children in the team. **Team, Coaches and team supporters should demonstrate Core Values throughout the season and during competitions/ events.**

The FLL competition has 4 main components: Core values, Robot Design, Robot Game, and Project.

You will learn more about Core Values in the **'Forming A Team'** chapter and about the project in the **'Caring about Community'** chapter. In this chapter we will learn about the Robot Game and most importantly Robot Design.

Robot Game, Core Values and Project are equally important for advancement of the team to the next Level.

Typically, your team will compete in the Qualifiers first and then advance to Regionals. Advancement in regionals will allow your team to register for the World Championship.

The FLL competition season begins in the month of May with registration opening in May. In August/ September the challenge is released and the field setup kit is shipped. Tournaments begin in October /November and the World Championship is held in March/April of Next Year.

Visit - http://www.firstlegoleague.org/challenge- for complete and up to date information.

Once you have registered, if you are a rookie team, you can buy the mat and game elements from previous year challenges. When I formed my team our regional FLL partners were selling some excess mats they had. You can also find mats for sale on eBay, Amazon and other online websites. Practicing on an older mat gave my team a distinctive advantage in understanding how the competition would be and what kind of missions the robot would have to complete.

The designers of the FLL mat and Challenge are very innovative so you should be prepared for a new set of challenges for every new season. The key is knowing the building blocks and that is what we will continue to discuss in this book.

ROBOT GAME

The Robot Game is played on a 4 by 8 feet table which is built as per the specifications provided by the competition rules. You should build your own practice table before the mat arrives in August / September and should immediately build the game elements and create the game setup as a team activity. Once you build the table, it can be used for multiple years.

https://www.firstinspires.org/sites/default/files/uploads/resource_library/fll/table-build.pdf

The mat is laid on top of the table and the robot performs missions from the challenge. For this particular challenge there are a total of 15 missions. In every match in the competition your team will try to complete as many missions as possible in **2 minutes 30 seconds,** based on the strategy you have decided.

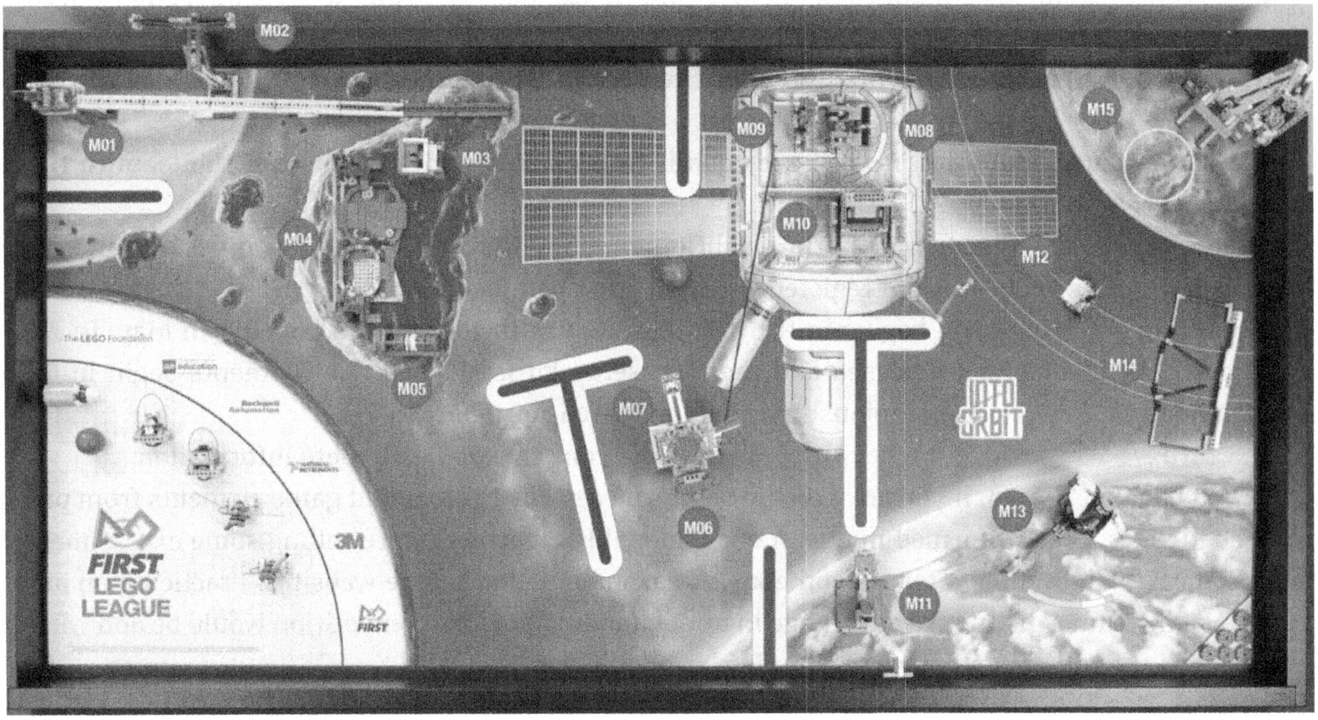

All the information about the challenge and Robot game can be found on http://www.firstlegoleague.org/challenge.
Coaches should always refer to the Coaches Handbook and the latest Game updates and Project Updates.

What happens during the Tournament?
During the tournament you play 3-4 matches. When you arrive in the morning at the event place, you are given a schedule of when your matches will be held and in which Pit? or at what table? You are also given a schedule for the team's Judging sessions for Robot Design, Project, and Core Values. During each match only 2 team members (Technicians) are allowed in the pit to launch the robot on the field (The rest of the team must stand back as directed by tournament officials, with the expectation of fresh Technicians being able to switch places with current Technicians at any time if desired).

The robot has **2 minutes 30 seconds** to complete challenges and gather points by completing missions. The robot has to start from the base and can return to the base as many times as needed but once the robot leaves the base it is in full autonomous mode (You are not allowed to touch the robot). Touching the Robot outside the base will result in a penalty- typically 3 points subtracted from your match score for every interference.

This is how the schedule looks.

East Bay Championship 2016v2

Pit #	Team #	Team Name	City	Affiliation	Game Round 1		Game Round 2		Game Round 3		Game Round 4	
1	[illegible]	[illegible]	San Mateo	[illegible]		RED 1		WHITE 2		WHITE 1		BLUE 2
2	[illegible]	[illegible]	Fremont	[illegible]		RED 2		BLUE 2		BLUE 1		WHITE 2
3	[illegible]	[illegible]	Fremont	[illegible]	10:30 AM Group5	WHITE 1	11:20 AM Group1	RED 1	2:00 PM Group1	BLUE 2	3:40 PM Group1	BLUE 1
4	[illegible]	[illegible]	San Ramon	[illegible]		BLUE 1		RED 2		RED 1		WHITE 1
5	[illegible]	[illegible]	Fremont	[illegible]		BLUE 2		BLUE 1		WHITE 2		RED 2
6	[illegible]	[illegible]	Fremont	[illegible]		WHITE 2		WHITE 1		RED 2		RED 1
7	[illegible]	[illegible]	Fremont	[illegible]		RED 1		WHITE 2		WHITE 1		BLUE 2
8	[illegible]	[illegible]	Hillsborough	[illegible]		RED 2		BLUE 2		BLUE 1		WHITE 2
9	[illegible]	[illegible]	Union City	[illegible]	10:40 AM Group6	WHITE 1	11:30 AM Group2	RED 1	2:10 PM Group2	BLUE 2	3:50 PM Group2	BLUE 1
10	[illegible]	[illegible]	Pleasanton	[illegible]		BLUE 1		RED 2		RED 1		WHITE 1
11	[illegible]	[illegible]	Fremont	[illegible]		BLUE 2		BLUE 1		WHITE 2		RED 2
12	[illegible]	[illegible]	Fremont	[illegible]		WHITE 2		WHITE 1		RED 2		RED 1
13	[illegible]	[illegible]	Fremont	[illegible]		RED 1		WHITE 2		WHITE 1		BLUE 2
14	[illegible]	[illegible]	San Ramon	[illegible]		RED 2		BLUE 2		BLUE 1		WHITE 2
15	[illegible]	[illegible]	Santa Clara	[illegible]	9:20 AM Group1	WHITE 1	11:45 AM Group3	RED 1	2:25 PM Group3	BLUE 2	4:00 PM Group3	BLUE 1
16	[illegible]	[illegible]	Fremont	[illegible]		BLUE 1		RED 2		RED 1		WHITE 1
17	[illegible]	[illegible]	Fremont	[illegible]		BLUE 2		BLUE 1		WHITE 2		RED 2
18	[illegible]	[illegible]	Fremont	[illegible]		WHITE 2		WHITE 1		RED 2		RED 1
19	[illegible]	[illegible]	San Francisco	[illegible]		RED 1		WHITE 2		WHITE 1		BLUE 2
20	[illegible]	[illegible]	Fremont	[illegible]		RED 2		BLUE 2		BLUE 1		WHITE 2
21	[illegible]	[illegible]	Fremont	[illegible]	9:30 AM Group2	WHITE 1	11:55 AM Group4	RED 1	2:35 PM Group4	BLUE 2	4:10 PM Group4	BLUE 1
22	[illegible]	[illegible]	Union City	[illegible]		BLUE 1		RED 2		RED 1		WHITE 1
23	[illegible]	[illegible]	San Jose	[illegible]		BLUE 2		BLUE 1		WHITE 2		RED 2
24	[illegible]	[illegible]	Castro Valley	[illegible]		WHITE 2		WHITE 1		RED 2		RED 1
25	[illegible]	[illegible]	Fremont	[illegible]		RED 1		WHITE 2		WHITE 1		BLUE 2
26	[illegible]	[illegible]	Fremont	[illegible]		RED 2		BLUE 2		BLUE 1		WHITE 2
27	[illegible]	[illegible]	Dublin	[illegible]	9:55 AM Group3	WHITE 1	1:15 PM Group5	RED 1	2:50 PM Group5	BLUE 2	4:20 PM Group5	BLUE 1
28	[illegible]	[illegible]	Danville	[illegible]		BLUE 1		RED 2		RED 1		WHITE 1
29	[illegible]	[illegible]	San Ramon	[illegible]		BLUE 2		BLUE 1		WHITE 2		RED 2
30	[illegible]	[illegible]	Cupertino	[illegible]		WHITE 2		WHITE 1		RED 2		RED 1
31	[illegible]	[illegible]	Cupertino	[illegible]		RED 1		WHITE 2		WHITE 1		BLUE 2
32	[illegible]	[illegible]	Fremont	[illegible]		RED 2		BLUE 2		BLUE 1		WHITE 2
33	[illegible]	[illegible]	Fremont	[illegible]	10:05 AM Group4	WHITE 1	1:25 PM Group6	RED 1	3:00 PM Group6	BLUE 2	4:30 PM Group6	BLUE 1
34	[illegible]	[illegible]	San Francisco	[illegible]		BLUE 1		RED 2		RED 1		WHITE 1
35	[illegible]	[illegible]	Fremont	[illegible]		BLUE 2		BLUE 1		WHITE 2		RED 2
36	[illegible]	[illegible]	Los Altos	[illegible]		WHITE 2		WHITE 1		RED 2		RED 1

When 2 team members (Technicians) get into the Pit area before the match they should inspect the field and make sure the **walls are smooth and the mission models are setup correctly.** If anything is out of place, politely suggest the referees to correct it. **Always make sure to calibrate the light and gyro sensors before the match begins**.

During the competition matches, you are playing with another team and although you are competing for first place in the robot game you are actually co-operating with the other team. If you do a common mission (see Challenge Handbook), both teams will score more points. Example of the cooperation mission is shown in the yellow highlight in the next picture.

Both teams play on tables placed side by side as shown in the picture below.

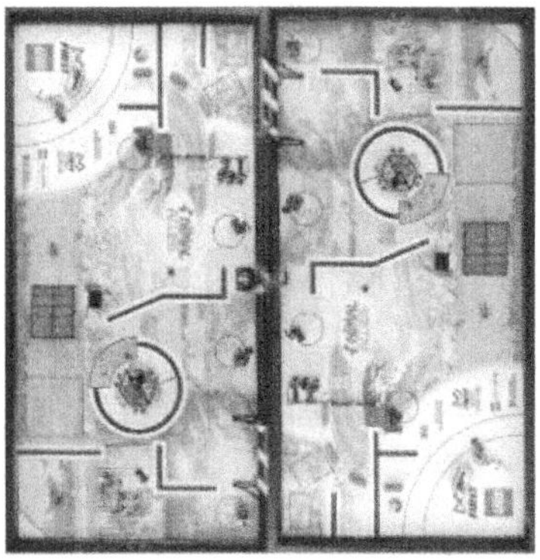

Examples of Missions

In the 2014-2015 'World Class' challenge the 'Search Engine' mission required the robot to push a slider to turn a wheel (fortune wheel) and based on a randomly selected color, pull the same colored loop out of the mission model. This was a highly complex mission and this difficulty allowed teams to score a maximum of 60 points

Search Engine 	**Required condition visible at the end of the match:** The color wheel has spun at least once. If a single color appears in the white frame, its matching loop is no longer touching the model. If two colors appear in the white frame, the remaining color's loop is no longer touching the model. Both "not desired" loops must be touching the model, in their holes. **Required methods, constraints**: Nothing has caused the color wheel to spin except the slider being pushed. **=Slider: 15 points** **Or Slider + Loop: 60 points**

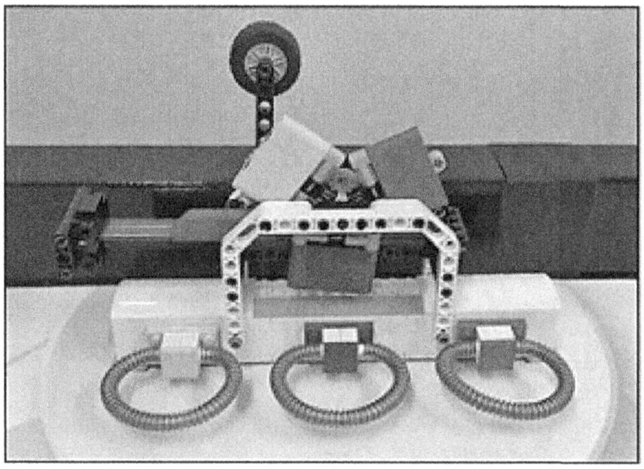

In 2012 the 'Transitions' Mission in the 'Senior Solutions' challenge required the robot to jump over a gap in the ramp and walk down the steps to score 70 points.

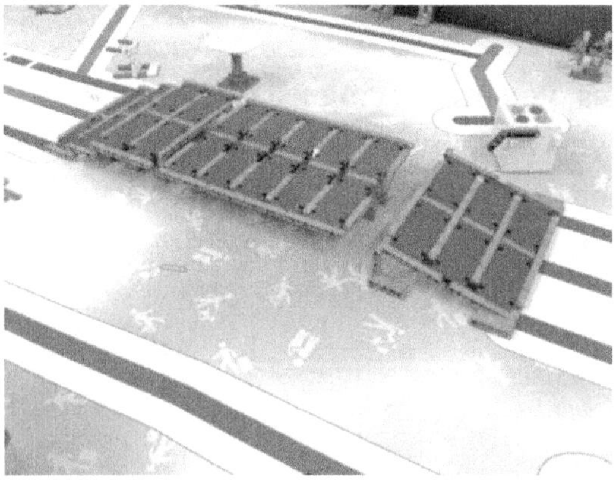

For the 2018 'Into Orbit' challenge's 'Space Walk Emergency' mission, the robot should place the astronaut in the Airlock chamber.

AIRLOCK CHAMBER

Empty - No points

Fully in 22 Points

Partially in 18 points

Scoring:

Robot Game Matches are scored by adding all the points for your completed missions and then subtracting your penalty points.

The best score out of 2 or 3 matches is taken and then your team is ranked thusly. There is typically a display near the game pit, where the scores and ranking of the teams are displayed.

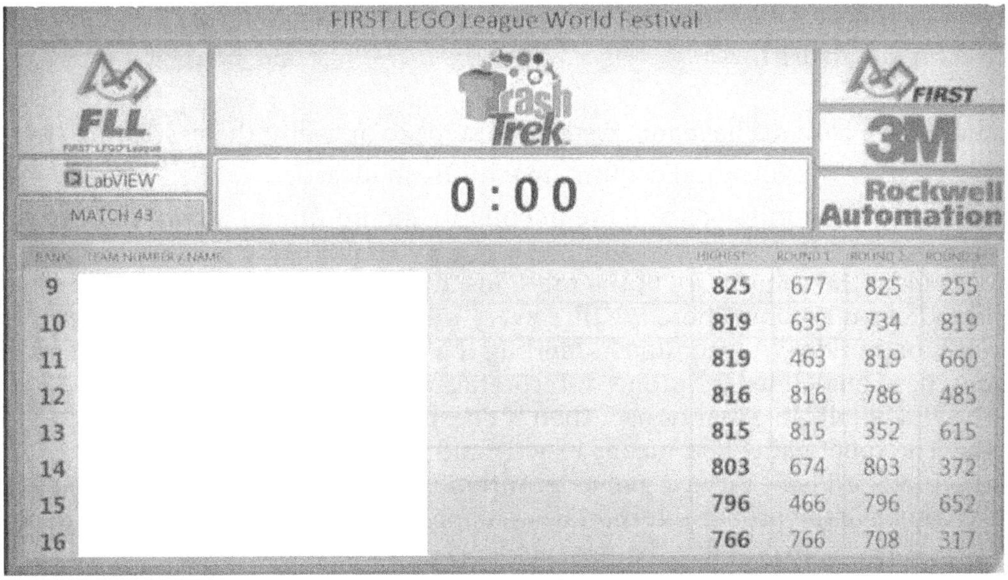

RANK	TEAM NUMBER / NAME	HIGHEST	ROUND 1	ROUND 2	ROUND 3
9		825	677	825	255
10		819	635	734	819
11		819	463	819	660
12		816	816	786	485
13		815	815	352	615
14		803	674	803	372
15		796	466	796	652
16		766	766	708	317

GAME STRATEGY

As a rookie team in 2013 we had no game strategy. What we did have was the desire to learn and adopt and that is exactly what has helped us over the years. I have developed a strategy that will work 50-70% time but out of the box thinking, experimentation, and learning from failures will perfect your game strategy.

Why do you need a game strategy? – TIME. You do not have an infinite amount of time for building and practicing. You only have 2 minutes 30 seconds to score the maximum amounts of points in the match. Planning and visualizing will allow your team to work faster and more efficiently.

1- How many 'robot runs' you will have in the match?
   One 'robot run' is when the robot leaves the base to perform missions and comes back to the base. So hypothetically you can have an infinite number of runs.
2- What your robot design will be?
3- How many missions you will be able to do?
4- How many total points you will be able to score?

Let us first think about the constraints you have in the competition.

1- There are only 2 minutes 30 seconds for you to complete the maximum amount of missions in a match
2- FLL or any other competitions only allow 4 motors. This limits how many activities you can do in one robot run during the match. You need 2 motors for the 'Drive Train' (To make the robot go from point A to point B), so you are only left with 2 motors to perform tasks.
3- Typically, you can do 1-3 tasks per motor, per run and 2 motors will allow you to do anywhere between 2-6 tasks in a single run
4- Based on my experience you can only do 2-5 runs in a given match with a 'Basebot – Attachment' Design. (This is the recommended approach for design and we will learn about a Basebot more in the upcoming sections)
5- The mat has mission models on it, so robot has limited space to maneuver.
6- As you get more away from the base, every turn the robot makes, adds a small deviation in the intended path due to drift.

All the best teams I have coached have followed these steps to arrive to the best game strategy. The most important part is creative thinking and coming up with fresh ideas.

1- (Explore) Know all the missions and the maximum and minimum points you can score for each mission.
2- (Imagine)Look at the complexity of the missions and first think about how the robot will accomplish those missions. There are three very important concepts to consider
   a. **Out of box thinking** – After understanding the mission requirements make sure that you follow these guidelines for proper interpretation
      I. If a detail isn't mentioned, then it doesn't matter.
      II. The robot game text means exactly and only what it plainly says.
      III. If a word isn't given a game definition, use its common conversational meaning.

      Once you have the proper interpretation, apply 'Out of the Box Thinking' to come up with various ways to accomplish the mission.

      Example: In 2016's 'Animal Allies' Challenge there were 2 missions dependent on each other. One was for the robot to get different colored food and another was to place the same colored food in front of different animals. There were 8 food pellets, 2 of each color, and total 4 colors. Based on interpretation, the team I was coaching, decided to get the food from the refrigerator in the first 'Robot Run' and bring it back to base. Then they sorted it manually, while robot was doing the second 'Robot Run'. Finally, then put the sorted food on a conveyor assembly on the robot to deliver it to the animals in the third 'Robot Run'. We did multiple missions in the first, second and third 'Robot Runs' but the refrigerator and food distribution was only one part of those runs.
   b. **It is all about the position of the robot.** How will the robot get in the right position next to the Mission Model? One example where this question is asked is in the 'Space Walk

Emergency' mission mentioned earlier in the book. How will the robot reach and position itself so it can lift the astronaut and place it perfectly in the airlock chamber?

c. **How will the robot do the task or tasks?** – What mechanism will be used to do this activity? Example: Is it an arm attached to the arm motor, an attachment, or a 'pincher mechanism' (We will learn this mechanism in later sections of this chapter) that will grab the astronaut?

3- (Imagine)Based on the complexity of the mission and it's point value, decide which missions you can do in 2 minutes and 30 seconds and rank them in an order that the whole team agrees with.
4- (Imagine)Decide the navigation path of the robot that will allow you to do 3-4 Missions in one 'Robot Run' and most importantly will allow the robot to return back to the base.
5- (Imagine)Once you have decided on 3 to 4 'Robot Runs' and a navigation path for each run, start thinking about what the robot should look like. Example: If you have decided on doing a mission that requires the robot to cross a hurdle then you will need ground clearance. Looking at the obstacles on the mat, you will have to decide how wide and long your robot needs to be.
6- (Imagine)Make sure that the size of the robot is possible. Based on my experience the most compact Basebot that can be built will be 6 inches wide and 6 -8 inches long.
7- (Imagine)Consider all of these factors to finalize the first iteration of the 'Game Strategy'.
8- (Create)Write it all down in an 'Engineering Notebook' and maintain it. Start building.
9- (Test)After you have designed and built the robot, continue experimenting and testing.
10- (Improve)Modify your strategy to suit the findings of your experiments.
11- Continue the process of Explore, Imagine, Create, Test, Improve, Share throughout the season till the competition date.
12- Thinking about a penalty as a way to get the robot back – This strategy may not always help you so keep this as a deep backup.

Continue to do these steps till you perfect your Game Strategy.

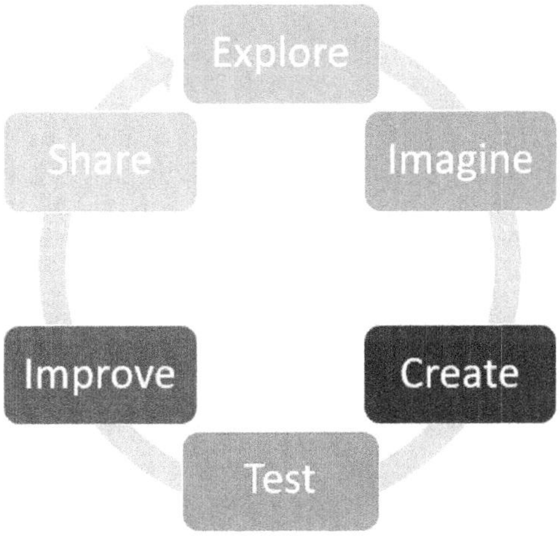

Considerations for Robot Positioning:

This is the most important point. For any missions you want to complete in the 'Robot Run', you have to make sure that you are able to perfectly position the robot next to the mission model (X and Y position). The following points should be considered for finding out if you will be able to do that.

1- Missions near the wall allow you to position the robot easily, as you can use mechanical means to continue in a straight line and you can use ultrasonic sensors to stop at a specific distance. With ultrasonic sensors, you have to watch out for obstructions. (Marked by yellow circles in the following picture)

2- Right Angled black lines easily allow you to position the robot in a perfect position, using color sensors and our 'Line Stop' program. (Marked by orange circles in the following picture)
3- Black lines perpendicular to the walls allow you to align robot using 2 color sensors and our 'Line align' program. (Marked by purple circles)
4- Long black lines allow you to position the robot using color sensors and our 'Line Follow' Program.
5- You have to make sure that the mat does not have any black spots between the robot's starting position in the base and the final black line where it is going to stop, align or line follow. If you see such a black spot, program the robot to run a few 'Move Tank' block rotations before running the program to detect the black line.
6- Every robot that you will construct will have drift. What is drift? – Drift is when the robot is programmed to go straight but slightly deviates from where it is going. This happens because of the fact that the two motors that are driving the wheels are slightly different due to manufacturing processes. This variability in robotic actuators and sensors is always going to be there and you will have to correct it programmatically (We have programmed 'gyro straight', 'straight using encoders' and 'Gyro straight My Block').

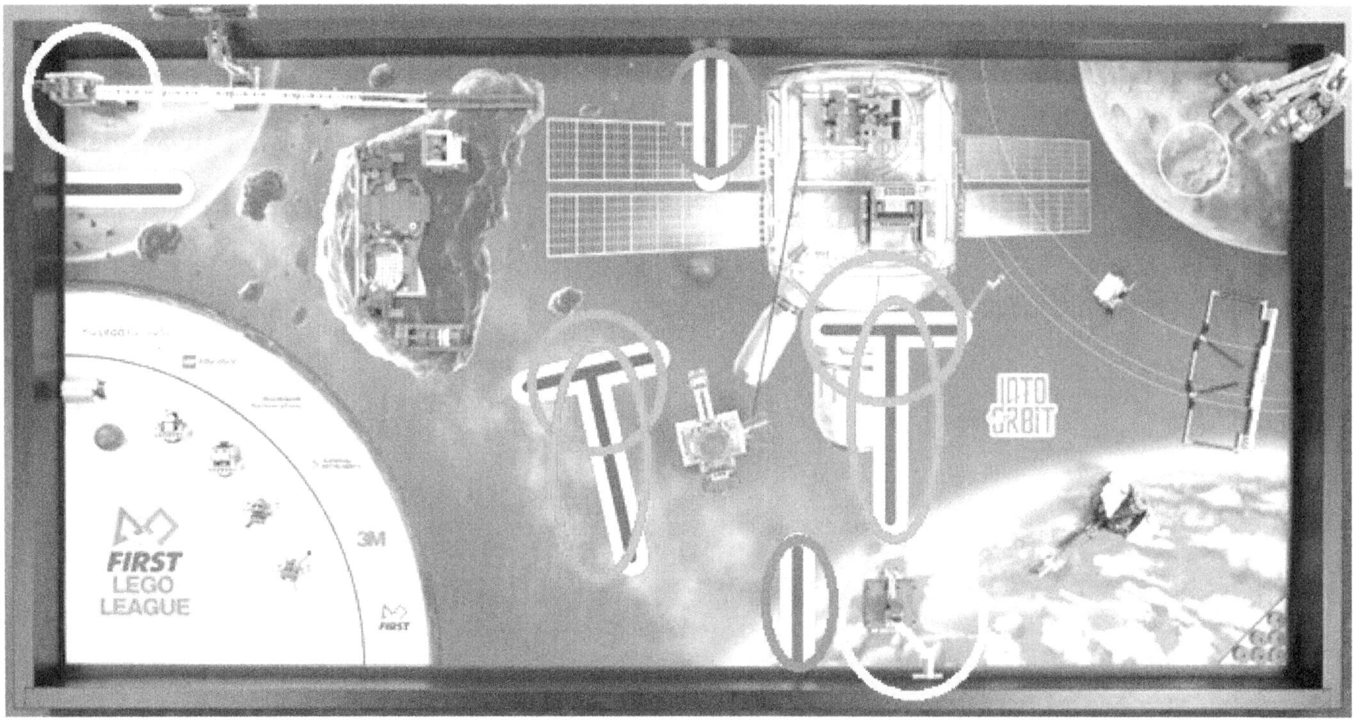

GAME STRATEGY EXAMPLES

Let us discuss some examples of what other team's 'Game Strategy' was over the years. Wherever the back arrows are not shown, the robot returned the same route it had come from.

2017 – Hydrodynamics

One of the highest scoring teams during this challenge had the three 'Robot Runs' shown below.

In the **First Run** (lightest grey or blue arrows, squares, and circles) they completed 2-Fountain, 3-Pipe Removal, 4- Pipe Addition, 5- Manual Covers, and 6-Water Treatment. They did preparation work for 1-Manure and collected the Manure in step 7. They used the wall to guide the robot and used a wide and rigid attachment for consistent runs. During Run 1 they prepped for the sludge mission (Denoted by square numbers). In this run they scored **90 points,** completing 5 missions, and setting up for 1 mission.

In the **Second Run** (light blue or medium grey arrows, and circles) they completed 8- Filter, 9-Pump Addition, 10- Flow and 11- Rain missions. In this run they scored **110 points**. Again, they used large wide attachments for reach and used the wall to guide and align the robot

In the **Third Run** (blue or dark grey arrows and circles) they completed 12-Water collection, 14-Fire, and 13-Flower missions. In this run they scored **145 points.** This was the most difficult run for the robot and the attachment used for this run was very small to allow the robot to maneuver into tight spaces on the mat. (two-wheel turns come in handy).

Total score – 345 points, which is a great score for this challenge.

Did you notice that they did not do any missions on the inaccessible part of the mat? This was another manual cover and pipe construction mission. Though these missions were the same as what they had previously done, they had to maximize their points in their allotted time. They also saved their hardest mission for last in order to avoid too big of a loss in points if one of their runs failed.

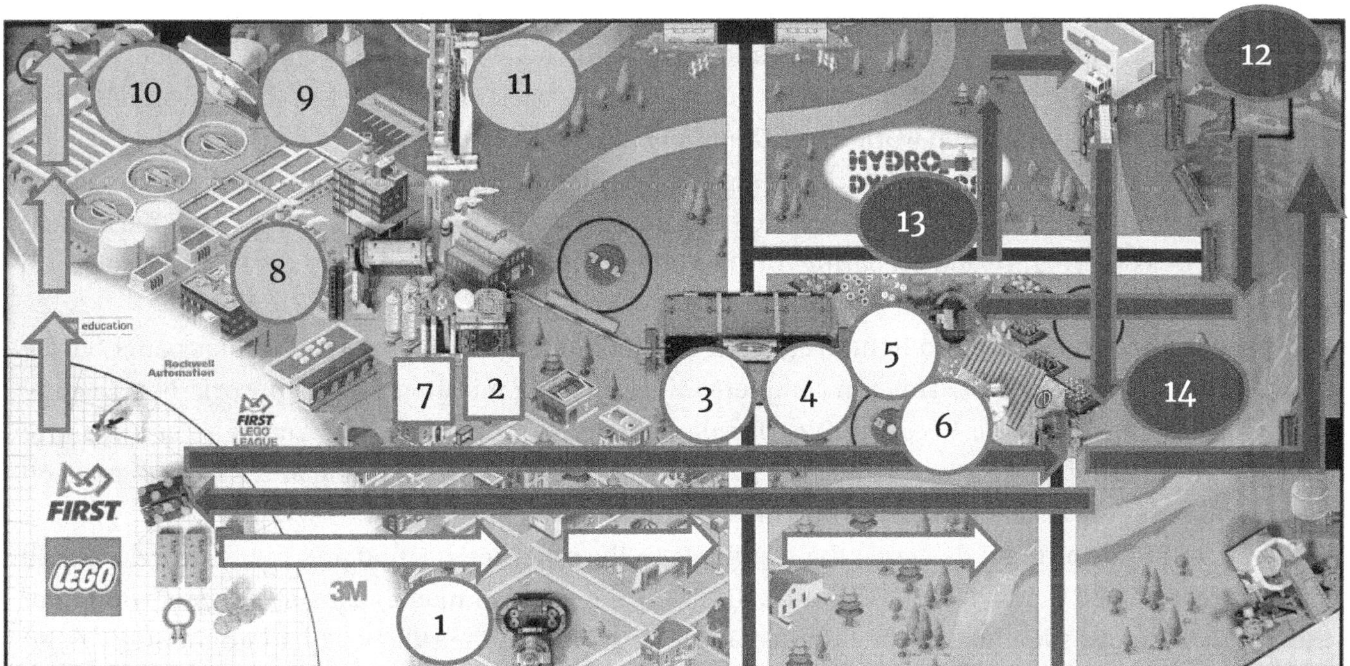

2016 – Animal Allies

This team's strategy below had 5 robot runs

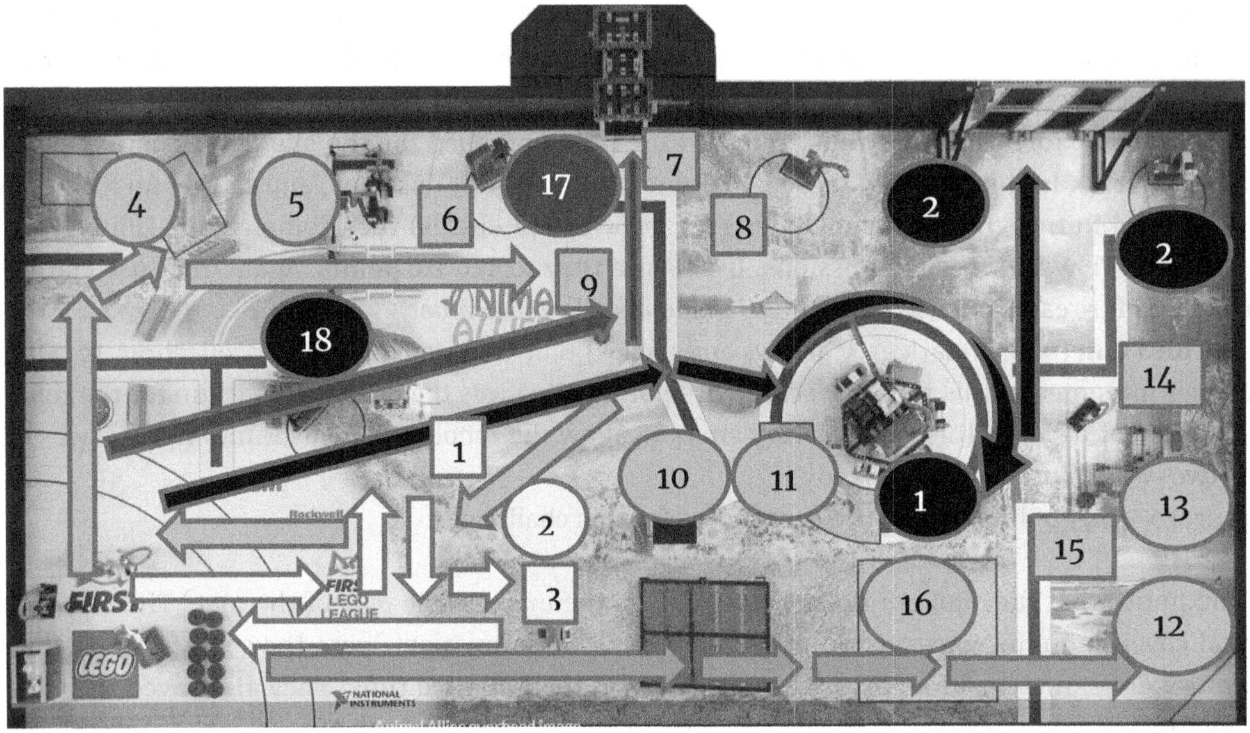

The **First Run** (lightest blue or very light grey) consisted of prep work for the feeding mission by retrieving the food out of the refrigerator (1), and getting the bee for the bee keeping mission (3). The team then completed the prosthesis mission by getting the pig back to the base (2). Run 1 scored them **9 points** but performed a lot of prep work to set them up for success later.

The **Second Run** (light blue or slightly lighter grey) was for dropping the shark tank for the shark shipment mission (4), completing the service dog mission (5), picking animals to prepare for the Animal Conservation Mission (6,7,8), and preparing for the training and research mission's (9). This second run scored the team **45 points.**

The **Third Run** (orange or medium light grey) used an attachment which crossed the solar panel hurdle and used the wall for alignment. This run completed the following missions and prep work: Bee Keeping (10), Pig Delivery (11), Camera Recovery (12), Panda Release (13), Collecting the zoologist and manure sample for the Training and Research mission (14 & 15), completing the Training and Research mission (16) and delivering the seal to the base. This run scored the team **78 points**.

The **Fourth Run** (blue or grey) delivered the 4 animals to the other team's mat and in the process paired 6 animals, scoring **120 points** (17). (There are 2 frogs on the mission model) **This strategy is where out of the box thinking was applied on the interpretation of the rules. The rule book had no mention about how many animals could be paired and the team interpreted it as no limit. Through this interpretation, they decided to pair all 6 animals and get 120 points. Keeping the animals and feeding all 4 of them, as part of the Feeding mission would have gotten them only 80 points and was also more time consuming. So, the option was between, get 80 points or get 120 points by interpreting the rules differently.**

The **Fifth Run (Black)** completed the missions of delivering the food to the gorilla (18), milking automation (19), delivery of food to frogs (20), and Bio-mimicry (21). The robot hung itself using a pneumatic mechanism. This run scored them **147 points. Total Score 399.**

2015- Trash Trek

During this year, teams used a lot of line follow programs. There were 4 total runs with a maximum of 712 points.

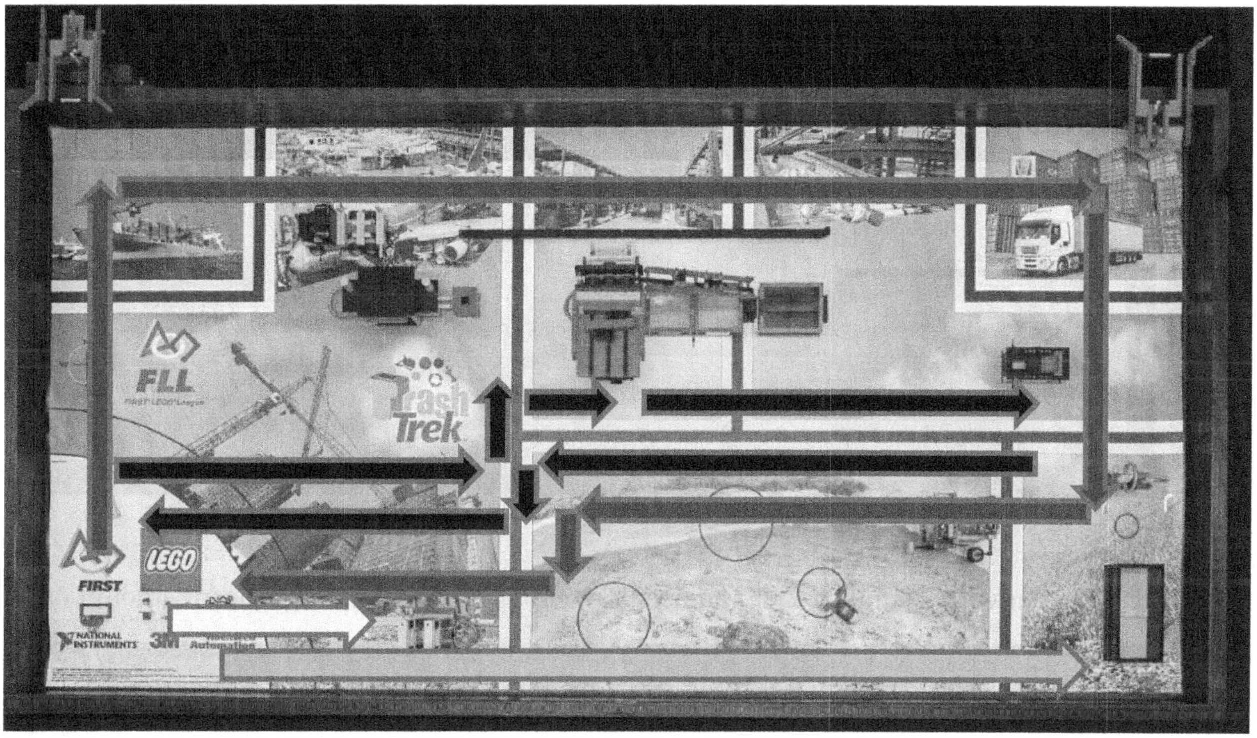

2014 – World Class

Teams divided the mat into 3 distinct zones and created separate attachments for each zone. This zonal approach allowed teams to score very high

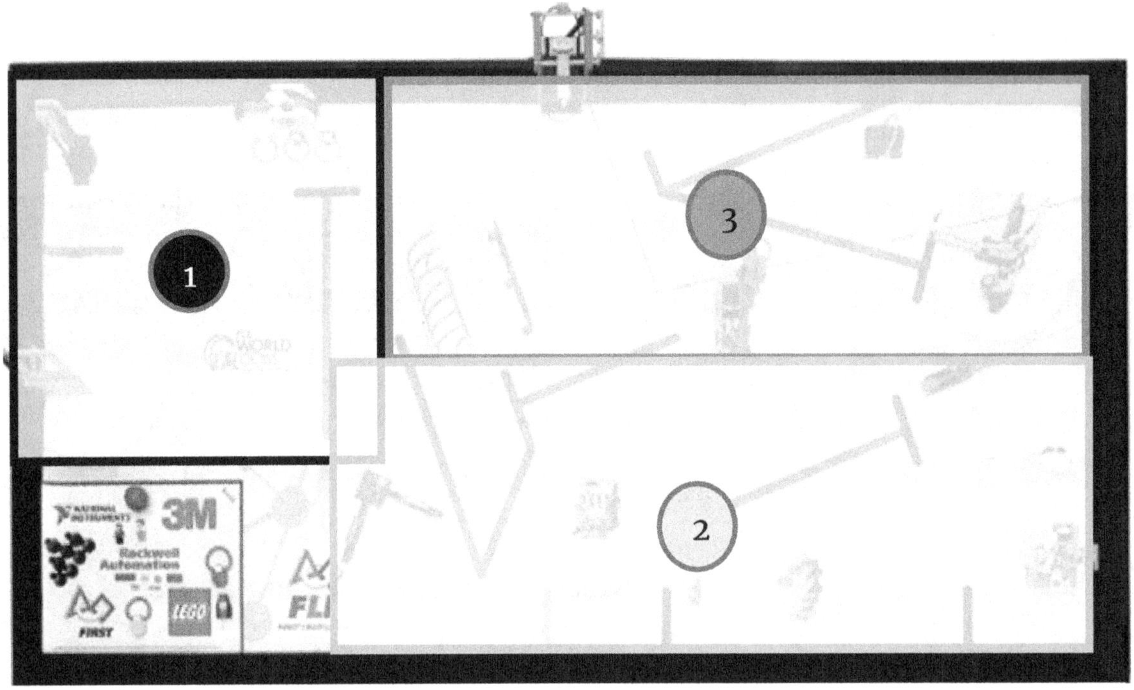

2013 – Nature's Fury

I practiced on this mat with a simple robot and used 8-9 robot runs to get a significant amount of points.

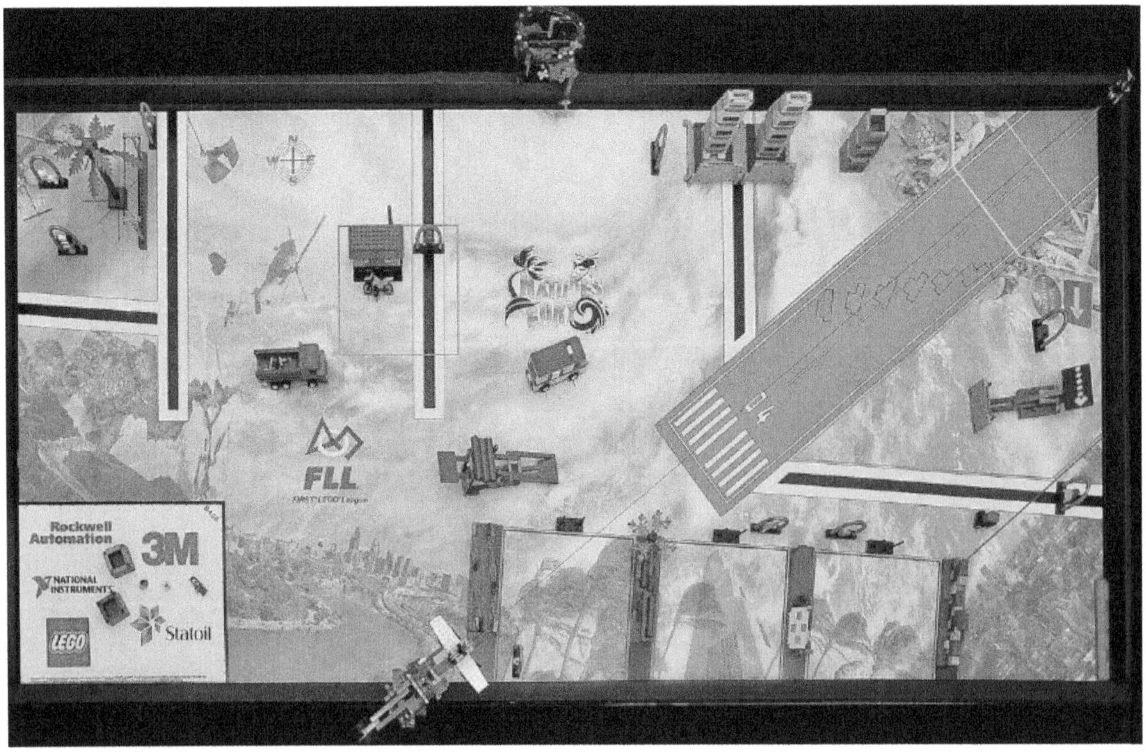

GAME PRACTICE

After your strategy is ready, ensure it is clearly written in the 'Engineering Notebook' and that all the team members understand it. In addition, include pictures of various 'Robot Runs' (which missions are going to be accomplished, score for each mission and total score of the run)

The best way to approach the strategy is to divide and conquer. Divide the team into sub teams. Example: 6 people teams turn into 3 sub teams of 2 team members each. Each sub team should decide which missions they are going to build, program, and practice.

Schedule practice for each sub team separately with an overlap of 30 minutes to 1 hour for team building and discussion.

Every sub team should make sure that any changes in the robot or changes in the strategy due to testing and improvement is documented in the 'Engineering Notebook' and discussed with other sub teams.

Take photographs of the robot during each practice session, so that you can easily reference back to old versions of your robot. Every practice run, program changes should be saved with a date in it for versioning. For example, if you are writing a program for a robot run to accomplish the 'Space Travel' mission as part of **Run 1** for the 'Into Orbit' challenge then you should name the project 'Into Orbit-run1-8-6-2018-Subteam1'. When you make a change in the program you should save it as a new project with today's date in the project name and the name of the sub team you belong to.

Remember to follow the rule of 3-time consistency, the robot should complete the mission 3 consecutive times with success to mark the mission as done.

Remember to follow this wheel to continually improve.

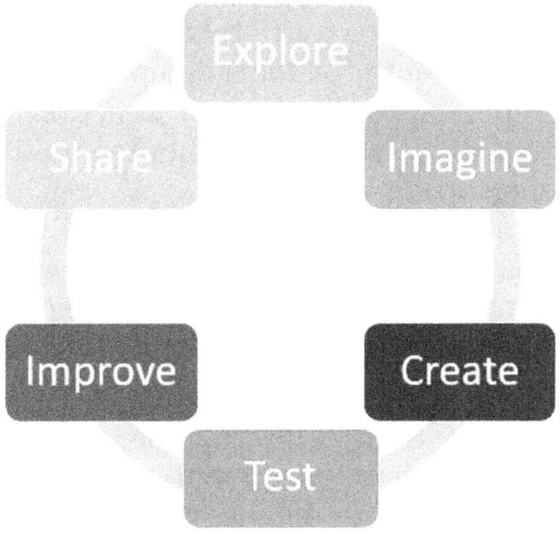

PREPARATION FOR TOURNAMENT

Make sure to Register early for the Qualifiers, as they are first-come-first-serve and the slots fill fast.

At least 4 weeks before the tournament, you should integrate all your programs and should start practicing for the tournament. The following are recommended activities for preparation.

When 4 weeks are remaining for the first Tournament:

1. Whole team should meet and decide the final runs for the robot and decide on the final score you want to achieve. Based on all the learning, testing and improvements you should have one more brain storming session to come up with any new ideas.
2. Coaches and Mentors should meet to finalize logistics like T-shirts, transportation etc....
3. Team should finalize the poster for their project and presentation.
4. Decide the game dry run schedule. **Game dry runs** are when you practice on the practice table in the same way you would compete on tournament day. (time limit and penalties applied)
5. Find out if there are any local scrimmages or invite other local teams for friendly matches.
6. Make sure all the project activities are complete.
7. Make sure the Qualifiers/ Championship registration is complete.

When 3 weeks are remaining for the first Tournament:

1. Continue with Game Dry runs and decide on technicians who will handle the robot during the matches. There should be a minimum of 2 teams. 1 main team and 1 backup.
2. Check the Challenge updates for new updates and make sure your robot meets all height requirements (12 inches if not specified otherwise- This requirement has only been changed once for Animal Allies).
3. Make sure your robot will always fit in the base with a height of 12 inches.
4. Read the Robot Game rules to make sure you are not in violation of any of them.
5. Check emails for instructions for the tournament from the organizer.
6. Complete all tasks requested by the tournament organizer.

When 2 weeks are remaining for the first Tournament:

1. Sort all your parts and keep them ready in boxes to take with you during the tournament day.
2. Make sure you have a power strip to take to the tournament
3. Check if there are other tournaments happening in your local area. Go and attend them to understand the rules and check out the strategies of other teams. This will help you to correct something that you might be doing wrong.
4. Again, check your emails for instructions
5. Complete all tasks requested by the tournament organizer.
6. Think about taking practice table to the tournament and decide on logistics.

The WEEK of the tournament

1. Prepare the 'Robot Design Executive Summary'. No more changes can be made to the robot
    a. Robot Facts: Share a little bit about your robot, such as the types of sensors and how many sensors you have, drive-train details, number of parts, and the number of attachments. The Judges also like to know about what programming language your team used, the number of programs, and the robot game mission where your team had the most success.
    b. Design Details:

i. Fun: Describe the most interesting part of your robot design as well as the most challenging parts. If your team has a fun story about your robot please feel free to share it in this section.
ii. Strategy: Explain your team's strategy and the reasoning for choosing and accomplishing missions through this strategy. Talk a little bit about how successful the robot was in completing the missions that were chosen.

c. Design Process: Describe how your team designed their robot and what process they used to make improvements to the design over time. Briefly share how different team members contributed to the design.
d. Mechanical Design: Explain the robot's basic structure. Explain to the judges how the robot moves (drivetrain), what attachments and mechanisms it uses to operate or complete missions, and how easily you are able to remove and attach attachments.
e. Programming: Describe how your team programmed the robot to ensure consistent results. Explain how the team organized and documented programs. Mention if the programs used sensors to ascertain its location on the field.
f. Innovation: Describe any features of the robot's design that the team feels are special or clever

2. Keep the part boxes ready.
3. Keep the project poster and presentation ready.
4. Keep the power strip and other items requested by the tournament organizer ready.
5. Get ready for a fun tournament.

WHAT IS A SUCCESSFUL ROBOT GAME?

If you are able to score the points in the tournament, that you had anticipated and practiced for, while having fun and following Core Values then you have succeeded in winning the robot Game.

WHAT IS A GOOD DESIGN?

According to the world's leading designers, the following principles are the 10 principles to follow for any good design:

1. **Innovative** – Originality, build something that solves the problem in a unique way.
2. **Design Usefulness** – Make sure every part of your design serves a purpose
3. **Understandable Design** – It is self-explanatory and well documented
4. **Reliability**– It performs the task it is meant to do consistently with low maintenance
5. **Thorough** – Nothing must be left to chance, every scenario should be accounted for
6. **Environmentally friendly** – Must be efficient and use the least amount of resources possible. If there is a way to use a more environmentally friendly material it should be used.
7. **Minimalistic** – Less, but better

Now let us understand what is a good FLL robot design as per the FLL Judges:

1. Mechanical Design -Durability- The robot has structural integrity and is able to withstand the rigors of its environment. This is very true for any robot. The degree of durability varies from application to application but the robot has to be durable for the operation it needs complete. For example, I once saw a small robotic arm of NASA's Mars Curiosity Rover that was on display at the 'Academy of Sciences' in San Francisco. The engineer from JPL who had designed it said that the cost to create it was in millions, but it could withstand extreme temperatures and still operate with high accuracy. Your robot should be able to withstand the rigors of all matches in the tournament. We will learn about it in 'How to design strong and efficiently' section of this chapter.
2. Mechanical Design – Mechanical efficiency –The design should have an economic use of parts and time and should be easy to repair and modify. This efficiency is necessary for all robots in the world. Again, think of where robotics is currently being used extensively in industry. It is being used in environments that have hazardous conditions, such as the use of a robot as the payload of a rocket going into space. These robots are used for a variety of necessary activities in space. Using parts efficiently reduces the weight and significantly decreases the cost. Similarly buying excessive FLL parts and excessively building will waste both time and money. We will learn about examples of building efficiently in 'How to design strong and efficiently' section.
3. Mechanical Design – Mechanization – The ability of robot mechanisms to move or act with appropriate speed, strength and accuracy for intended tasks. This includes the proper drive train and motor attachment constructions for the intended use of the robot. This determines the accuracy of the robot and is essential to winning the competition. We will learn more about this in the 'Basebot' and 'Attachment' sections.
4. Programming – Programming Quality - Programs are appropriate for the intended purpose and will achieve consistent results. We will learn this in the 'Programming for Competition' section.
5. Programming – Programming Efficiency - Programs are modular, streamlined, and understandable. We will learn this in the 'Programming for Competition' section.
6. Programming – Automation / Navigation – The ability of the robot to move or act as intended using mechanical and/or sensor feedback. This includes the use of 4 types of sensors and mechanical programming. We will learn about this in the 'Programming for Competition' and 'Mechanical Programming and Mechanical Guidance' sections.
7. Strategy and Innovation – Design process – How your design process has progressively improved the mechanical and programming aspects of the robot? We will learn this in the 'Design Strategy' section.
8. Strategy and Innovation – Game Strategy – This is one of the most important aspect judges look at and we have covered it in the 'Game Strategy' section.
9. Strategy and Innovation – Innovative Design -The creation of new, unique, or unexpected feature(s) (e.g. designs, programs, strategies or applications) that are beneficial in performing the robot's specified tasks. This you can achieve by understanding the game rules, Out of the Box thinking and experimentation.

DESIGN STRATEGY

The most important principle for design is innovation. Your team is going to create a robot that will be unique across all teams. Innovation allows you to find solutions, which nobody has thought of before, to solve the most difficult problems.

Your strategy should include understanding the basic laws of physics and mathematics that will apply in designing and building of robots.

Some of the basic things you should know are:

1. The center of gravity is the point where you can balance the robot. At that point all the surrounding weight is equal. – Lower and 'in the center' is better.

2. Ground clearance is the distance between the underside of the chassis and the ground. It determines the height of the obstacles the vehicle can drive over without scraping them and is important because once the robot scrapes an obstacle it may move in an unpredictable path.
3. Every object in motion takes time and distance to stop- The faster the robot is going, the more distance required to stop it. Even though the EV3 motors are servo motors and will stop within a 1 degree of accuracy, the momentum of the robot will push it forward.- Very important in a programming aspect.
4. Similarly, every rotating part takes time and distance to stop.
5. Torque is the turning force applied to any object. If you are lifting a heavier object more toque is required. There is a limit to the torque a regular motor can supply, but this limit can be exceeded using a gear train.
6. Power is the product of speed and torque. You will notice that motors are able to lift more weight if the arm gains some rotational speed before lifting the weight. Power is measured in watts and LEGO motors can deliver 0.021 W to 2.38 W of power.
7. Friction is the force that resists movement between two surfaces. For example, the robot's tires and the mat create friction
8. Traction is grip of the tires on the mat's surface. More traction means better grip and less slippage. Reduced slippage allows for more accuracy in predicting how the robot will travel.
9. Backlash is the gap between 2 coupled components (example: Gear Teeth). Typically backlash cannot be measured but is useful to know. A smaller gap is always the best. For gear to gear coupling, a 32 teeth gear to 32 teeth gear will produce less backlash and will produce more accurate robot movement than a 4 teeth gear to 4 teeth gear coupling.
10. Wheel diameter determines the distance the robot will cover (Circumference = Diameter X 3.14). The bigger the wheel, the faster the robot.

11. A minimum of 3 wheels are required to support any object you want to move. (A 2 wheeled vehicle needs balancing).
12. Having more wheels increases the weight carrying capability of vehicle but reduces its ability to turn quickly, reliably, and accurately.

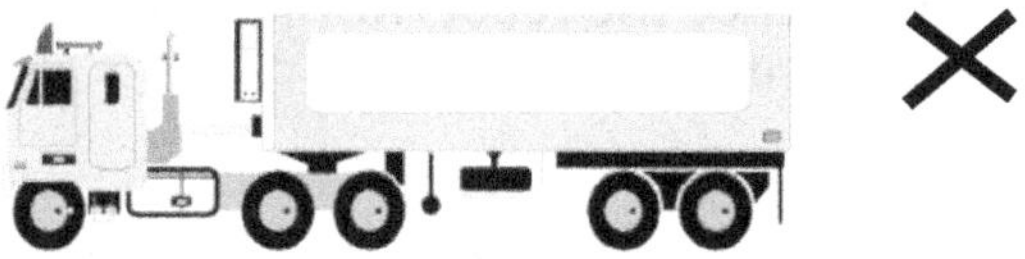

FLL Robot Design Considerations:

1- The design should be modular and able to use a limited amount of motors to accomplish different missions.
2- Due to the 2 minutes 30 second time constraint, making any changes to the robot between robot runs needs to be done quickly and your robot design has to support that. (Ex: changing attachments).
3- Color sensors should be placed one stud above the mat for proper detection of light.

4- Place 2 color sensors in front of and close to the wheels to allow for proper line following and line squaring.
5- Ultrasonic sensors should be placed 1 to 1.5 studs above the mat.
6- Gyro sensors should be placed in between the 2 wheels and should be positioned properly.

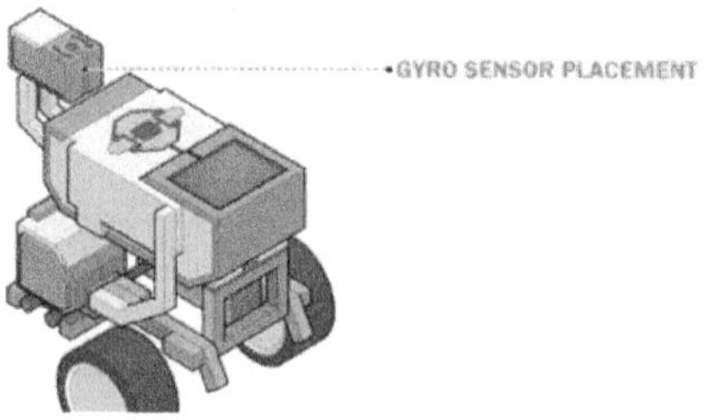

7- To reduce drift, non-driving wheels should be ball wheels or plastic wheels without the tire rubbers. 3 wheels are recommended compared to 4 wheels as a 3-wheel design helps in reducing drift and makes robot turning more reliable.

Design strategies that worked for teams I mentored was very simple. They considered how much time they had for the qualifier competition, parts they had with them and based on that they decided what type of robot to build.

If you are 1-3 months away from the first qualifier and your team has the budget to buy additional parts adopt a strategy similar to the one mentioned below:

1. Buy Additional parts – You will need lot of additional parts for attachments.
2. Construct the Basebot – based on your game strategy (size, shape, sensors)
3. Divide the team into multiple sub teams and each team then constructs their own attachments to the Basebot to complete their allocated 'Robot Run'
4. Test the Basebot and attachments and continually improve your design. Each sub team should make sure that Basebot changes should be communicated to other sub teams.
5. Do Dry Runs close to the tournament.

If you are just a month away from your qualifiers or you do not have the budget to buy additional parts– No need to worry just adopt a strategy like the one mentioned below

1. You can take the robot we have built as part of exercises earlier in this book and modify it, making sure it has 4 motors and 4 sensors. I have provided those details in the 'Basebot' section.
2. Allocate missions you want to complete to various team members.
3. Have a game strategy of completing 1 to 2 missions per robot run, by attaching mission-specific arms to the arm motors using axles.
4. Test the robot and make improvements.
5. Always do dry runs close to tournament.

ADDITIONAL PARTS TO BUY

The robot you will build has to be innovative and useful in completing missions. To build a reliable robot you will have to purchase additional parts and come up with fresh ideas. Recommendations in this book are based on my experience and will save you the frustration of running out of certain important pieces. You should buy the parts based on your team's budget. I have specified few parts as essentials and a few parts as 'good to have'. These pieces are not necessary but will make your robot more efficient and can be useful in certain situations.
Over the years various FLL teams have used simple and complex robot structures to complete missions. Let us look at a few examples of competition robots.

The next picture shows a robot completing missions on the 'Animal Allies' Mat. This robot was within base regulations in the base but then extended its components to finish the missions. As you can see it uses a lot of beams, frames, gears, wheels, and many many connector pegs.

This robot used pneumatic parts as actuators(motors). The white cylinder-like structure is the air reservoir that stores pressurized air for pneumatics.

This robot shown in the next picture is using a conveyor belt to complete the 'sorting' mission and the pneumatic actuators are being used to complete other missions.

The next picture shows a robot that used the weight of the wheels to balance the weight of its arm. It uses a lot of frames to have the cantilever arm pick up the animal mission models.

Looking at the examples provided in the previous pictures, you will need additional parts to allow you to build more complex structures. If possible, you should buy and experiment with these parts to build a versatile robot that can complete almost all the missions. In my opinion any list that is provided will not be a complete list of all the parts your team will need but you can stock your team's storage bins in such a way that you will be ready for most scenarios. Now, let us look at the storage bins I have and discuss which additional parts you will need.
Before we begin, you should take stock of how many parts you have and then decide how many additional parts you need after looking at the recommended quantity in the book.
The prices given in the recommendations and websites are bound to change and I have no control over them. Prices are for the team to understand the approximate amount.

Storage Bin-1

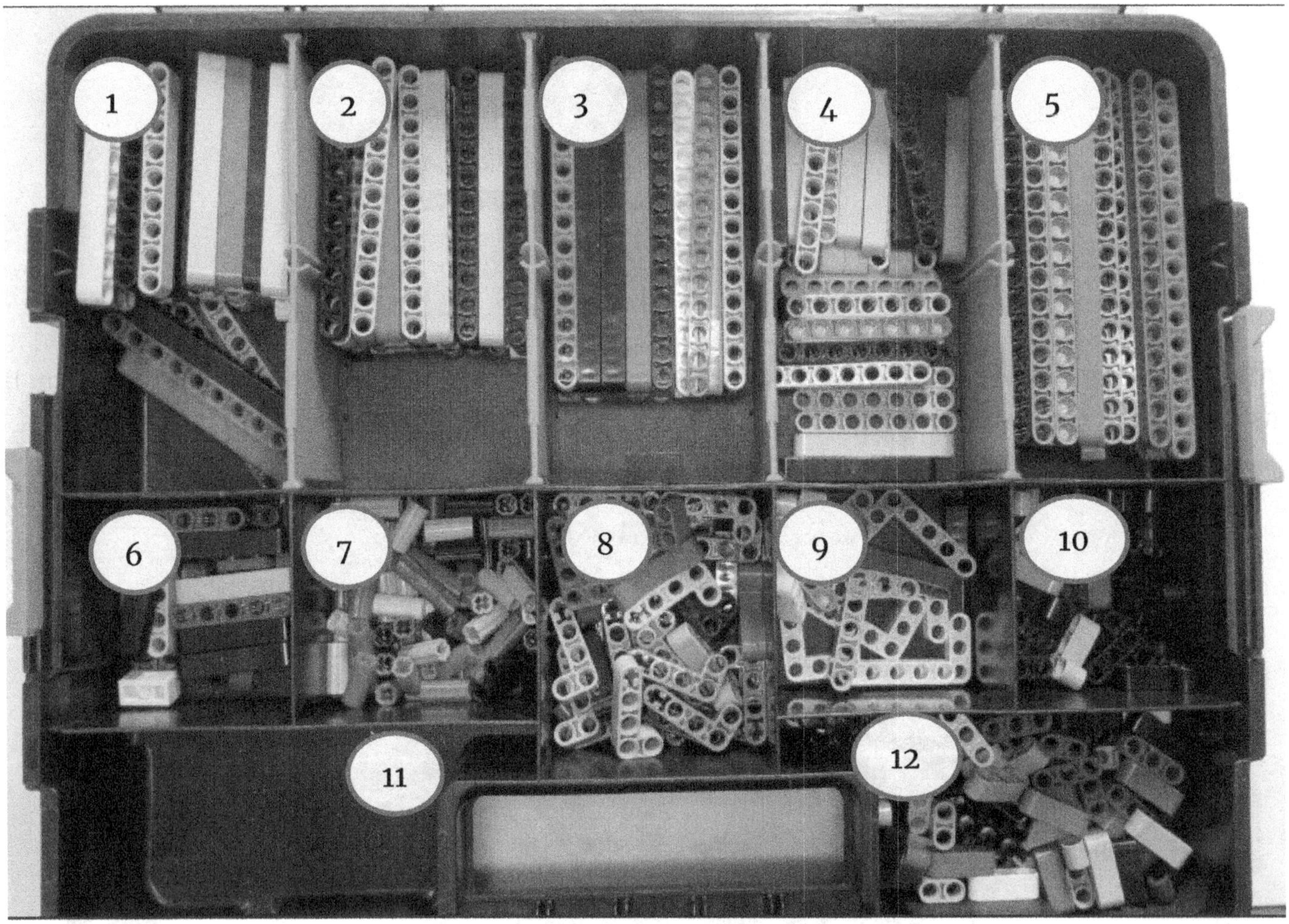

1- 9 Module beams 4211866 -50 total - $9+shipping on **Brickowl.com**
2- 11 Module beams 4611705 -50 total -$16+shipping on **brickset.com**
3- 13 Module beams 4522934 – 100 total - $30 +shipping on **Bricklink.com**
4- 7-module beams 4495930– 100 total - $30 +shipping on **Bricklink.com**

5- 15 Module beams 4542578 -150 total - $32 + shipping
6– 5 Module beams 4211651 – 100 total - $4 + shipping
7- Bushing axle extender 4513174 – 40 total - $1.20 + shipping
8- Angular beam, 2x4-module 4141270 – 50 total - $3 + shipping
9- Angular beam, 3x5-module 4211713 – 150 total - $15 + shipping
10- T-Beam, 3x3-module 4552347 – 30 total - $3 + shipping
11- Empty
12- Beam, 3-module 4142822 -100 total
12- Beam with cross hole, 2-module 6006140 -50 total
12- Beam, 2- Module 4211862 – 20 total
12- Rubber beam with cross hole, 2-module, black 4198367- 10 total

Storage Bin -2

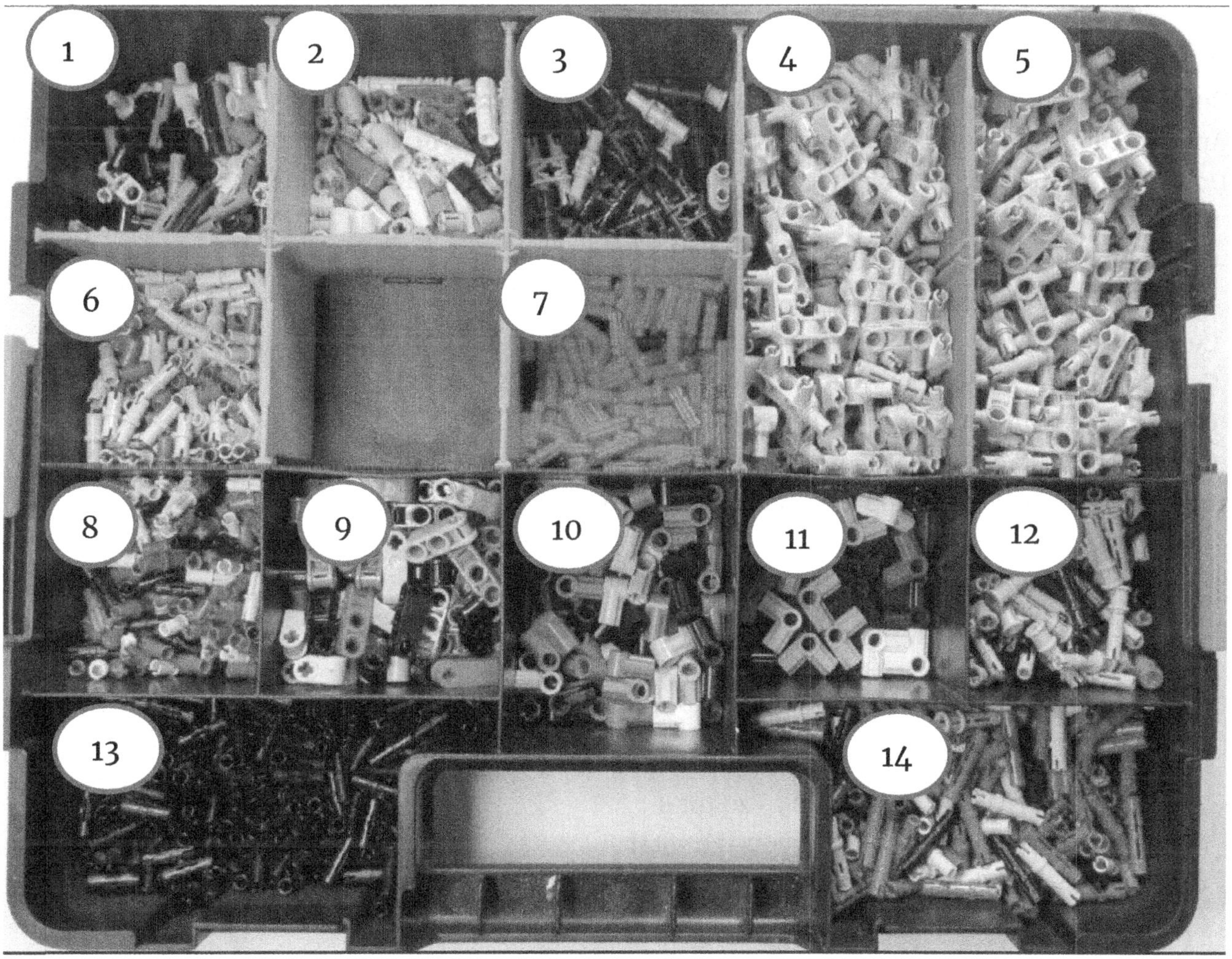

1-Double connector peg, 3-module,4560175-20 total
1-Single Bush 2Module, **6073231** (very useful)- 30 total

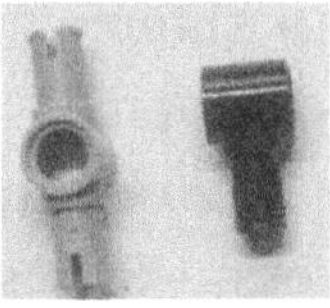

2-Tube 2-module 4526985 – 10 total
2- Pointer- 3-module 4173941- 10 total (good for gear stopper),
2- Bushing ½-module yellow 4239601 -100 total
2- Bushing 1-module grey 4211622 -100 total. -$20 + shipping

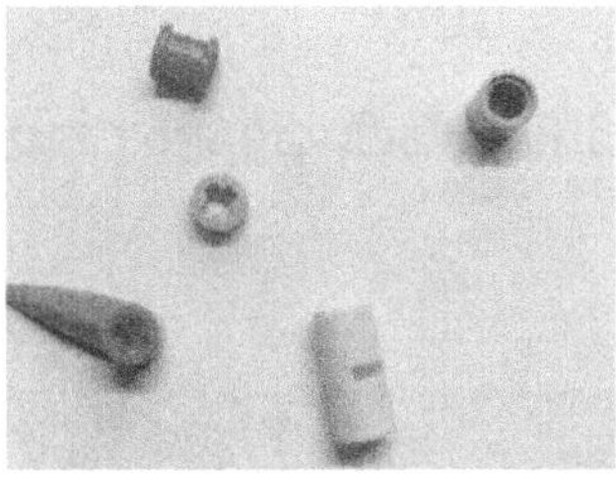

3-Double pin connector with axle hole -4119589 -24 total - $5 on eBay or Amazon
4-Angular connector peg,3x3-module, 4296059 -50 total- $25 – **bricklink.com (very useful)**
5-Double connector peg,3x3-module, 4225033 -50 total -$20 - **bricklink.com**
6- Connector peg, 2-module, grey 4211807 -50 total
6- Connector Peg W. Knob 4143005 -20 total
7- Axle, 2-module, 4142865 -50 total
8- Connector peg with axle, 2-module, beige, 4666579- 50 total
8- Connector peg with friction/axle,2-module, blue 4206482 -100 total
9- Cross block, 2-module, grey,4211775 -30 total
9- Cross block, 3-module, dark grey 4210857- 50 total
9- Double cross block, 3-module, black, 4121667 -30 total

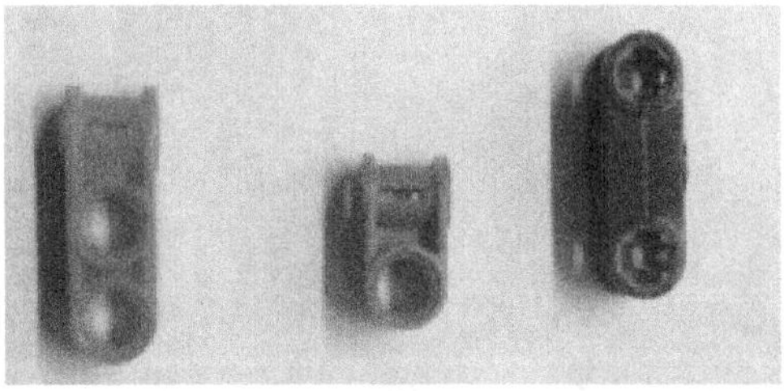

10- Angular block 1, 0°, black, 4107085 -20 total
11- Angular block, 6 (90°), black 4107767 -30 total
12- Connector peg with bushing,3-module, 4140806 -60 total
13- Connector peg with friction,2-module, black 4121715 -400 total (you can never have enough of these)
14 - Connector peg with friction,3-module, blue 4514553 -200 total

Storage Bin-3 (Grey numbers are nice to have)

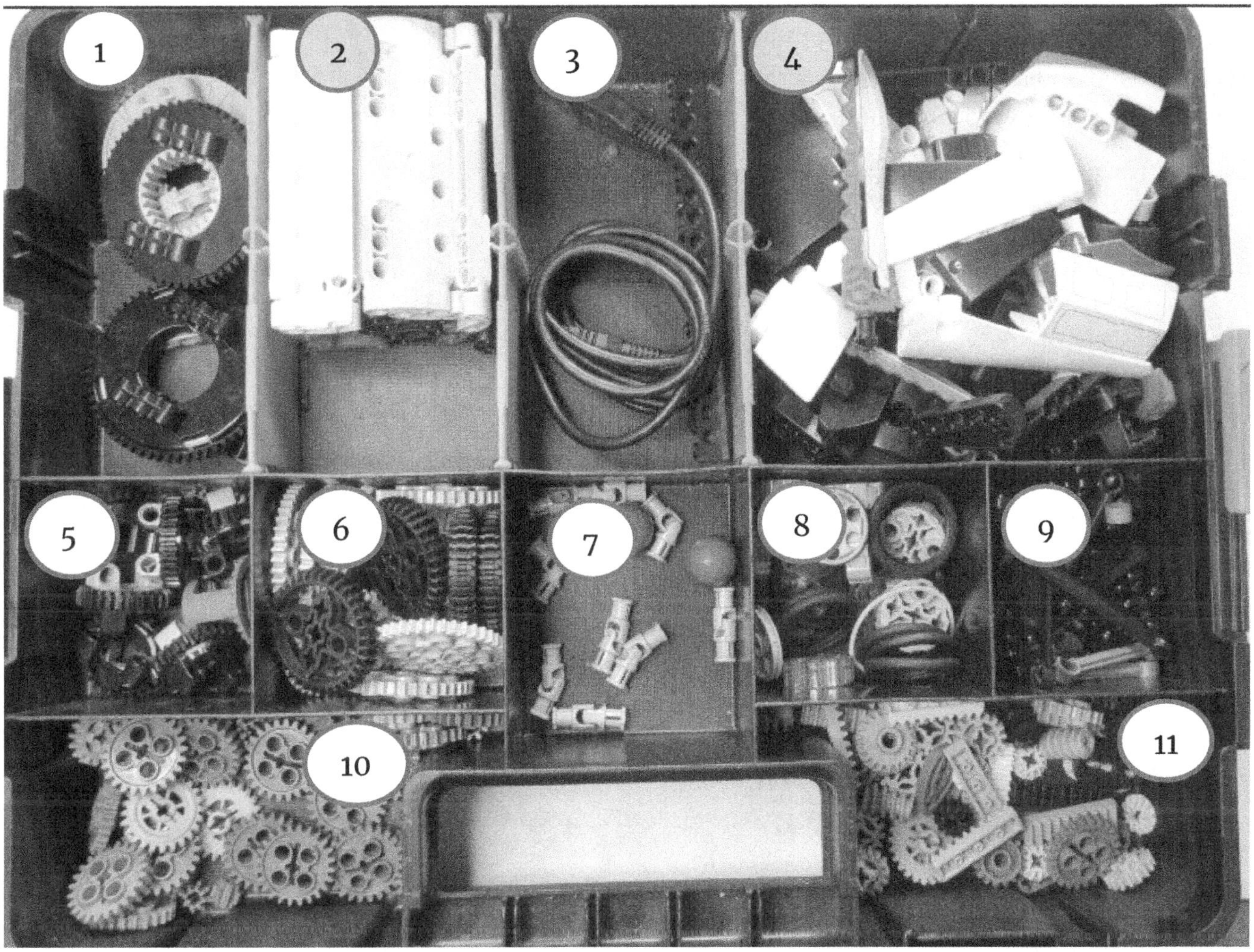

1-Turntable 4624645 - 3 total- $8 + Shipping
1-Black Gear Rack 1 x 13 with Axle and Pin Holes 64781 -10 total
2-Bowed Panel 6031916 – 10 total (nice to have)
3- USB Cable 6036901-1 total – (comes with core set)
4- Right curved panel 5x11-module 4543490, Left Curved Panel 4541326, Left curved panel 3x5-module 4566251, and Right curved panel 3x5-module 4566249(comes in core set – nice to have)
5- Turntable top and bottom 28-tooth black 4652236 & 4652235 - 4 total -$10 - bricklink.com
5-Technic, Gear Differential with 28 Bevel Teeth 4525184- 8 Total - $16 (very useful) - bricklink.com
6- Gear, 40-tooth, grey 4285634 -40 total - $25 - Good for transferring motion
6- Double bevel gear, 36-tooth, 4255563- 30 Total –$25 - Good for changing direction of motion
7-Propeller Shaft 4525904 – 10 total – Good for changing direction of motion.
8-Hub, 24x4 mm, 4587275 – 40 total – Used in wall follow and as third wheel.
8-Tire, 30.4x4 mm, black 6028041 -10 total
8- Weapon Barrel 4654432 -10 total
8- LEGO Rubber Band 33 mm , 25 mm, 20 mm 4544151, 4544147,4544140 – 10 total /each – Brickowl.com

9- Gear, 4-tooth, black 4248204-60 total- Good for changing direction of motion
9- Ball with cross axle, 4211375 -30 total
9-Ball with friction snap– 4184169- 50 total
9-Technic Weapon barrel 4654432 –5 - rarely used
9-Track Rod 6M 4629920 – 20 total

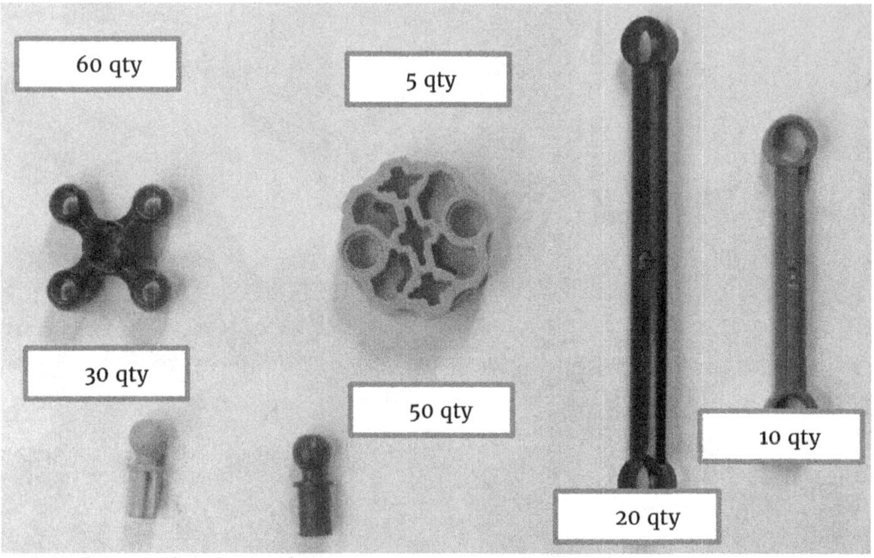

10 and 11 refer the next picture for Quantity.

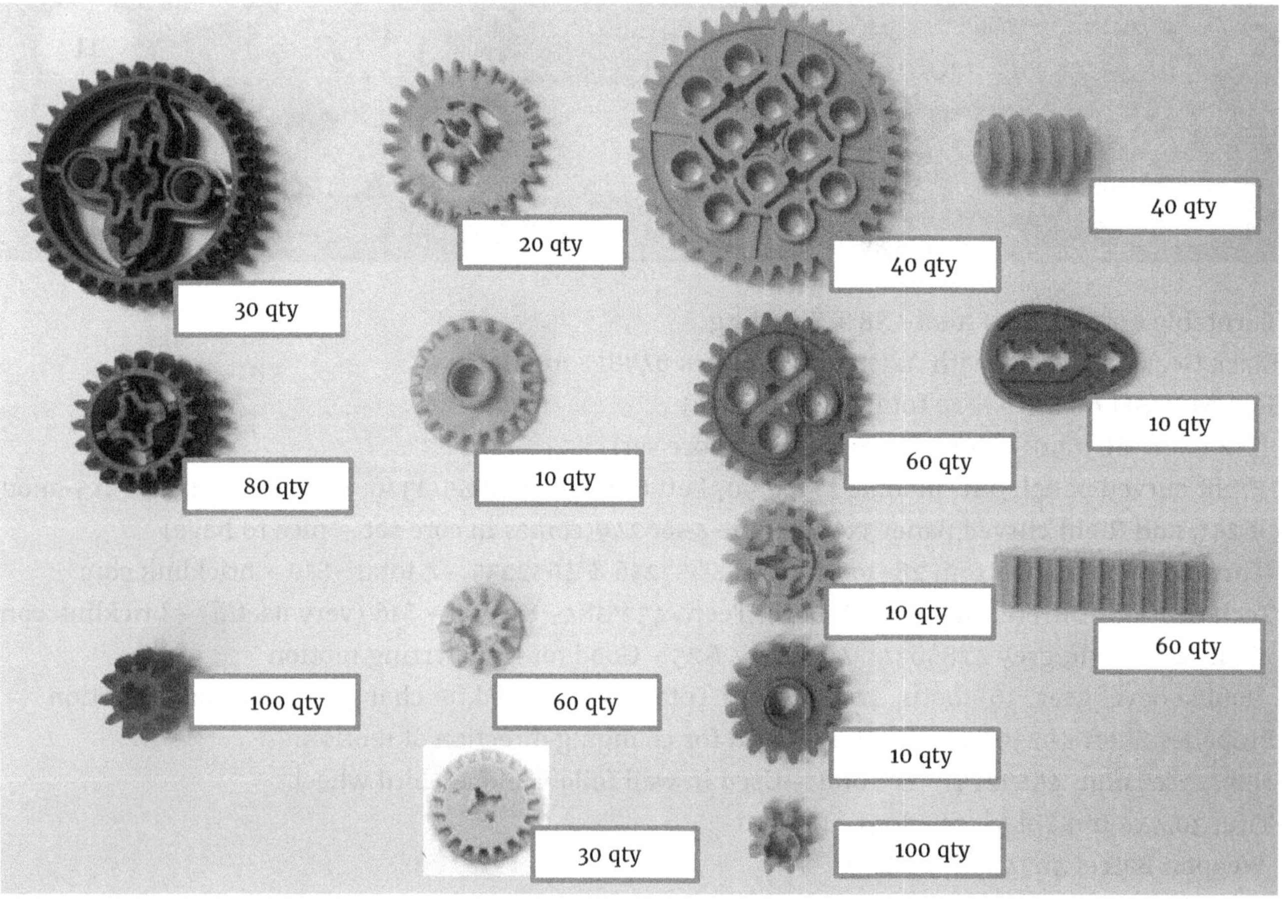

10 –Gear, 24-tooth, dark grey 4514558 – 60 total
11- Double bevel gear, 20-tooth 4177430- 80 total
11- Double bevel gear, 12-tooth, black 4177431 – 100 total
11-Gear, 16-tooth, grey 4640536 – 10 total
11- Bevel gear, 12-tooth, beige 4565452 – 60 total
11-Gear, 8-tooth, dark grey 4514559 -100 total
11-Worm gear, grey 4211510- 40 total
11-Bevel gear, 20 teeth 6031962 – 30 total
11- Bevel gear, 20 teeth with pin hole 4558690 – 10 total
11- Rim narrow 6044729- 20 total (not in the picture)
11 – Toothed bar 4205760 – 60 total (very useful when used with stud full beams)

Storage Bin-4(Grey numbers are nice to have)

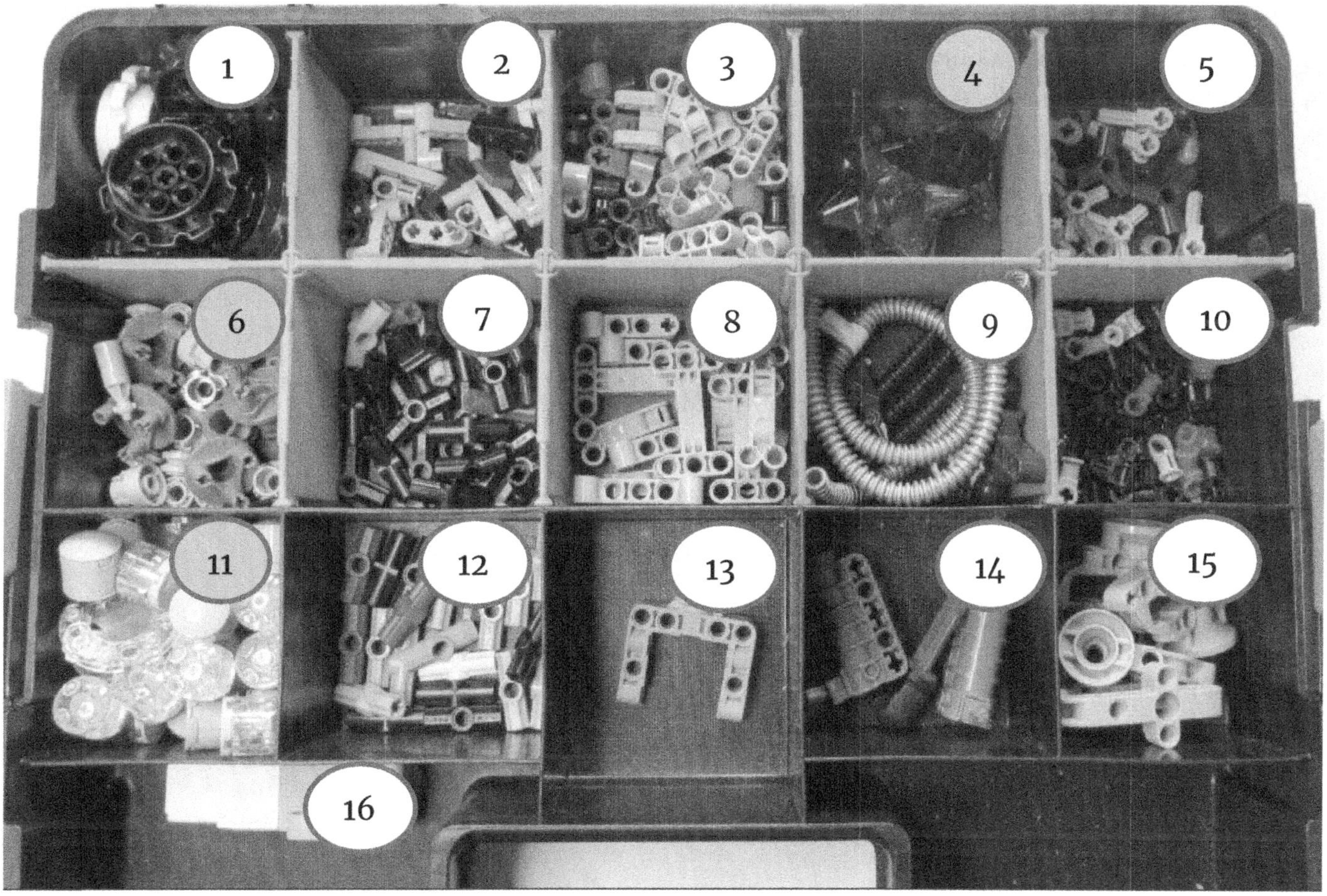

1- Sprocket 4582792 – Used for conveyor belt -10 total
2- Connector peg with handle 3-module 4563044 - 4 total (useful connector)
3- Cross block, 2x2-module 4140430 -10 total (useful connector)
3- Cross block, 3x2-module 4538007 – 6 total – included in core set (useful connector)

3- Cross block fork, 2x2-module 4162857 -12 total – (useful connector)
3-Cross Block/Form 2X2X2 – module 4610371 – 6 total – (useful connector)

4-Half Spike Ball 46027626 – Included in core set– Nice to have.
5- Technic Pole Reverser Handle 4216055 -10 total
5- Beam 1M W. 2 Cross Axles 90° 6005331 – 20 total
5- Technic, Axle and Pin Connector Triple 6005755 – 10 total
5 - 3-spoke angular block, 3x120° 4502595 -20 total

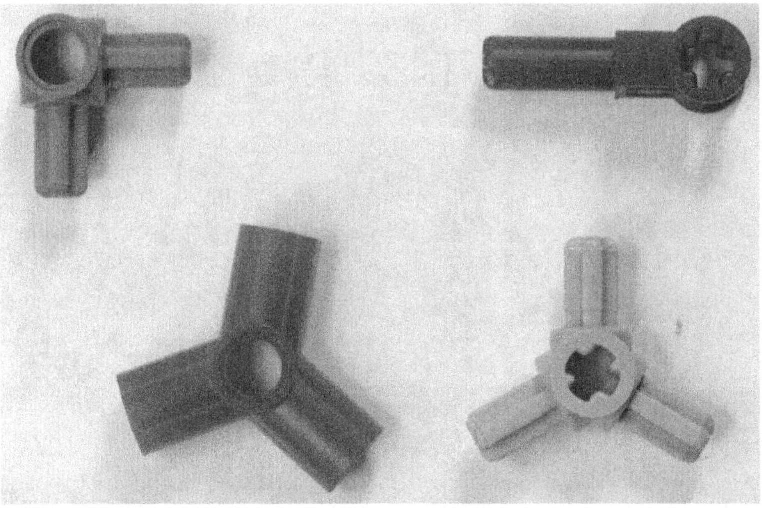

6 - 3 Snap Gear block 4610378 – nice to have
6- Steering CV Joint 4268659 – nice to have
6 - Technic, Transmission Driving Ring 4278957 – nice to have
6 - LEGO Technic - Extension Ring Driving Ring 32187 – nice to have

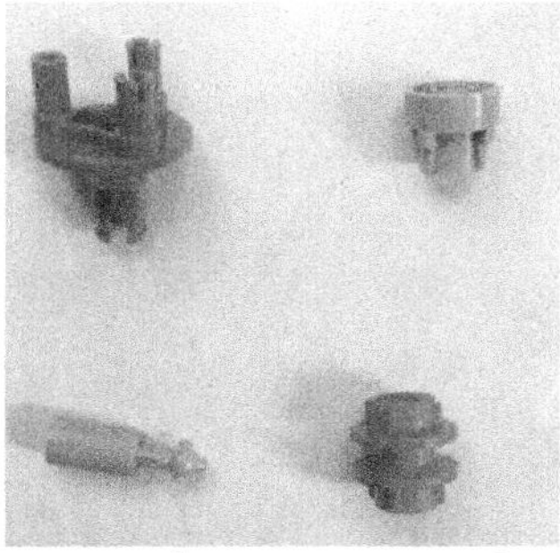

7- Axle and Pin Connector Angled #5 - 112.5 degrees 4107084 – 20 total
7- Axle and Pin Connector Angled #3 - 157.5 degrees 4107082 – 20 total
8- Technic Cross Block 2 x 4 (Axle Hole/Pin/Pin/Twin Pin) 4652234 – 10 total
9- LEGO hose – Multiple variety -https://www.brickowl.com/catalog/LEGO_category/tubes
10 - Axle Connector with Axle Hole 4107081 – 30 total
11 – Brick, round 2 x 2 with Axle Hole 4178398 – 10 total – can be used for sliding smoothly on walls
11- Slide Shoe Round 2X2 4278359 -10 total - can be used for sliding smoothly on walls
12- Angle Connector #2 (180°) 4107783 – 40 total – good to connect axles
13- Steering Ball Joint Large Open with C-Shape Pivot Frame 4610379 – 4 total – very good for motion transfer
14- Competition Cannon with Arrow – 2 total – Good for shooting balls.
15 – Gear block 4610377 – 4 total – Good for creating drive trains.
16 – LEGO Motors – ideal 4 large motors 45502
The following picture is example of a drive train created using the above parts.

Storage Bin-5 (Grey numbers are nice to have)

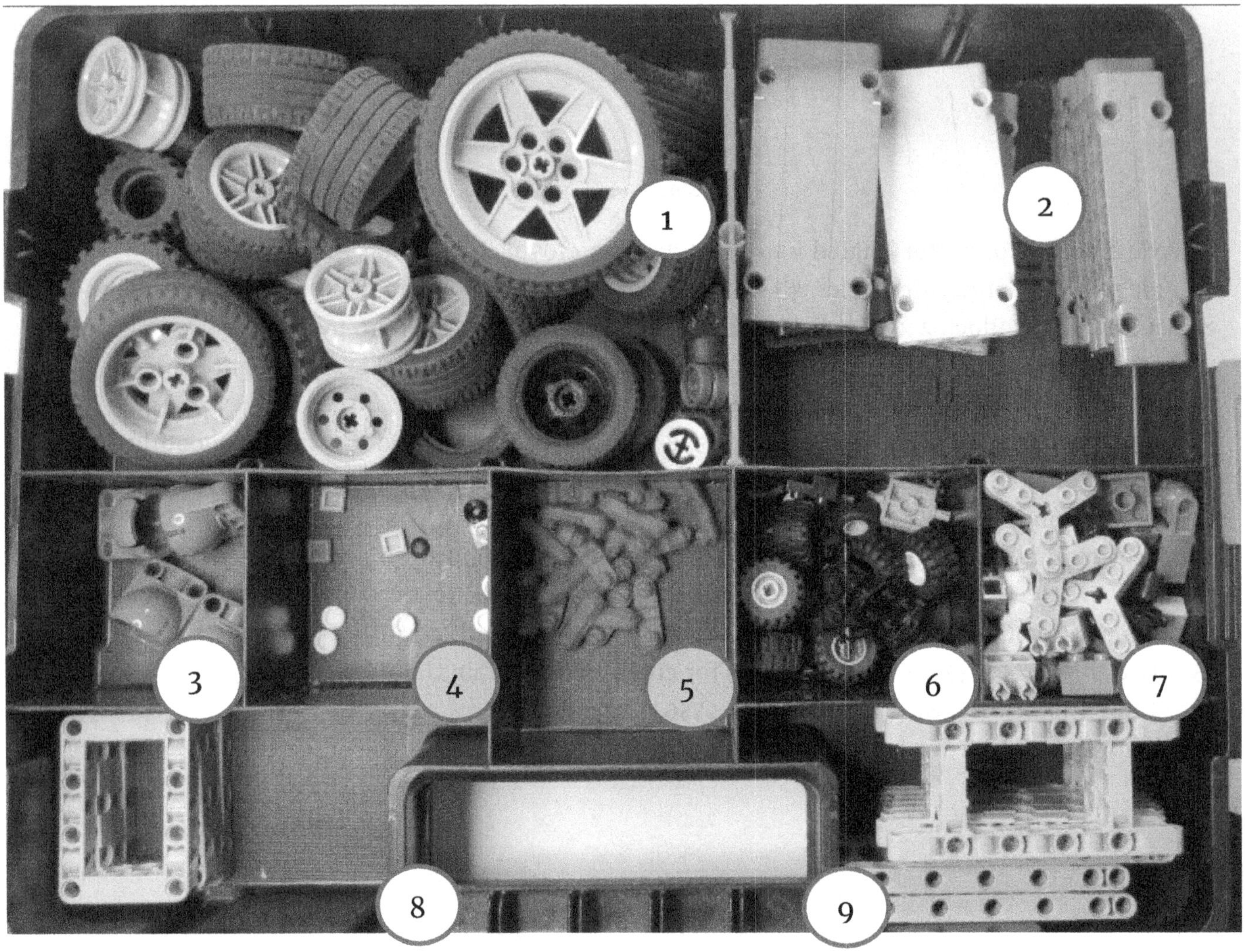

1- Hub, 43.2x26 mm, 463409 – 4 total – (included in core and extension set)
1- Low profile tire, 56x28 mm, black 6035364 – 4 total (included in extension set)
1- Wheel 30.4mm D. x 20mm with No Pin Holes and Reinforced Rim 4297210 -3 total (included)
1- Tire 43.2 x 22 ZR 44309 – 3 total (included in extension set)
1- Wheel 56mm D. x 34mm Technic Racing Medium, 3 Pin Holes 4211845 – 4 total (included)
1- Black Tire 68.8 x 36 ZR – 4614801 – 4 total (included in extension set)
1- Wheel Technic Street Bike 81mm D. x 28 51378 – 2 total – I recommend these wheels
1- Tire Technic Street Bike (8420) - Narrow, Front 51380 – 2 total – I recommend these tires
1- Wheel 61.6mm D. x 13.6mm Motorcycle – 2903 – 2 total – nice to have
1- Tire 81.6 x 14.2 Motorcycle Z Racing Tread 6596 – 2 total – nice to have
1-Wheel 30mm D. x 14mm (for Tire 43.2 x 14) 56904 – 4 total – can be used as third wheel
1-Tire 43.2 x 14 Offset Tread 56898 -4 total – nice to have
1- Wheel 41mm Znap Thin Tread -4 total – I recommend these wheels if you are building low sitting robots.

1- Tire 41 mm Directional Tread -2 total – I recommend these tires if you are building low sitting robot.

2- Technic Panel 1 x 5 x 11 - Dark Bluish Gray 64782 – 70 total – essential
2- Flat Panel 3X11M 6055627 – 30 total - essential
3 - Steering Ball Joint Large Receptacle 92911 -2 total
3- Ball Steel 18mm 99948 – 2 total
4- Empty
5- Link Tread Attachment, Double, Rubber 6036424 – 60 total.
6- Wheel 18mm D. x 14mm with Axle Hole, Fake Bolts and Shallow Spokes – 30 total – used extensively in mechanical wall follows.
6-Wheel with Split Axle hole 3482 – 20 total -used in mechanical wall follows
6- Wheel 18mm D. x 14mm with Pin Hole, Fake Bolts and Shallow Spokes 55981 – 20 total- used in mechanical wall follows

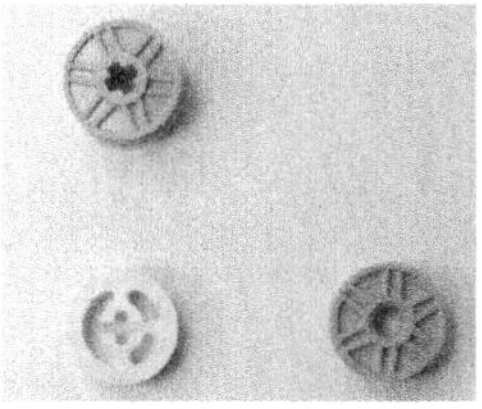

7- Stud full parts – nice to have
8- Technic, Liftarm 5 x 7 Open Center Frame Thick 64179 -50 total – essential
9- Technic, Liftarm 5 x 11 Open Center Frame Thick 64178 – 20 total – essential

Storage Bin-6 (Grey numbers are nice to have)

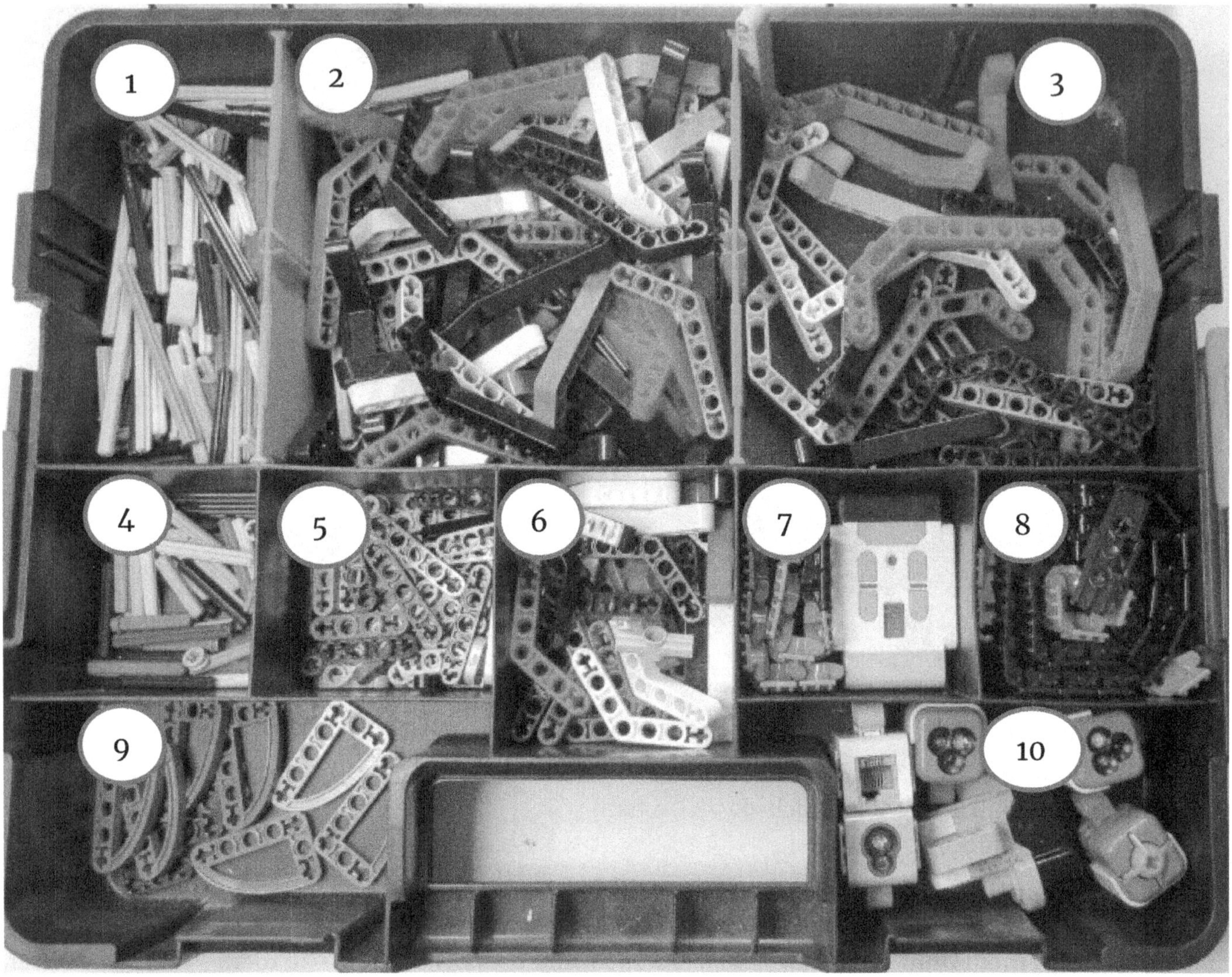

1- Axle with stop, 8-module, dark grey 4499858- 20 total
1- Axle, 5-module, grey 4211639- 20 total
1- Axle, 6-module, black 370626 – 20 total
1- Axle, 7-module, grey 4211805 -20 total
1- Axle, 8-module, black 370726 -20 total
1- Axle, 9-module, grey 4535768- 20 total
1- Axle, 12-module, black 370826 -10 total
1- Axle, 16- module 50451 -4 total
1- Axle, 32 Module 50450 -2 total – nice to have
2- Angular beam, 3x7-module, grey 4211624 -30 total
3- Double angular beam, 3x7-module, white 4495412 – 40 total
4- Axle with stud, 3-module, dark beige 6031821 -20 total- you can attach the beam using a stud
4- Axle with stop, 4-module, dark grey 4560177 -40 total- very useful

4- Axle, 3-module, grey 4211815 -20 total
4- Axle, 4-module, black 370526- 20 total
4- Cross Axle 5,5 With Stop 1M 4508553 – 20 total
4- Axle 4module with Center Stop 99008 -20 total

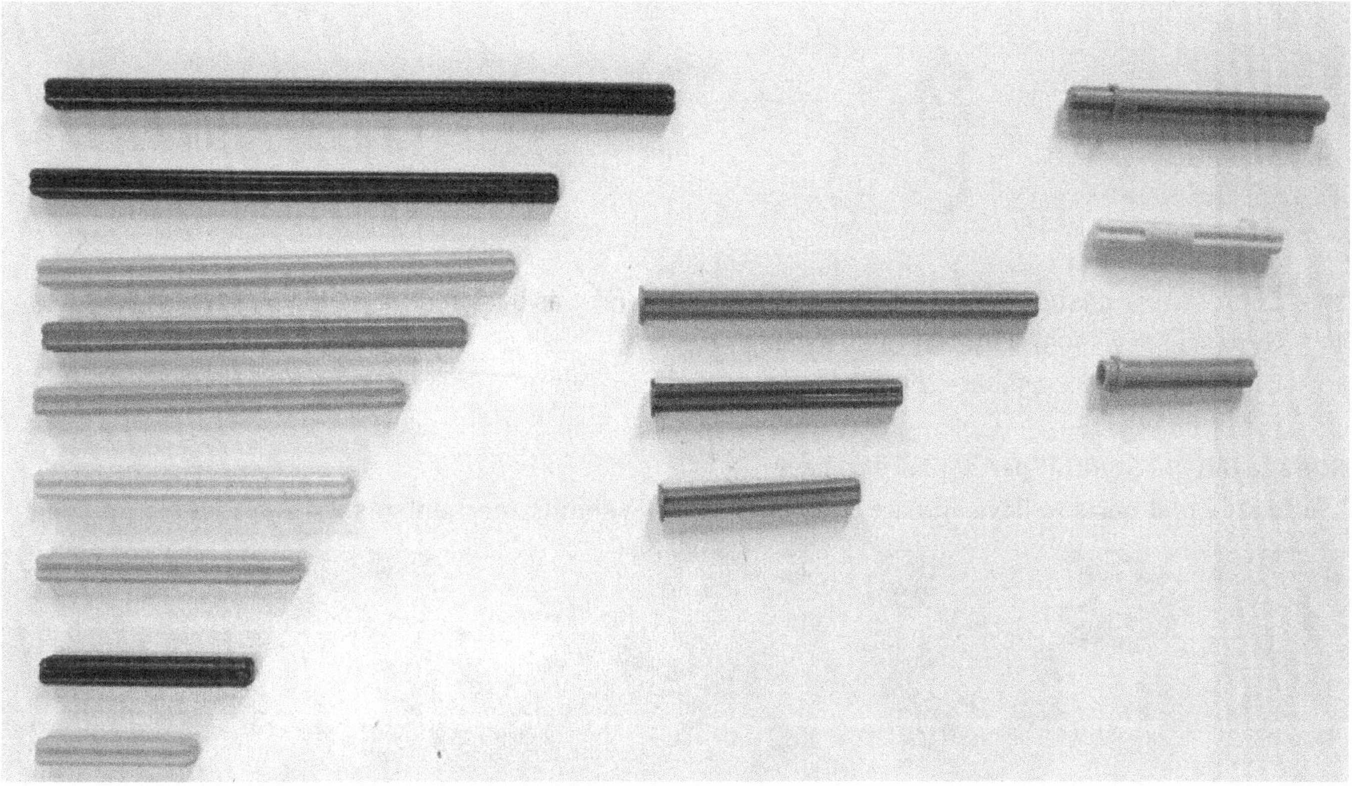

5- ½ beam, 2-module, black 4164133– 20 total
5- ½ beam, 3-module, black 4211566 – 20 total
5- ½ beam, 4-module, black 4142236 – 20 total
5- ½ beam, 5-module, black 6020286 – 20 total
5- ½ beam, 6-module, black 32063 – 20 total
5- ½ beam, 5-module, black 32017– 20 total

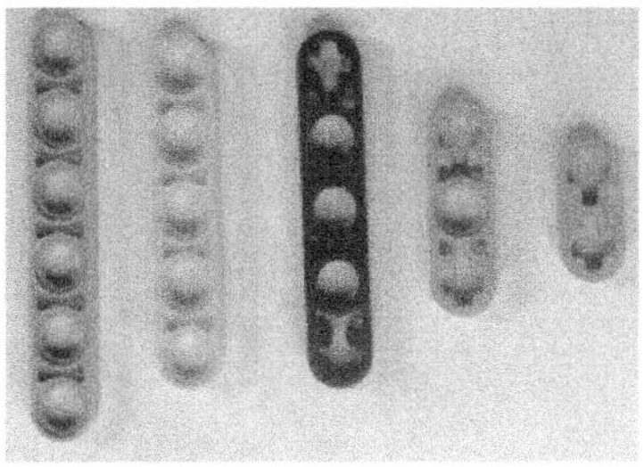

6- Angular beam, 4x4-module, white 4509912 -20 total
7-Track Element, 5x1,5 6014648 – 60 total – used for conveyor belt or track belt
8- Track Element, 5x1,5 6014648 – 60 total – used for conveyor belt or track belt
9- ½ triangle beam, 5x3-module, grey 6009019 -20 total

9- Half Beam 5 x 7 Bent 90 degrees with Curve 32251 -20 total
9- TECHNIC LEVER 3X3M, 90° 32056 -20 total

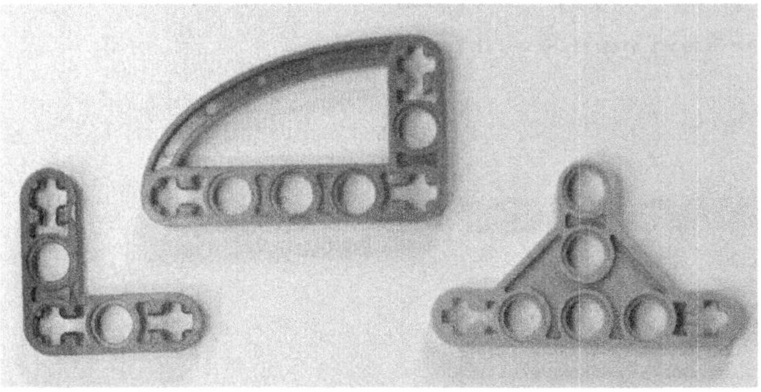

10 – Color sensor 45506 – 4 total – 2 for use on robot and 2 as backups
10 – Gyro sensor 45505 – 2 total – 1 as backup
10 – Ultrasonic Sensor 45504 – 2 total – 1 as backup

Storage Bin-7- Studfull parts – Nice to have
These are great parts to have and are useful for creating sliding mechanisms.

Stud full parts can be used in component assemblies where you do not want a strong connection. One example is when you need bins to hold something on the mat that you will later be delivering.

The following parts are studfull parts that you can typically use. I would not recommend buying these parts except the beams, but you can use them if you have them from old LEGO creations.
You should buy stud full beams, as they have the ability to connect to studless beams to create a long extender arm.

The next picture shows how to create a part of the extender arm.

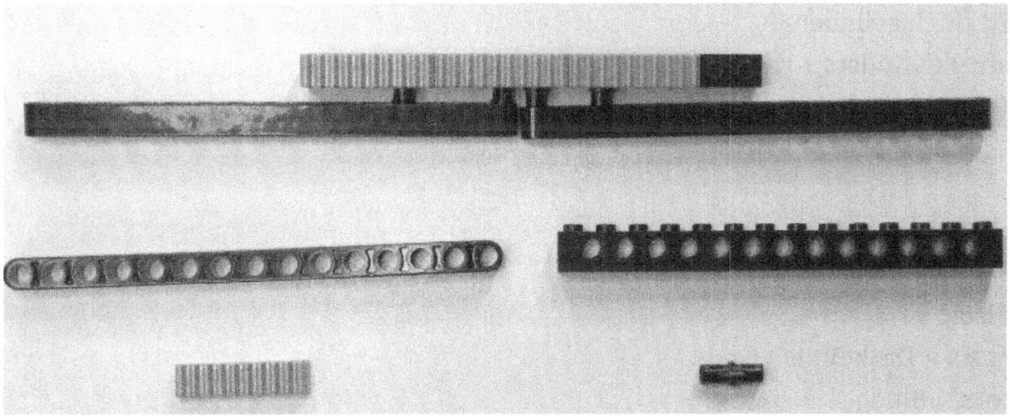

Storage Bin-8 – Pneumatic Parts, Rope Cord, Weight Bricks and Magnetic Parts.
LEGO Pneumatic mechanisms are allowed in FLL competition. These are very helpful in performing missions and can be used as actuators in addition to the 4 motors that are allowed. I recommend buying the following kit from eBay or Amazon.

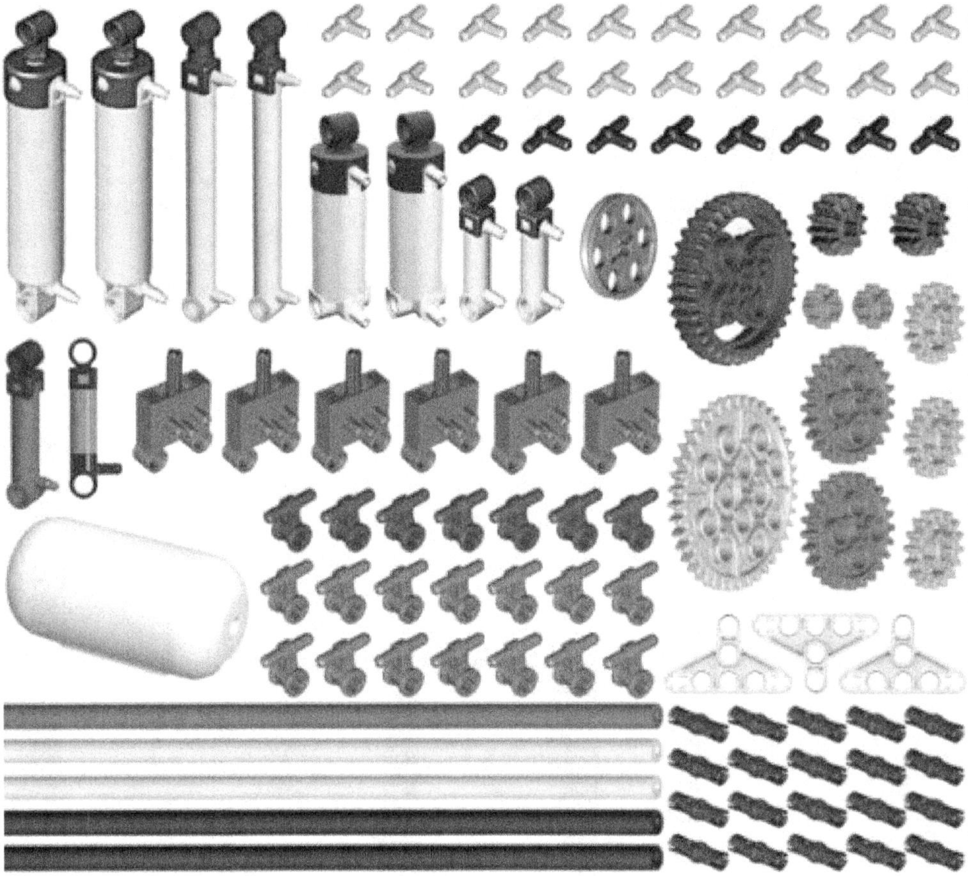

1 Air Tank
2 LEGO extra-long thick cylinders
2 LEGO extra-long thin cylinders
2 LEGO standard thick cylinders
2 LEGO thin (mini) Cylinders
2 Mini Pumps (6 and 5.5 studs long)
6 Switches
1 Pulley
11 Gears
20 T Fittings - Light Bluish Gray
8 T Fittings - Black
14 Hose connectors - Dark Bluish Gray
7 Hose connectors - Blue

3 Technic triangles
20 Technic connector pins
204cm (80 inches, 6.6 feet) Black LEGO compatible hose
204cm (80 inches, 6.6 feet) Yellow LEGO compatible hose
204cm (80 inches, 6.6 feet) Blue LEGO compatible hose

You should also buy 1-2 extra Air tanks depending on how many attachments will be using pneumatic actuators.

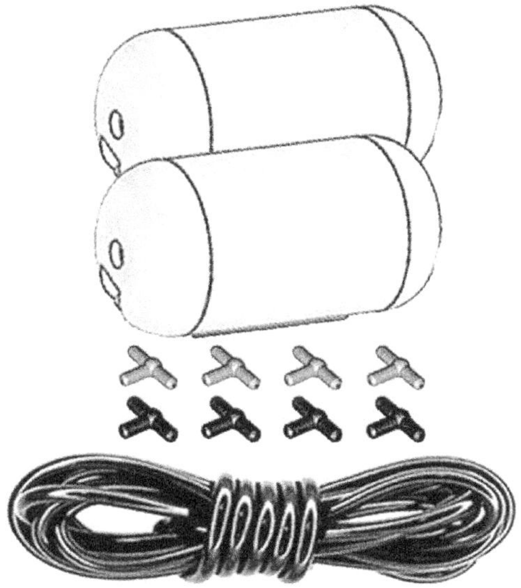

You should also buy the LEGO rope cord kit. Few uses of rope cords are listed below:
1- Rope cords can be used to convert the movement of the robot on the mat into rotational motion, by pulling on the rope cord wound on the spindle.
2- Rope cords can be used to tow game elements back to base.

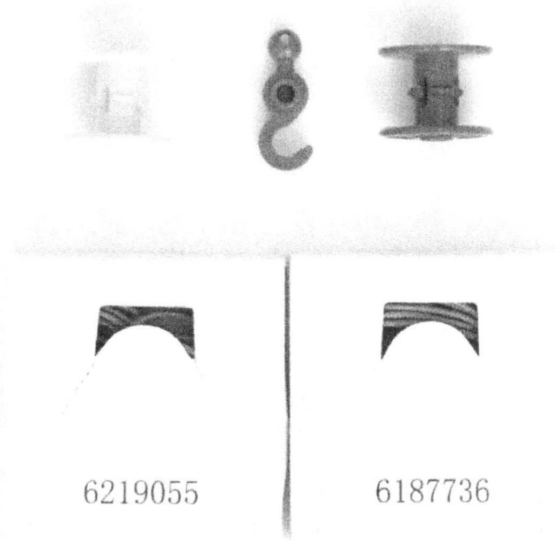

LEGO Magnetic parts and Weight bricks: –nice to have
Magnets can be used for all kinds of attachments, releasable items, breakaway components, and more.

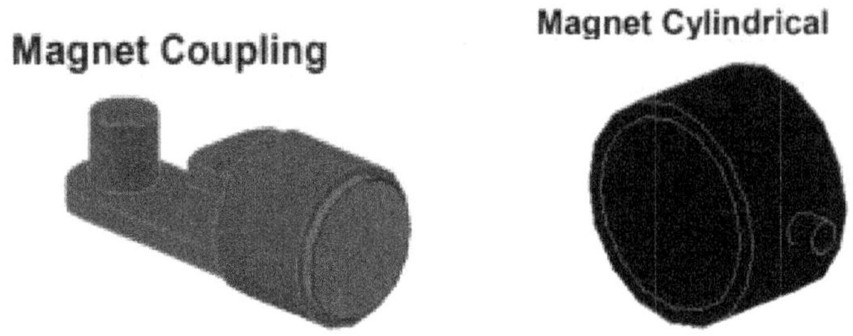

Weight Bricks are useful in balancing weight when using attachments.
LEGO Brick with weight 73090b

We have been through a lot of parts, but it is always fun to have LEGO mini figures, different hats, caps and hairs as shown in following picture.

HOW TO DESIGN STRONG AND EFFICIENTLY

Simplicity is the key to any good design. To achieve simple and reliable robot designs you will have to understand both common and specialized LEGO components.
Let us start with the simple structural parts that will create the backbone of the robot(chassis) and then we will move on to building moving assemblies.
For building the robot consider the right parts and always remember that assemblies break at the weakest point of contact. Strengthening these weak points with more connections make your robot much sturdier.
The next pictures show how to connect 2 beams properly. When you want to connect 2 beams and form a long arm always connect the beams to each other using a third beam.

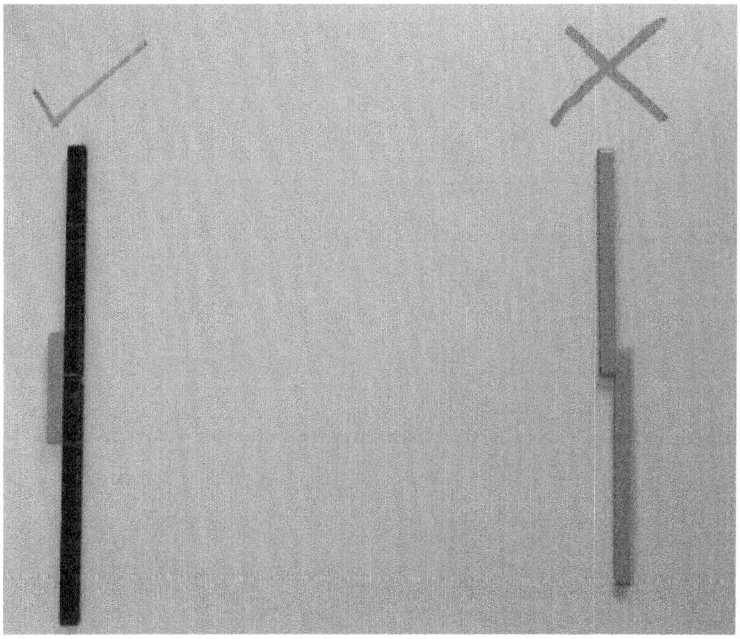

When you want to connect 2 beams at a right angle make sure to use the angular beams you have seen in storage bin-1 slot 8 or 9. Refer to the following picture.

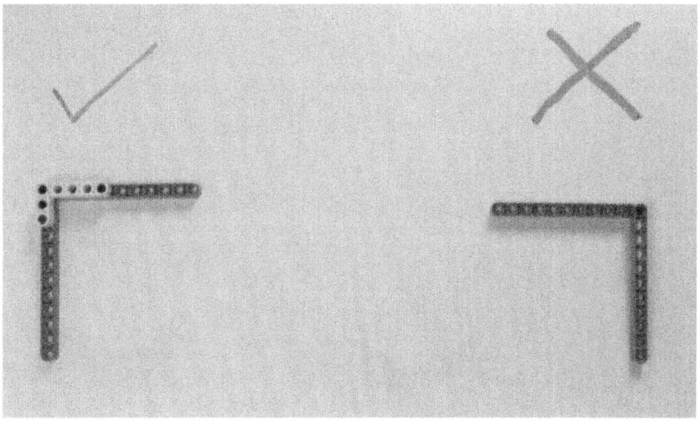

For creating squares or rectangular structures always use frames or plates. If you are running out of those use the angular connector pegs 3x3 shown in storage bin-2 slot 4.
Refer to the following picture. Another way is to use axles with axle connectors with axle holes from storage bin-4 slot 10

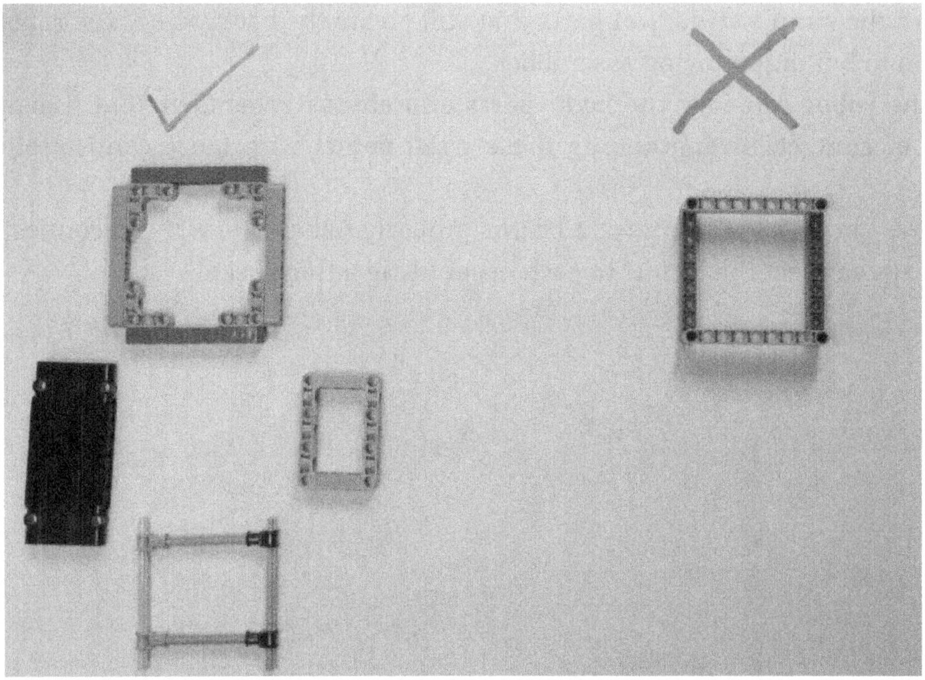

For connecting angular beams with a cross hole, you can use the 2-module axle. For connecting 4 beams you can use the weapon barrel part.

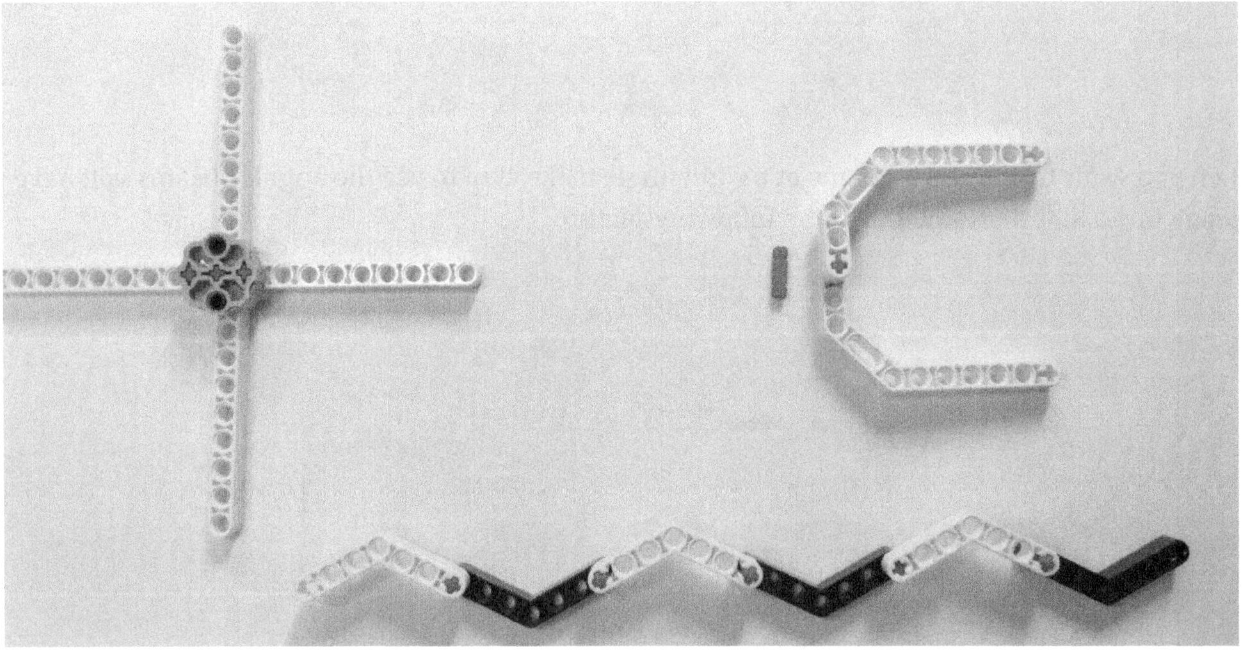

The picture after the next picture shows the main structural parts you will use to construct your robot. You should print this picture and paste it on your wall to refer to it when you are building the robot. Knowing the parts, you can use greatly enhances your ability to construct a strong and efficient robot.
All the parts shown in the next picture allows you to build rigid structures. The connectors shown are friction connectors.
Large motors and bricks can also be used as part of structural components.
You will use 3 different set of parts or combination of parts to construct your robot.
1st SET: Frame, plates, beams and friction peg or connectors- This is a very strong combination and is very helpful for building sturdy robots.
2nd SET: Stud full parts- these are good for quick construction but cannot be used for very rigid structures. This is not recommended for the structural part of the robot but can be used to plan the robot
3rd Set: Axles and Axle Connectors- These create very rigid structures if put together correctly

The following picture provides you a brief idea of how these components can build a cube.

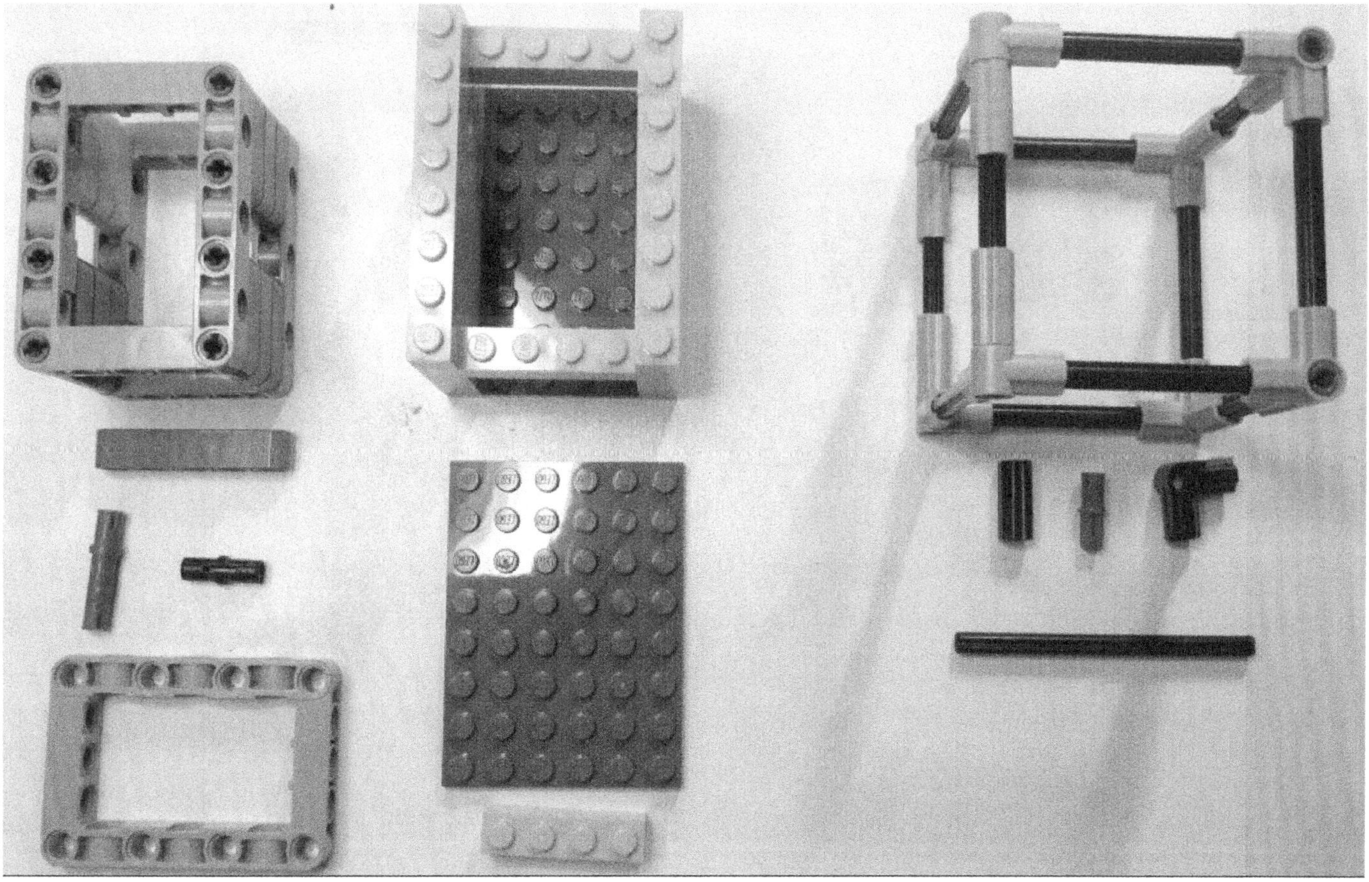

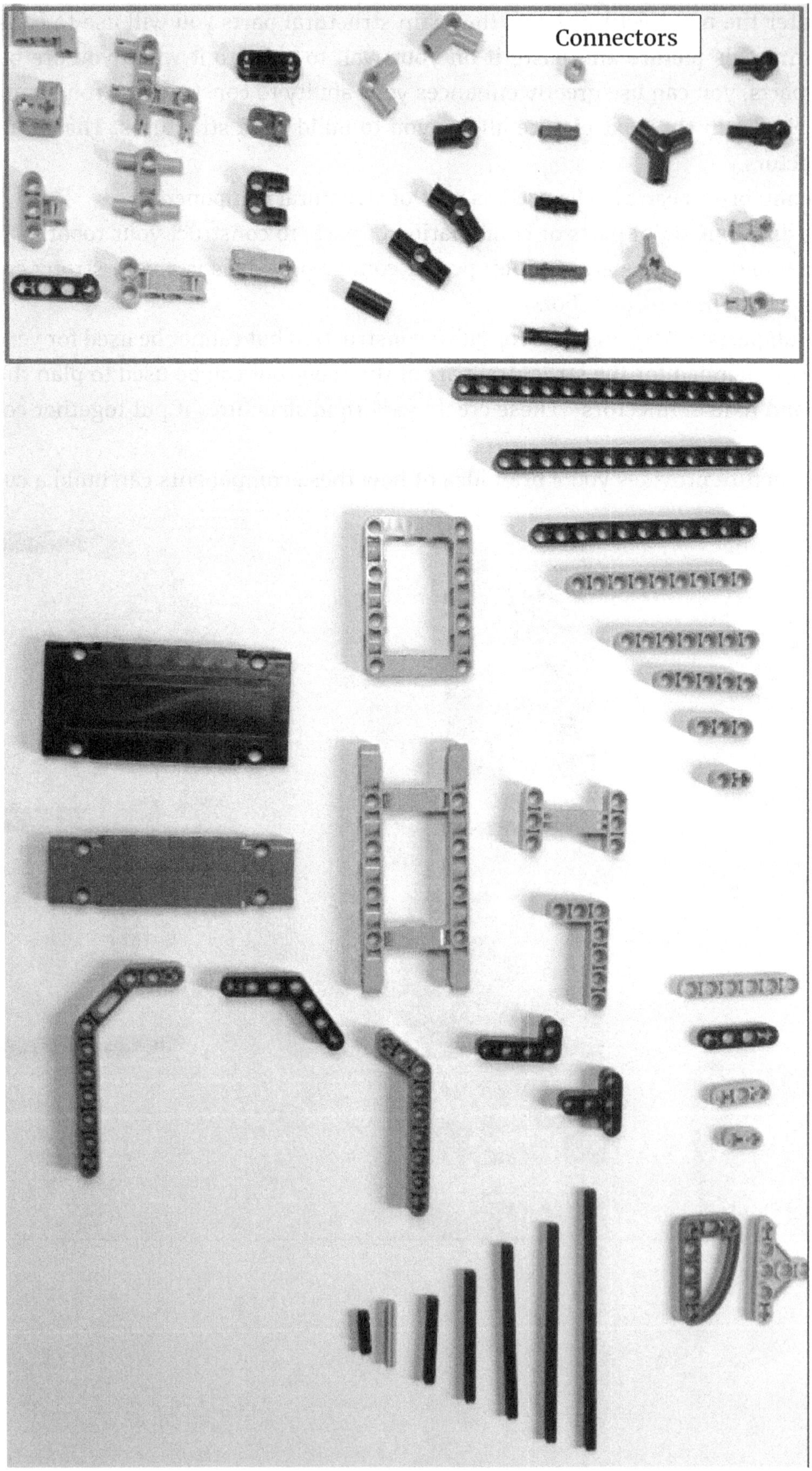
Connectors

You will learn more about structural construction while building the recommended Basebot and example attachments.

For constructing strongly coupled moving parts on the robot, use the following ideas.

Gear coupling -1 (same direction)

In the following picture you are building an assembly of gears to transfer rotational motion from one point to another using a simple normal gear coupled with a bevel gear.

Gear coupling -2 (transfer the motion into a different direction)

While running your robot, you will often transfer motion from one direction to another. This assembly helps with that.

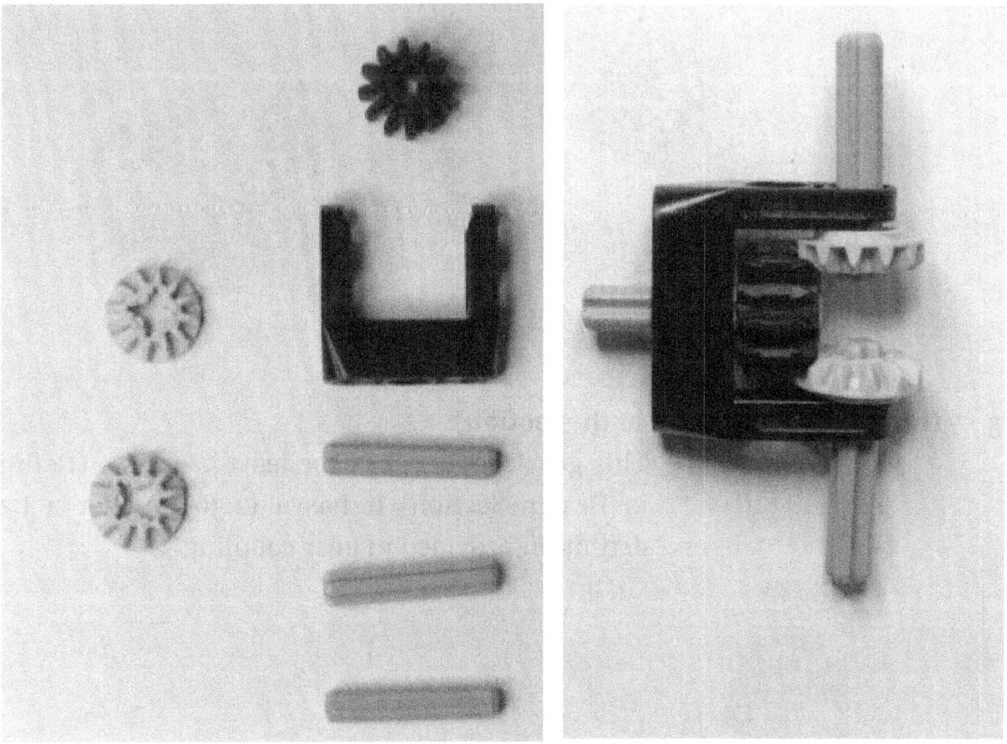

Gear coupling -3 (transfer the motion into a different direction)

This gear coupling increases the torque and changes the direction. When you couple a 12 teeth gear with a 24 teeth gear, there will be two rotations for every one rotation of the motor. This is called the **gear ratio** (Ratio 1:2)

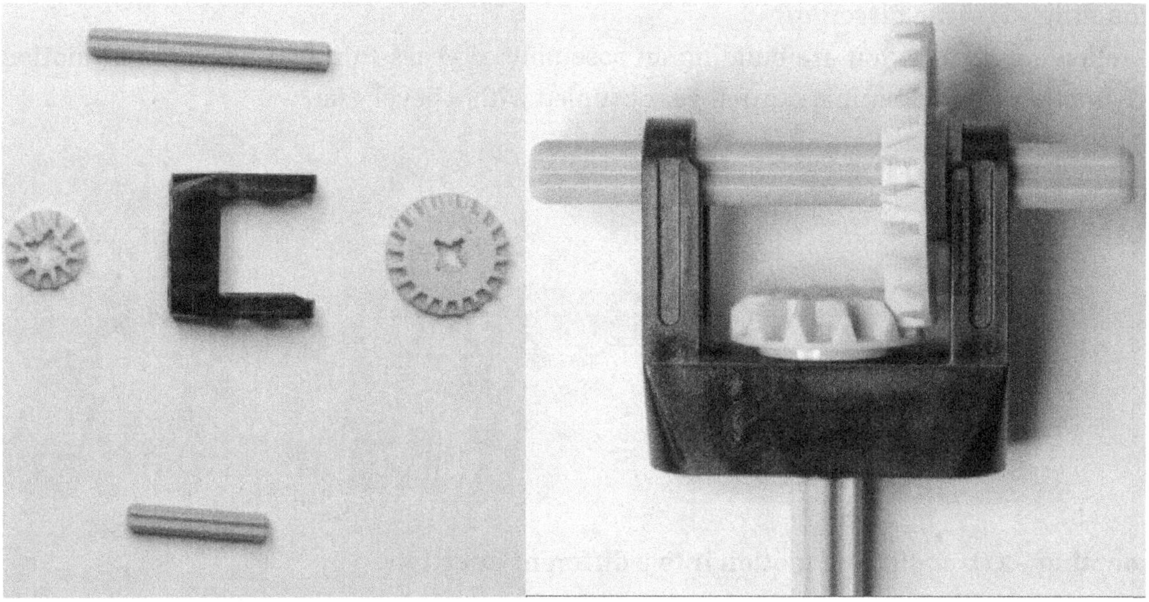

Gear coupling -4(same direction)

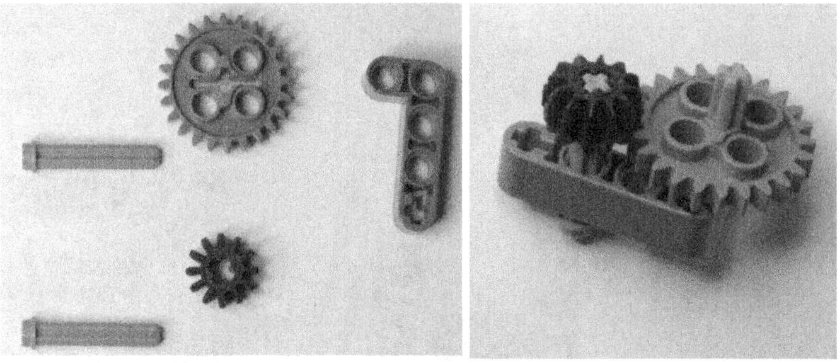

Gear coupling -5 (transfer the direction of the motion)

This gear coupling has the least backlash. (Definition provided in Design Section) It has a 12:36 ratio or a 1:3 ratio. (Ratio definition provided in gear coupling 3)

Gear coupling -6 (transfer the direction of the motion)

Gear coupling -7 (transfer the direction of the motion)

Gear coupling -8 - Strong high torque converter

This assembly drives a worm gear that turns a 40 teeth gear. One rotation of the worm gear causes only one of the teeth on the normal gear to turn. So, 40 worm gear rotations results in one full rotation of the 40 teeth gear. This ratio is 40:1. A ratio where the first number is higher than the second number means the motion is slower but the torque is higher. With a 40:1 ratio, the torque on this mechanism is extremely high. With more torque the mechanism is able to lift heavier objects.

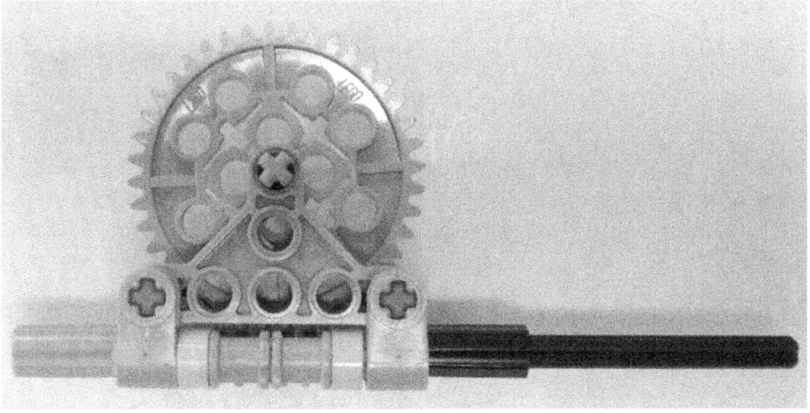

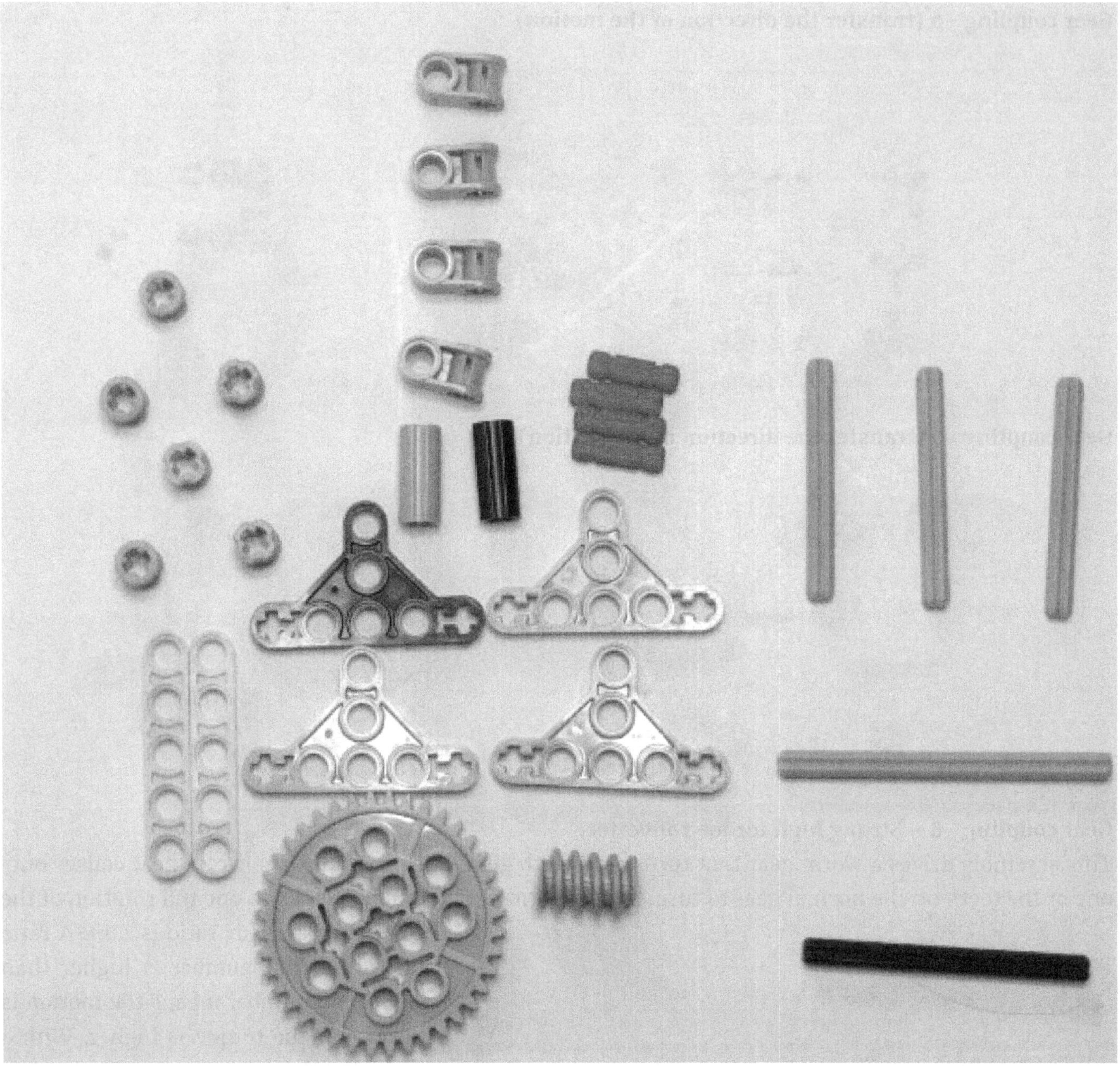

Steps to build are shown in next picture.

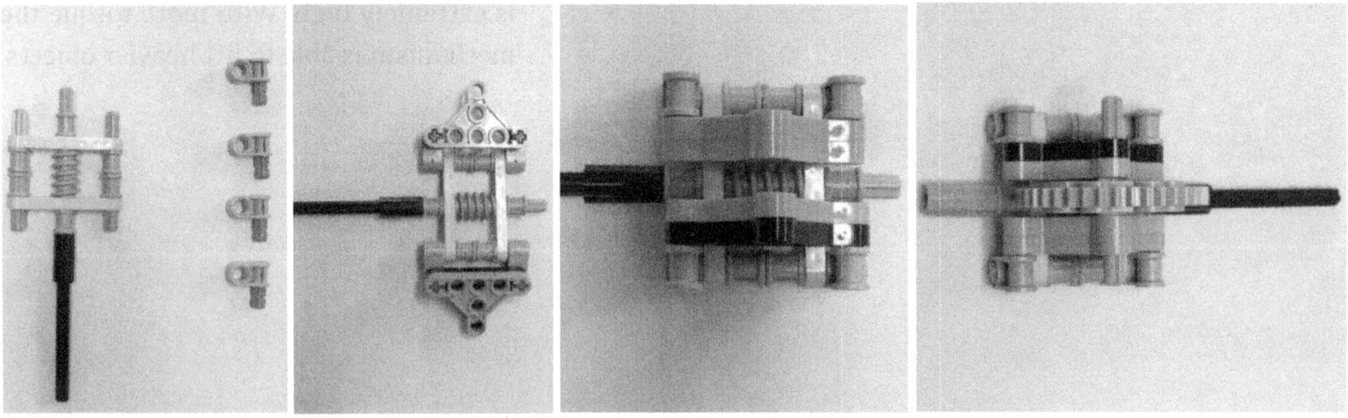

Gear coupling -9 (Strong medium torque converter)

What do the pieces look like to you at the bottom? Is it spooky? I arranged them to look just like a skeleton. This gear coupling allows conversion of motion from one direction to another, but the ratio is 1:8, as we are using an 8 teeth gear. Before you move on think about whether this ratio will increase the torque or will it increase the speed?

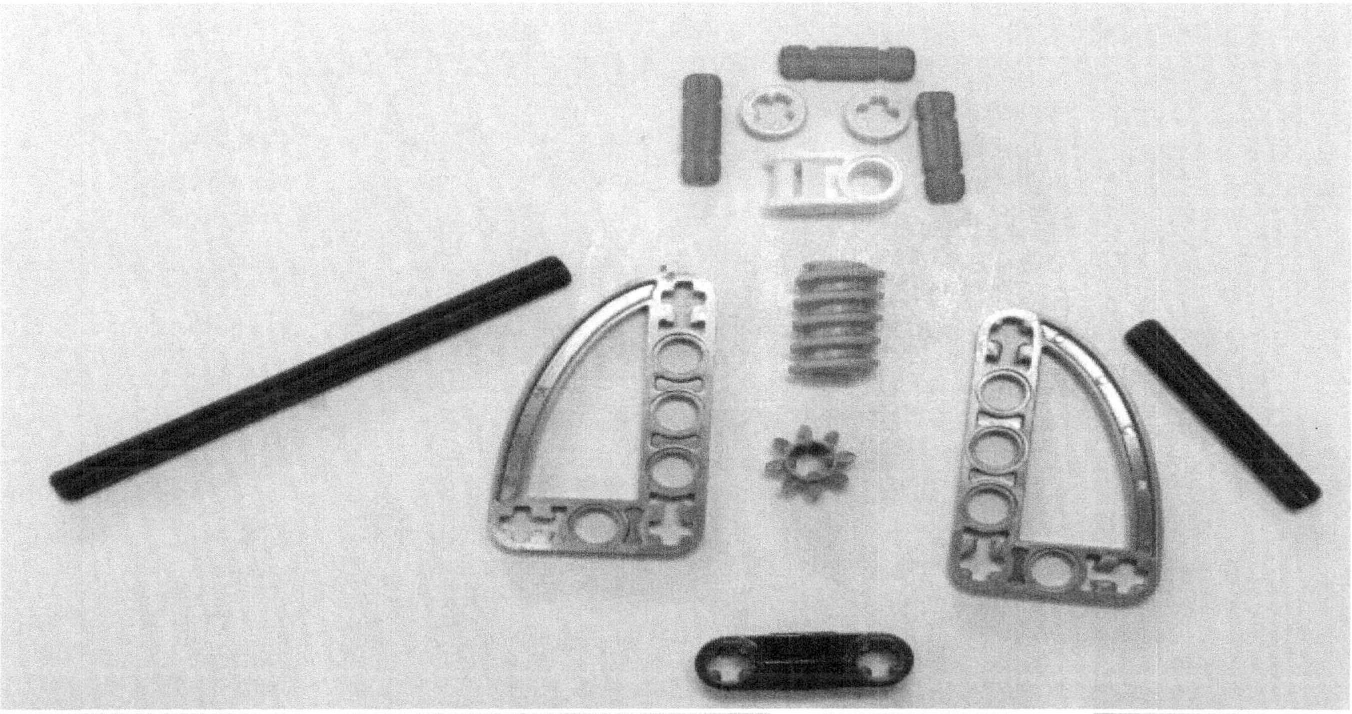

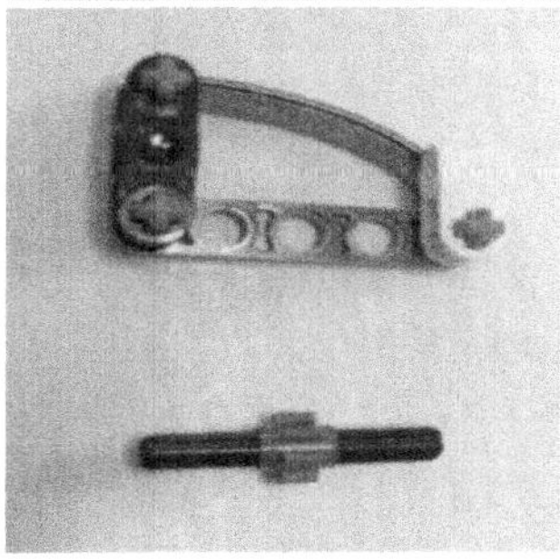

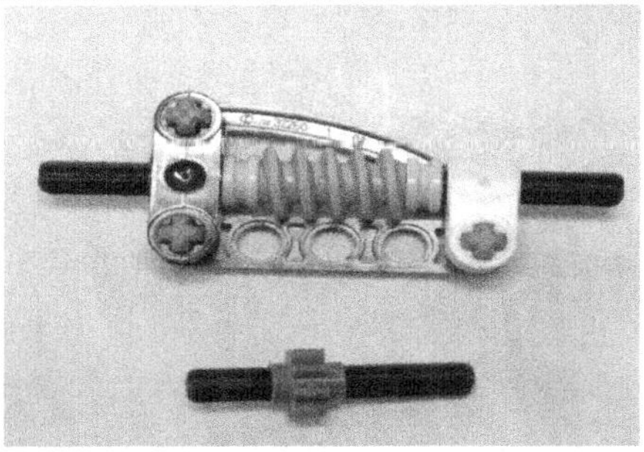

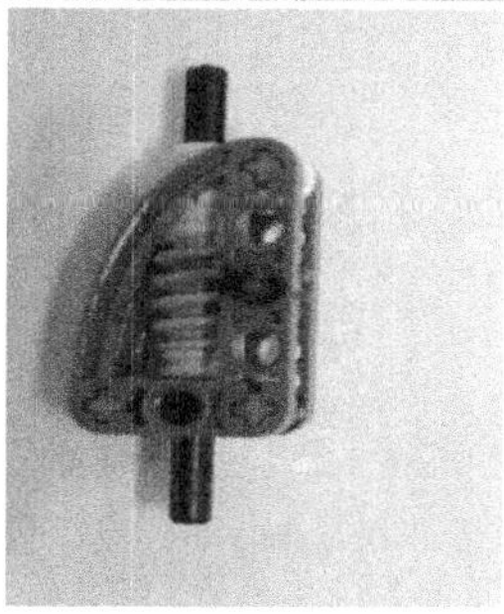

Gear coupling -10 (Strong very high torque converter)

This gear coupling transfers motion in the same direction but increases the torque significantly.

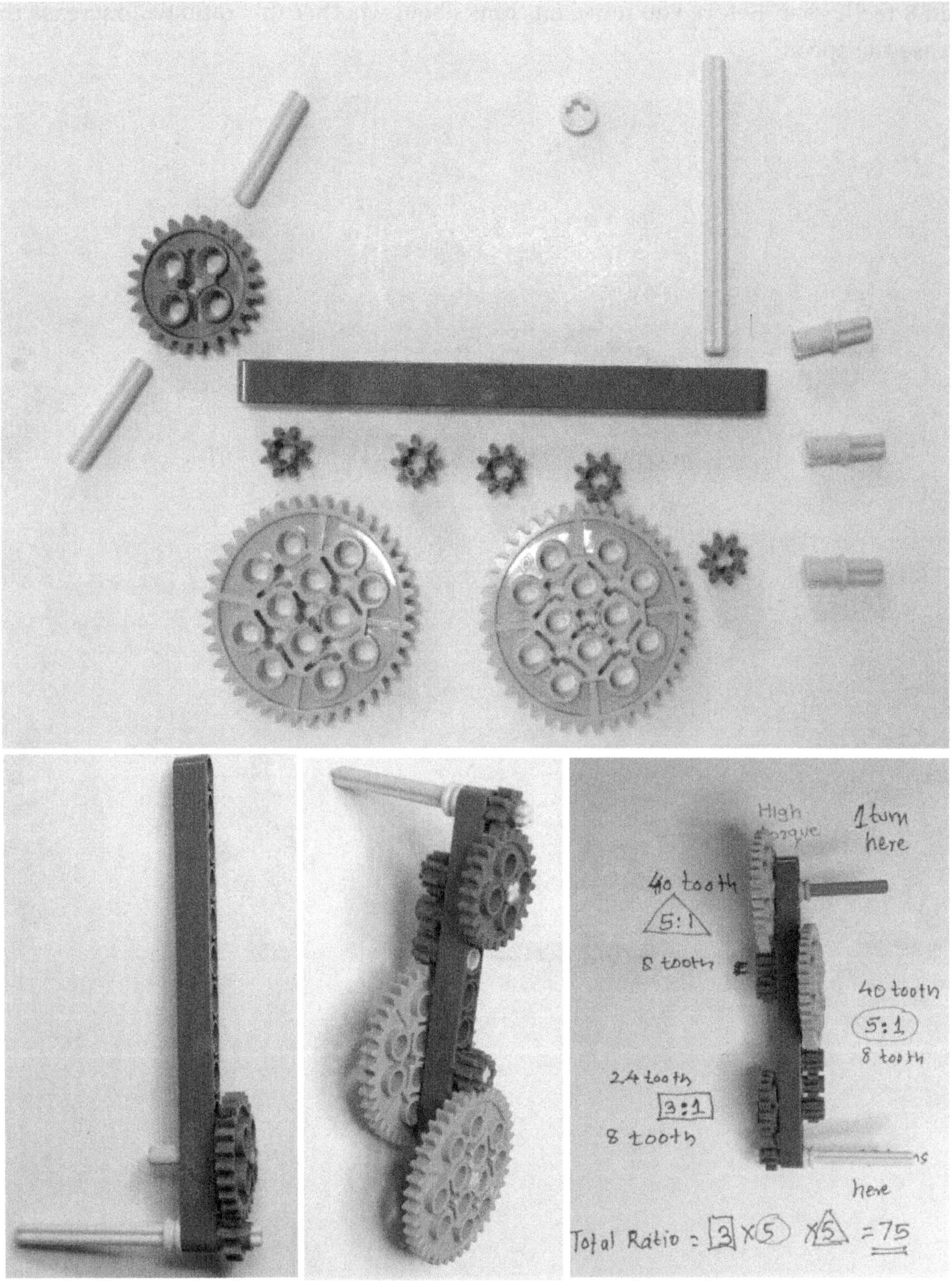

Ball wheel assembly:

The ball wheel is useful as a third wheel and the following pictures show how to build a modular ball wheel assembly that can be attached to any robot.

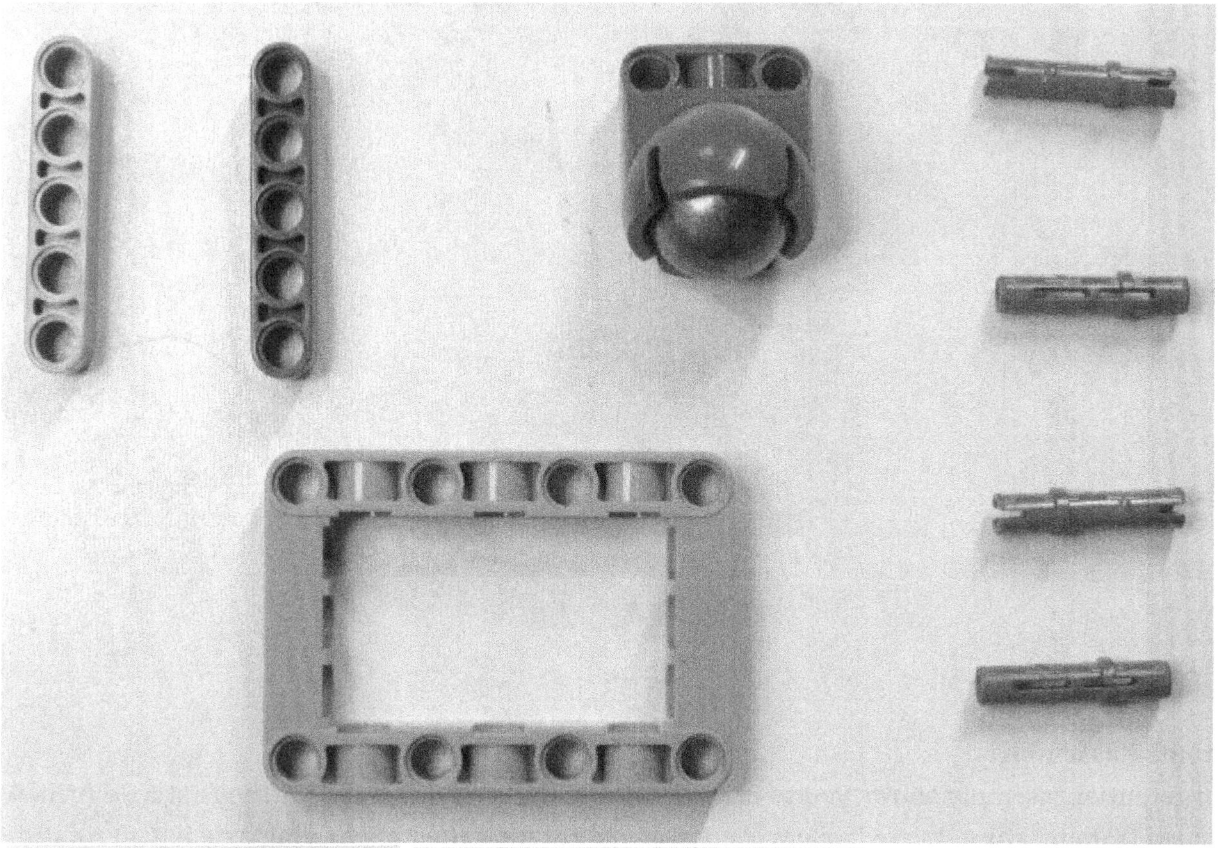

Universal Joint:

Universal Joint allows the motion to be transferred in any direction if the angle between the 2 axles is between 140 -180 degrees.

In constructing this assembly you have to fit the round ball shape structure into the ball wheel component. This is shown in the next few pictures.

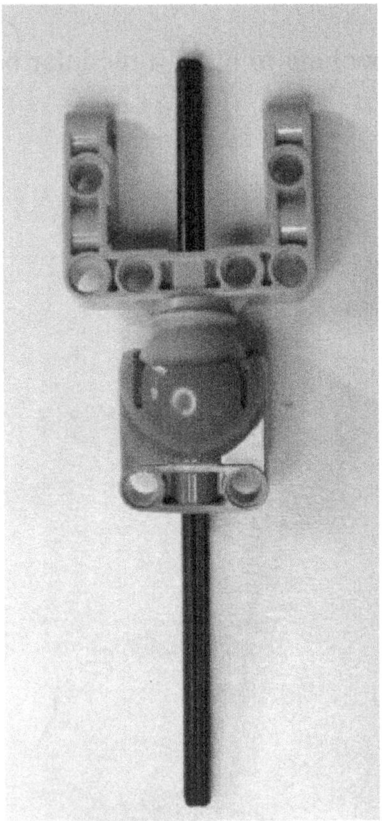

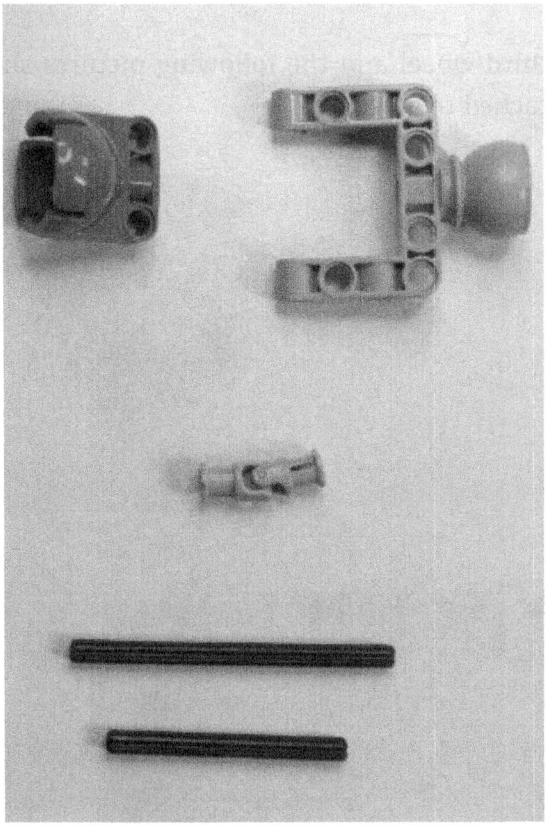

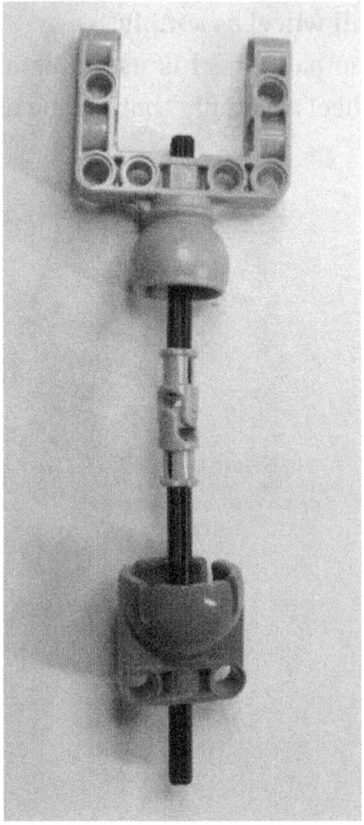

Differential assembly:

The differential assembly allows you to drive 2 axles using only one motor If the first axle (yellow axle) is stopped from rotating, the red axle will continue to rotate if the grey driving axle is still rotating. This can be used to drive 2 activities from one motor during a robot run.

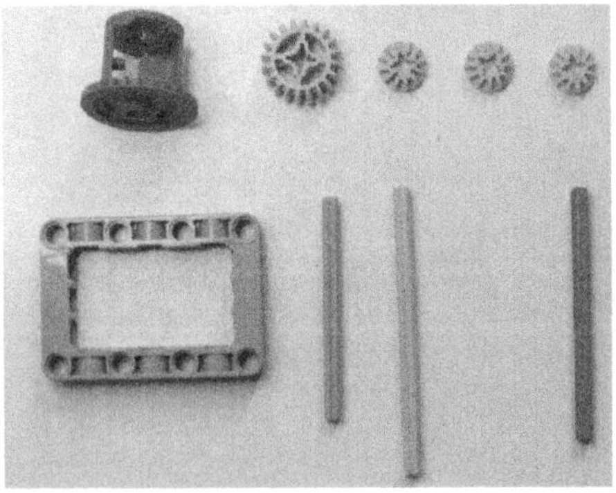

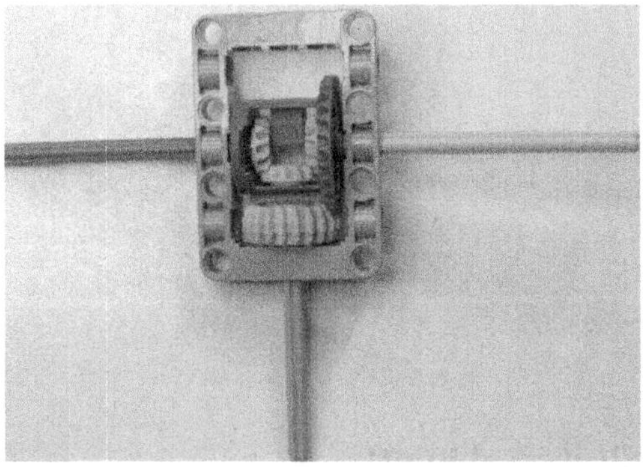

Convert rotational motion into linear movement:
This assembly is one of the ways to transform rotation into linear movement. I have attached pictures to show you how linear movement is created. We will see one more example of rotational motion conversion in the 'Attachments' section.

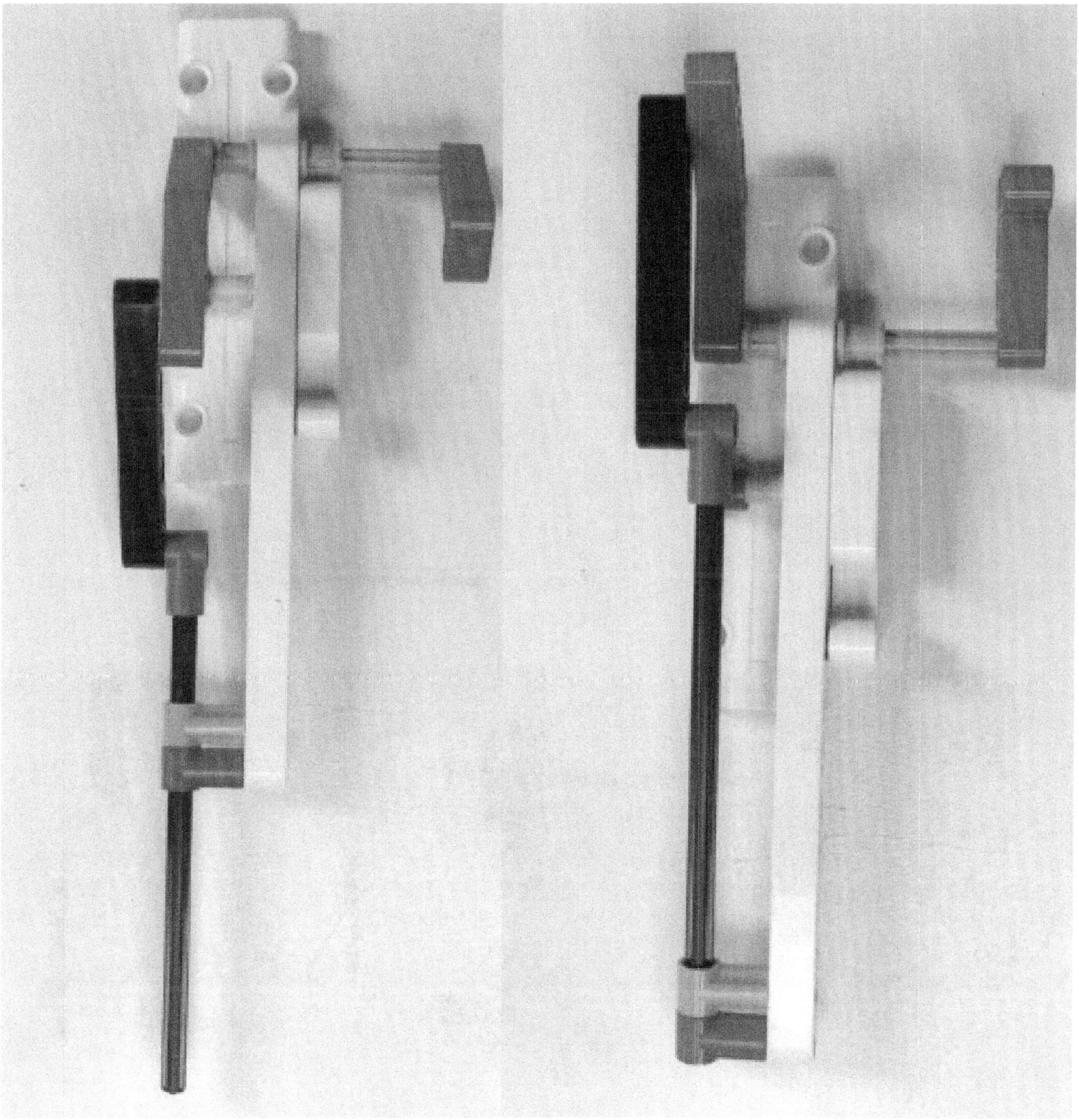

Convert rotational motion into linear movement -2:

The motor can be connected to the grey axle and when it rotates the black axle will be pushed out. The white plate is attached to stop the mechanism from going in the opposite direction. 2 small angular beams connect the plate to the white beam.

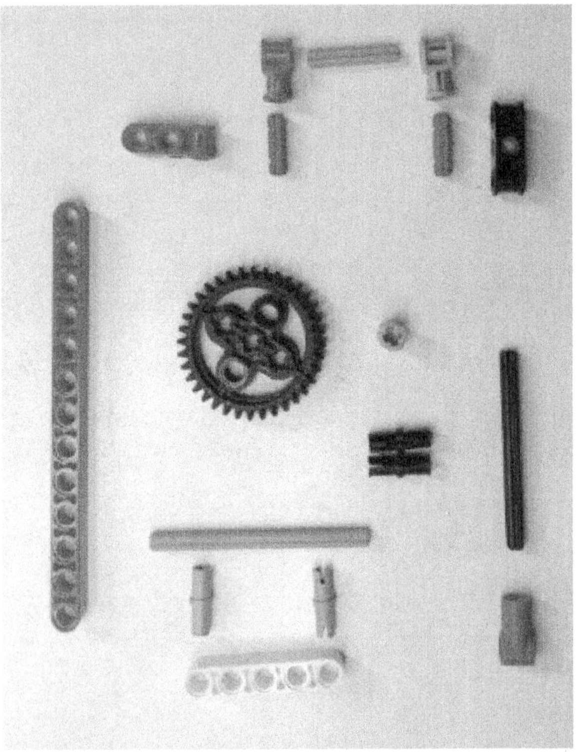

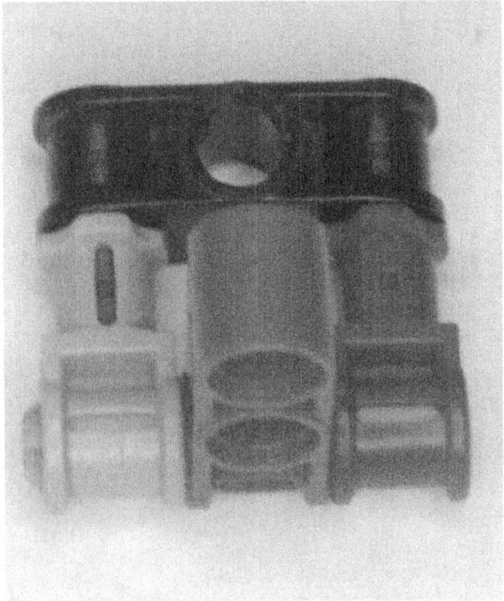

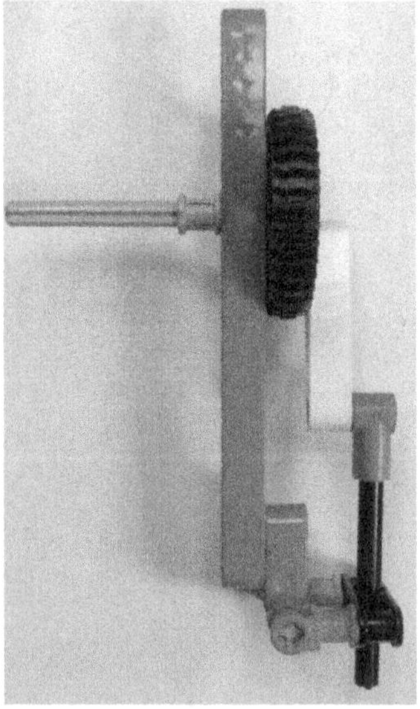

Transmit rotational motion over a long distance:
The following assembly can be used to transmit rotational motion over long distances.

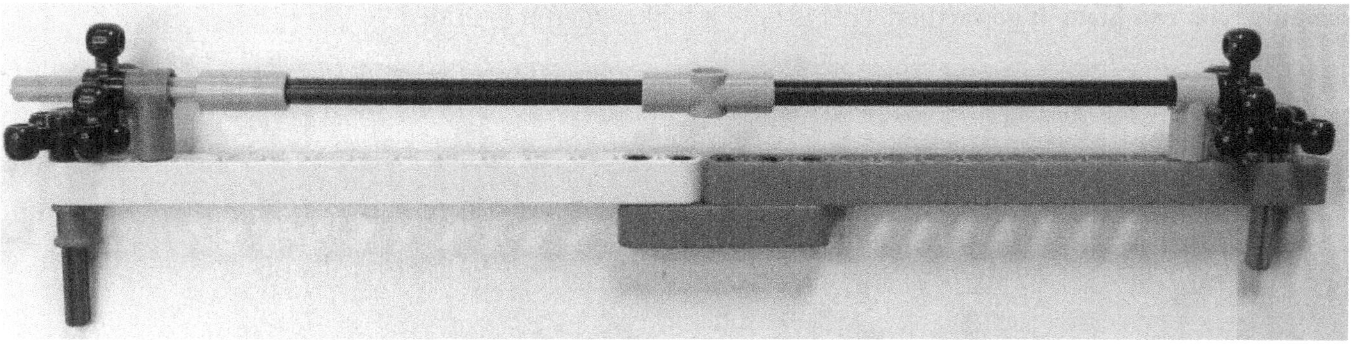

Parallel bar assembly:
This assembly can be used to lift pieces in such a way that it keeps those pieces parallel to the ground You can attach an axle to the top angular beam and anything picked up by that axle will not slide up or down the axle.

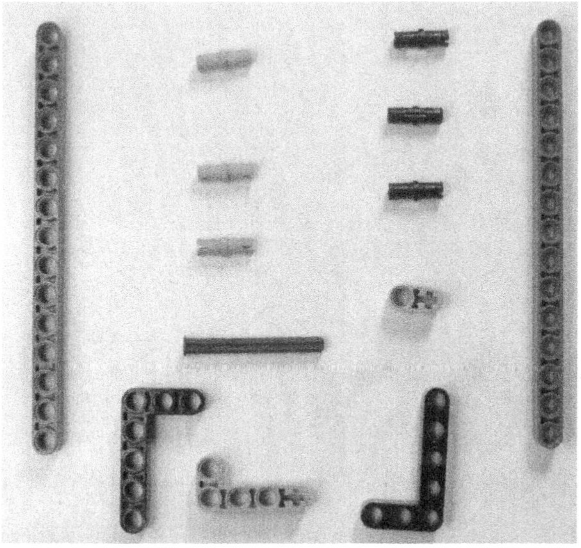
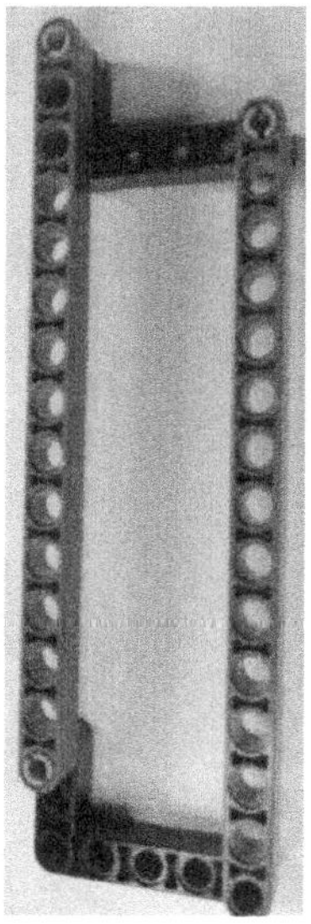
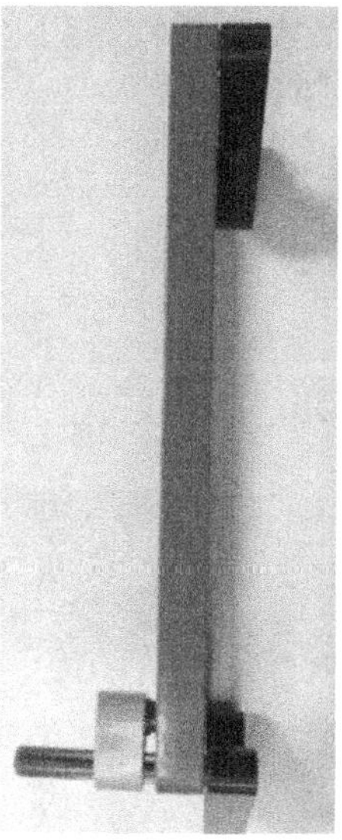
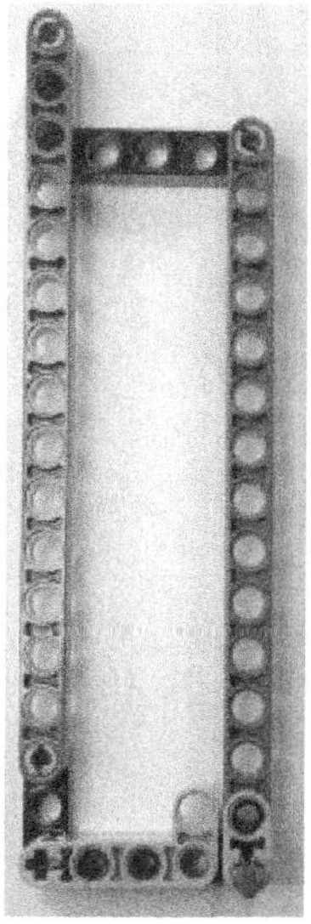

Parallel bar assembly in action

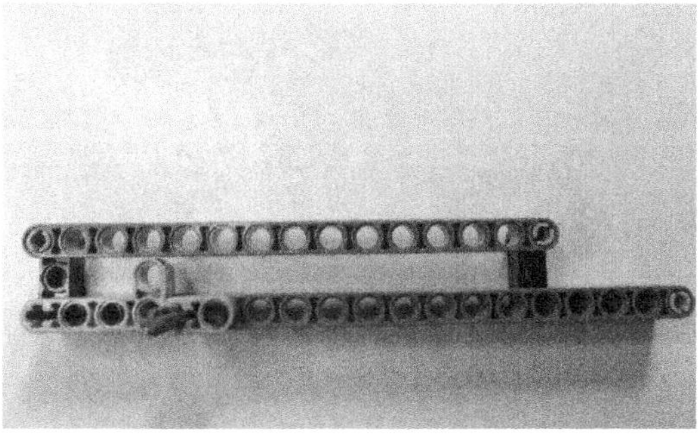
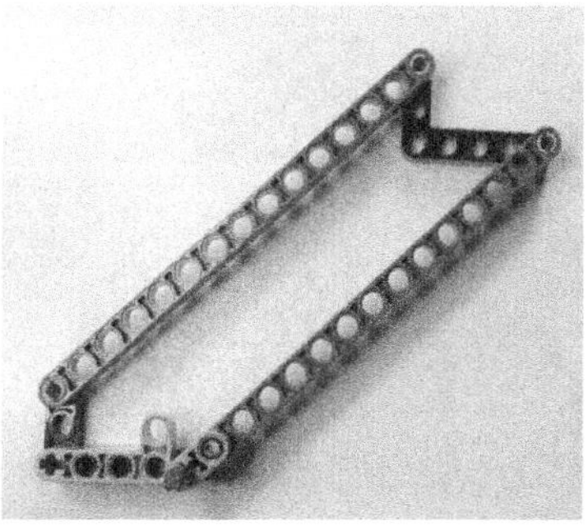
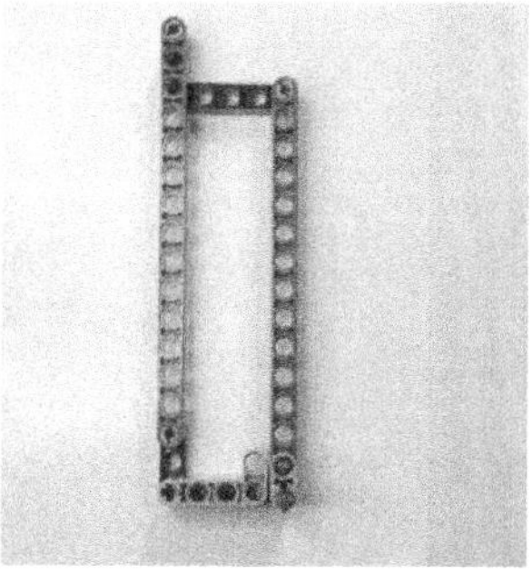

Sturdy scissor link or extender:

This scissor link can be used to extend an arm out, which can go up to 3 ft in distance. The folded extender in the next picture is 4 inches long but extends up to 15 inches long. By adding more links to this assembly, you can make it go farther. This is how it looks when it is folded.

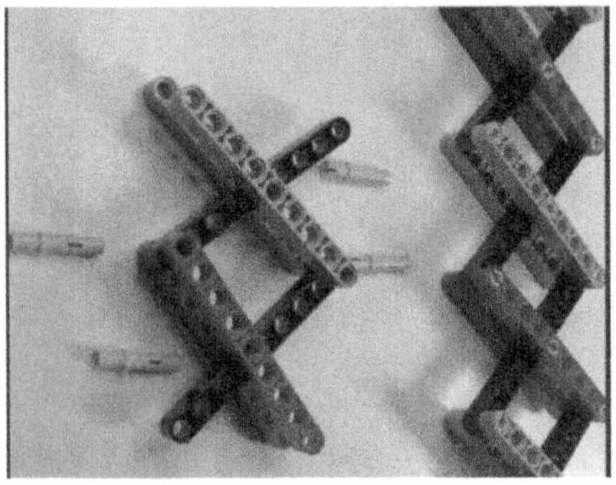

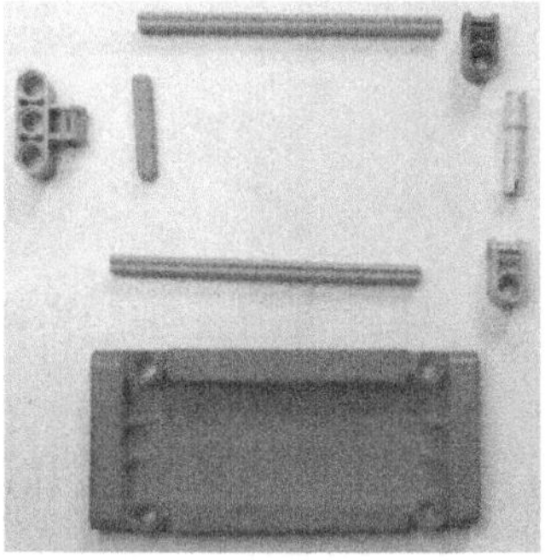

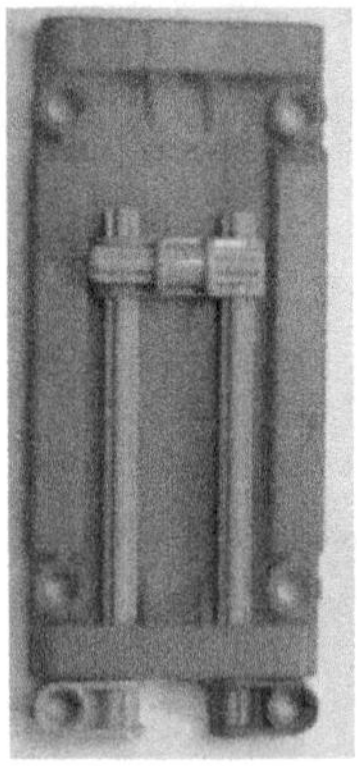

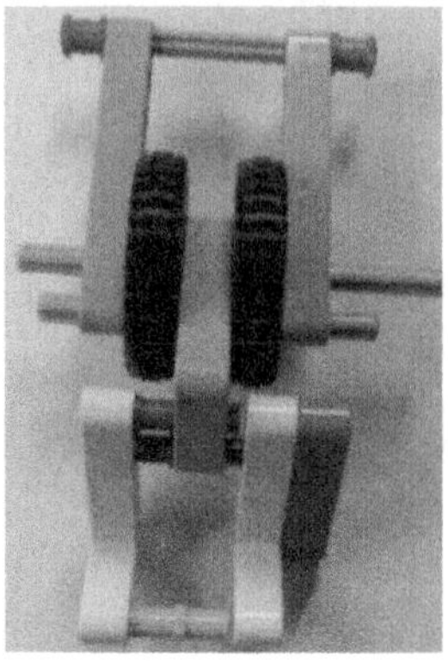

This is how it looks when opened.

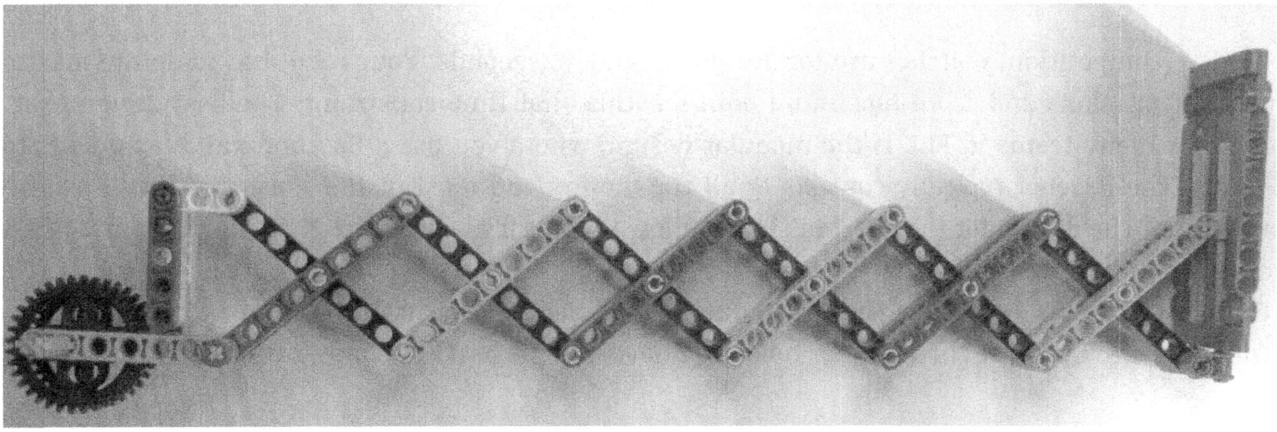

Next picture takes closer look at the mechanism that operate the scissor.

BASEBOT

In the FLL competition, matches are for 2 minutes and 30 seconds. Your robot has to do the maximum amount of missions and score maximum points within that time constraint. The best design that has worked for many teams in FLL is the modular design, where you use a Basebot and attachments to do missions. The Basebot typically consists of all the motors and most of the sensors you will use in the competition. The design for the Basebot should allow for an easy way to attach and take out attachments. There are 2 options for Design.

Option-1 -You can create the Basebot and the attachment shown in this section and next section. OR

Option-2- You can use the learning robot you have built as part of 'Chapter-1'

Option-1-Basebot

Basebot design should follow all the good robot design requirements that you have read in the 'Design Strategy' section.

One of the most common designs for the Basebot is a square or rectangular Basebot which can then be fitted with hollow box like attachments.

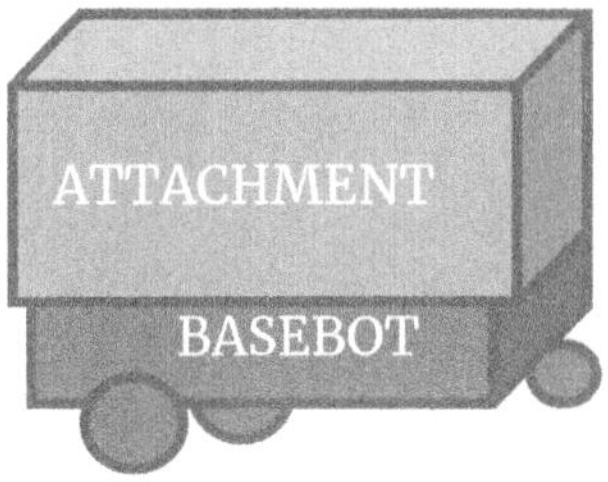

The Basebot you are about to build will require additional parts. I have listed these parts earlier in the book. This Basebot design has been successfully used by many teams I have mentored, and you can certainly make changes after you build it to allow the Basebot to meet the requirements of your game strategy for a particular FLL Challenge.

The Basebot consists of a total of 9 different assemblies put together to create a sophisticated Basebot.

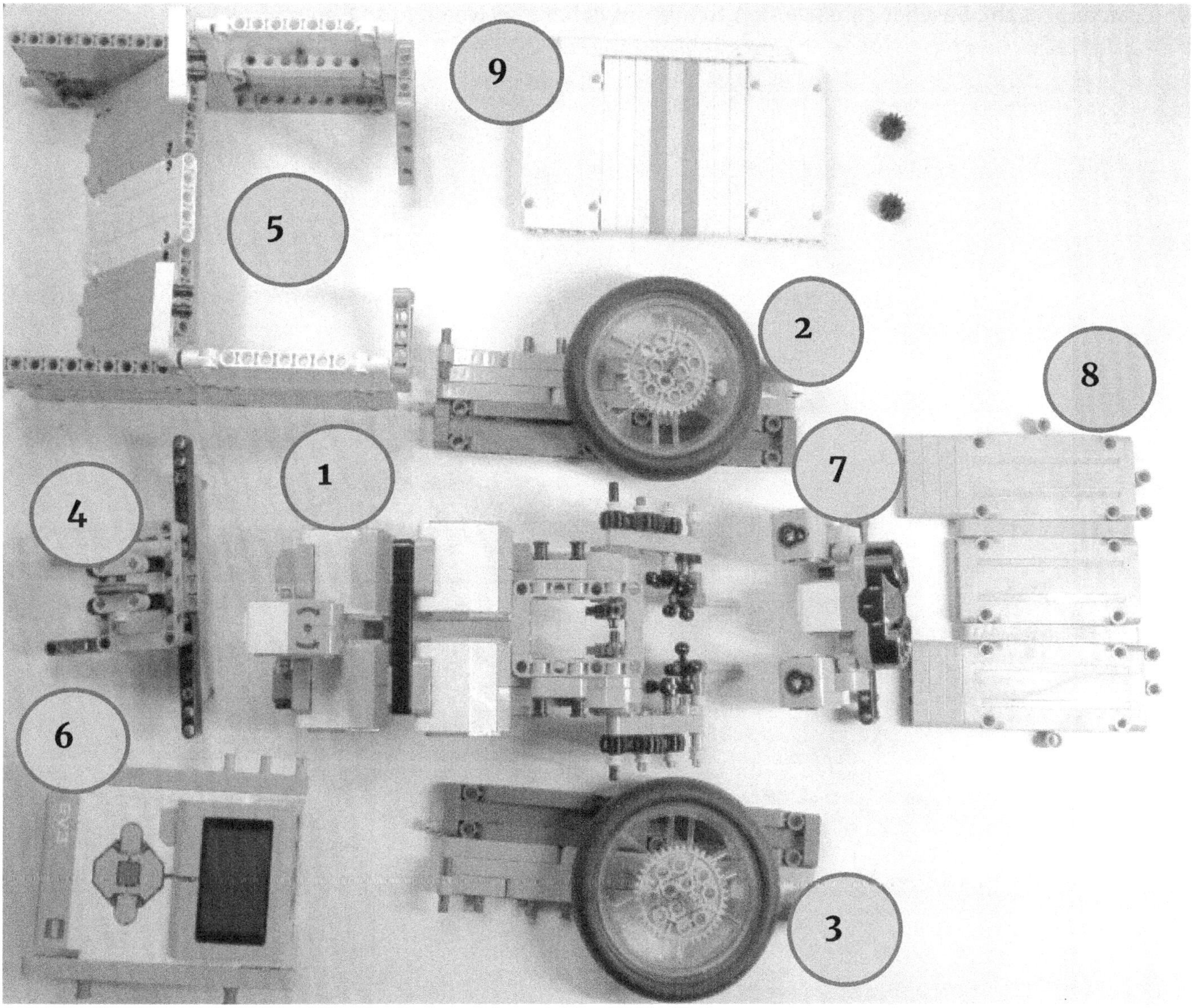

This is how the Basebot will look after the construction is complete. Provided that you have all the parts, you can expect the Basebot construction to take anywhere between 3 to 12 hours.

1- Motor and gyro sensor assembly

Collect parts shown in the next picture. The parts used in the 2 gear assemblies are shown later in the book. Precision is required in building this assembly as it is the heart of the Basebot, it determines how the wheels are placed and it allows the robot's structure to form. The Basebot is very compact and because of that the tolerances for error are very low.

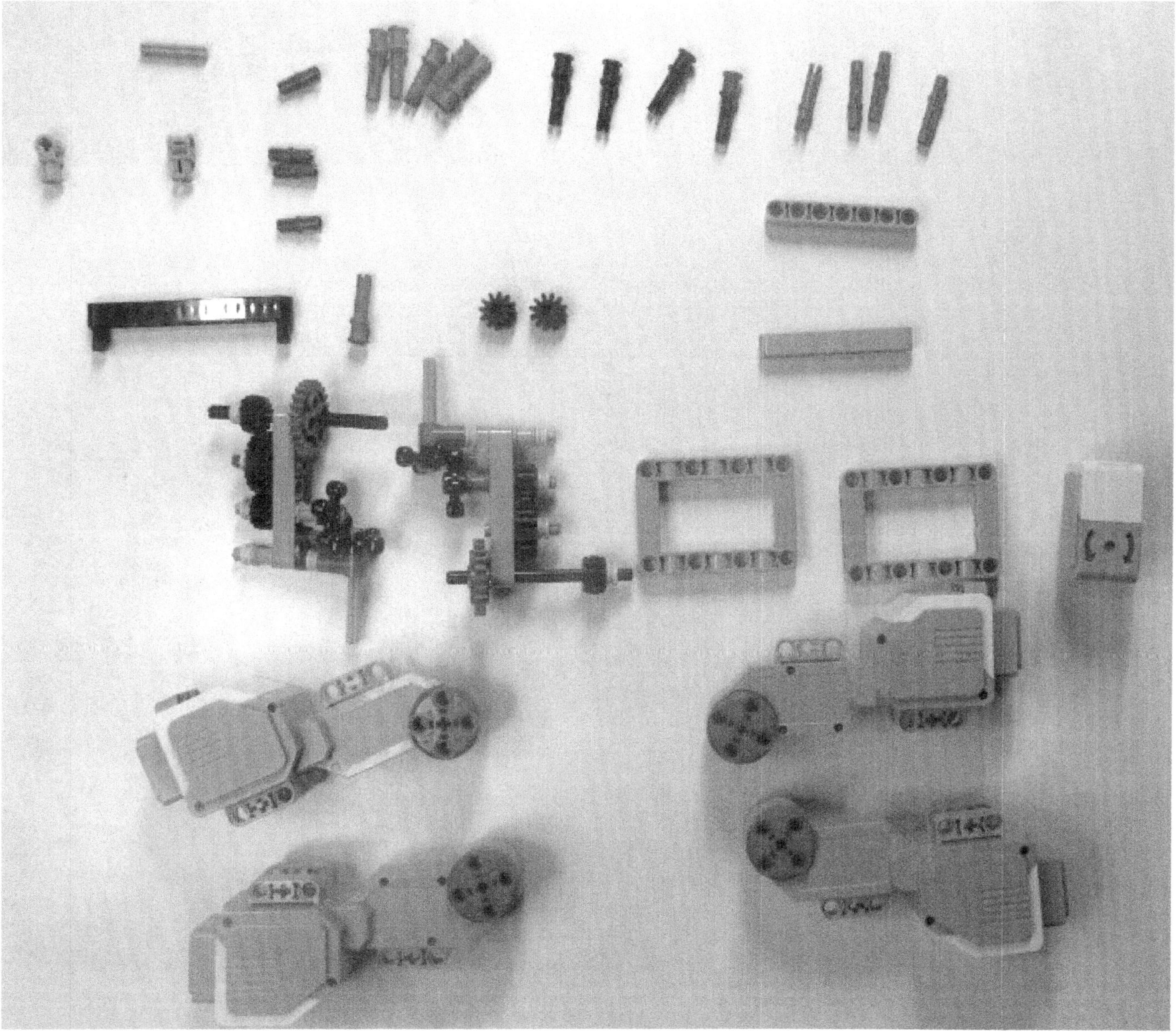

Start building as per the instructions below.

Precisely connecting the 2 motors with one hole overlapping each other is very important.

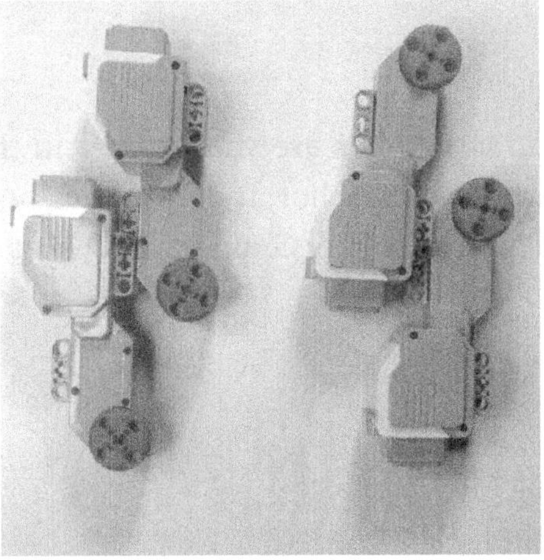

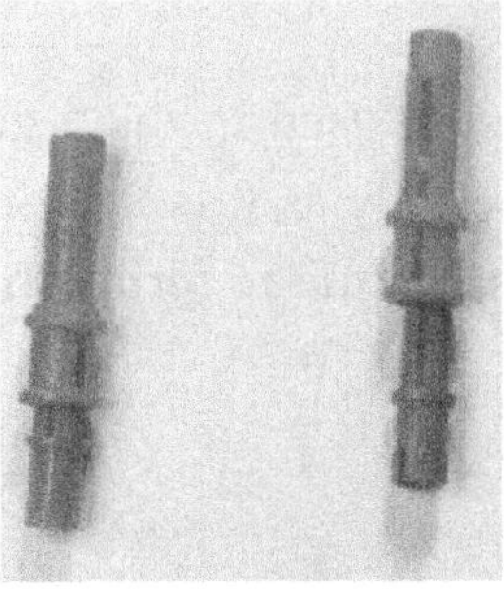

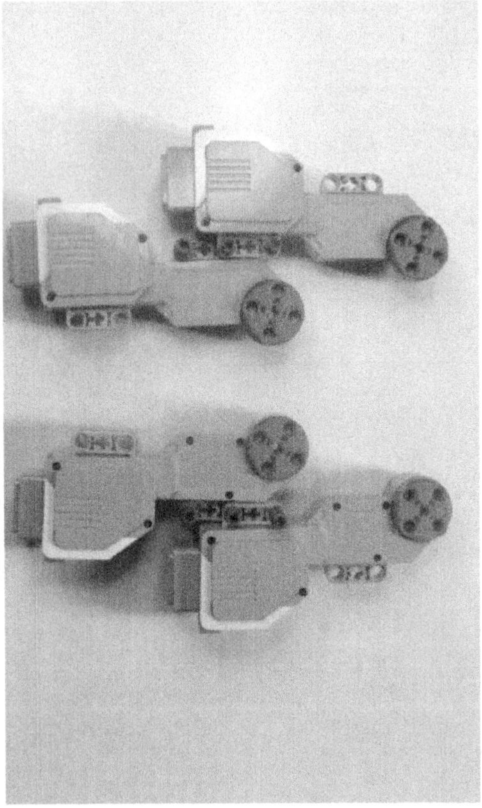

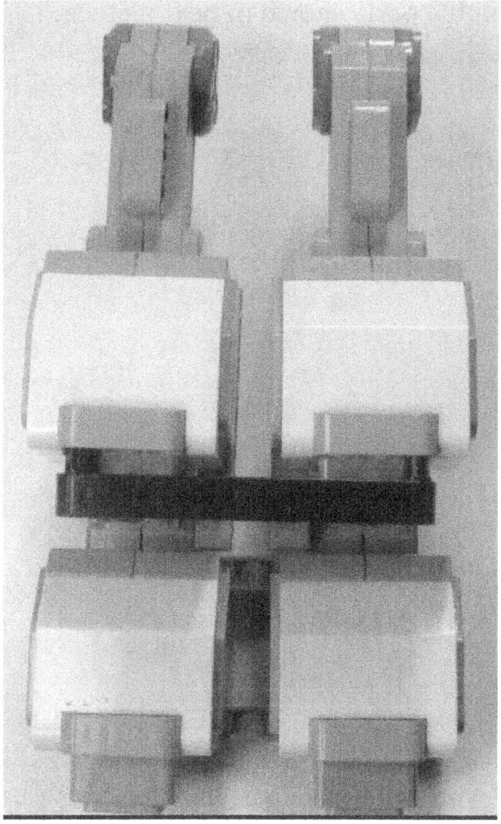

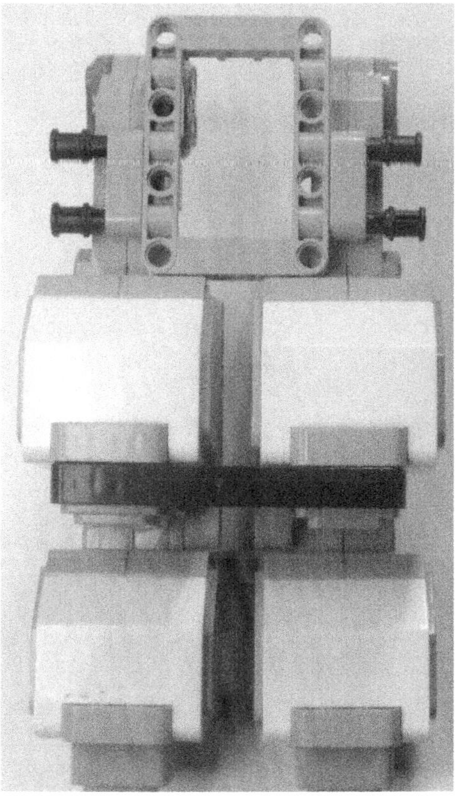

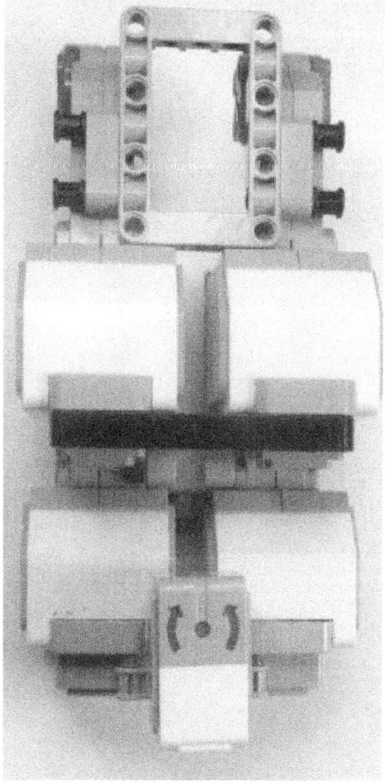

Gear sub-assembly parts shown in next picture.

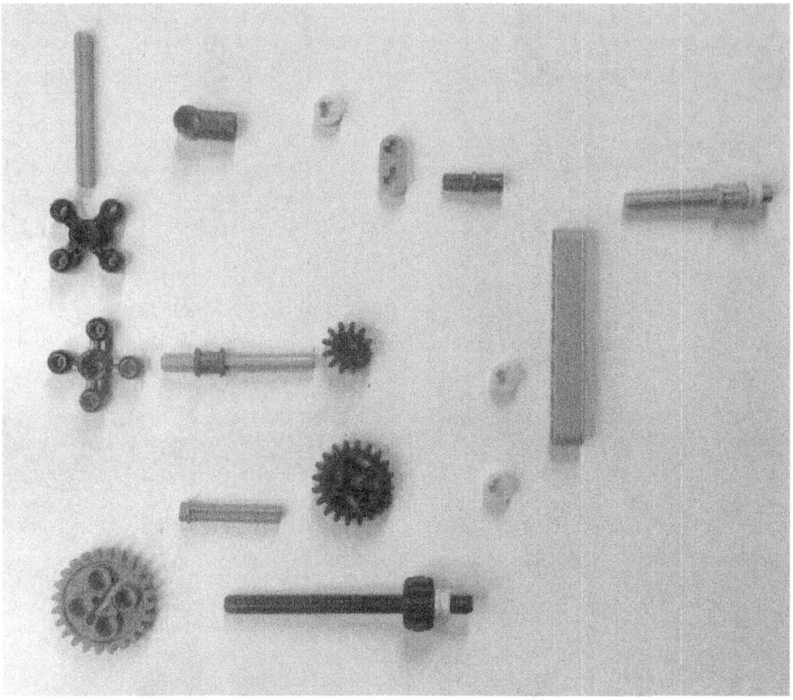

As you can see, you will be using a lot of methods you learned in the 'How to Design strong and efficiently' section in this gear assembly. You will also be improvising on the assembly you had learnt in 'Gear coupling -7'.

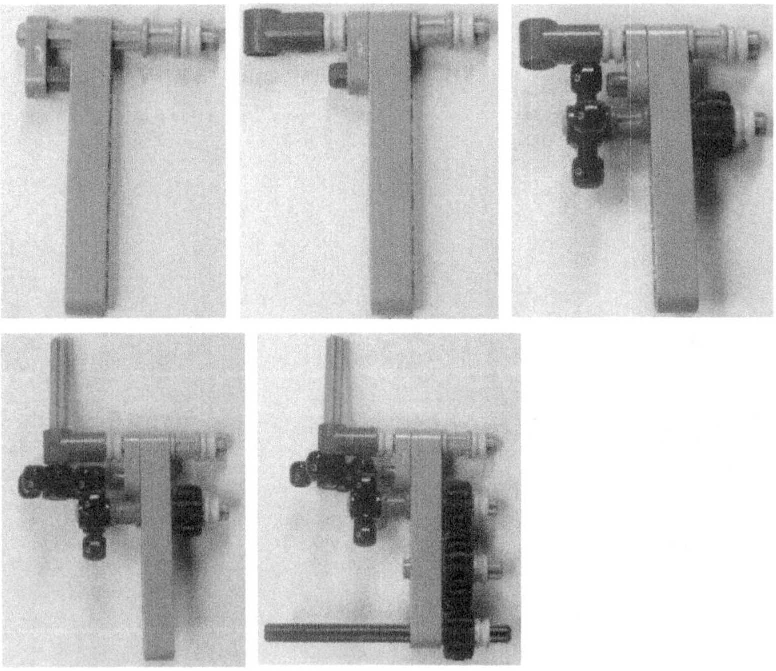

Attach the gear sub-assembly to the arm motor.

2- Wheel assembly (1st wheel)

Use the wheels and tires that you have ordered as per my recommendation in 'Additional Parts to Buy' section.

1- Wheel Technic Street Bike 81mm D. x 28 51378 – 1 total,

1- Tire Technic Street Bike (8420) - Narrow, Front 51380 – 1 total

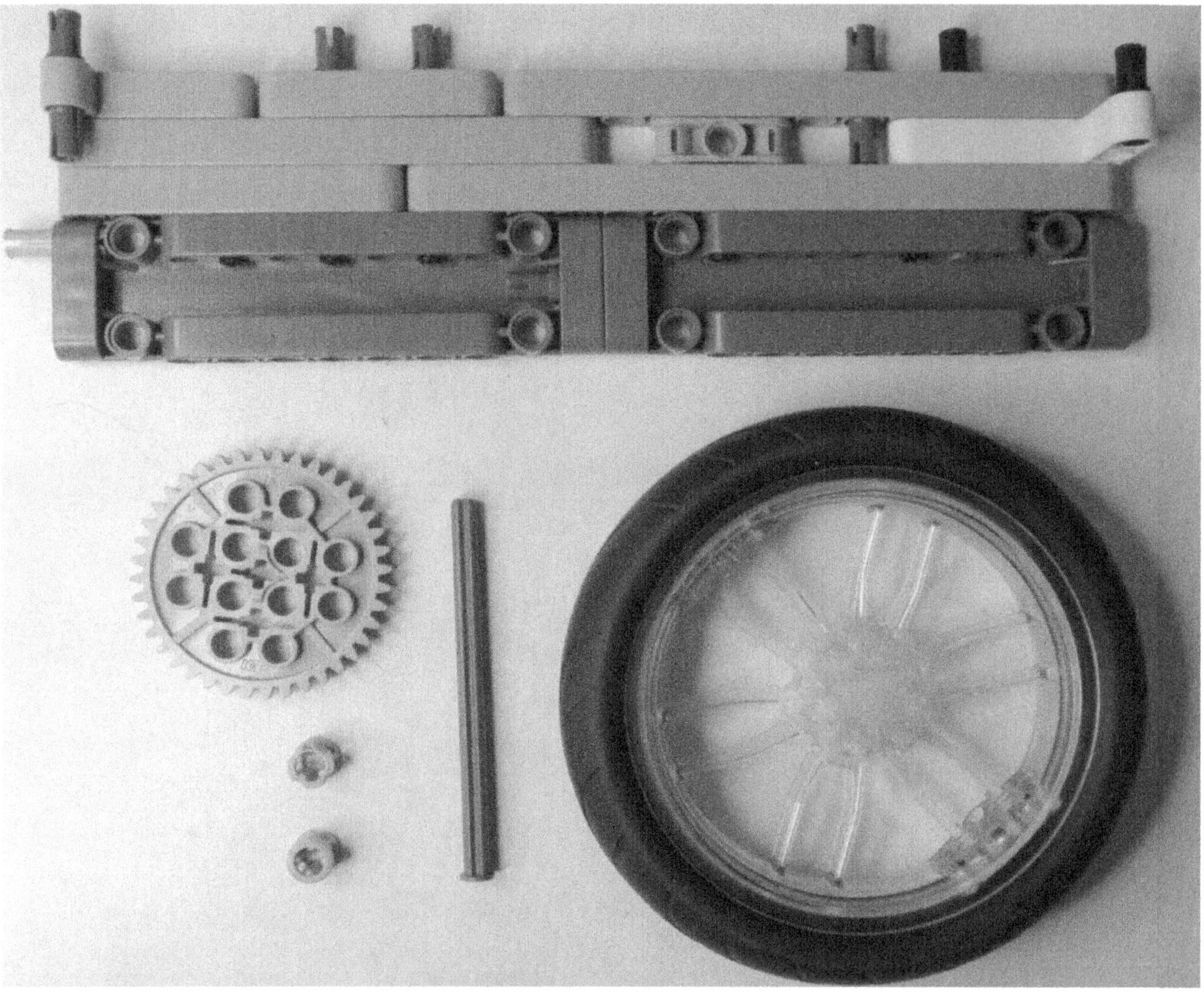

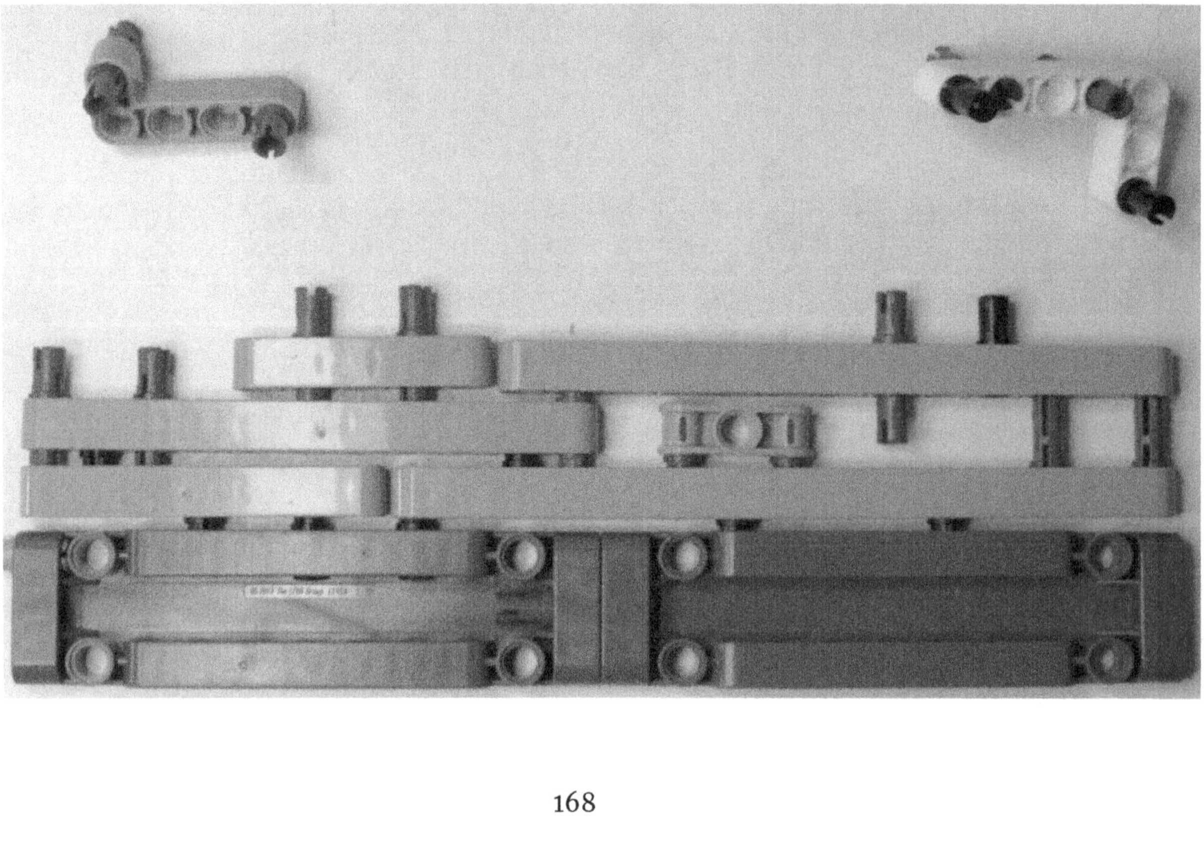

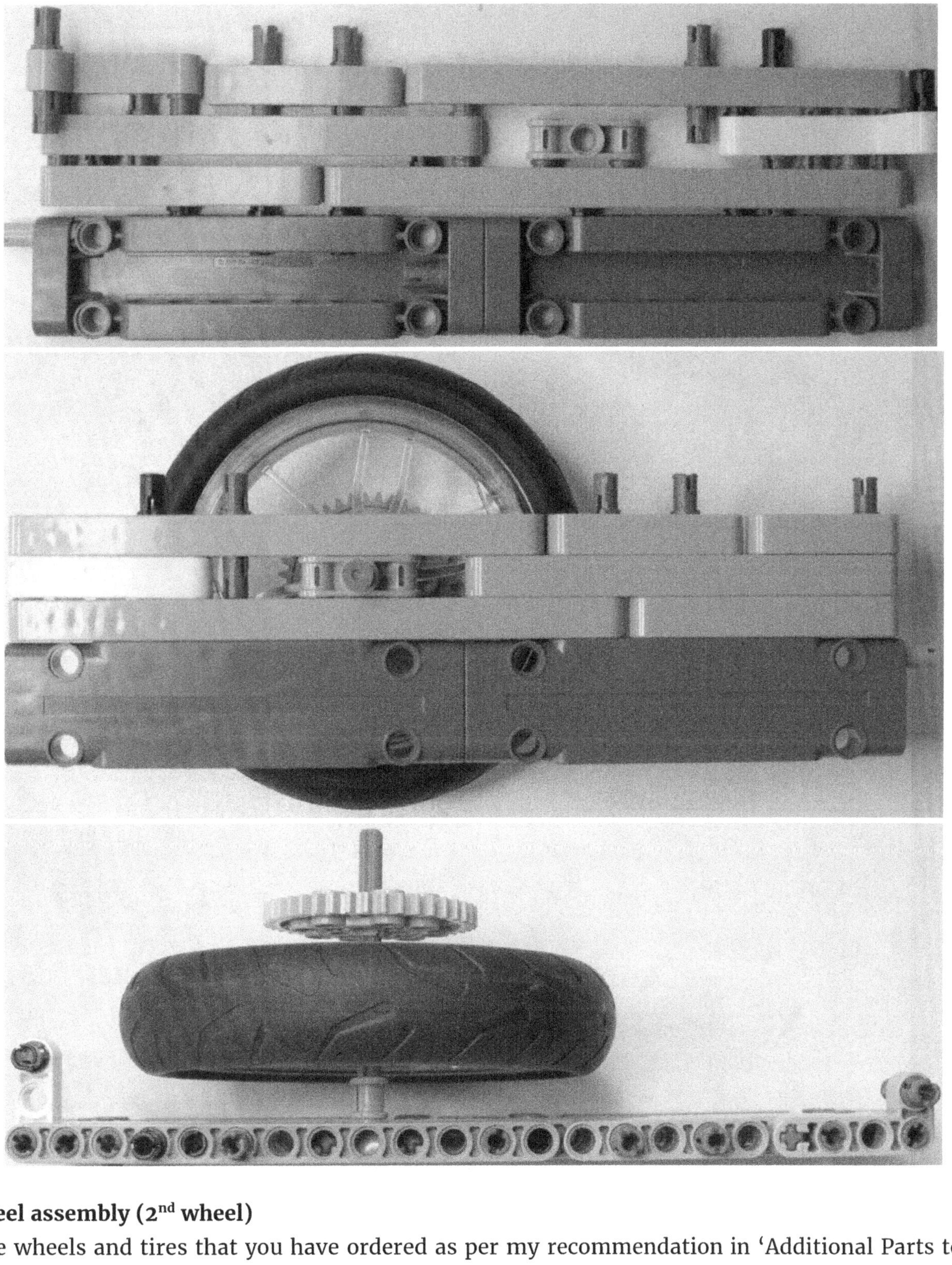

3- Wheel assembly (2nd wheel)

Use the wheels and tires that you have ordered as per my recommendation in 'Additional Parts to Buy' section.

1- Wheel Technic Street Bike 81mm D. x 28 51378 – 1 total

1- Tire Technic Street Bike (8420) - Narrow, Front 51380 – 1 total

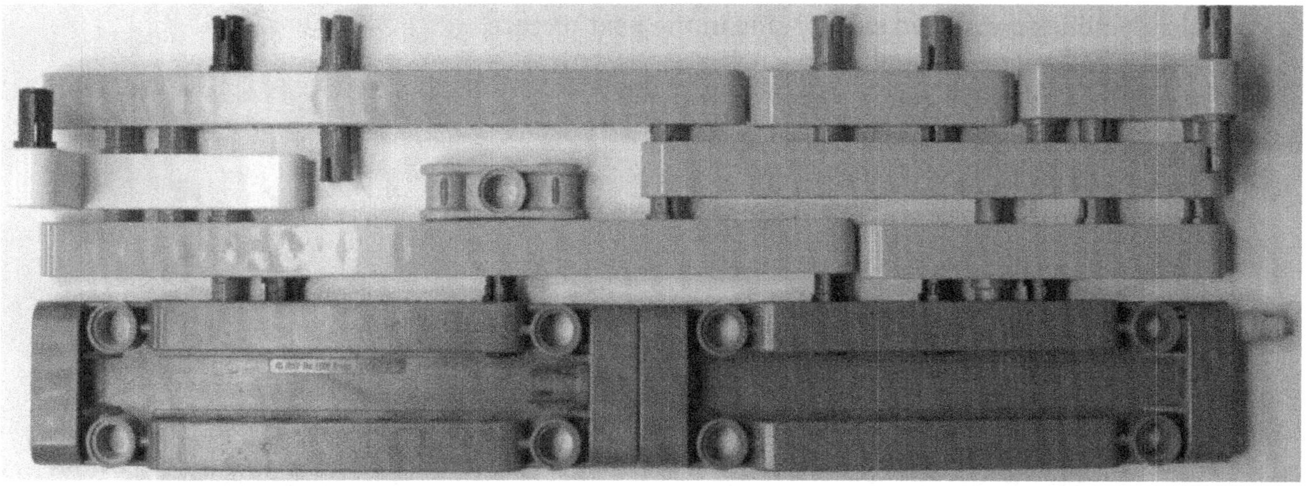

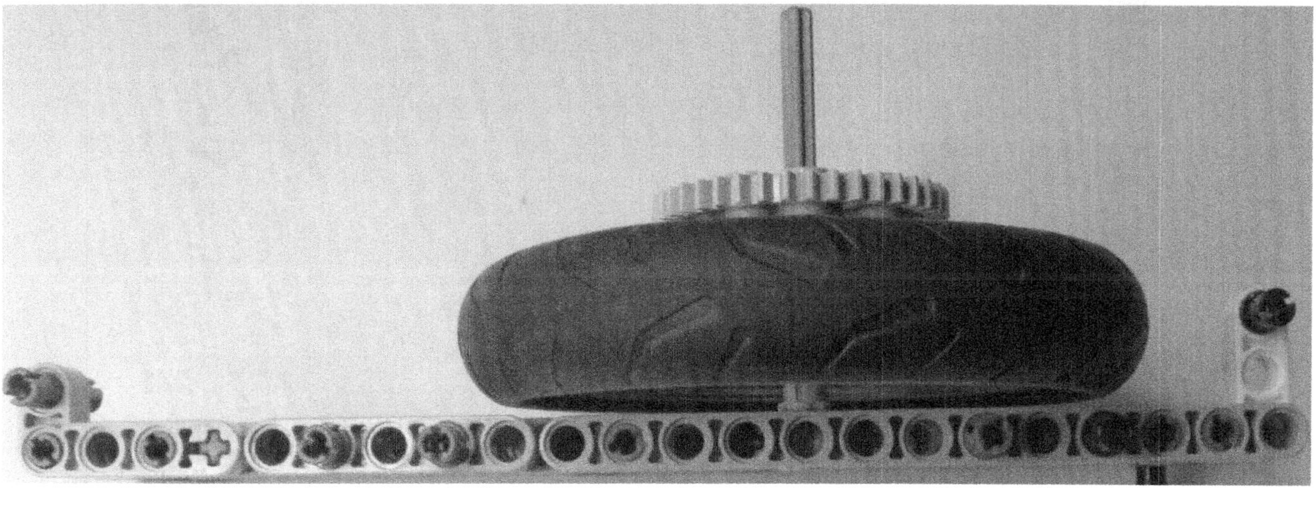

The 2-wheel assemblies are shown side by side in the next picture.

4- Third Wheel Assembly

You will be using the same wheel assembly you used on our training robot or you can use the ball wheel assembly. Just connect it to a few more parts as shown in the next pictures.

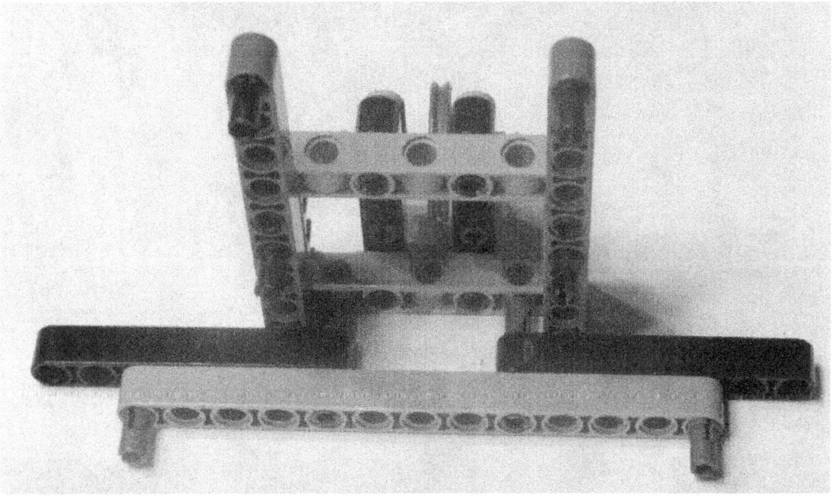

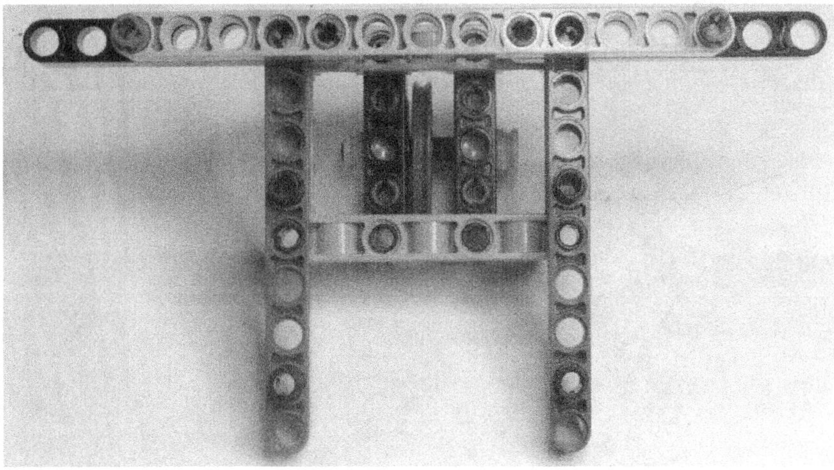

Connect all 3-wheel assemblies to the 'Motor and Gyro Sensor Assembly'. Make sure to push the motor axles all the way in. Squeeze the Wheel assemblies at the point shown.

This is the upside-down view of the back of the robot. Connect the 'third wheel assembly' as shown in the picture.

This is how the Basebot chassis should look after this step. It should be 19 peg holes wide, including corners and should be 22 peg holes long including corners. Having a perfectly rectangular shape is essential.

This is how the Basebot chassis should look from the front and back.
Front:

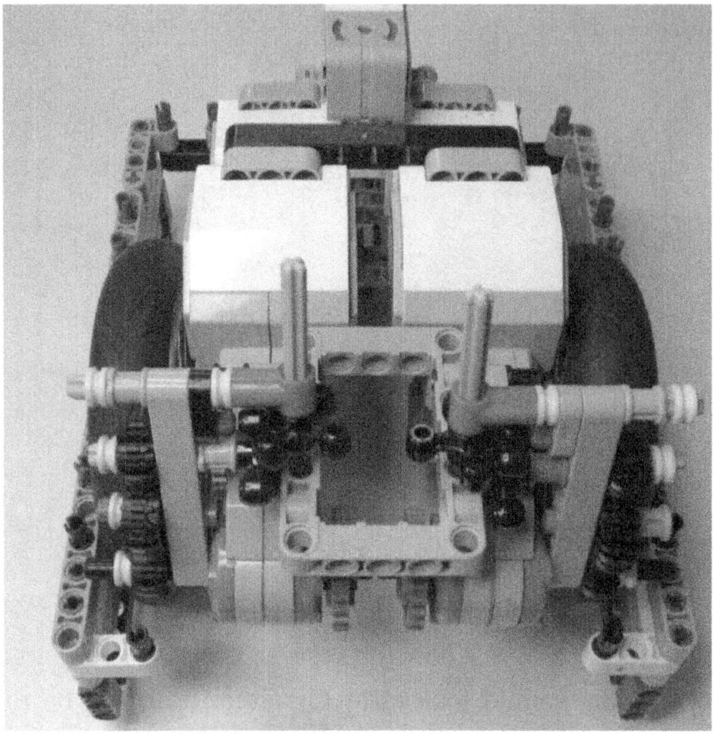

Back:

5- Body frame assembly

Construct the following using plates, beams and other parts as shown in the next picture.

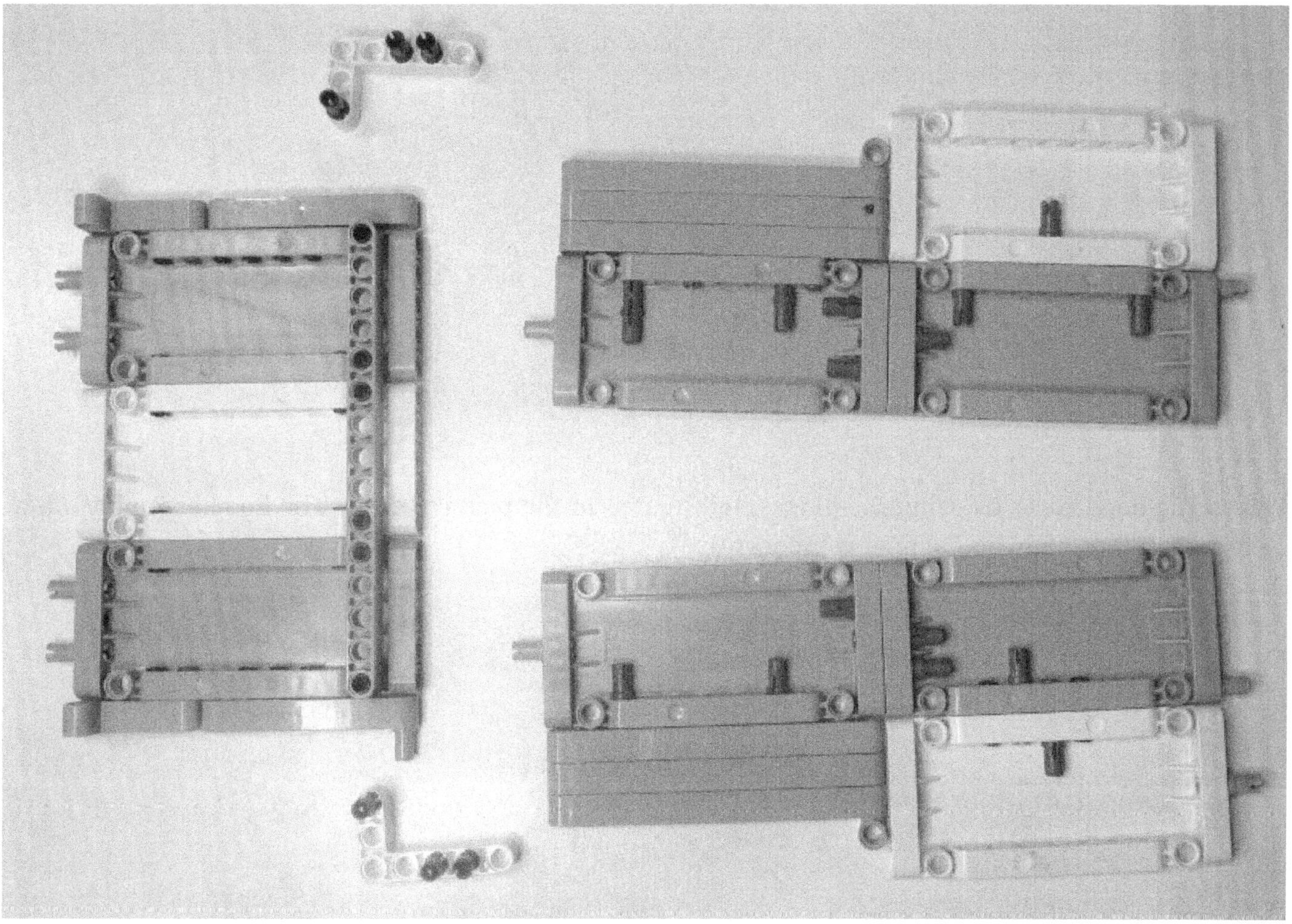

Attach the body frame assembly walls to the Basebot chassis. The Left wall attachment is shown in the next picture.

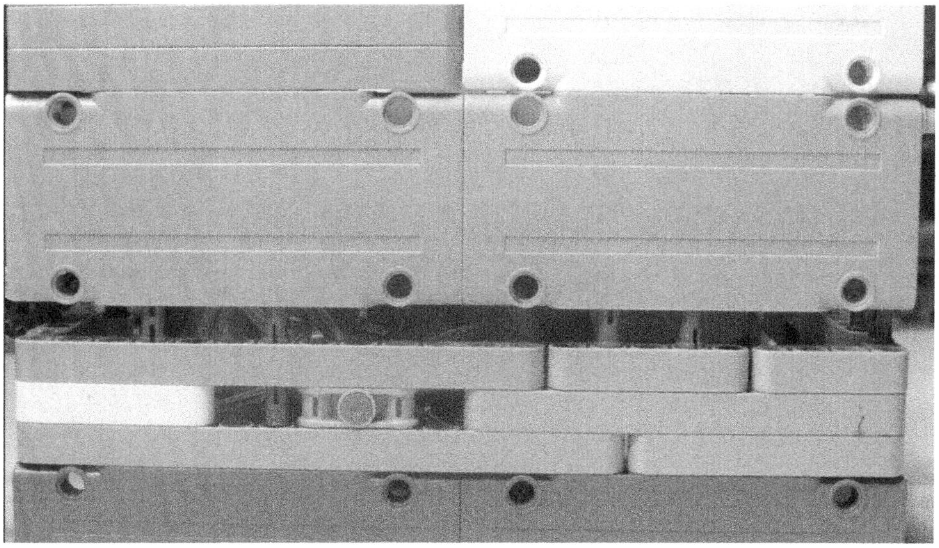

The Right wall attachment is shown in the next picture.

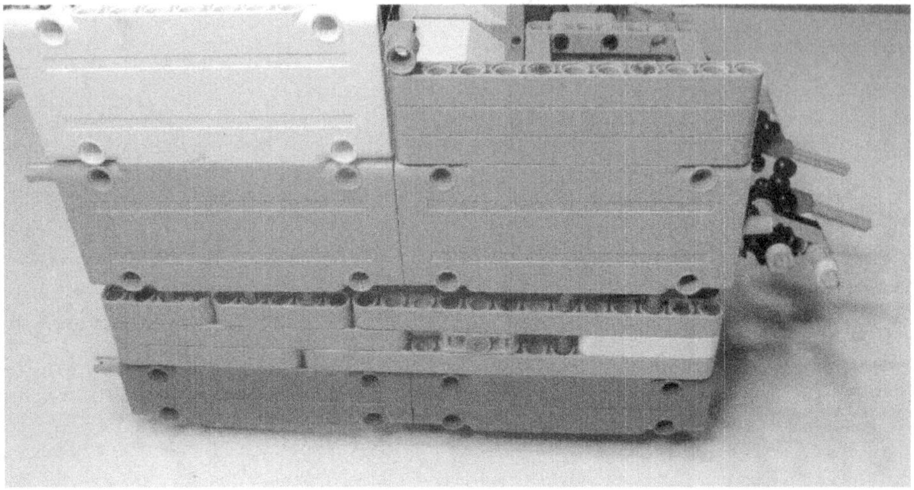

Attach the hood cover by using the hinges highlighted in the picture below. The hood assembly allows easy access to the Basebot' s inner components.

Attach the 2 angular beams to hold the Brick assembly.

6- Brick Assembly

Construct the brick assembly as shown in the next picture. The brick assembly construction will allow you to change the batteries easily.

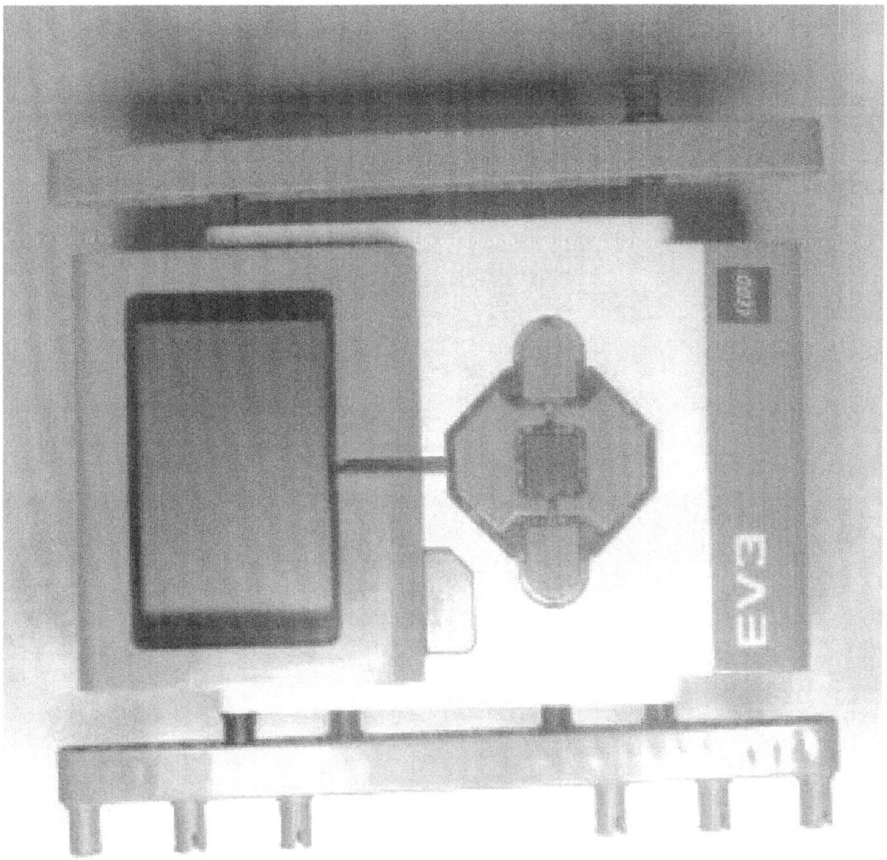

7- Sensor Array Assembly

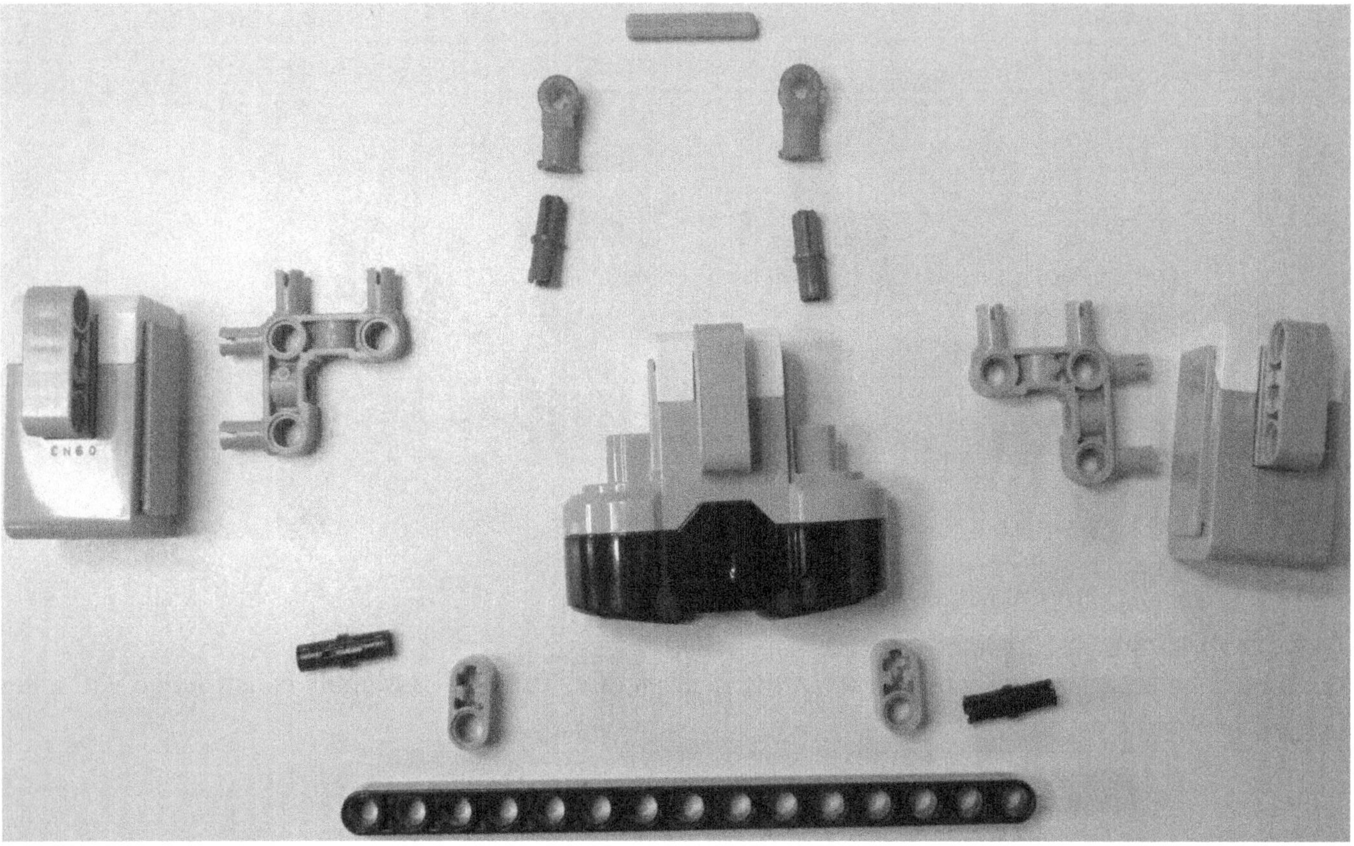

Next picture shows how the entire assembly looks once constructed.

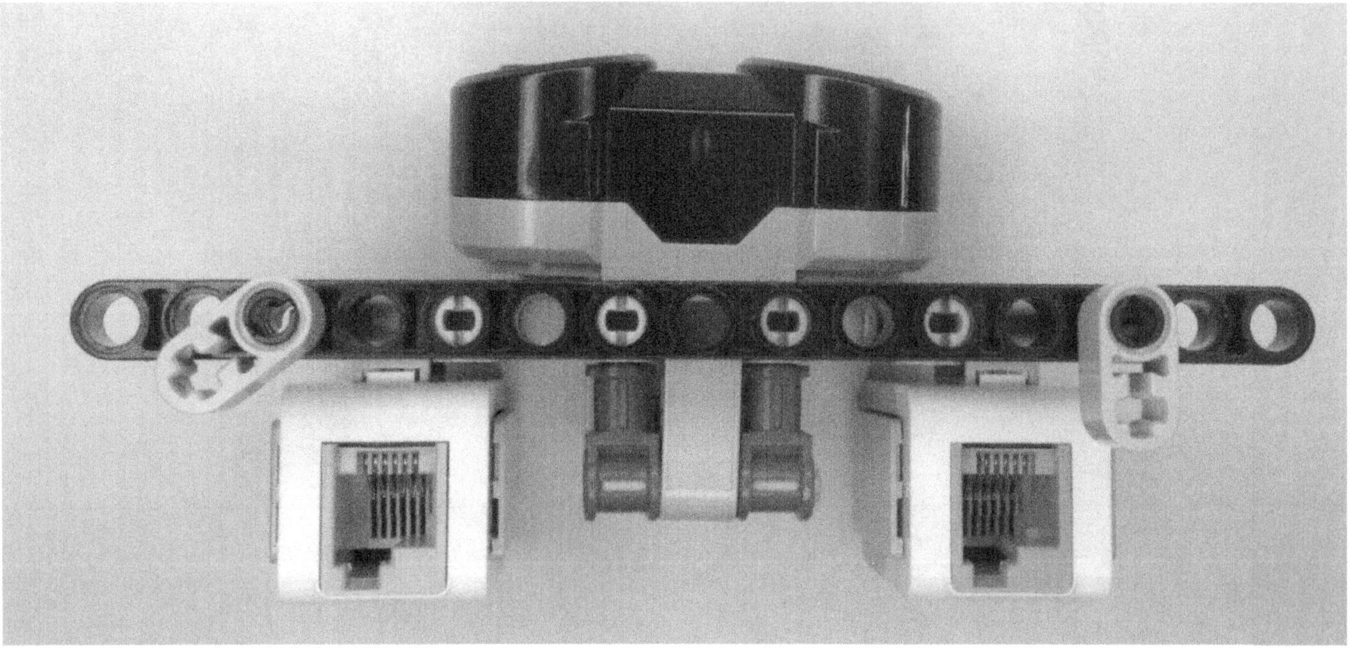

The two angular connectors are connected to the color sensors and the ultrasonic sensor is attached using the axle. The axle goes in the third peg hole of the ultrasonic sensor. Initially the assembly may not seem rigid but once the angular connectors are attached to the beam, the assembly will strongly fix the color sensors' and ultrasonic sensors' positions.

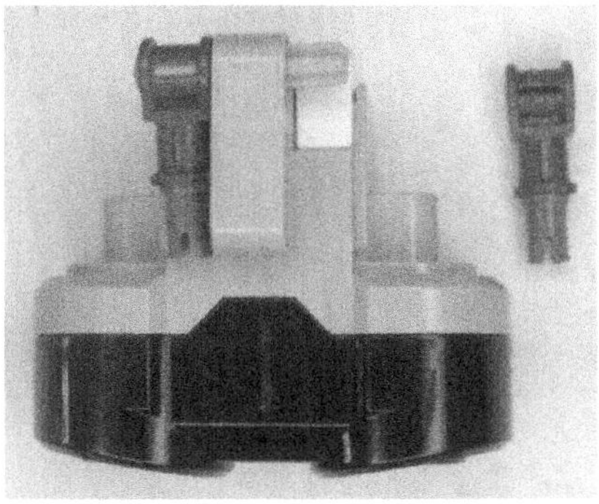
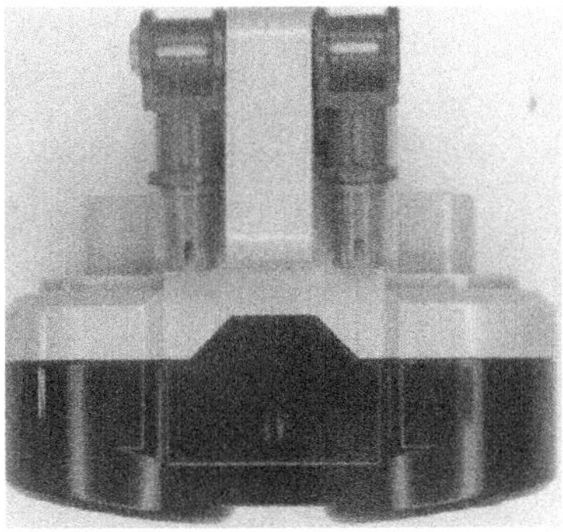
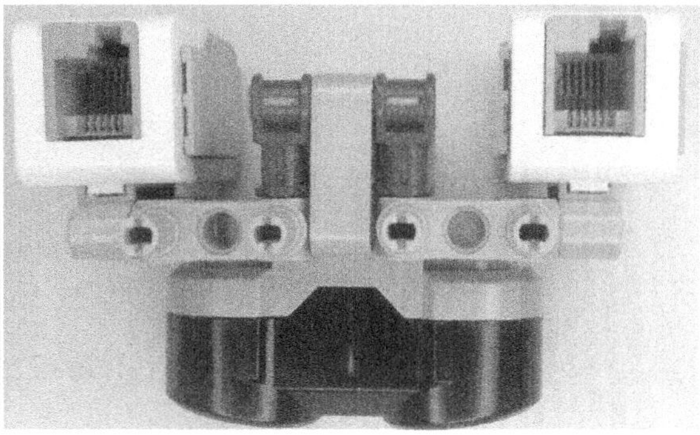

Attach the beam to the assembly. The top 2 2-module beams are only for support and are connected to the beam by 1 peg each.

Route all the sensor wires through the gap between the two motors.
Connect all the wires to all the motors and the sensor array (except the gyro sensor) and keep it ready for the brick. You should tag the wires with small stickers.

Connect all the wires to the brick and then connect the brick assembly to the Basebot. At this point the wires will create deformations in the walls, but the Basebot' s perfect rectangular cube shape will be restored once all points of physical connection between the Basebot housing and brick assembly are completed.

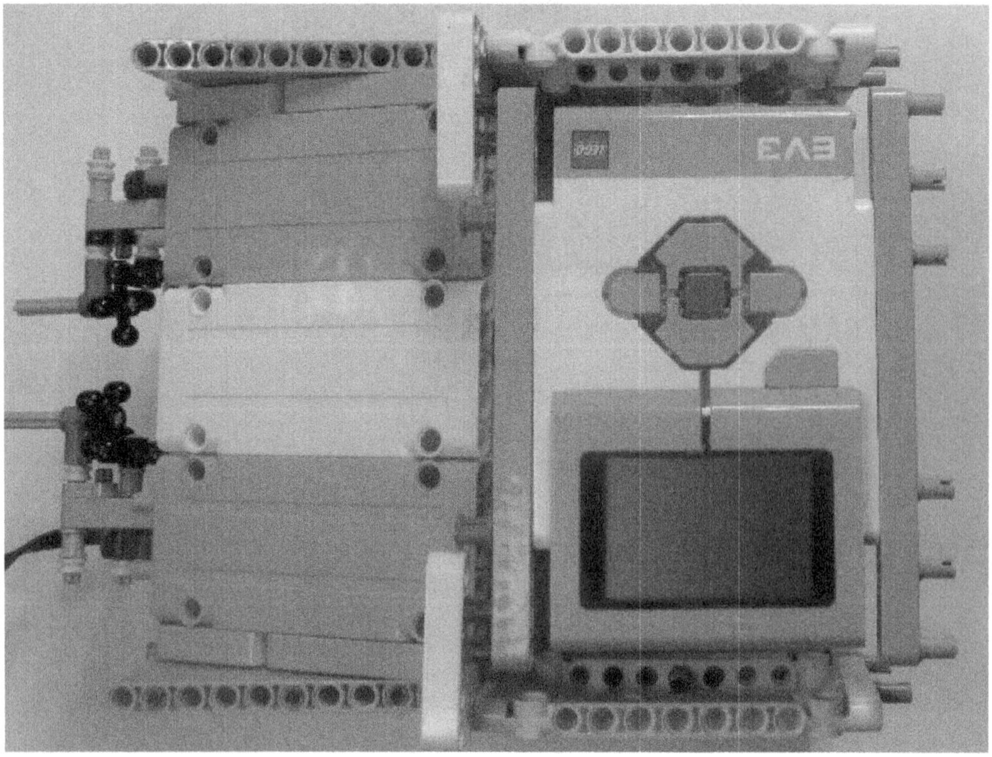

Finally connect the Brick assembly from the back using 2 frames. At this point your Basebot should look like a perfect rectangular prism.

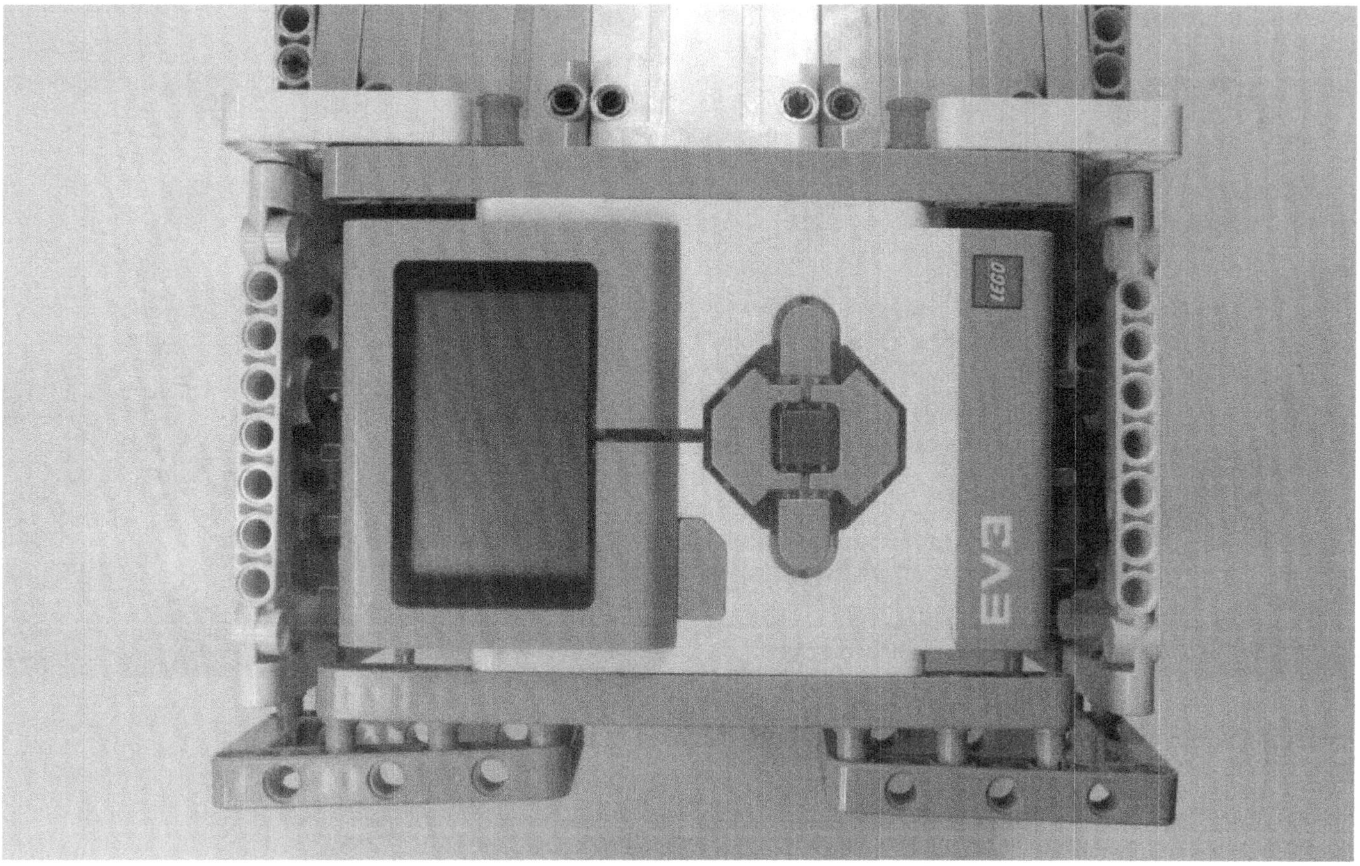

Connect the sensor array to the front angular beams of the Basebot chassis.

Insert the arm assembly axles into the front hood cover.

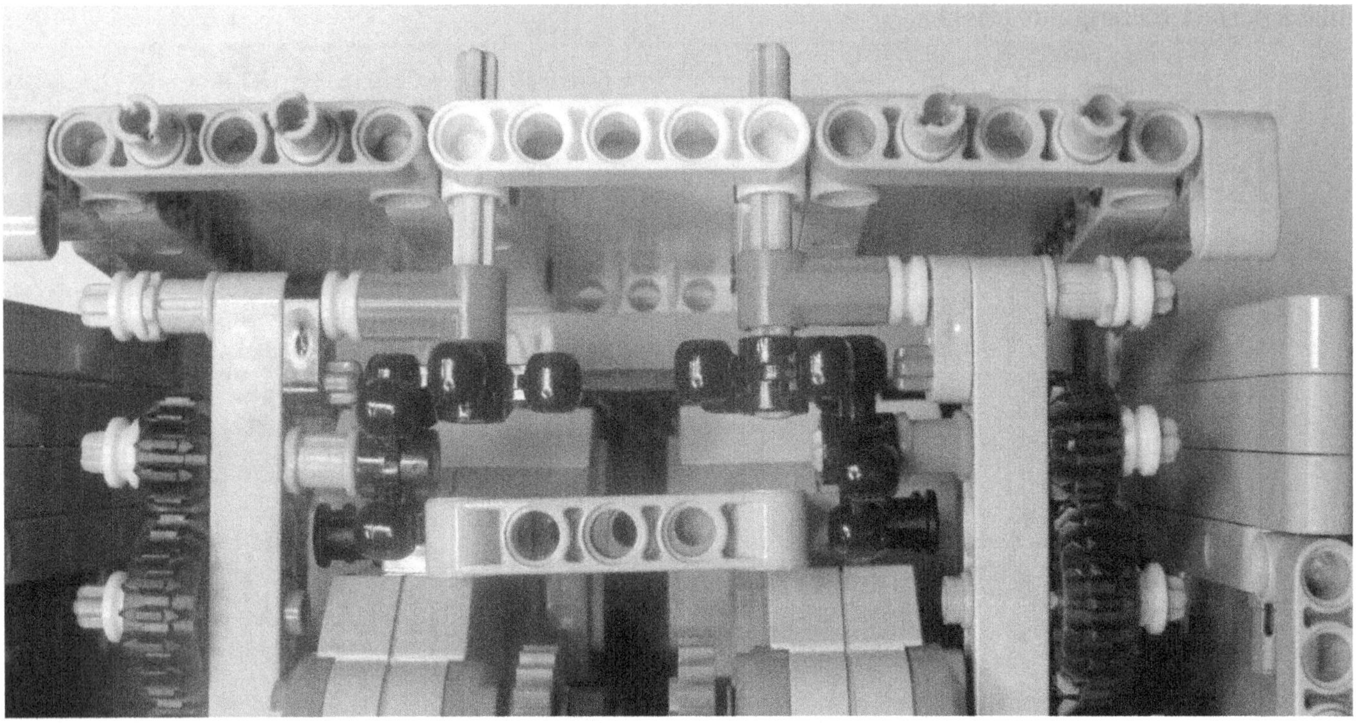

Attach the bevel gears, making sure to support the axle from the bottom.

Make sure that wires are routed properly. Use friction pegs and axles to securely route the wires.

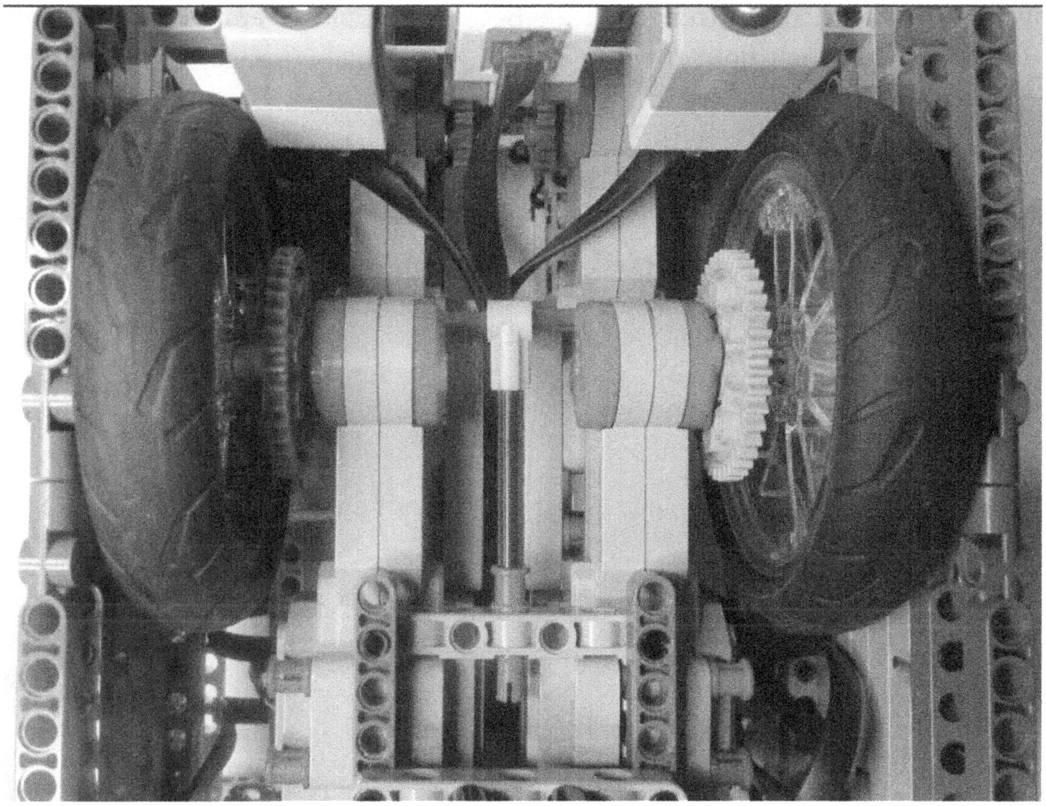

8-Front cover assembly

Construct front cover as shown in the picture and attach it to the Basebot.

The front cover provides structural strength to the Basebot and blocks ambient light from reaching the color sensors. To have accurate light intensity readings, the color sensors should be shielded from ambient light.

9-Back cover assembly

Construct the back-cover assembly and connect the Gyro sensor before attaching the back-cover assembly. The back cover provides easy access to the Gyro sensor for 'Hot Resetting' the Gyro sensor by disconnecting wire and re-connecting them after 1 minute, while the Brick is still 'ON'.

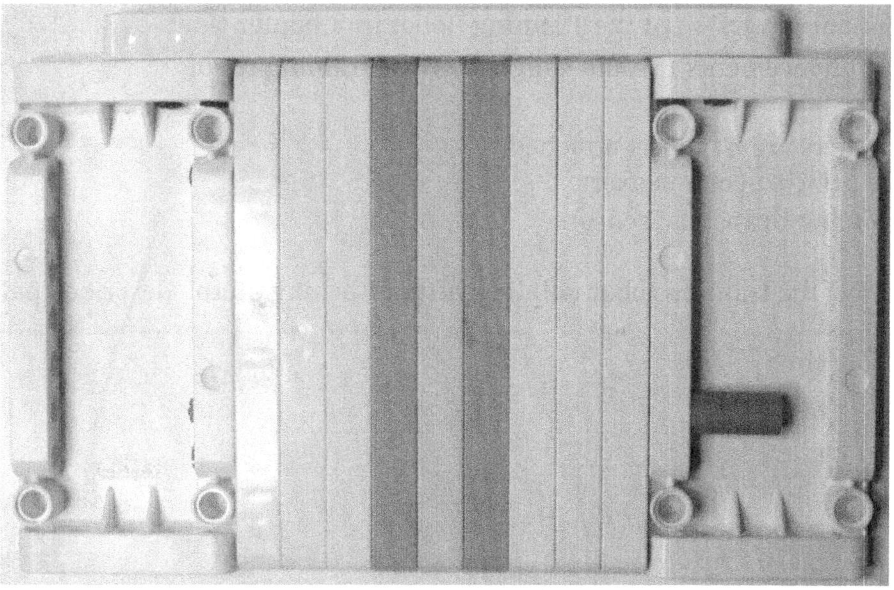

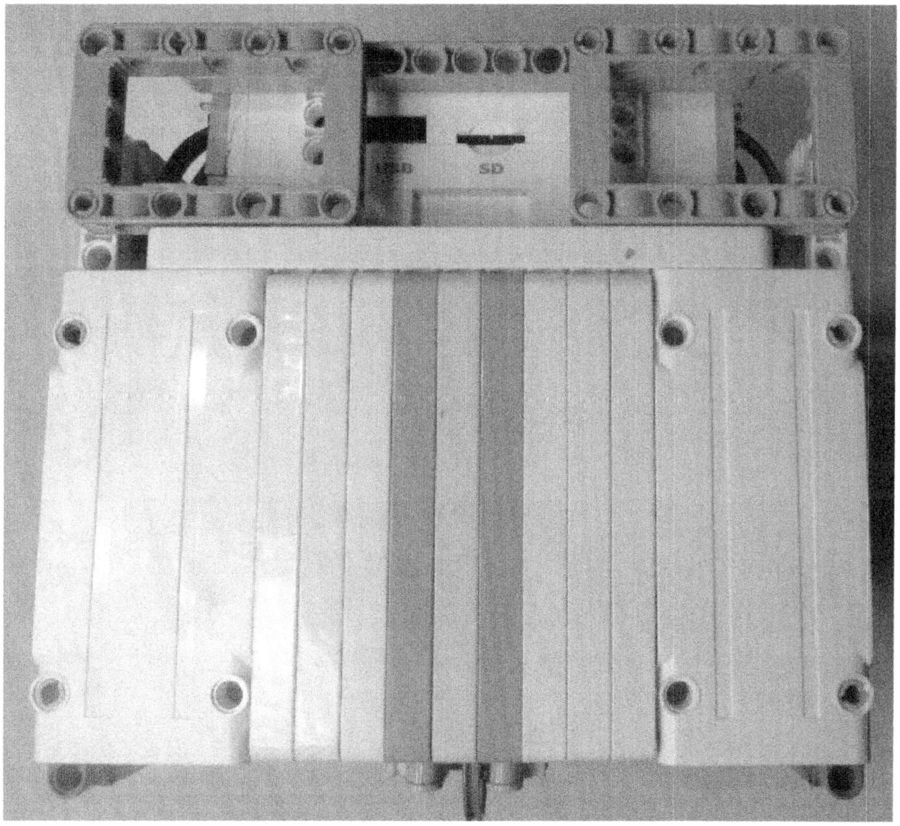

Turn on the Basebot and program it to move forward 8 rotations. Resolve any issues related to drift by checking loose wheels and wires that may be touching the wheels.

Option-2- Use an enhanced version of the Training Robot in 'Chapter One'
The following is the enhancements I would suggest for the training robot

1. Make sure there are 4 motors attached.
2. You should attach 2 color sensors
3. Gyro sensor and Ultrasonic sensors

Next picture shows how the training robot will look after attaching all the described parts

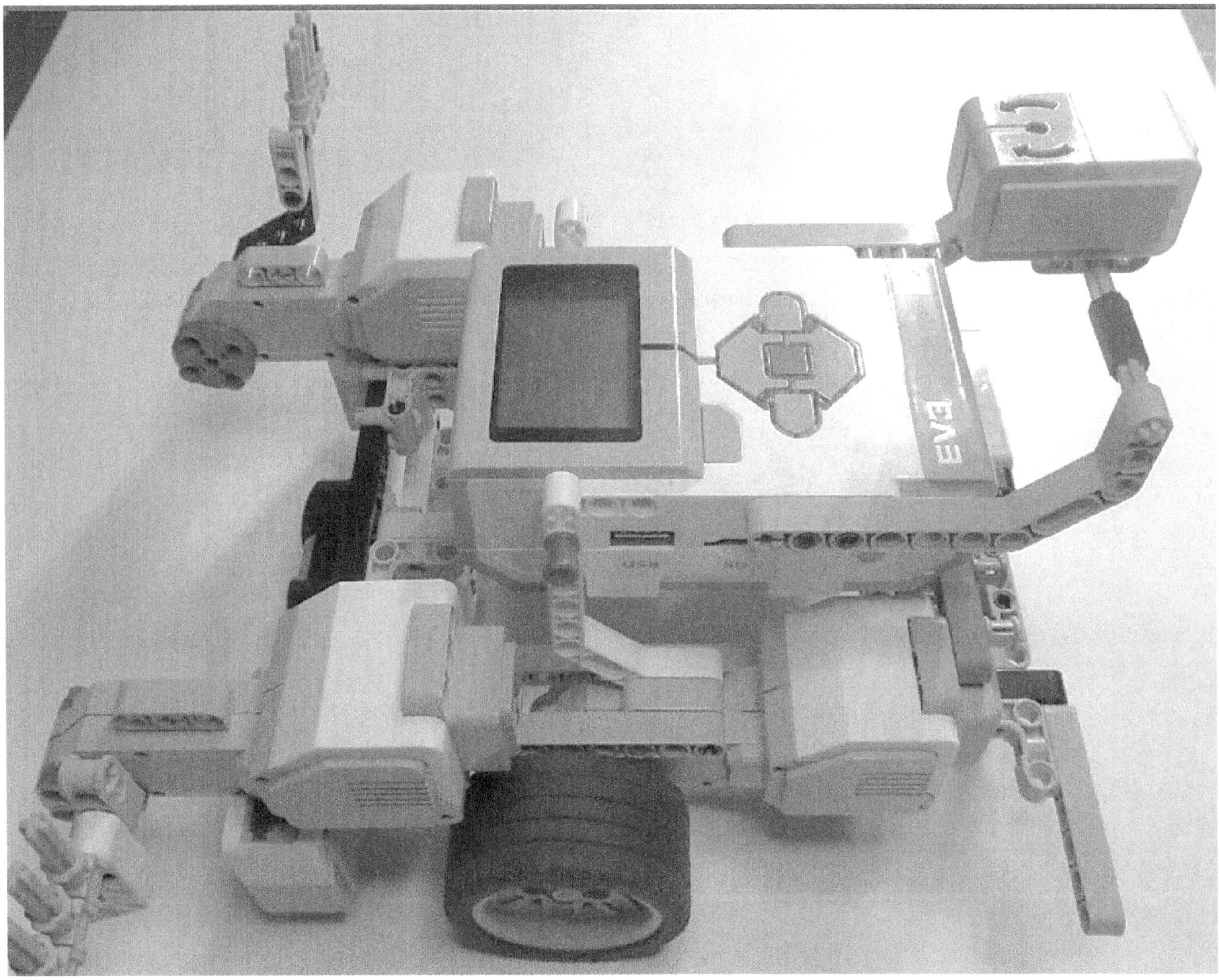

To enhance the robot, follow these steps

1- Attach the following parts or assemblies to the training robot as shown in the next picture. These parts will make the robot more robust by adding a chassis design and supporting the wheel axles at 2 points to prevent bending. In addition, you will also be changing the way the arm motors are attached and will be making that connection more rigid. You will also need to attach 2 color sensors to the robot, right in front of and close to the wheels in front. During the competition, you need to align the robot properly with the wall to start the robot run. To achieve this, you should attach 2 beams at the back to allow for good wall alignment.

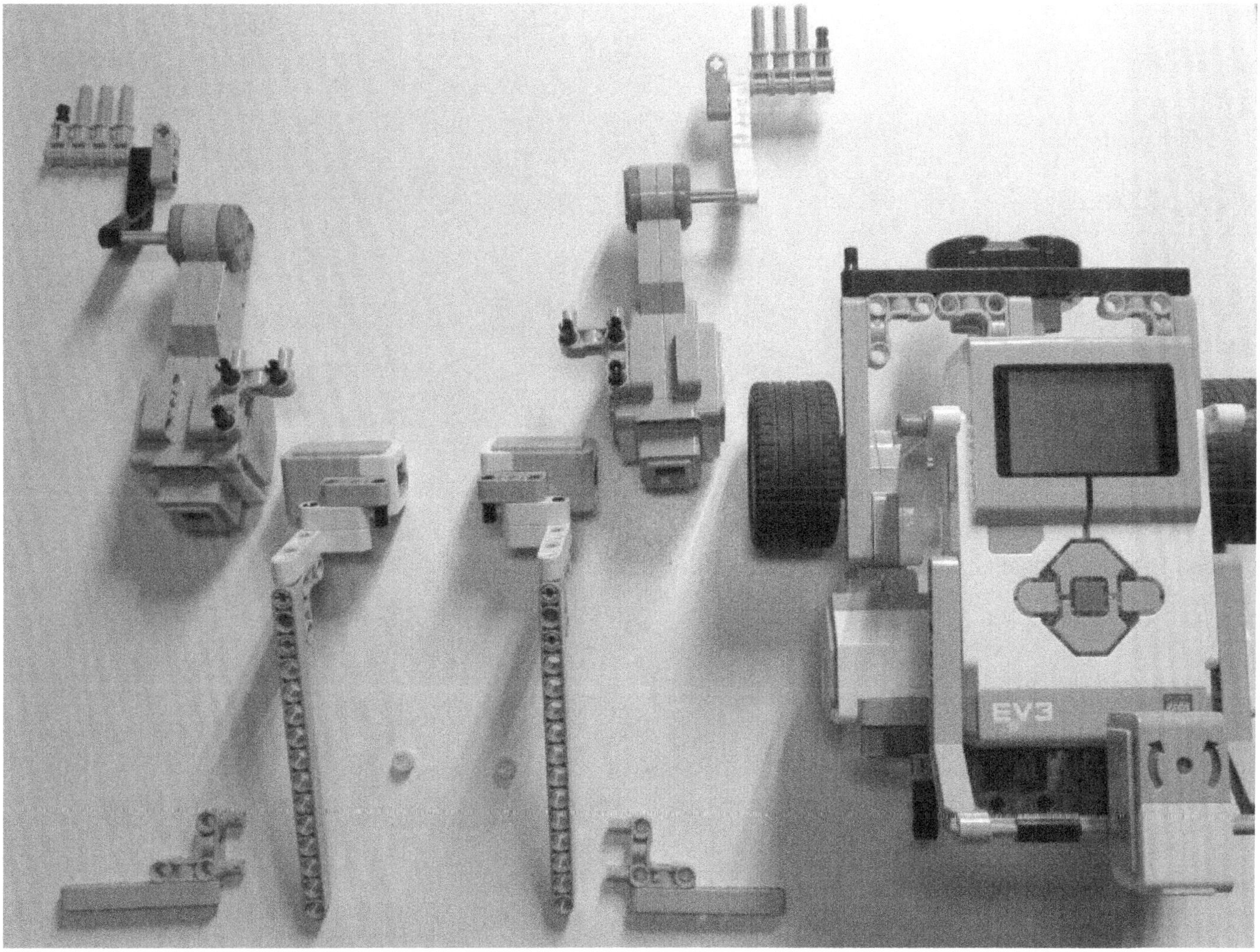

Let us attach the wall aligners first.

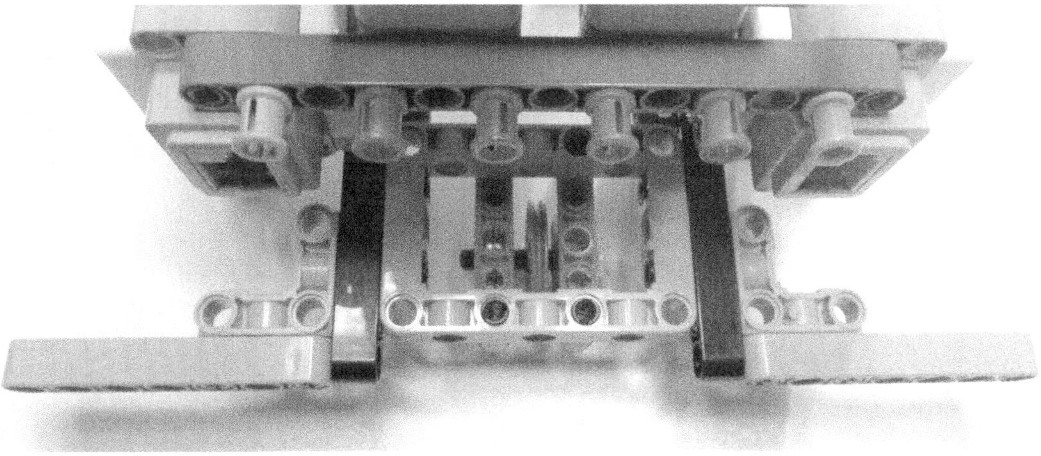

Create 2 sets of the chassis beam and color sensor assemblies.

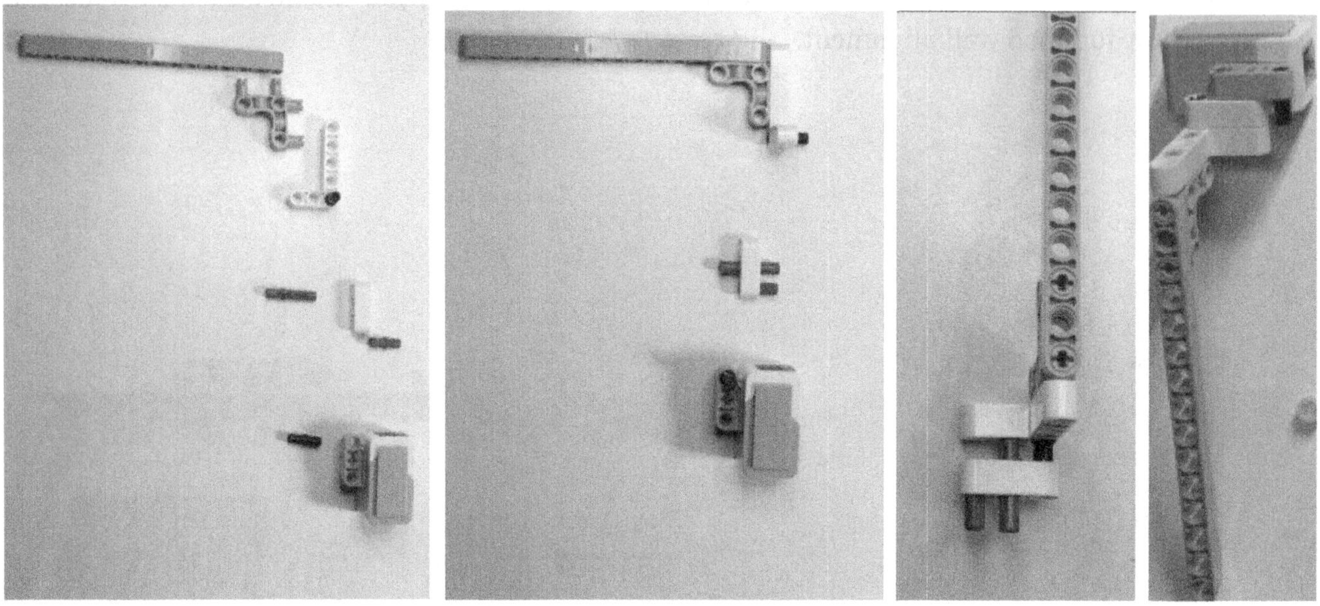

Attach the left chassis and color sensor assembly(left).

Complete attaching both chassis and color sensor assemblies

Attach both the arm motors.

For option 2 you will keep attaching new arms or arm assemblies to the motors for every robot run.

ATTACHMENTS

In this section I will show you how to create the attachment shell and also cover some of the major activity assemblies you will use in your robot runs such as the claw, lift, conveyor belt, pneumatic, and box activity assemblies.

I would recommend creating one shell for each of your robot runs. If you have decided on 3 robot runs, you should create 3 shells so that you can create 3 distinct attachments. Using the same attachment for 2 different runs saves time but usually the location of the activity assemblies needed changes.

The following picture represents an example of what you might take to the competition. Attachment-1 has a conveyor belt, box, and claw activity assemblies but the assemblies' relative positions are different than how they are positioned on Attachment-2.

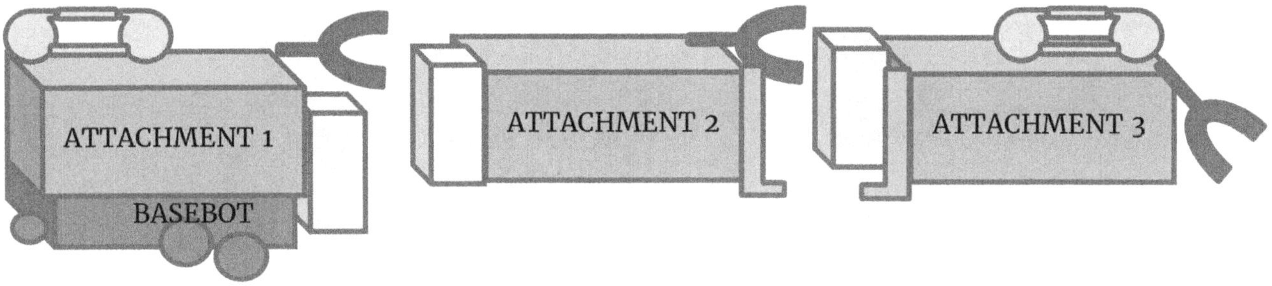

The final attachment shell is shown in the next picture. It will have smooth walls on the inside to easily slip it on top of the Basebot. It will also include wheels on one of its sides to allow the robot to perform a wall follow, if required.

You can always use less plates on the attachment shells but you should make sure that you are still able to easily change attachments within 10 seconds.

Attachments may need preparation for certain activity assemblies before the run. For example, you may need to put something in the box activity assembly, to deliver it on a certain part of the mat. If the piece you are going to put in the box is already available in the base then you should prepare your activity assembly before the match starts. If the piece you are going to put in the activity assembly is only going to be available in the base after then first robot run, then you will have to prepare the activity assembly of the next attachment between runs. Making the preparations as smooth and fast as possible is always recommended.

Typically, you should avoid any sensors or motors on the attachments, as that will require you to connect the wires to the brick as part of your preparations. The only exception is the first attachment, which you are allowed to put on the Basebot before the match starts as all preparation can be done ahead of time.

Wall-1 construction:

Construct Wall-1 as shown in the next picture.

Wall-2 construction- Inner wall:

Create Wall-2 as shown in the next picture.

Wall-3 (Front wall)
Create Wall-3 as shown in the next picture.

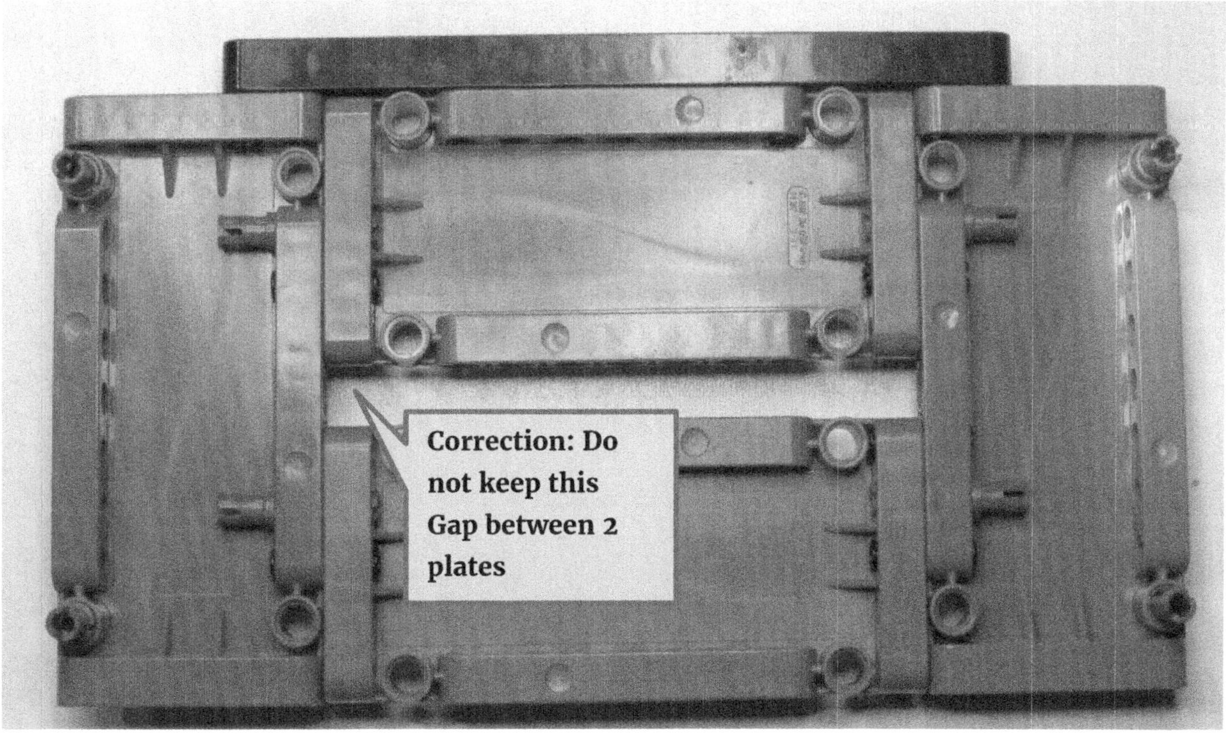

Attach Wall-2(Inner wall) to Wall-3 as shown in the next picture.

Attach Wall-1 to the Wall-2/3 assembly.

Create the front wall sliding wheel assembly and attach it to the black and green wall junction.

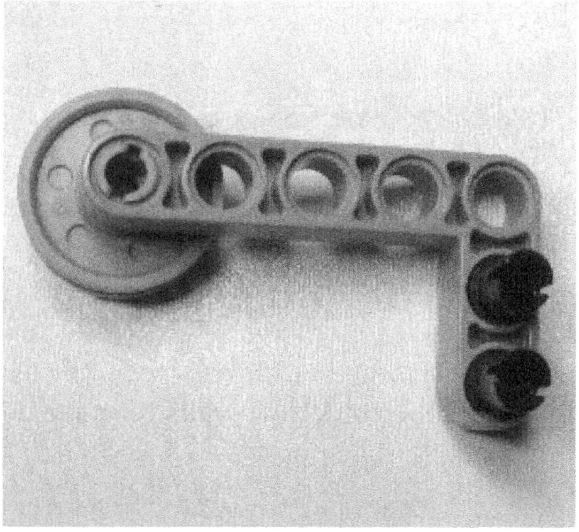

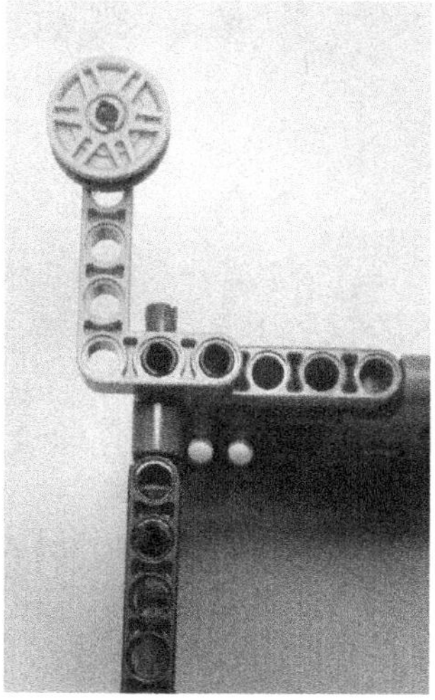

Create the Wall-2 (Outer wall)- (2 plates only) and attach to the wall assembly.

Prepare the remaining 3 outer wall plates. Use the non-friction axle pegs to attach the wheels to the plate peg holes. Finally, attach the 3 Plates to the wall.

Prepare the 2 large angular beams and attach them to the conjoined walls to make perpendicular joints sturdy.

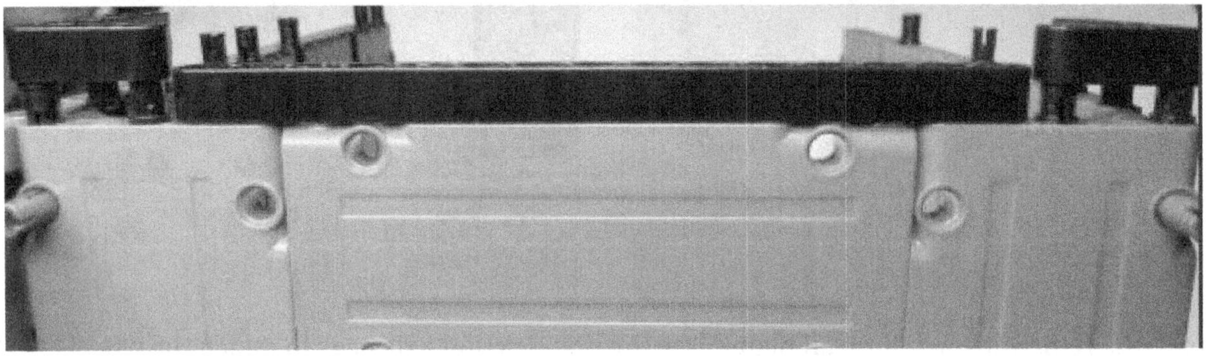

This is how the assembly should look after these steps.

Create the Brick Surround walls: This is the top portion of the attachment that surrounds the brick of the Basebot.
Assemble this together:

Also assemble these subassemblies.

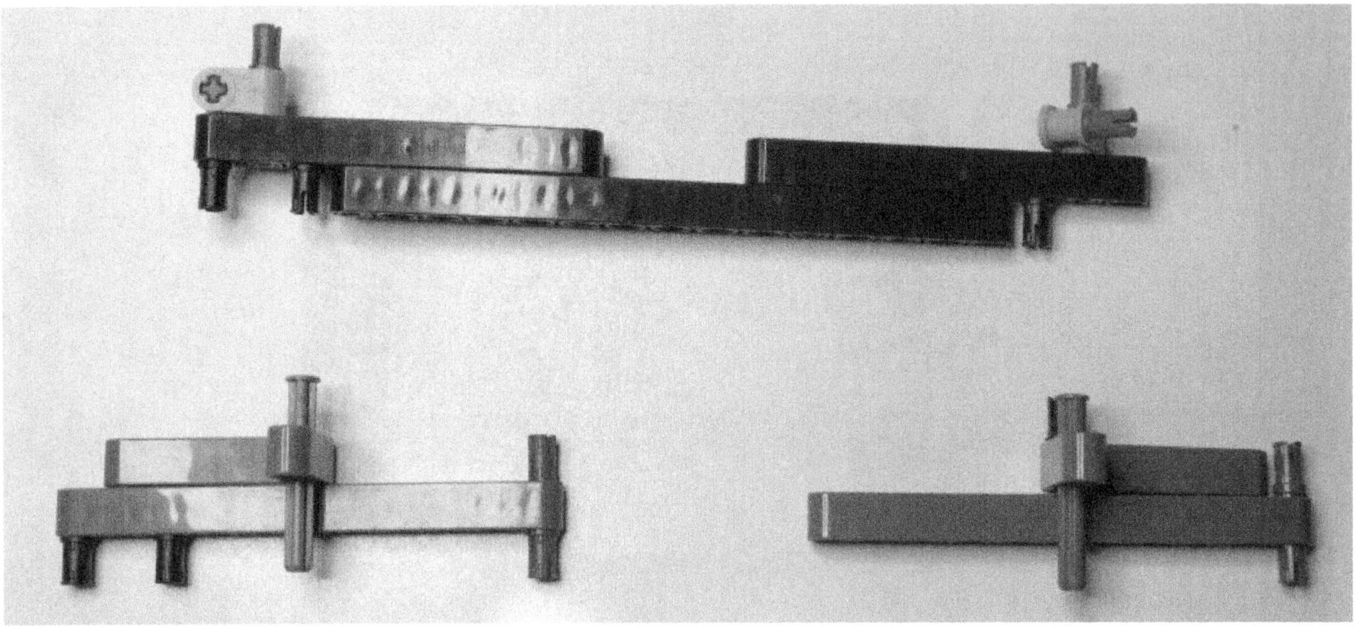

Connect the parts together as shown in the next pictures.

Connect diagram -1

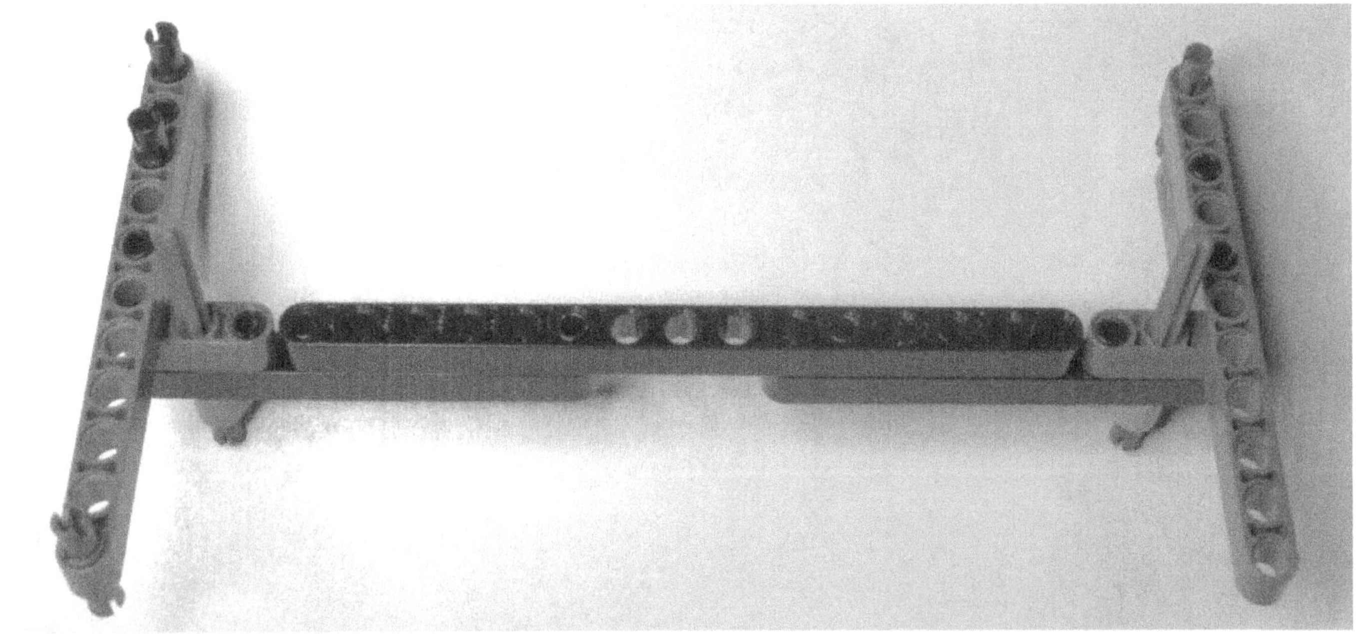

Connect diagram-2

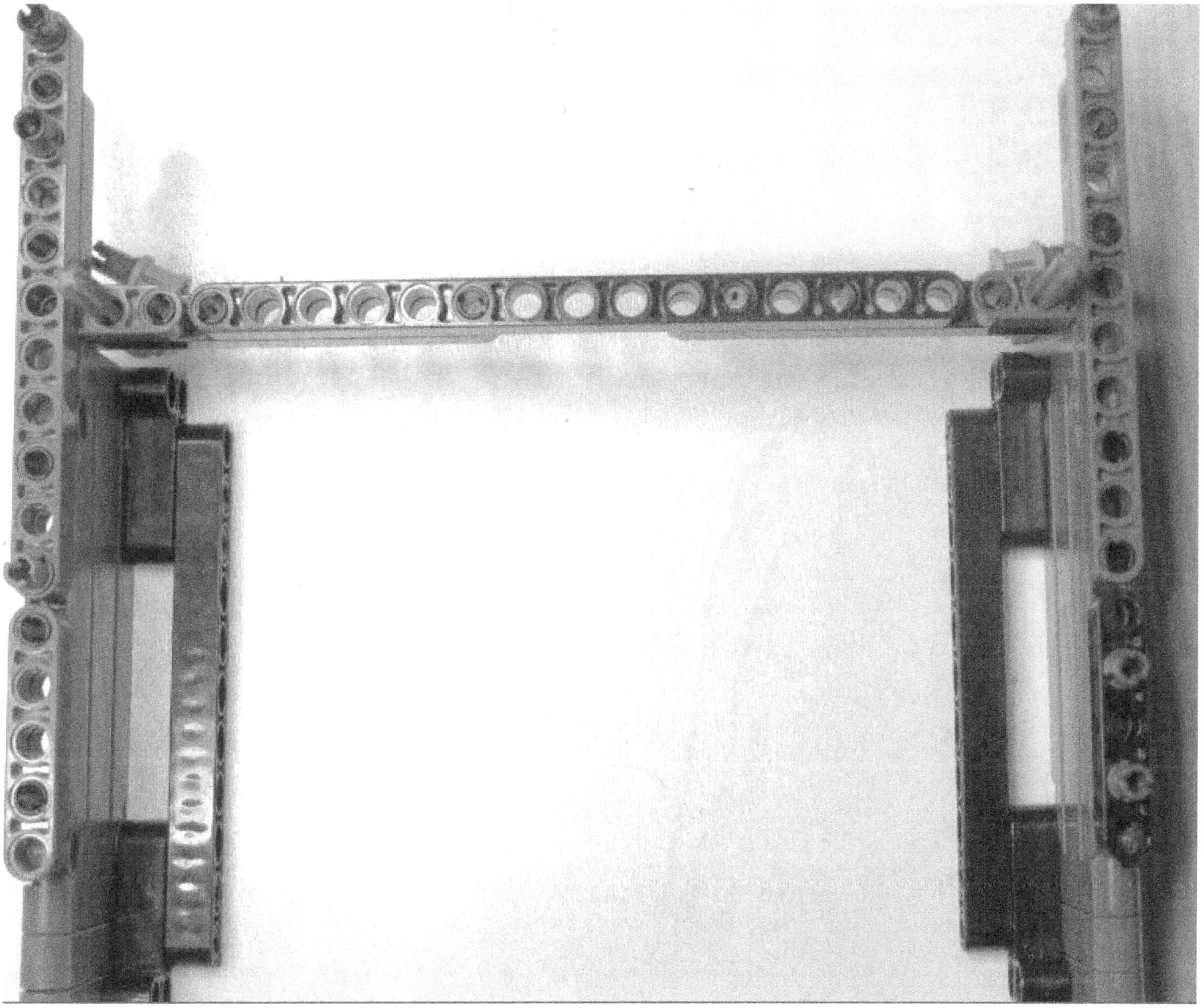

This is how it should look from the top

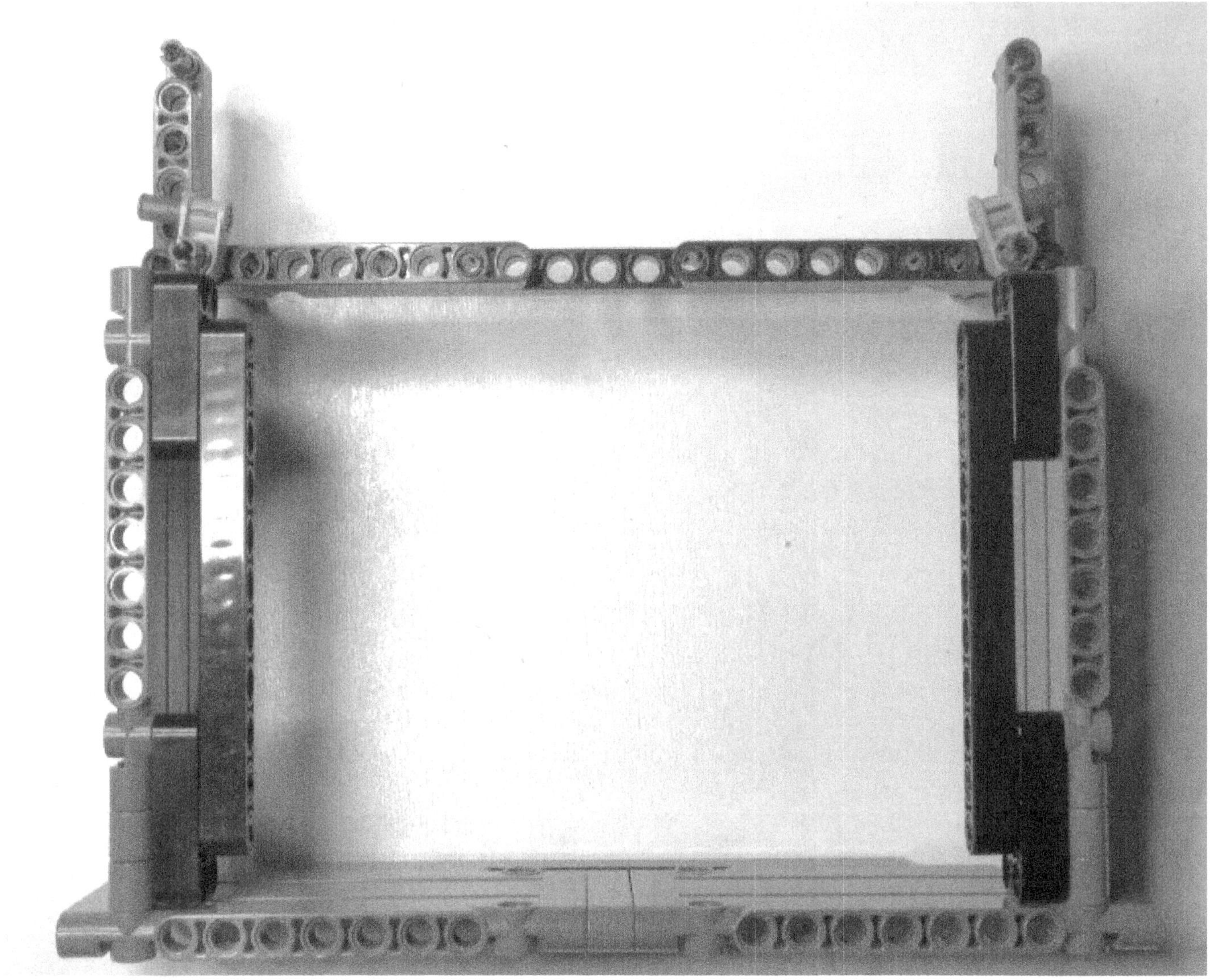

Connect the friction pegs to the plate as shown in the next picture.

Connect the brick surround assembly to the 3-wall assembly to form the final shell structure.

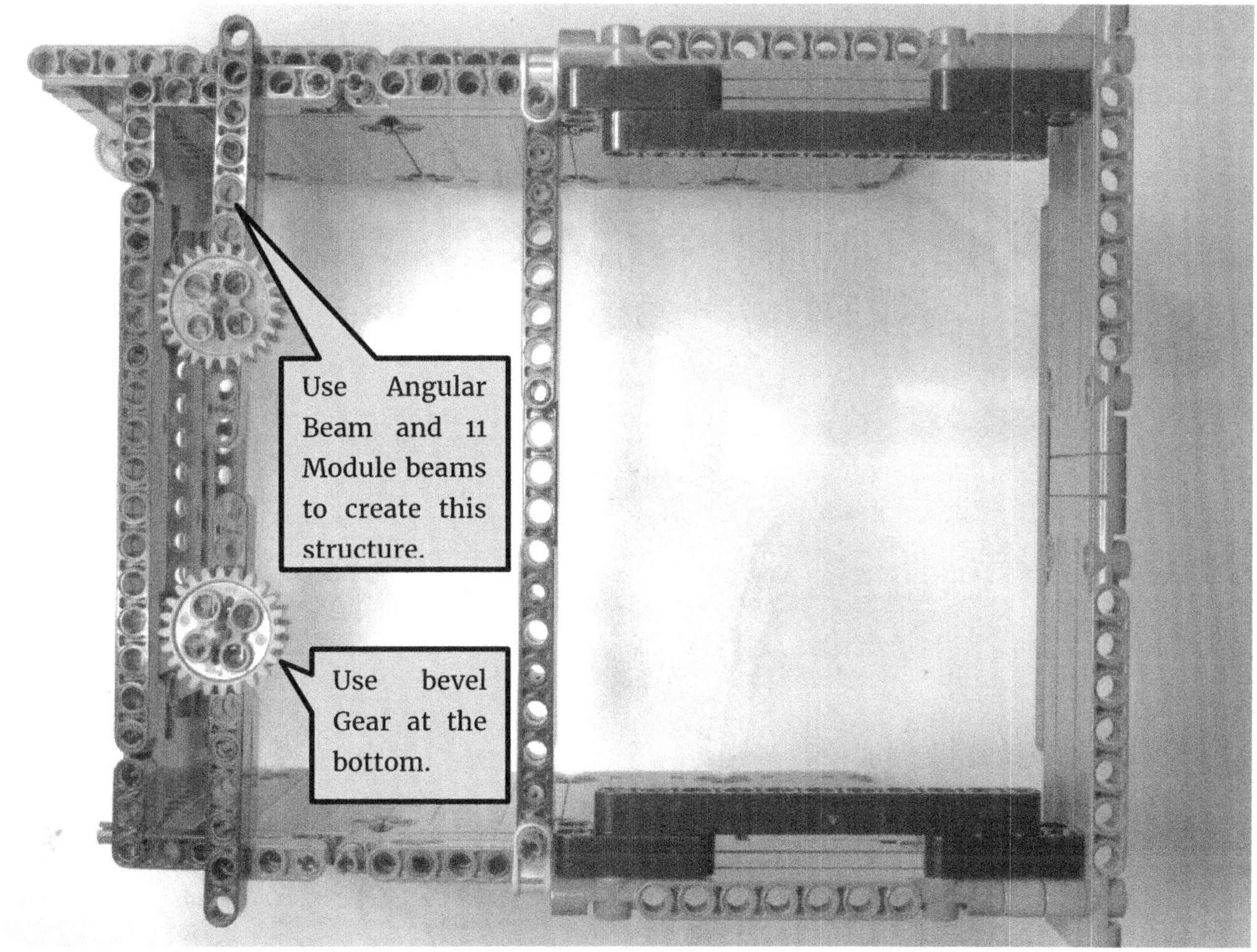

This is how the attachment should fit on the Basebot. The addition and removal should be very smooth.

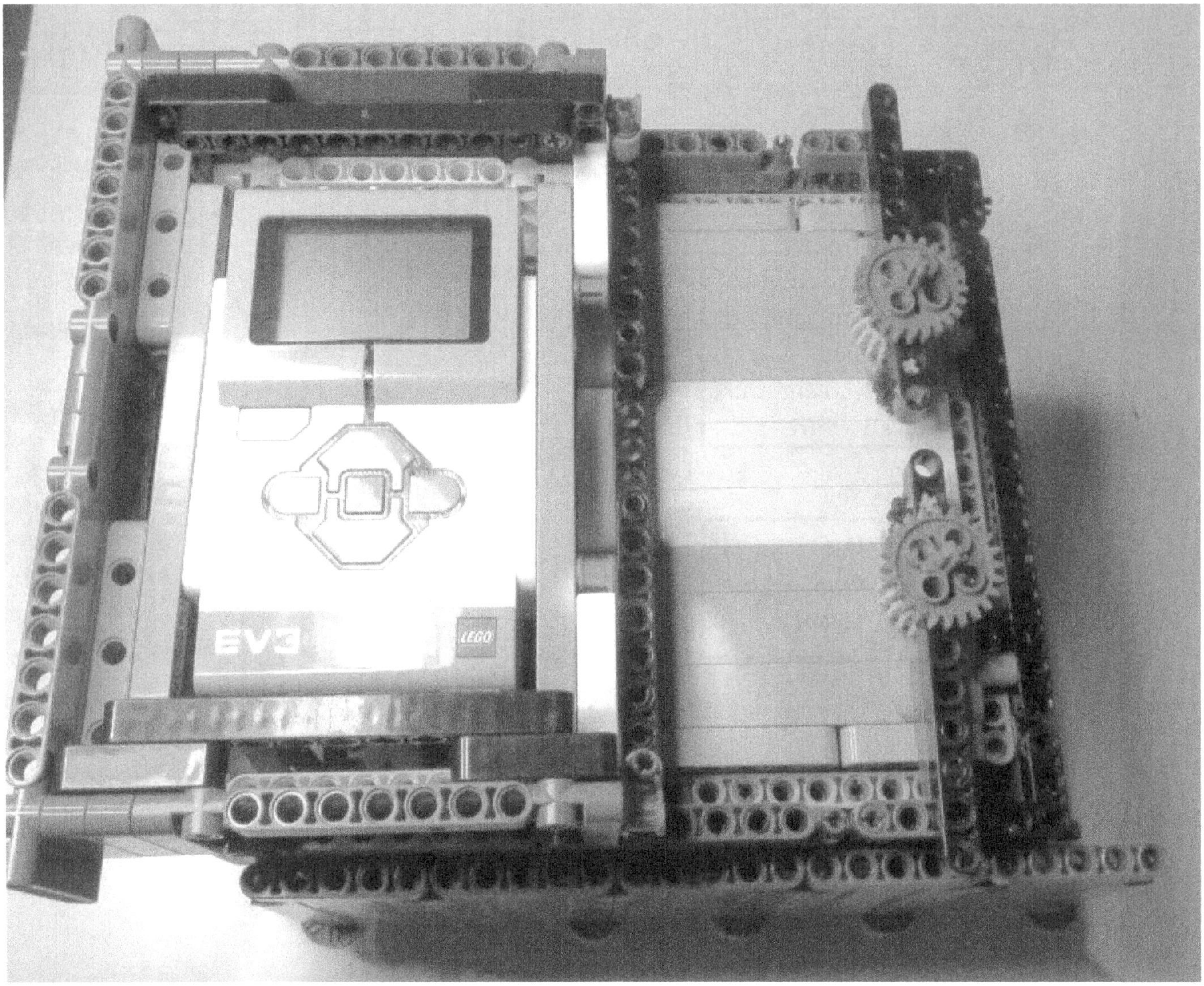

The bevel gear of the attachment should align perfectly with the Basebot' s driving bevel gear and the top of the axle of Basebot bevel gear should be inside the peg hole as shown in the adjacent picture.

The reason for having both axles of the bevel gears (one from the Basebot and one from the attachment) pass through the black beam is to ensure no slippage of gear teeth during operation. This is the most important reason why you should use the horizontal coupling of gears compared to the vertical coupling. Achieving robust vertical coupling during change of attachments always takes extra time and effort.

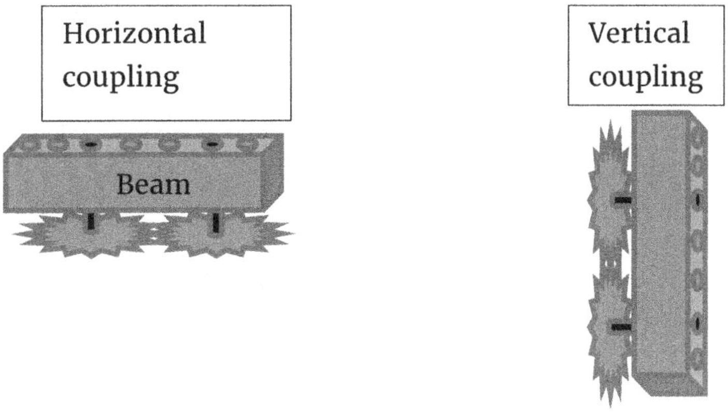

To build attachments that can perform missions you have to attach the activity assemblies to the attachment shell at the proper position and orientation
Activity assemblies can be of 2 types
1- Active assemblies are driven by one of the attachment bevel gears or pneumatic systems.
2- Passive assemblies can perform activities without using arm motors or pneumatic systems.

Active assembly -1 - Claw

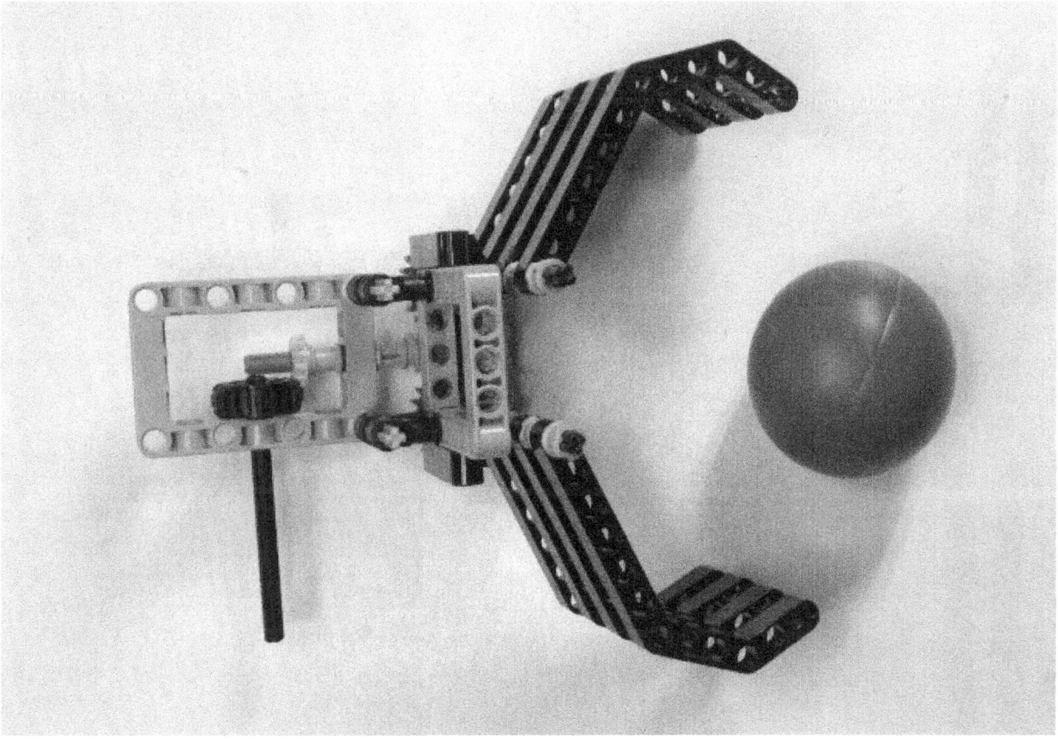

The grabber or claw assembly allows the robot to grab objects and release them at a desired location.

The next picture should allow you to build the claw assembly but I have also included additional details to help you out

The following picture shows the subassemblies or parts you will need to build the claw.

The 2 claw arms have a staggered alignment of double angular beams to allow the beams to pass through each other, when the claw closes.

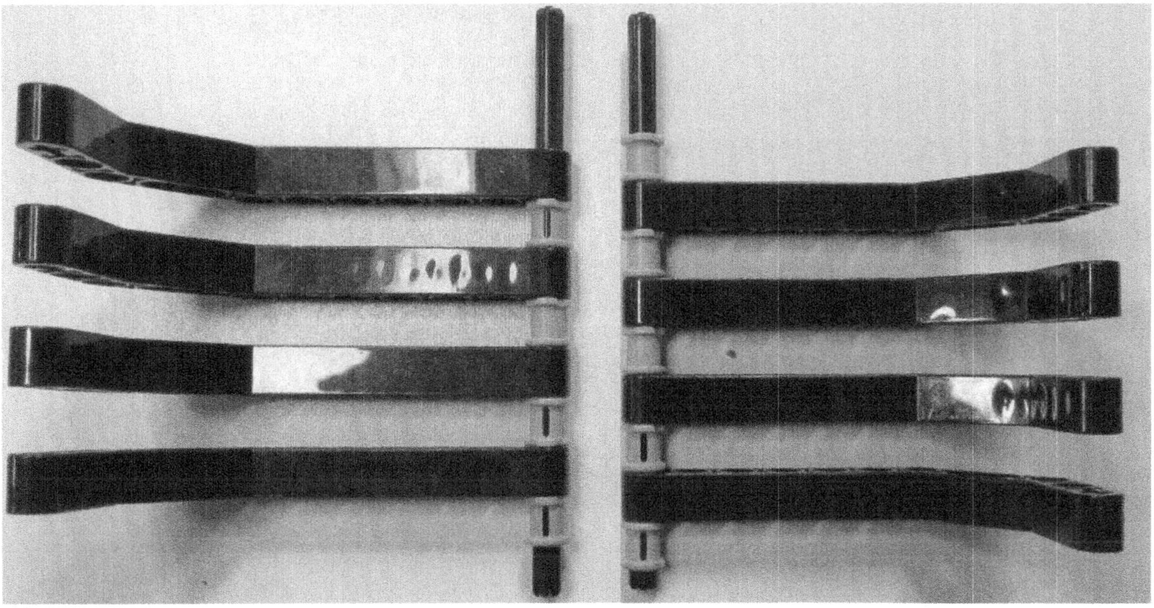

Construct the claw arms holding assembly. The structure has to look exactly the same as the next picture to allow the worm gear to perfectly mesh with the 24 teeth gear.

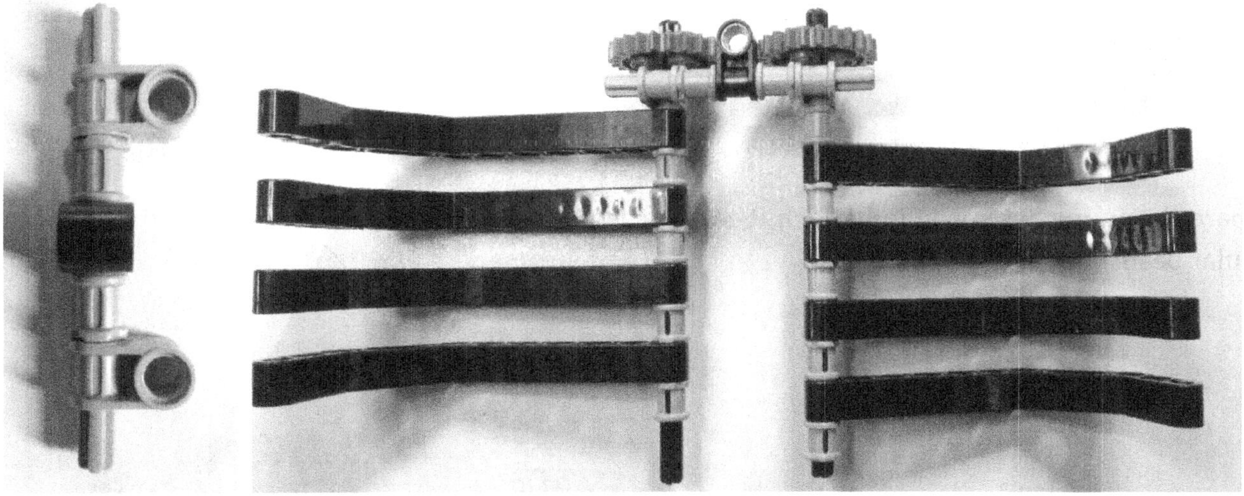

Attach the Bevel gear using the axle with a stopper.

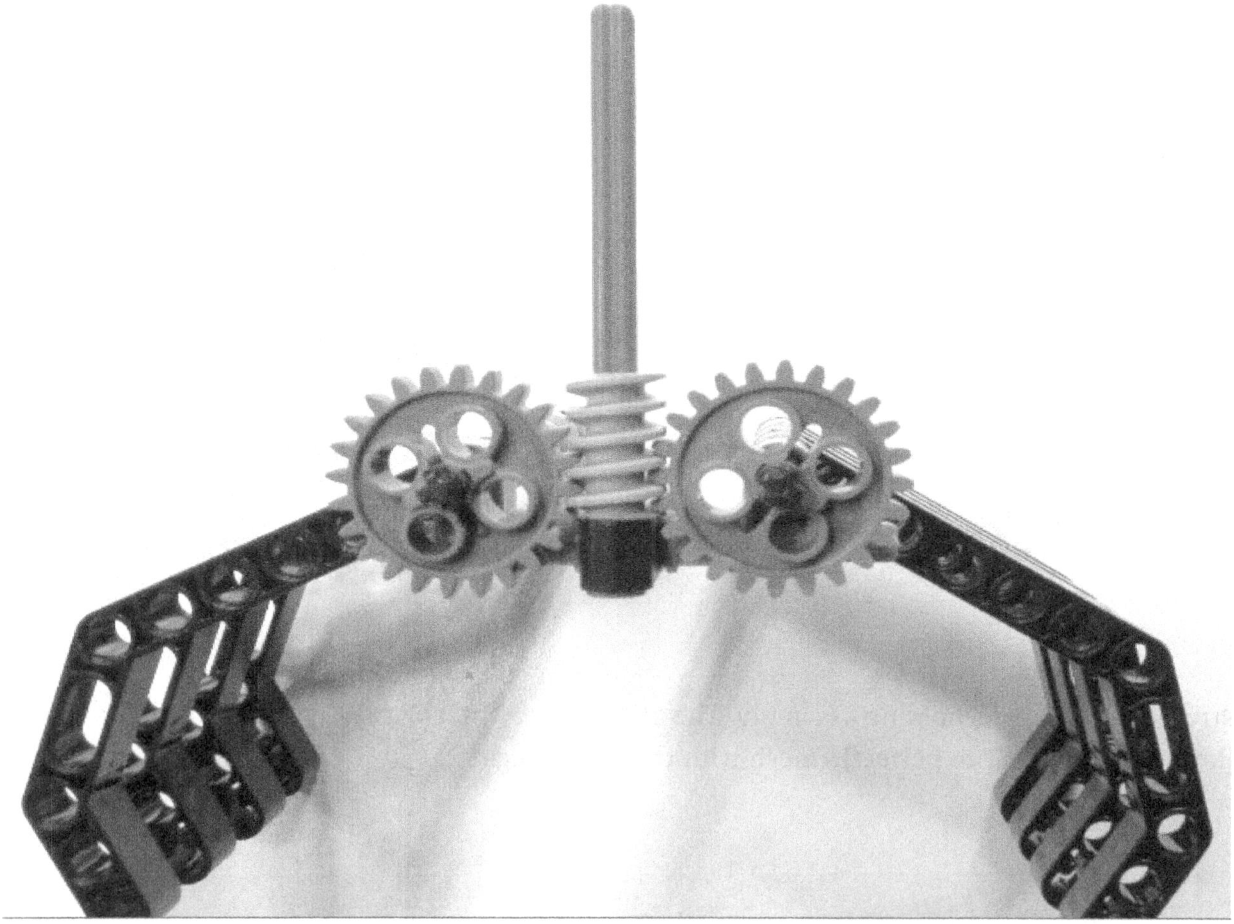

Prepare the frame assembly and attach it to the claw by merely inserting the axle in the third hole of angular beam

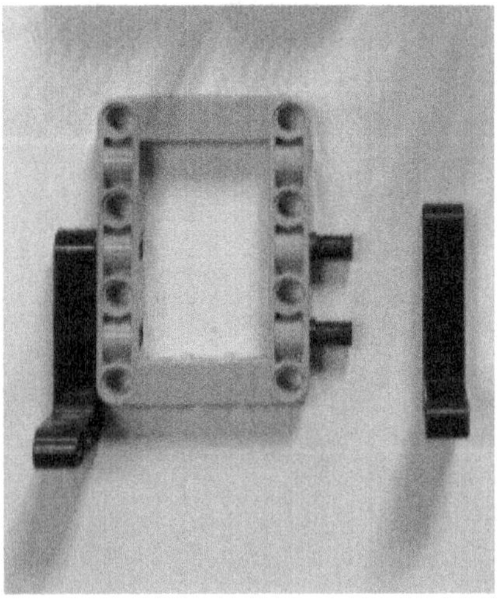

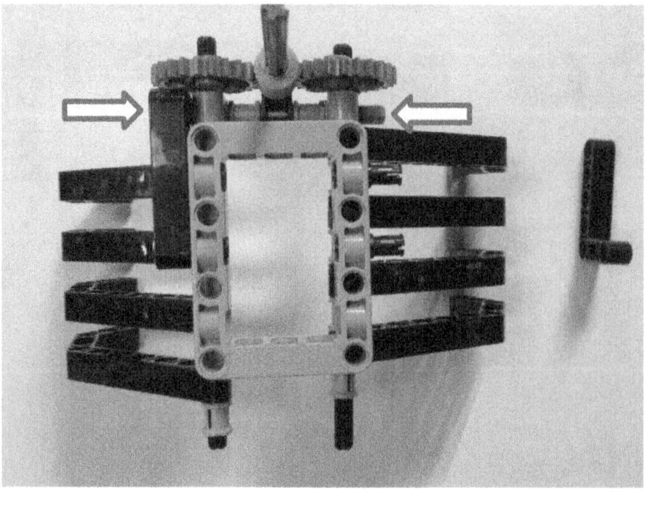

This is how the assembly should look. The 2 angular beams attached to the frame will hold the axle of the claw.

As shown in next picture prepare the second frame and attach it to the assembly.

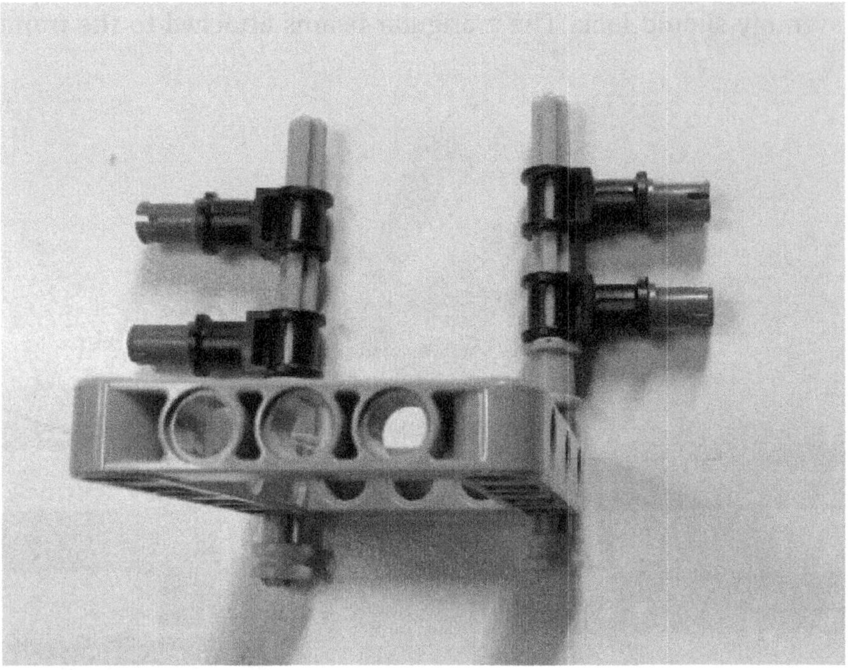

Complete the motion transfer gear configuration component shown in the next picture.

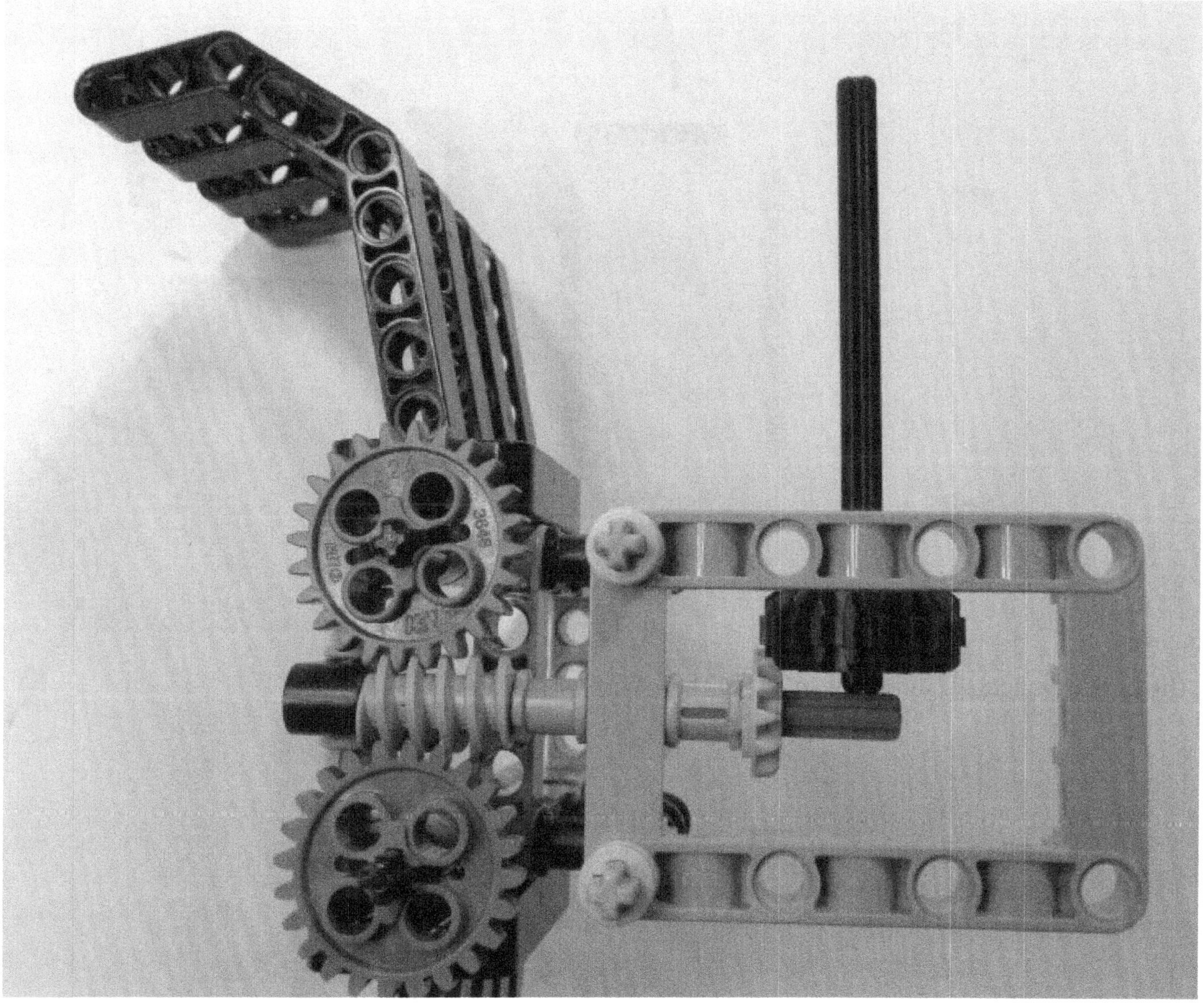

Active assembly -2 – Lifter:

This assembly can be used to lift mission models. Use parts shown in the next picture to build the lifter assembly.

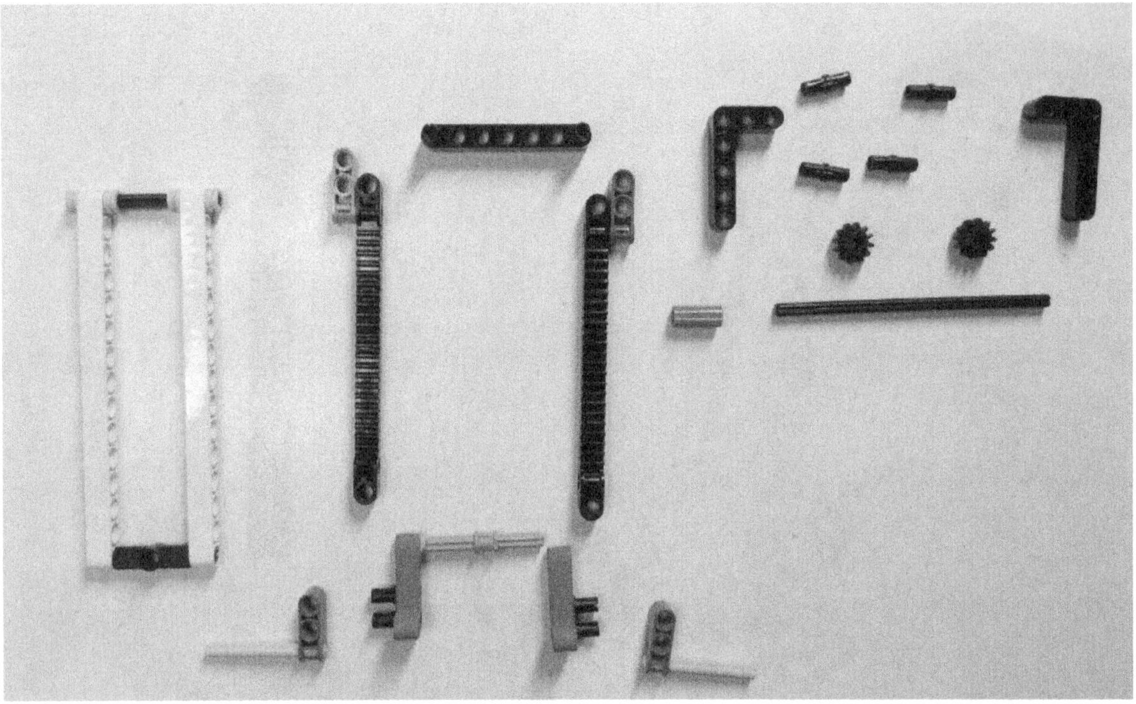

The next few pictures show how to attach these parts.

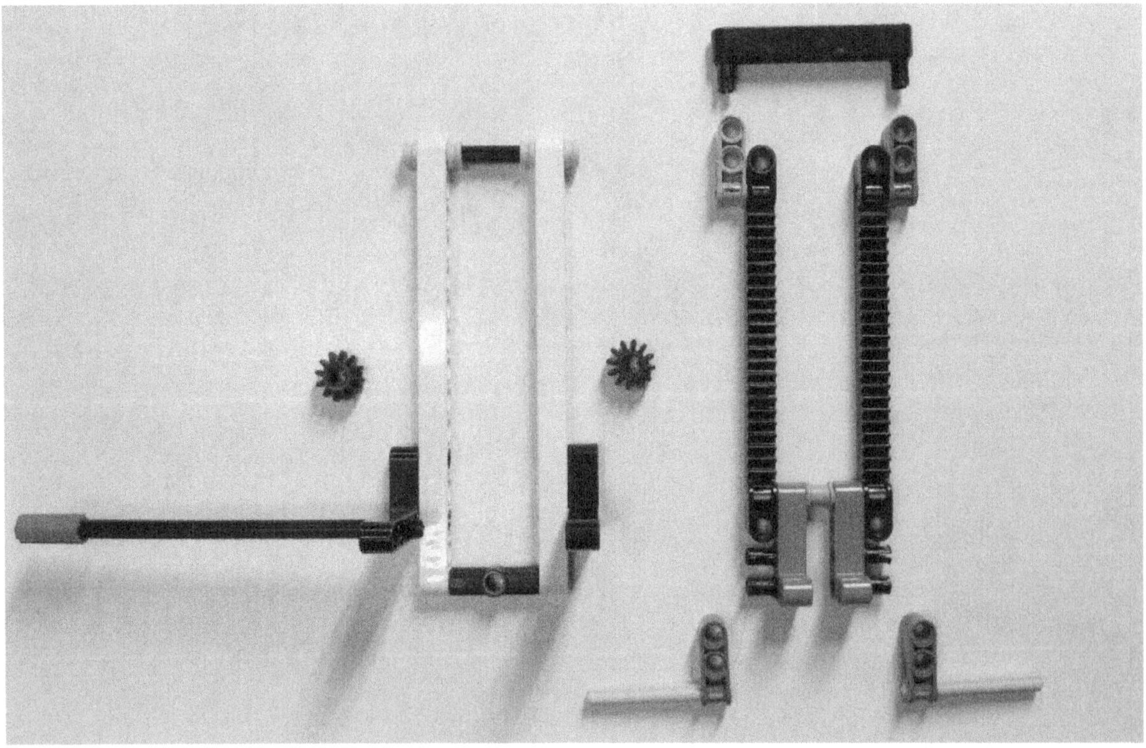

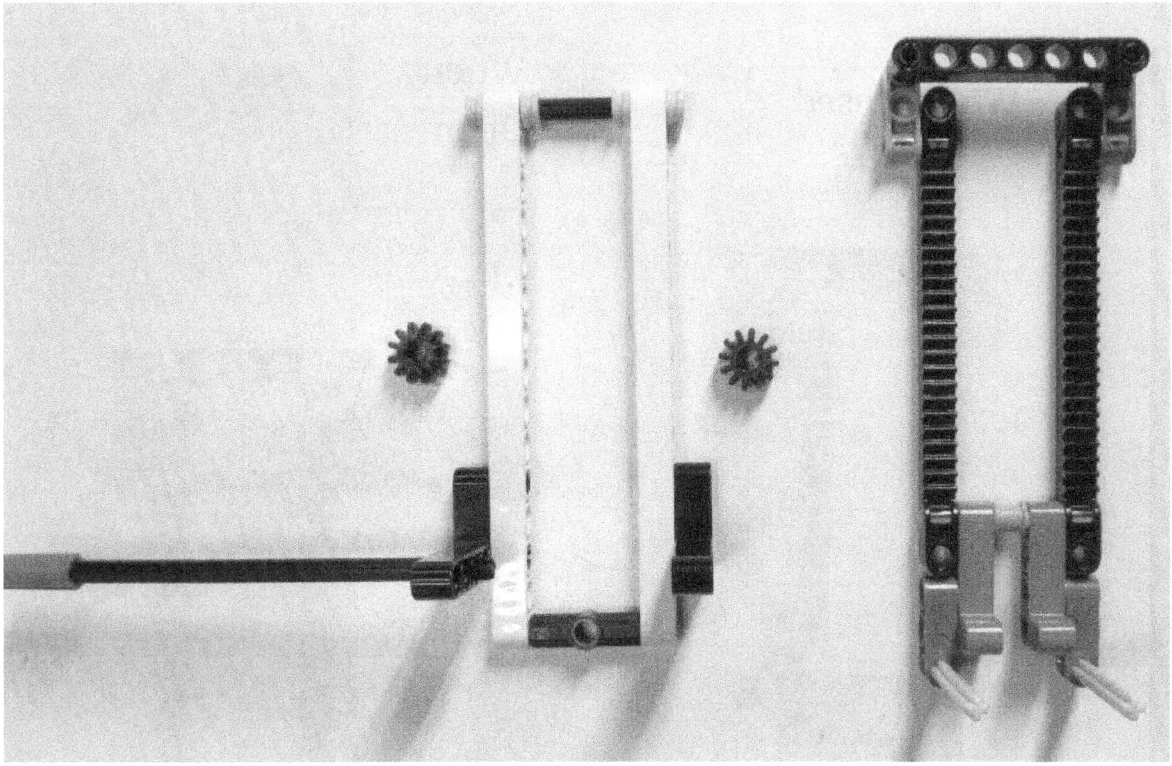

Insert the axle and attach the gears on the axle to sandwich the rack between the gear and the beam.

This is how the lifter assembly looks in action.

When closed

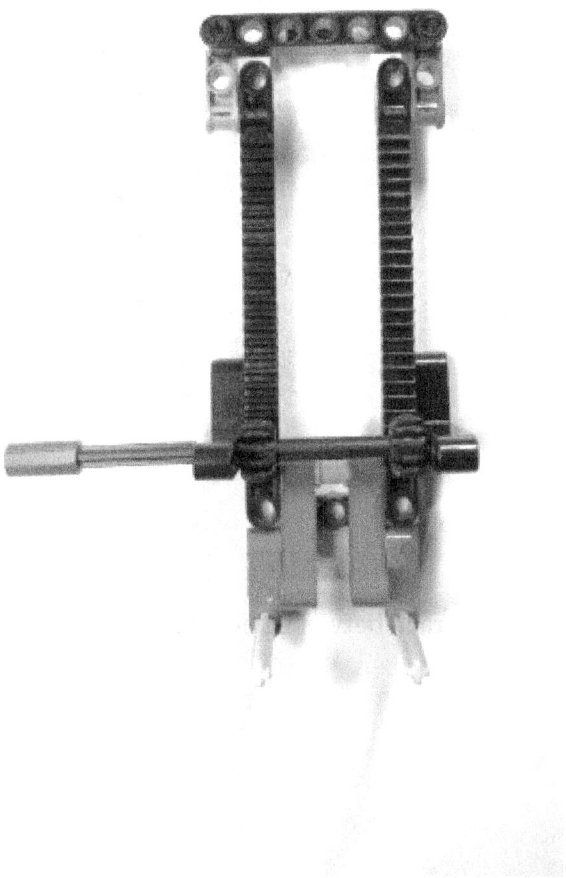

When Open

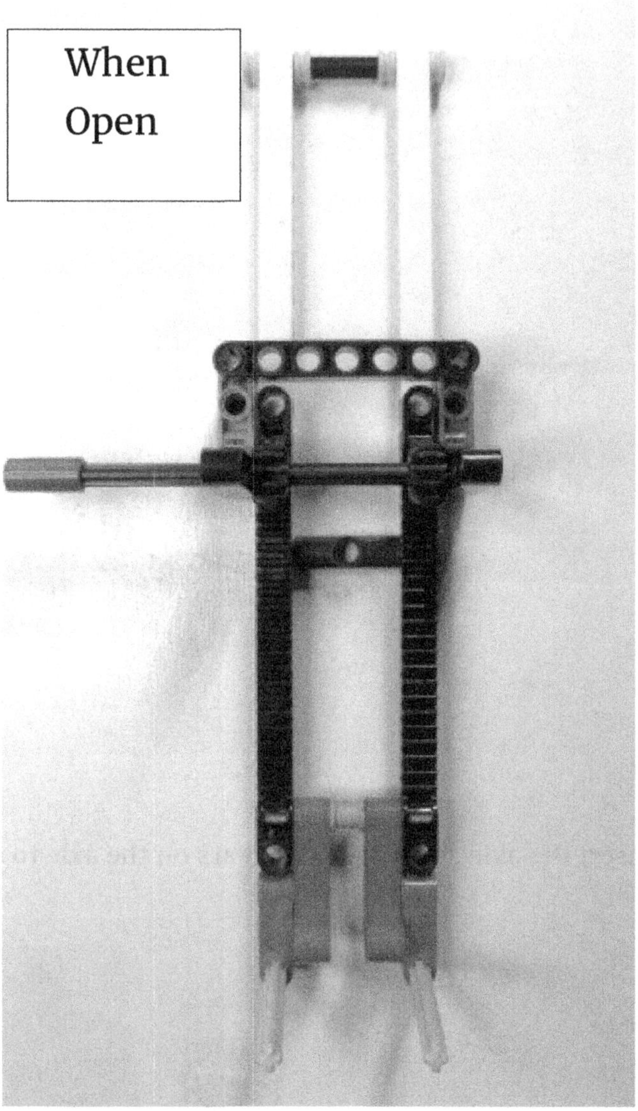

Active assembly -3 – Box assembly with door.
This assembly can be used to carry mission models from the base and deploy them on the mat.
Use the parts shown in the next picture. In this assembly you are going to use all 3 categories of parts that we have covered in this book: Studfull, Studless and Axle parts.

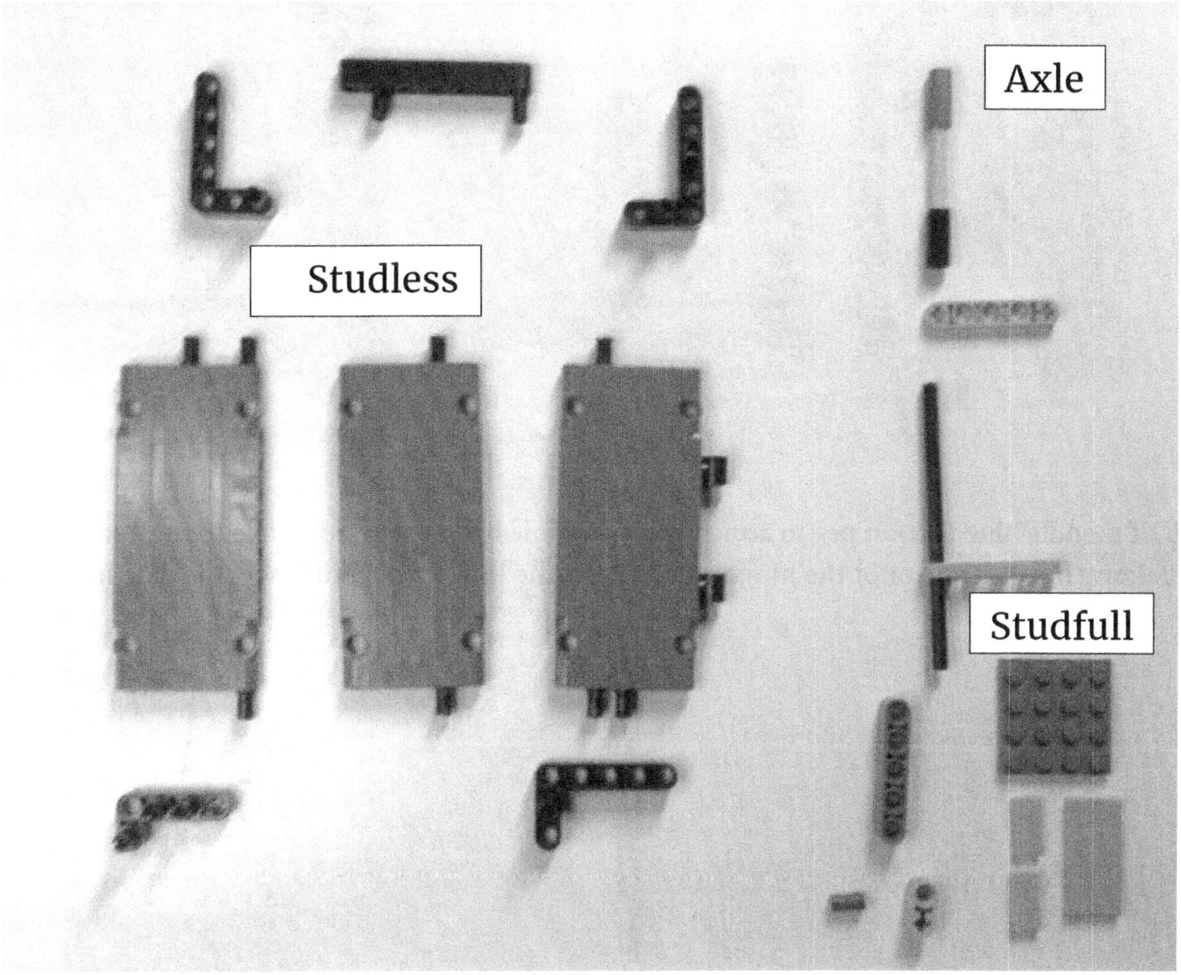

Construct the box. Use the angular beams to connect the plates and create a smooth bottom floor using the Studfull parts.

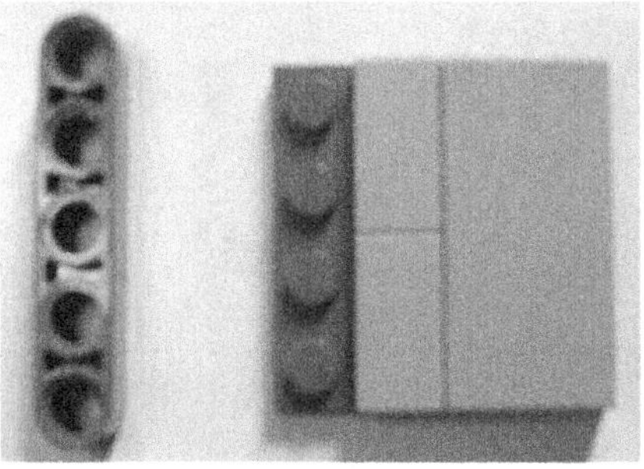
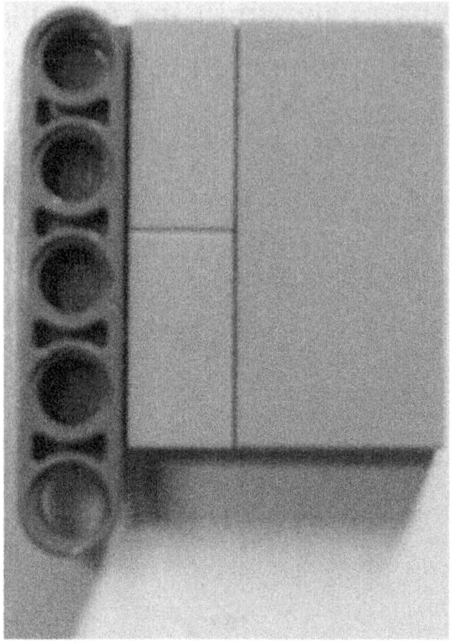

Use the half module blue friction peg to attach the 2-module beam with cross hole to the 5-module beam. This will allow the attachment of the hinge axle. Attach the hinge axle and insert the axle into the hinge holes

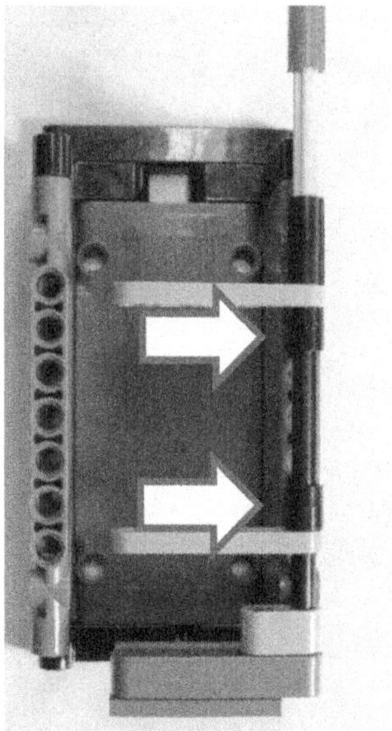

.

The box assembly in action

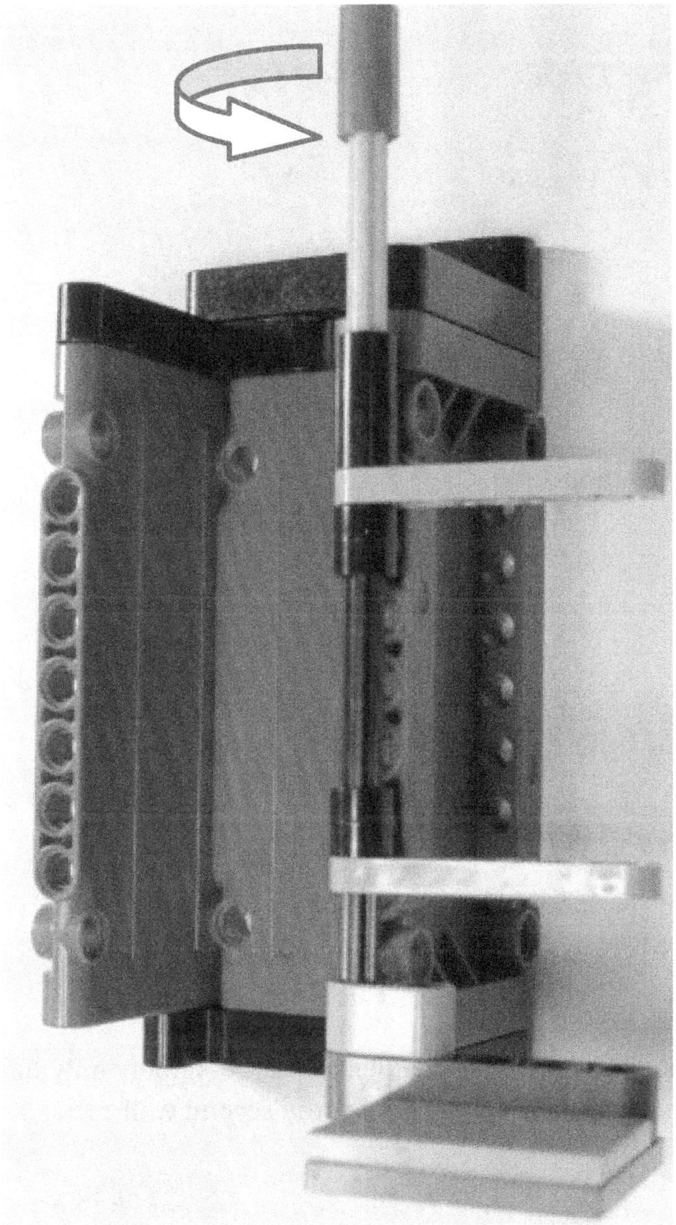

Active assembly -4 – Conveyor Belt.

The conveyor belt is another good way to deliver mission models to a specific location on the mat. Use the parts shown in the next picture.

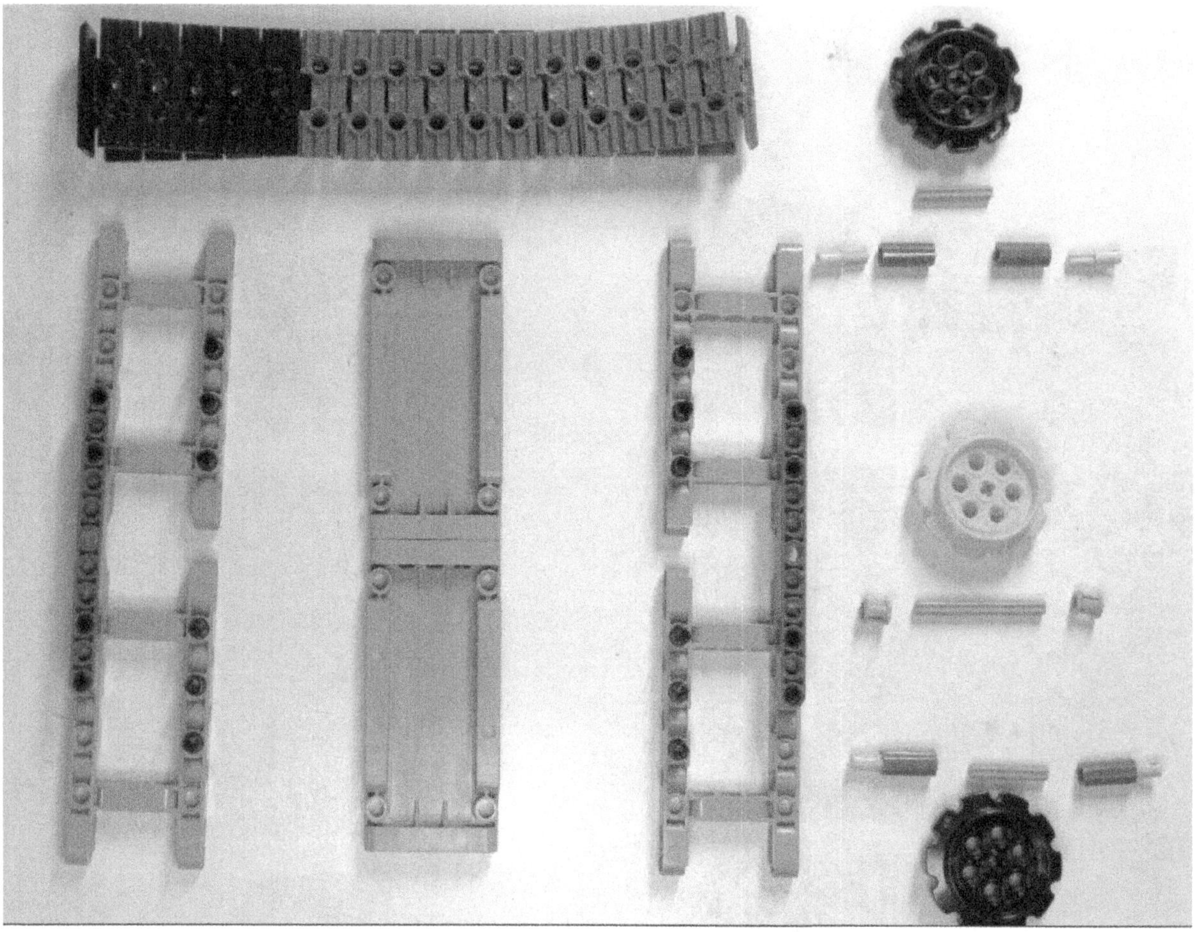

Connect the plates to the side wall (First side wall)

Prepare the 3 sprocket assemblies as shown in the next picture. The middle sprocket assembly only has one axle and 2 one module bushings. Attach the sprockets to the wall. Connect the second wall.

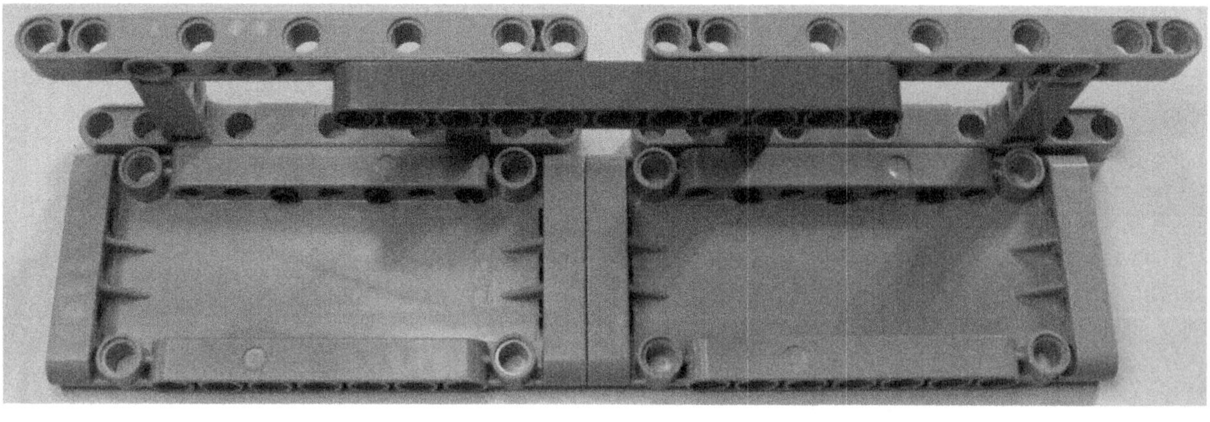

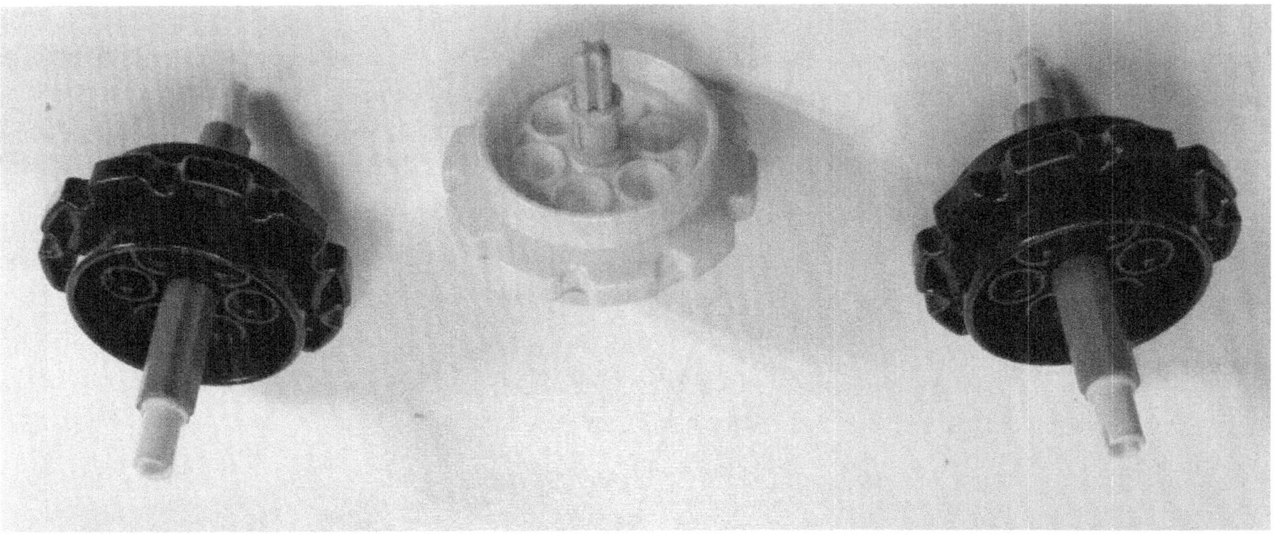

Run the conveyor belt inside the sprocket assembly, by inserting it below the sprockets, as shown in the next picture. The conveyor belt is made up of 34 track elements. The conveyor belt may seem loose but it needs to be that way to rotate freely.

Conveyor belt in action.

Passive assembly -1 – Collector.

This assembly allows the robot to capture objects on the mat by moving forward but traps the object once its inside the area.

Passive assembly- 2 – Grabber.

A similar concept to the collector but it catches the objects and do not allow them to fall on the mat once caught.

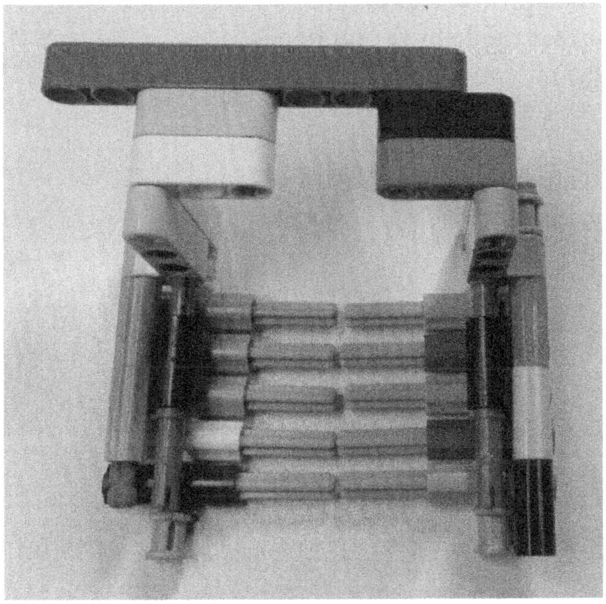

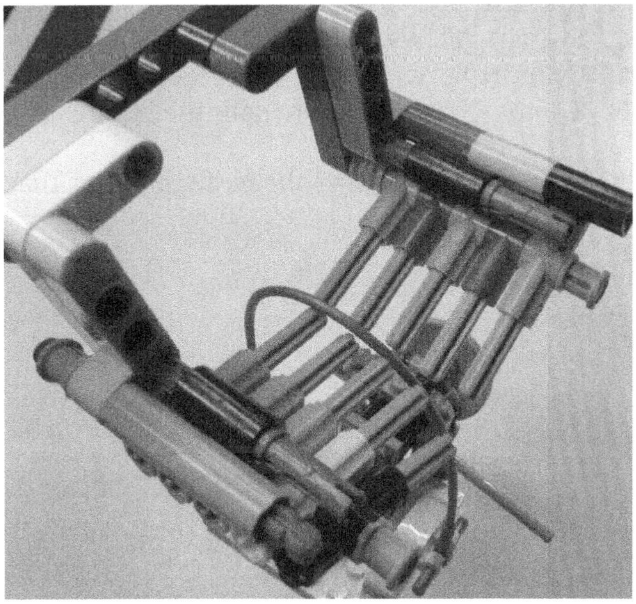

Pneumatic assembly:

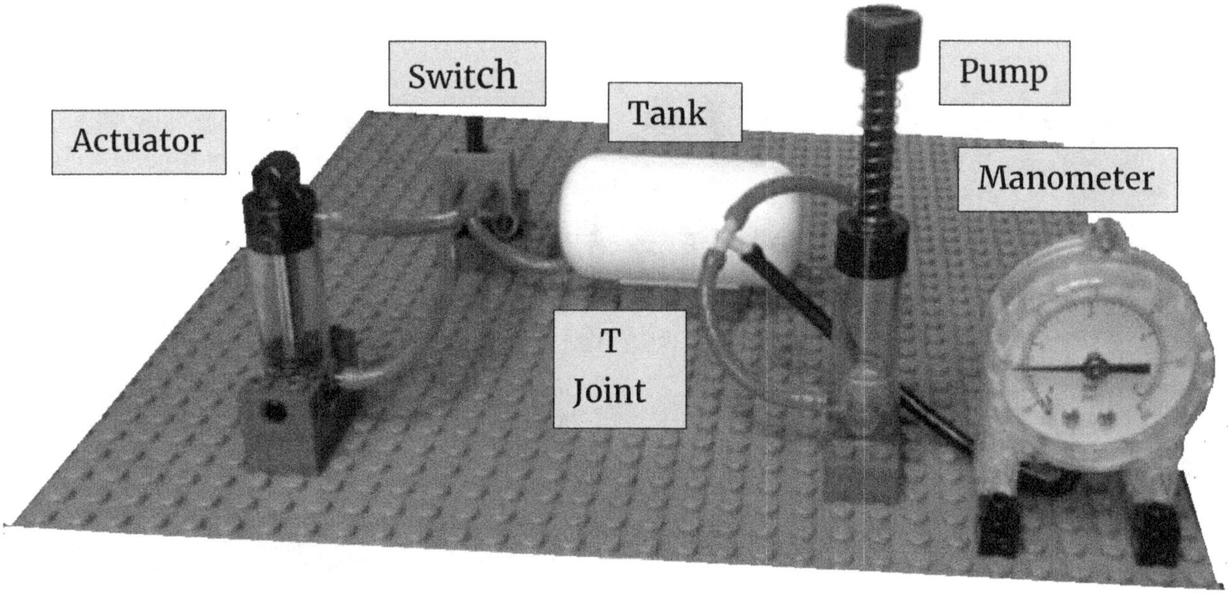

The pneumatic assembly consists of tanks, switches, Pumps, Actuators and an optional Manometer.

1. Tank –Stores the pressurized air. The tank has 2 tube like structures where you can connect the inlet and outlet tubes. It has peg holes to attach the tank to the robot.
2. Pump – Uses a spring-operated pump to pump the air into the tank. The pump should be attached to the attachment and should be used to pump air into the tank before starting missions.
3. Manometer- Manometer is used to measure the air pressure. This will allow you to make sure the right pressure is pumped into the tank before the start of the match.
4. Switch- Allows you to switch into extend mode, retract mode or off mode.
5. Cylinder or Actuator – This is used to drive the mission you are performing.
6. T Joint – This is used to split the air pressure between 2 devices.

The following picture shows the basic cylinders that are available for you to use.

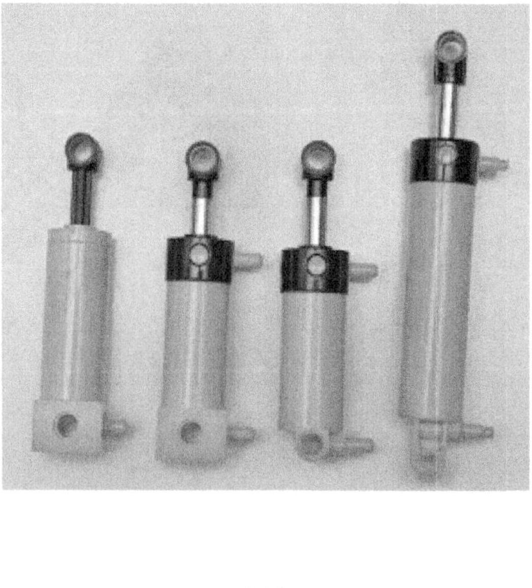

These are a few examples of how pneumatic assemblies can be used for activities like lifting or grabbing game elements.

Pneumatic assembly-1

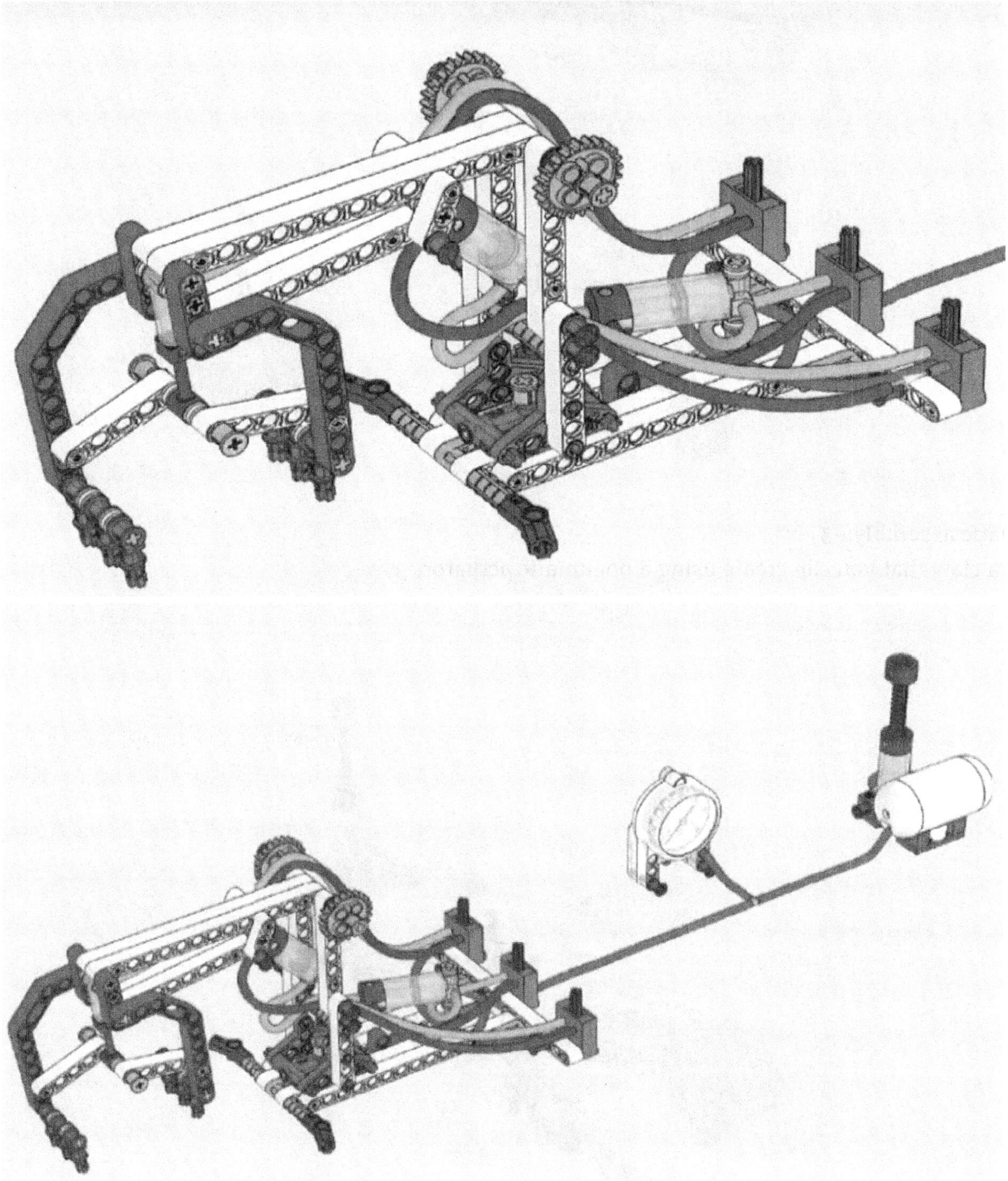

Pneumatic assembly -2

You can use the scissor extender you have built and drive it using the pneumatic actuator.

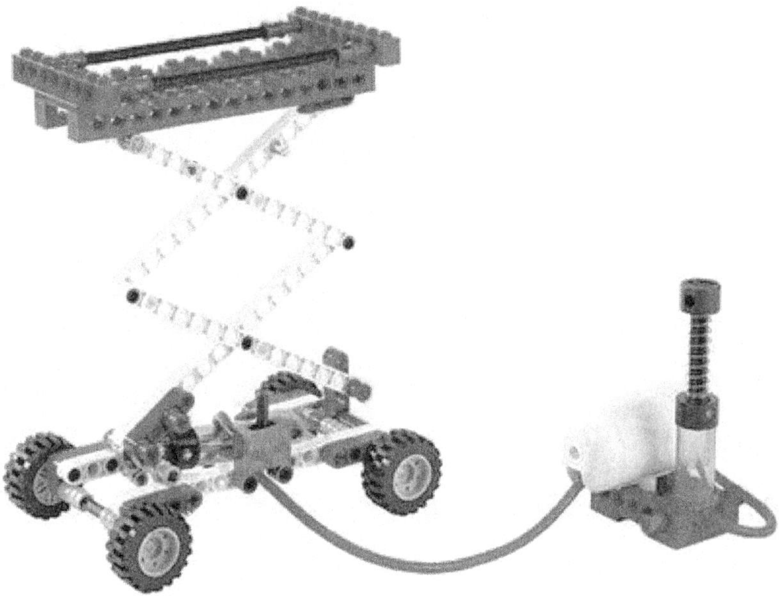

Pneumatic assembly -3

This is a claw that you can create using a pneumatic actuator.

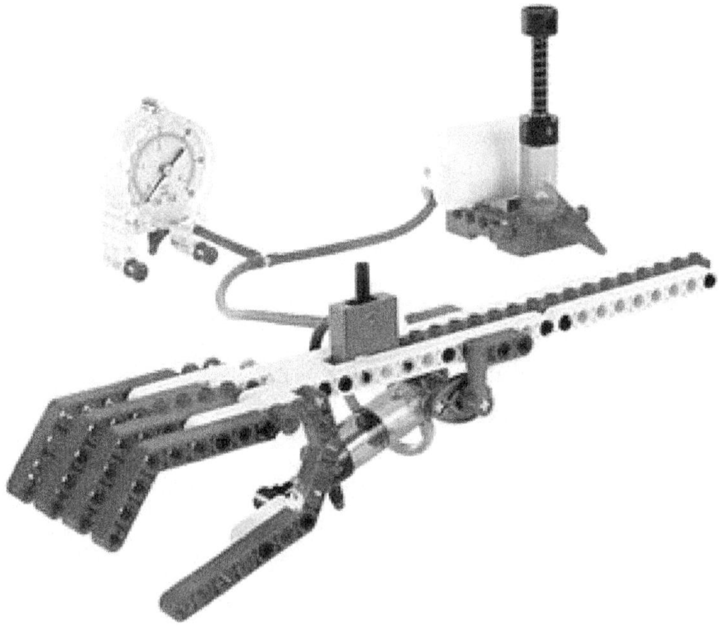

Pneumatics is an integral component of current gas driven car engines. You can build many complex mechanisms using pneumatic actuators. LEGO also offers a pneumatic Education set 9641 for around $80 that you can use in the robot build.

Assembly using LEGO rubber band belt:
I have used rubber band belts very effectively and very frequently to store energy on the robot assembly. This stored energy can later be converted into motion. Rubber band belt assemblies can be passive (Triggered by the robot hitting a wall) or you can use one motor to trigger multiple rubber band assemblies, making them active.
The big axle with the bushing is holding the poking assembly from getting released. The stretched rubber band belt is storing the energy.

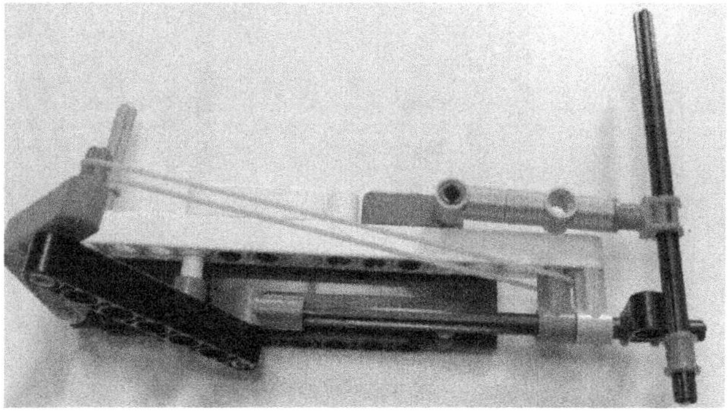

This is how it looks from the sides

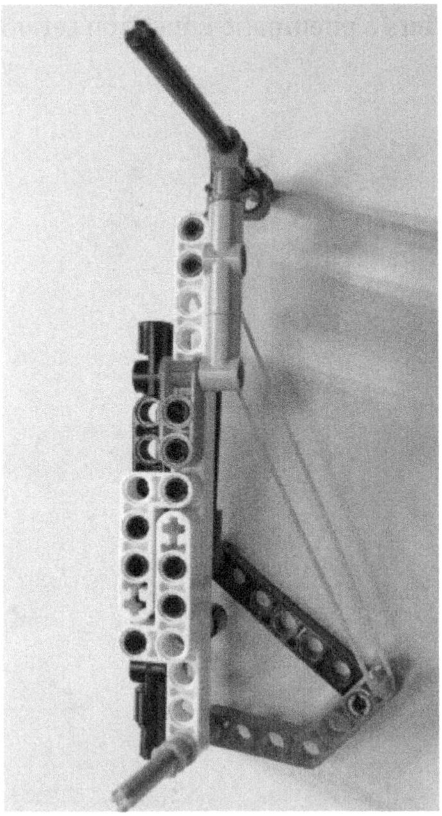
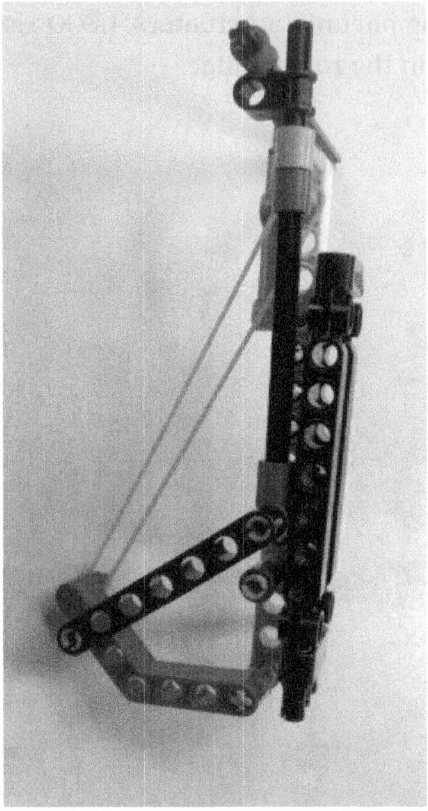

The rubber band belt assembly in action.

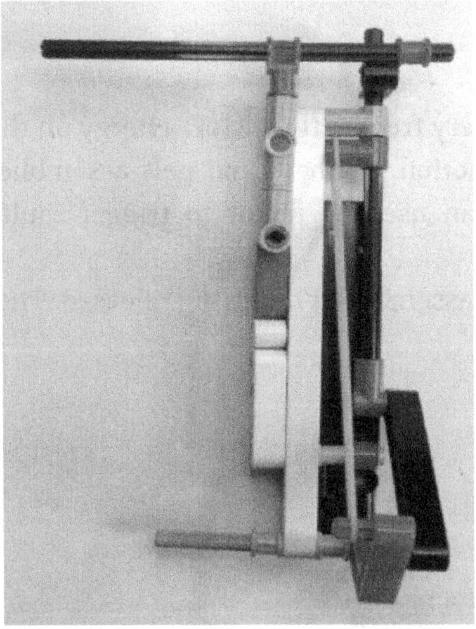
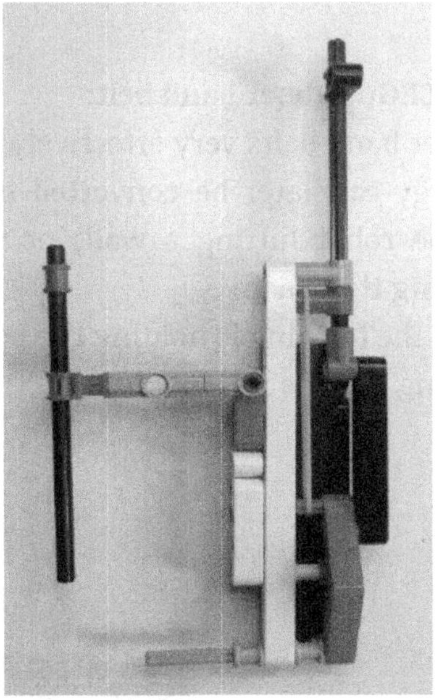

PROGRAMMING FOR COMPETITION

Any robot that you will create will only be as good as its programming. You are already familiar with programs that are commonly used in competitions (Chapter 1 -3).
You have also learnt what a good design should be in the 'What is a Good Design?' section. Let us explore how to apply those good design principles for competition programming

Programming Quality – Programs you will write will need to be appropriate for their intended purpose and will have to achieve consistent results. This can be achieved by making sure that you have a clear understanding of these 2 questions:
1-How the robot will position itself in order to complete a mission?
2-What the robot will do to complete the mission after it is positioned?
Strategy plays a significant role in making the right choices and once you have decided on both of these points you should use the right programs to achieve quality results.
Example – You have decided to use the 'T' on the mat to position the robot in a certain way. Your program should include the Myblocks 'curveLF_IN' or 'curveLF_OUT'. You should also use the line squaring Myblock that we will discuss later in this section. Your program should be able to achieve the same results 3 times in a row.

Programming Efficiency – Your programs will need to use Myblocks (modular programs), will need to efficiently use loops and switches (streamlined), and will need to be well structured with comments (understandable).
Example – 1
The following program is a Myblock that you have created. This is how every program should look.

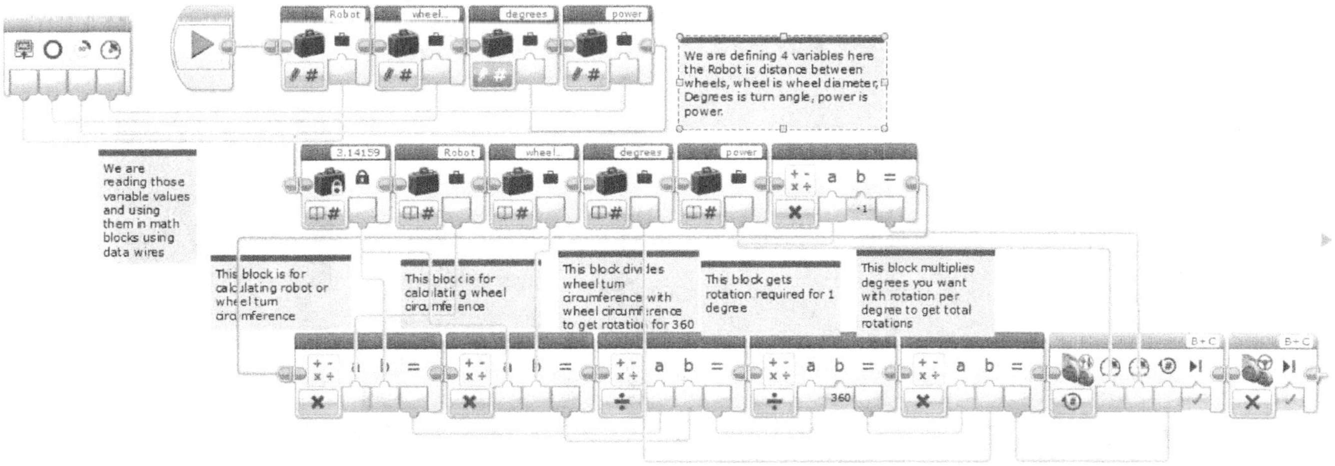

Example-2
A simple way of having less math blocks in the program is to calculate the circumference and use circumference as a parameter instead of wheel diameter. This will make your programs look less cluttered and will make them more streamlined.

Automation / Navigation – Use wall navigation and sensors extensively. Using sensors allows your program to be versatile and less dependent on changes in the physical conditions of the mat
The key to using sensors is understanding the limitations of the sensors, appropriately and frequently calibrating the sensors and keeping in mind that variability is part of the game.

Design Process – Maintaining the Engineering notebook diligently and making progress as you go through the Explore, Imagine, Create, Test, Improve, and Share cycles will certainly provide you a leg up in the design process judging session.

Innovative Design - Creation of new and unique programming features that will help you complete the missions is the most important aspect of the competition judging. This you can achieve by understanding the Game rules, thinking outside the box, and experimenting with your robots.

From a programming stand point you know a lot by now. There is one more Myblock that will help you immensely in competition programing.
Create a new program in 'Chapter three – Myblock' and name it 'Line squaring'. This program will allow you to align your robot perpendicular to any line. The next picture shows the robot aligned perpendicular to the line. This can be achieved by using 2 color sensors as you have in the Basebot and the 'Line squaring program'

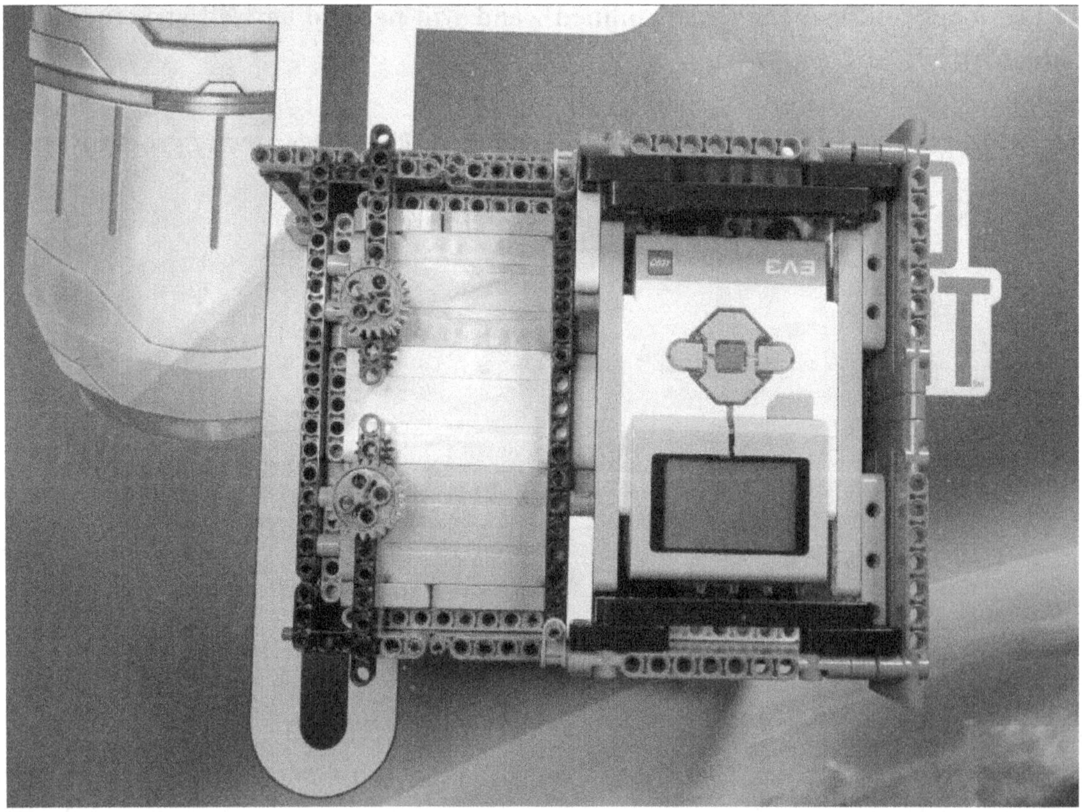

Create the program as shown in the next picture

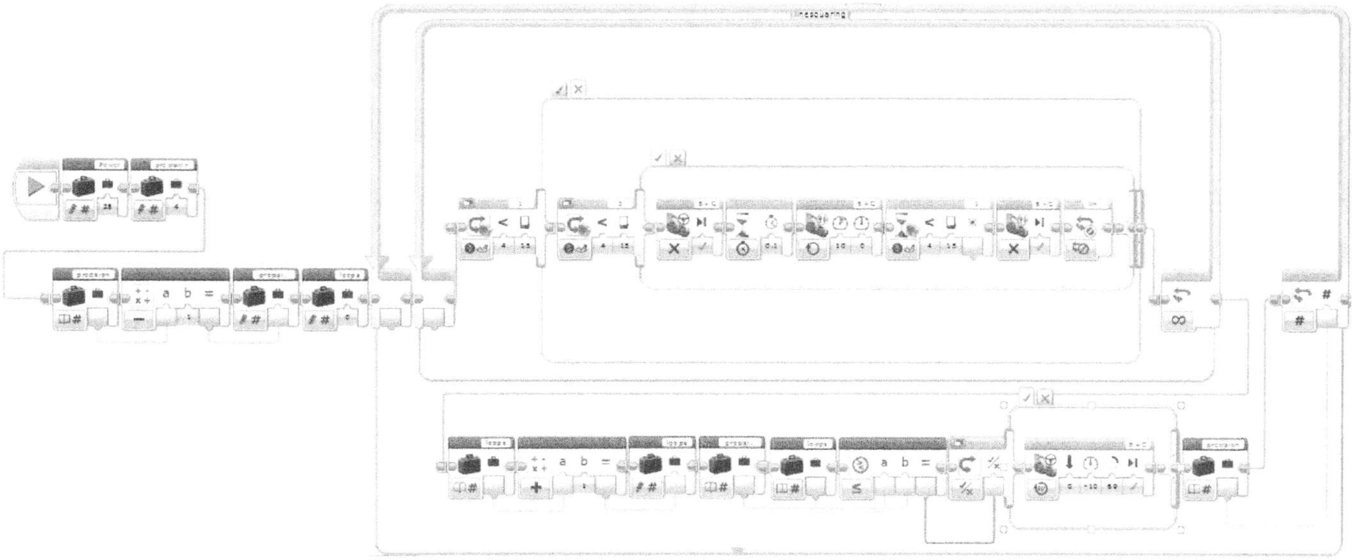

Here is the expanded view of this program:

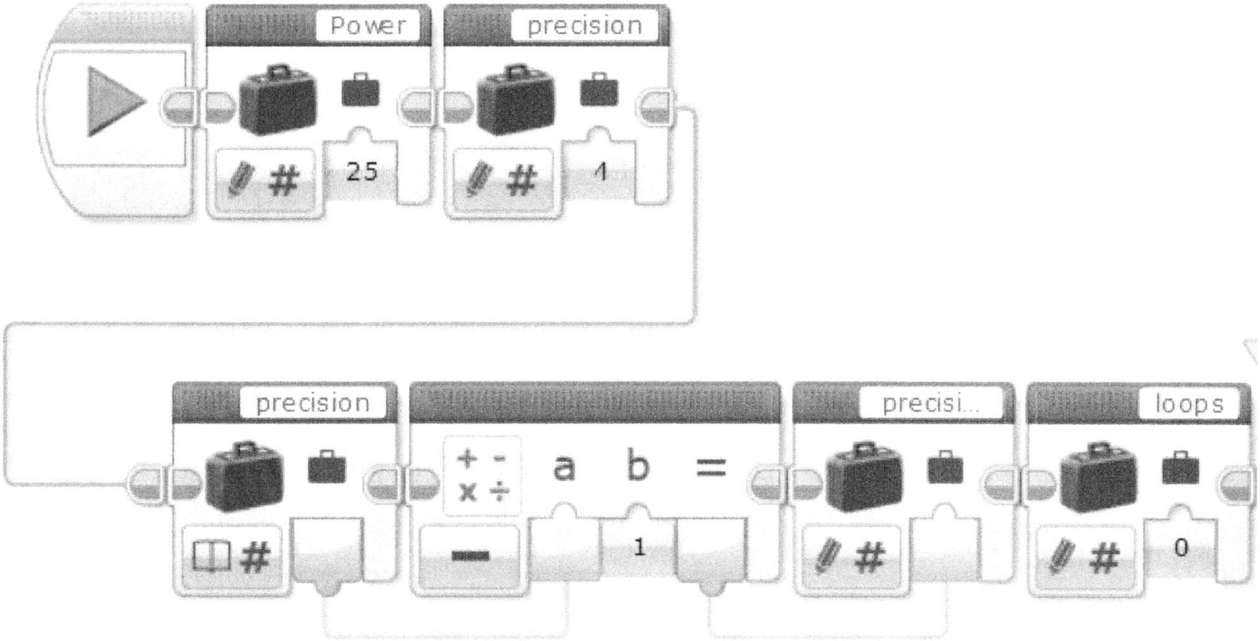

Inner Loop – True part of the switch.

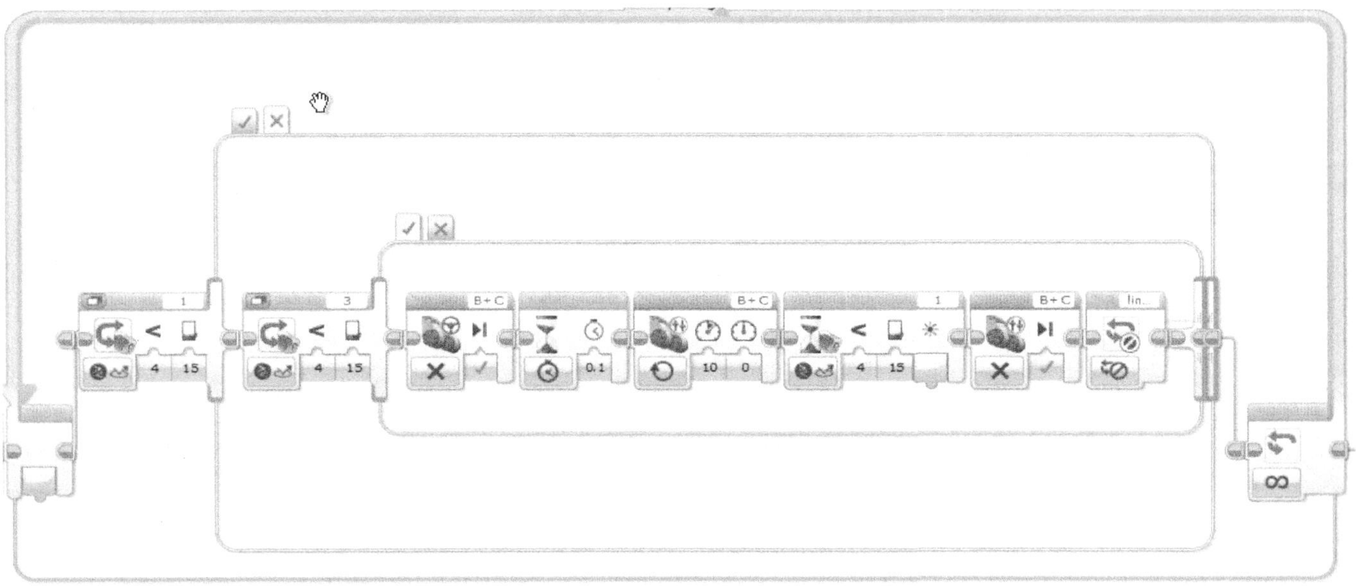

Inner Loop – False part of the switch.

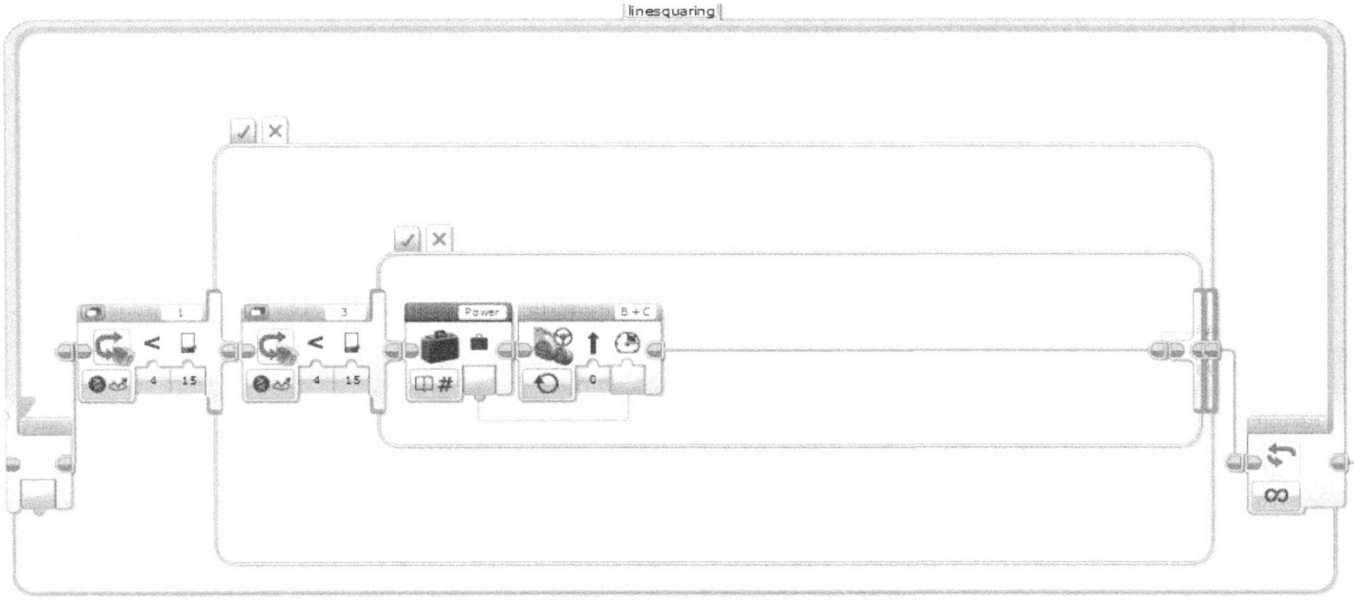

Other blocks in the outer loop that are connected to the inner loop. The 'True' part from the switch statement.

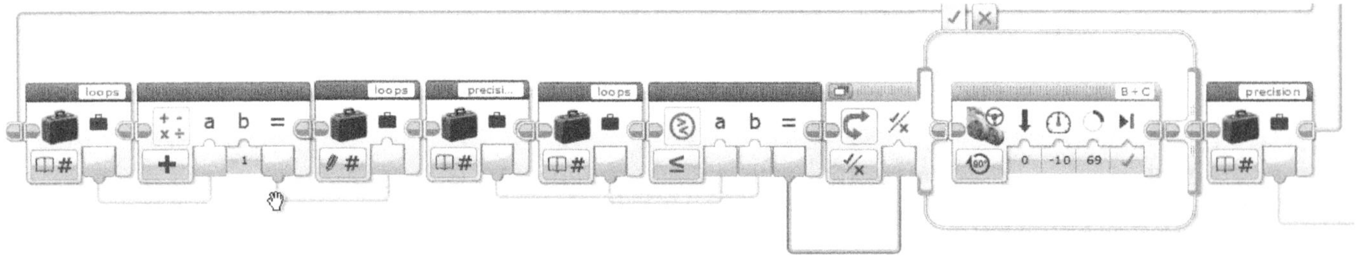

Other blocks in the outer loop that are connected to the inner loop. The 'False' part from the switch statement.

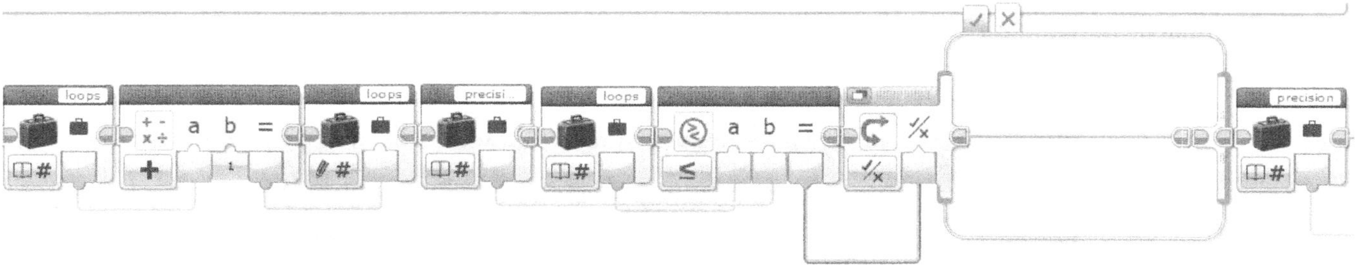

Convert this program into a Myblock called 'LineSquaring'.

This program takes power and precision as it's parameters. Precision is the number of times the outer loop will be executed to perfectly align the robot. You will have to decide precision based on the approaching angle of the robot to the black line. If the angle is close to perpendicular, a smaller precision value will work.

Now let us understand the process of programming as your team is getting ready for competition. Every sub team should create their own projects with the common Myblocks exported and imported in each project. Any change to the Myblock programming should be discussed between the sub teams.

Once the sub teams have perfected the programs and there are 4 weeks left till the competition, your team should combine all the programs into one project. The number of programs in this final project will be equal to your competition robot runs.

One day before the competition you should delete all the programs in the brick and the 'back up' brick. Then load the final project programs into both bricks.

Before going for the first match you should run your programs in reverse order. This process can be executed with the robot in your hand. This will allow the programs to be queued in the right order for you to run during the match.

Always request the referees to allow your team to perform calibration of their color sensors on the match table mat.

MECHANICAL PROGRAMMING AND MECHANICAL GUIDANCE

The best example of mechanical programming is in music boxes. A music box or musical box is an automatic musical instrument in a box that produces musical notes by using a set of pins placed on a revolving cylinder or disc to pluck the tuned teeth of a steel comb. The cylinder is the program here.

The spikes on the cylinder are placed (or programmed) in such a way that they create a tune.
The key here is that the music box drum is driven by a single axle. You can use same concept in your robot to drive multiple activities by using a single motor. You will have to use this in conjunction with pneumatic, spring and rubber band mechanisms as the programming cylinder will only have enough power to trigger these mechanisms.
Here are 2 simple mechanisms I have used to do mechanical programming.
The LEGO musical box shown in the next picture.

Yellow axle at top

Red axle at top

This mechanism allows you to operate 4 switches (the switches are operated by axles hitting the switch mechanism) at different points in time using a single rotation from the side red axle.
The pictures below show how the mechanism is built.

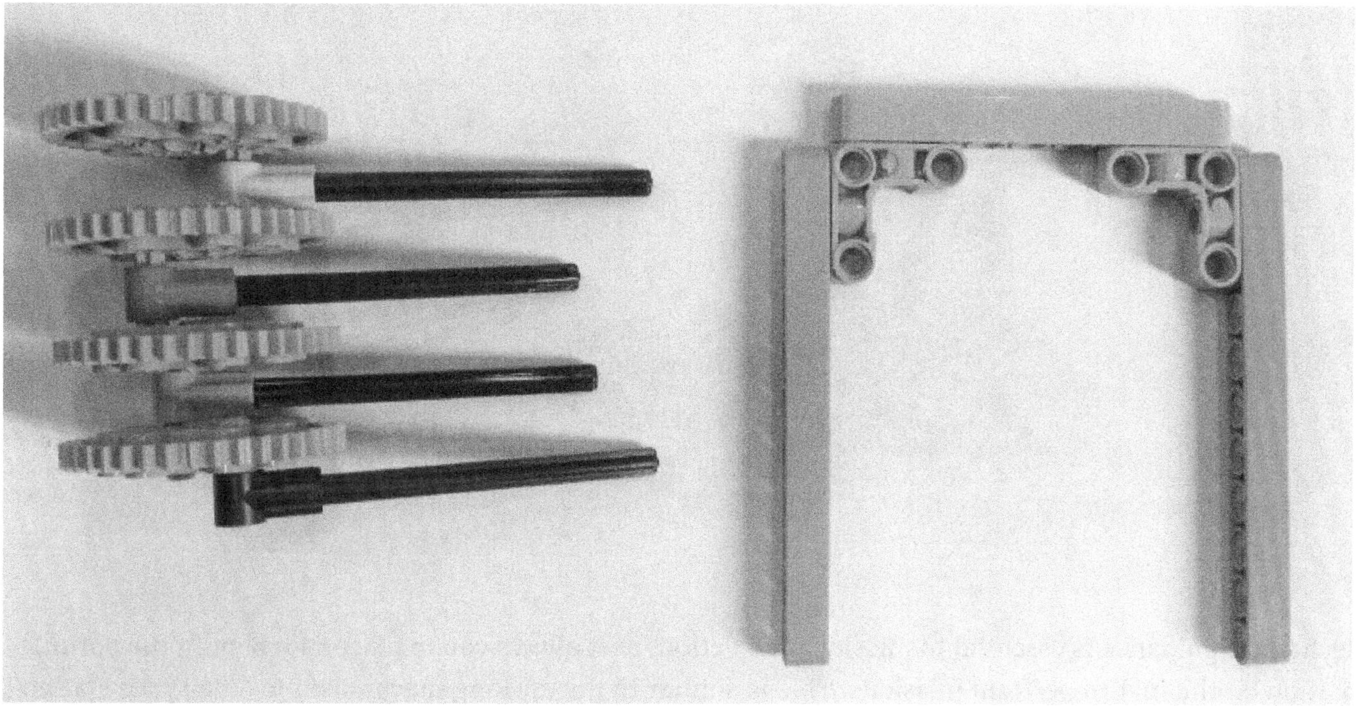

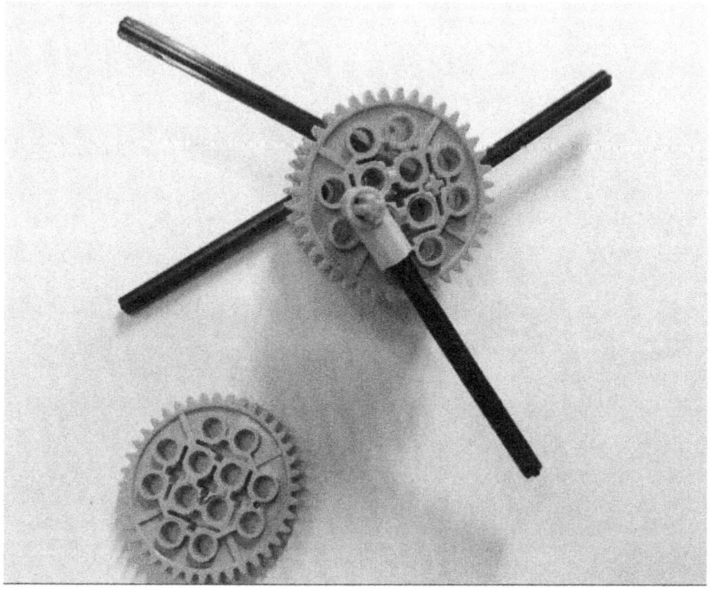

A similar mechanism can be built using cam gears as shown in the next picture.

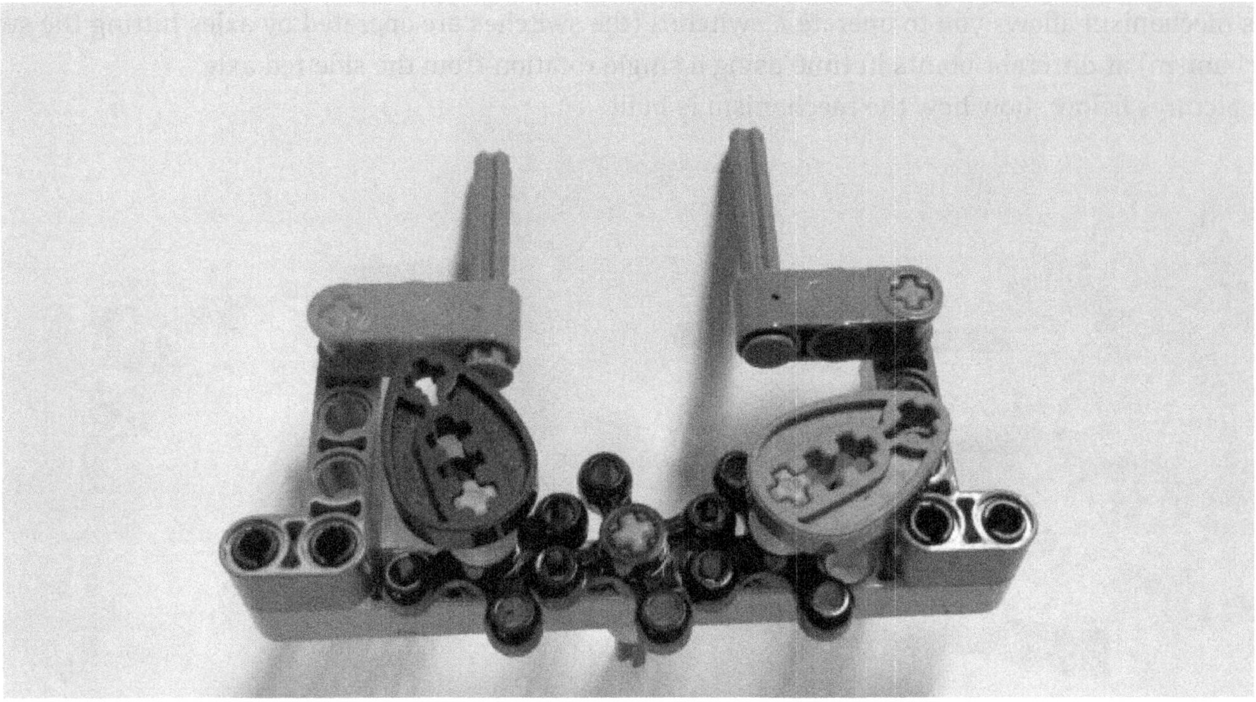

Mechanical guidance is essential to mission completion, as it allows you to place the robot in the optimal position on the mat to perform missions. This is similar to the docking mechanism for the space station modules shown in the next picture.

The next pictures show how you can use angular beams or axles to create the guidance mechanisms.

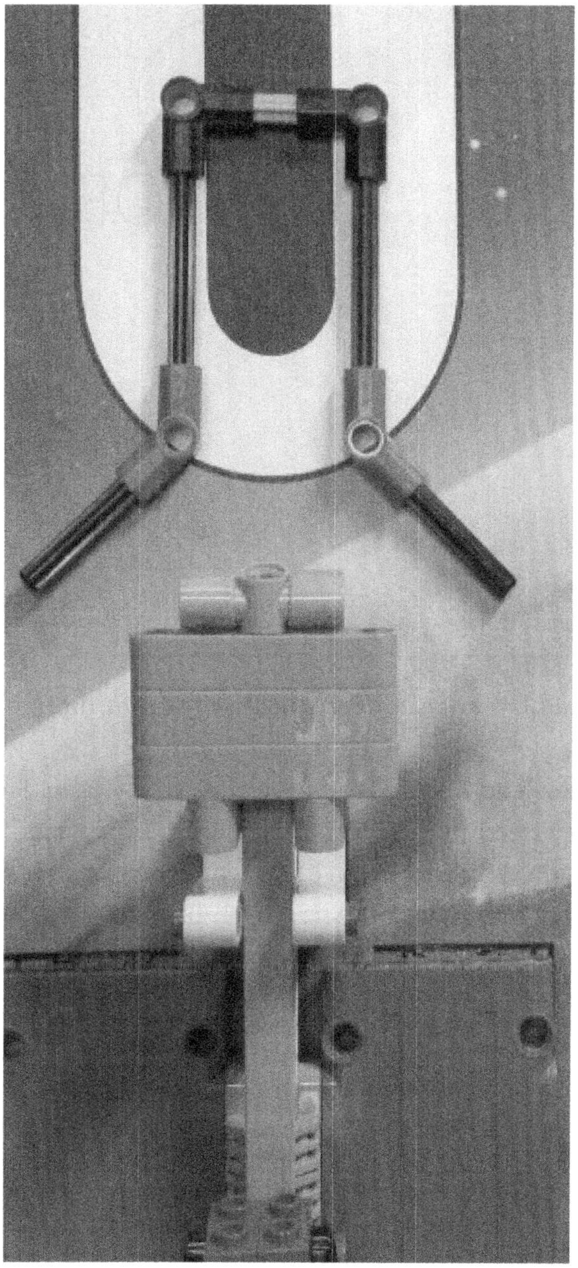

FORMING A TEAM

Core Values

T.E.A.M means Together Everyone Achieves More.
—FLL

THE TEAM

An FLL team can be formed with a minimum of 2 kids to a maximum of 10 kids, 1 Head Coach, and 1 Co-Coach.

The Head Coach-Registers the team. He or She will also act as a facilitator to help the team wherever they need help as per the guidelines provided in the Core Values and Coaches handbook. In addition to head coach each individual team can create a structure to further guide the team. For example, the head coach along with the co-coach may create a structure like the one shown below:

- **Co-coach**- Responsible for supporting the head coach.
- **Robot Game and Robot Design coach**- Robot Design coach is responsible for guiding the team about missions, helping them create small working teams, and helping them if there is a persistent problem
- **Project Coach**- Responsible for guiding the team for the Project portion – helping with the Challenge topic, helping them in their research, and arranging presentations based on the team's directions. A student in sixth grade may not be able to arrange a presentation at a school or library, but a parent will be able to do that easily. If you require more help or advice feel free to contact me at advaitmarathe.com
- **Core Values Coach**- Responsible for coaching kids through FLL Core Values. These coaches will step in if a problem arises between team members.
- **Treasurer (Money Manager)**- Responsible for managing finances of the team. This includes costs such as splitting costs for travel, food, parts, etc.
- **Program Manager** – Helps team create a schedule, based on their availabilities. This will need participation from all parents as team members will probably not be able to drive.

Factors to be considered while forming a team:

I get this question quite often from parents when I teach robotics. Here are some general factors which should be considered.

- **Age and Grade** – In general, kids should be of similar age (one or two years younger or older) Make sure all members are able to participate based on your region.
- **Residence Location**- All the team members should be able to attend scheduled and some spontaneous team meetings. One factor that I saw challenging was the commute. If parents and team members can commute in an acceptable amount of time, residence location should not matter too much. In general, kids living nearby within the radius of 10-30 miles can commute better and meet the meeting deadlines better than kids living farther away.
  As the team approaches competition day, teams tend to spend hours working and could possibly go into the night. In this situation it really helps if team members who commute live close by.
- **Interest and commitment**: Every team member needs to be committed to the competition. Through my experiences I have seen that this usually means spending at least 3-4 hours per week and around 6 -8 hours per week near competition time.
- **Coaches commitment**- Coaches will also need to commit 2-4 hours per week for guidance and overall team logistics, like travel, food, and commute.

NAMING THE TEAM

After the team is formed, the team should spend some time getting to know each other. They should have some team bonding sessions and should have some time to figure out what everyone is interested in.

Once the team knows each other the next **main step** is to **name the team**. The team should start brainstorming ideas about what they want to name their team. This activity is a good way to start promoting core values and I have always seen teams having fun in this part of the FLL competition.
A sample strategy for teams to carry out this exercise is to tell each team member to come up with 3 team names along with the explanation for those names **(This is a very common judging question- What does your team name represent?).**
Then, start voting and let the team members know that they aren't allowed to vote for themselves. Ask each team member to vote for the other team members' names by ranking them from 1-3. Whatever team name receives the maximum number of votes will be the final name of the team.

REGISTERING THE TEAM

After forming the team, the designated head coach registers the team with FIRST LEGO League.
Registration includes paying the registration fee, ordering the EV3 kit and field challenge kit, and registering the team to local qualifiers.
Average registration costs are around $300 - $400, which includes registration for local qualifiers.
Registration cost includes the registration fee and the challenge set (Field Mat and mission parts).
The costs not included in this are the costs for travel, snack/food, and buying the actual EV3 set.

TEAM RULES AND AGREEMENT

For every competition/tournament, there are rules for the competition/tournament itself. For FLL, establishing some ground rules and an agreement to follow those rules is key to preparing, participating, and winning the tournament.

It is good practice to have some ground rules developed by the head coach for the team.

Here is a sample handbook of some ground rules and agreements:

Sample FLL Team Handbook

- Everybody is equally important and contributes to the success of the team.
- All team members are required to uphold core values.
- Everybody should embrace FIRST Core Values throughout the FLL competition journey.
- Team meeting timings are subject to change with one-week prior notice. Changes can be Because of:
  - 3 or more people having problems in keeping the Regular Team meeting slot.
  - No team members available on Public Holidays
- Other coaches and parents need to inform head coach if they are planning to miss a team meeting a week in advance unless team member is not well. Inform the group about your absence.
- A task assigned to you means you own the detailed planning and execution of the task and timely delivery.
- Any team member requiring an extra time slot other than scheduled team meetings should work with coach for scheduling time.
- Kids are responsible for Mission Set-up and Clean-up. It should be supervised by volunteer present at the team meeting. This helps in keeping all the missions and their pieces together. Otherwise, there is a good chance of losing mission pieces
- For safety reasons, Field Table Setup should be the responsibility of the Parents.
- Each family will pool in initial $XXX towards Team Funds.
- Team funds will be used for:
  - Team registration and season field set up kit, LEGO parts, Batteries
  - Snacks for kids after team meetings
  - Project props, poster boards, costumes
  - Tournament expenses
  - Celebrations/ Fun activities

SAMPLE VOLUNTEER TASKS

Job Type	Volunteer Job	Volunteer Name
Treasurer	Manage Team Fund	
	Snacks after class, Tournament food and lunch	
Set up	Field set up, Batteries, Parts	
Project Core Values	Develop Project Schedule including project prep schedule, meeting venue... Project Prototype, Props and Costumes Core Values Guidance and activities	
Bot Design / Bot Game Bot Game	Guidance for Missions Design, attachments, programming Guidance with persisting mat problems	
Tournament/ Team Spirit	Tournament Logistics and waivers, table decoration, Team T-Shirts, Team Spirit/Cheer and team Celebrations	

Sample Team Meeting Schedule

Team Meeting	Day	Timing	Address
Robot design / Missions	For e.g. Thursday	7.00 PM to 8.30 PM PDT	
FLL Project	For e.g. Sunday	3.00 PM to 4.30 PM PDT	
FLL Core Values	For e.g. Tuesday	7.00 p.m. to 8.00 PM PDT	

Vacation Calendar

Team member	Vacation Start Date	Vacation End date
Member name		

TEAM LOGISTICS

Communication channel

After the team is registered, the next step is to decide how team members and parents are going to communicate regarding challenge updates, information, competition dates, questions, and logistics.

Coaches and parents can come up with a common communication avenue based on comfort level and accessibility. I have found that a Google Group is the best way to communicate as it works with any emails. We have used this method in our team when I was participating and I have also recommended this to new FLL parents.

Field Table and Practice Location:

To start working you will need a working field table as this is where all the missions are performed.

Team should decide where they are going to set up the field table and practice area. It could be a coach's, parent volunteer's house, school rooms, etc. The designated location should have space for the table (8 feet by 4 feet) and space for building, designing, and programming. For more information about the table check out the FLL Challenge website. Once everything has been decided, the team can start working on building the table at the designated location.

For safety purposes, this field table building exercise should always be supervised by coaches and/or parent volunteers. This process will take a lot of materials and will involve using power tools. MAKE SURE that team members are safe while using dangerous tools.

For information regarding building instructions, please refer to following link from the FLL website.

https://www.firstinspires.org/sites/default/files/uploads/resource_library/fll/table-build.pdf

Fun Team building activities

One of the key components of FIRST LEGO League is teamwork. Lead coaches and parent volunteers can (actually should) plan some team building activities with team members.

Examples of activities include bowling, hiking, scavenger hunts, or movies.

Team Information Sheet

Every registered team must send a team information sheet before the qualifiers. This sheet is used by FIRST to learn more about your team. This should include your FLL team name, fun facts about the team, their working style, and any other relevant information you may have.

Here is an example of a sample information sheet that we have prepared.

	Name	Description
Team	Team name and Team number	Describe your team Your Team strengths, FLL Core values Team learned and followed, Example of Gracious professionalism and Coopetition Fun facts about your team
Robot	Robot Name	Robot Design description
Project	Project Name, Prototype name	Short description of your project problem solution and learning

Registering for local region tournaments

There is a separate registration step required to register to local regional tournaments. The process is similar to registering for a qualifier.

Design and Ordering T-Shirts

On the competition day, it is recommended that team members wear unique t-shirts.

Team members can come up with t-shirt designs around three weeks before the tournament. Parents can help the kids to order the designed t-shirts. If there are any other accessories you want to add make sure to leave three weeks for the items to ship to ensure you get them by competition day.

Attend qualifiers happening before your tournament

One of the best tips I have is that your team should attend qualifiers before your tournament. We did that before our tournaments and it helped us immensely. The main goal of this visit is to cheer friends or other teams on and confirm the understanding of the rules. Coaches and parent volunteers can decide the day and date based on the regional tournament schedule. Going to tournaments beforehand can help you catch some mistakes in the understanding of the rules.

Tournament day

It is the big day. The day to demonstrate your team's work on the robot design, project research, solution and most importantly Teamwork!!!

Team members should show core values throughout the day as though the judges were following them throughout the preparation. (Remember judges will enter the Pit Area)

Team appreciation and celebration

Whatever the results are from the competition, always celebrate your team's hard work, and dedication. This will help in keeping team's morale up and encourage them to participate in future FLL competitions.

FLL CORE VALUES

Core Values is one of the most important aspects of the FIRST LEGO League Competition.

Core Values describes a way of working together, respecting each other, and helping each other.

The following are the FLL Core Values that each team participating in the tournament should embrace.

Coaches, Team Members and parent volunteers will express the FIRST philosophies of Gracious Professionalism® and Coopertition® through FIRST Core Values:

Discovery: We explore new skills and ideas. What matters most is what your team has discovered during this FLL season in all aspects of the FLL competition- Project Challenge, Robot Design, Missions, Programming. It could be new skills, innovative ideas, effective strategy, etc.

"What we discover is more important than what we learn" -FIRST

As for me I have learned so much from participating in tournaments and mentoring FLL teams. These competitions have helped me find my passion in robotics and have helped me explore new, more complex concepts.

Innovation: We use creativity and persistence to solve problems. Finding an innovative solution for the project objective, and creating a new strategy was one of my favorite parts of the competition. While working, the team should make sure it writes down all their original ideas in the engineering notebook. For any one given problem, there is more than one solution and the team must be able to analyze the solutions and pick the best one. This analysis was very useful to me down the line.

Impact: We apply what we learn to improve our world. Coming up with a problem for the FLL project question will make the team think of problems that the world is facing and how finding a solution for those problems will help people. Analyzing the impact of problems and the impact of the solution will help teams communicate their approach to the judges. Some FLL projects have turned into real life initiatives that have helped change the world.

Inclusion: We respect each other and embrace our differences. Team members should always respect each other and other teams.

"Teams recognize that both friendly competition and mutual gain are possible, on and off the playing field."-FIRST

The main objective is how your team listened to and considered ideas from everyone and made each team member feel like a valued part of the team. Share with the judges how you worked together and accomplished more than you could have by working alone.

Teamwork: We are stronger when we work together. One of the key components of FLL is Teamwork. It is a team competition for a reason. What matters most here is how successful the team is at getting things done. The judges will test how a team will make decisions, solve problems, set goals, learn and use time management, and self-correct if a team veers off course.

Fun: We enjoy and celebrate what we do!

CORE VALUES JUDGING

Core Values is judged throughout the tournament:

Teams will need to show gracious professionalism® and coopertition® throughout the tournament-During the robot game, core value judging session, practice, and in general across their entire FLL tournament, judges are watching you.

Please refer to Core Value judging rubrics from FLL website.

https://www.firstinspires.org/sites/default/files/uploads/fll/first-LEGO-league-rubrics.pdf

Teamwork Judging process:

Teams will meet with the Core Values judges in a separate room sometimes a separate building of the same venue. Coaches or mentors are not allowed in any of the judging rooms. Judges will generally **give the team one activity** to complete in 5 minutes. They will instruct a team on what they need to do but it is up to the team to figure out a solution. The main characteristic that judges are looking for is how well team members interact with each other and how they solve the problem as a team.

The Core Value Activities can be anything – Some examples from previous years include:

- Building a structure out of pennies, craft sticks, or pipe cleaners
- Create a skit to sell a newspaper
- Sorting Core Values in any order and explaining the reasoning behind the orders
- Building a LEGO structure as a team but each team member can only use one hand
- Solving a puzzle

After the team activity, Judges will ask questions about the activity. Some sample questions they ask are-

- Did you enjoy the activity?

- How did the team come up with the solution?
- How did they come up with the strategy?
- Was there any disagreement regarding solutions and how did you resolve them?

Apart from the activity, judges will ask general questions.

Sample core value questions

Could you share your Core Values Poster with us?

Inspiration:

Discovery

1. What's the most important thing you learned this season?
2. Would you still do FLL even if there were no awards? Why?
3. If an FLL team can't attend an event because there isn't one nearby, is FLL still worth doing? Why?
4. Do any of your team members mentor others? If so explain.
5. What was the most surprising thing you learned this season?
6. Which aspect of FLL did your team like best? Least?
7. How did your team decide which aspect of FLL to do first?
8. Describe any struggles your team had making sure they addressed all 3 aspects (Project, Robot, Core Values) of FLL.
9. How would you describe your team?
10. How did your team decide its name?
11. What's the most important thing we should know about your team?
12. What does your team do when it is having a bad day?
13. How does your team share with others your excitement and enthusiasm?
14. Do you participate on any other teams (i.e., sports, debating, chess club, drama club) and, if so, is there anything different about your FLL team experience?
15. Tell us what you have learned about FLL and how you think it will help you in the future.
16. Name one of the FLL Core Values and explain how your team uses it (or could use it) outside of FLL.
17. Who can give me an example of a way they used an FLL Core Value this year on their own away from the team?
18. Does anyone have an example of someone they know (on the team or off) using FLL Core Values in a way that impressed you?
19. What were your team's goals this season?
20. How did you decide on your team goals?
21. Tell me about a problem you had on your team and how it was resolved.
22. Tell me about how your group makes decisions together.
23. What do you do when your group doesn't agree?
24. How does your team solve problems that come up?
25. Does your team have a set of rules? If so, what are they, and how are they enforced?

Efficiency

1. How did your team decide what to do each time you met?
2. Did your team get everything done this season that you set out to do?
3. How does your team manage its time?
4. If we gave your team one more week to work together, how would you use it?
5. Tell us about the roles each of you had on the team and how this worked.
6. How did you decide who would do each role?
7. What happens if a team member is not getting his/her job done?
8. Can someone else do your job? What happens when someone is sick?
9. Do you have team leaders? If so, explain how that works.

10. What's the most important thing you learned from your coach?
11. What does your team do when it gets stuck?
12. Describe a situation when your coach helped you. What did he/she do?
13. What makes a good coach?
14. What kinds of things does a coach need to know?
15. What would your team do if it didn't have a coach?
16. How did your coach help the team be successful?
17. How does your team get its ideas?
18. How does your team decide which ideas they will pursue?
19. Tell me about one thing each of you contributed to the team.
20. What do you do when you don't like someone else's idea?
21. What does Gracious Professionalism mean to you?
22. How do you show Gracious Professionalism when you relate to your team? To your coach? To others?
23. How do you make someone feel valued when you talk to them?
24. What example of Gracious Professionalism have you seen another team do today?
25. If you saw something happening to another team and thought it wasn't fair, what would you do and why?
26. Explain how Gracious Professionalism is like good sportsmanship. And how is it different?
27. Can you give an example of Gracious Professionalism that your team displayed this season?
28. Competitions can sometimes be stressful. How does your team prepare each other or maybe other teams to get ready for a big event?

Judges look for:

1. Confidence and enthusiasm of team members.
2. Concrete descriptions and examples.
3. Are team members listening to each other and to the judges? Are they interrupting each other or waiting their turn?
4. Are team members looking at the judges when they speak or at team members when they are talking?
5. Is everyone answering questions or just a few?
6. Do they encourage each other to participate?
7. Does the team look to the coach for direction?

CORE VALUE AWARDS

In the regional tournaments, there is only one core value award given to teams.
In the championship tournaments, the following core value awards are presented
There are three (3) Core Value trophies awarded at the Championship Tournament:

- Inspiration Award
- Teamwork
- Gracious Professionalism

"The **Inspiration award** celebrates a team that is empowered by their FLL experience and displays extraordinary enthusiasm and spirit" -FIRST

Judging Criteria:

- Discovery
- Team Spirit

- Integration

Inspiration Award Possible Judge Questions:

1. What were your team's goals this season?
2. Tell me about a problem you had on your team and how it was resolved.
3. How does your team manage its time?
4. Tell us about the roles each of you had on the team and how this worked.
5. What's the most important thing you learned from your coach?
6. Describe a situation when your coach helped you. What did he/she do?

"The **Teamwork award** recognizes a team that is able to accomplish more together than they could as individuals through shared goals, strong communication, effective problem solving and excellent time management." -FIRST

Judging Criteria:

- Effectiveness
- Efficiency
- Kids Do the Work

Teamwork Possible Judge Questions:

1. What's the most important thing you learned this season?
2. Would you still do FLL even if there were no awards? Why?
3. How did your team decide its name?
4. What's the most important thing we should know about your team?
5. Name one of the FLL Core Values and explain how your team uses it (or could use it) outside of FLL.
6. Who can give me an example of a way they used an FLL Core Value this year on their own away from the team?

"The **Gracious Professionalism award** recognizes a team whose members show each other and other teams respect at all times. They recognize that both friendly competition and mutual gain are possible, on and off the playing field."-FIRST

Gracious Professionalism Judging Criteria:

- Inclusion
- Respect
- Coopertition

Possible Inclusion Judge Questions

1. How does your team decide which ideas they will pursue?
2. Tell me about one thing each of you contributed to the team.
3. What does Gracious Professionalism mean to you?
4. How do you show Gracious Professionalism when you relate to your team?
5. What example of Gracious Professionalism have you seen another team do today?
6. If you saw something happening to another team and thought it wasn't fair, what would you do and why?

OTHER WAYS TO SHOW CORE VALUES

"Swap" Items:

Some teams choose to give out "swap" items at tournaments. These items are completely optional. They are items that you swap with other teams to show gracious professionalism and teamwork to others. "Swap" items may include

- Stickers
- pencils with the team name
- erasers
- key chains
- small goody bags

Fliers and or other paper creations with information about the team or the team's project is a great way for your team to introduce themselves to other teams at tournaments and show Core Values

Pit Area:

Teams typically prepare items to decorate their pit areas at tournaments

- Posters
- Display boards
- Balloons (Latex-free)
- Tents and large displays!

This is one way a team can show off their fantastic season to spectators and other teams

Tournament Apparel:

Teams typically wear t-shirts with their team name/colors. Many teams choose to wear hats/wigs or other items of clothing to represent their team's spirit and purpose.

Handshakes/Cheers/High 5's:

Some teams choose to come up with different handshakes, cheers, and high 5's all in the spirit of teamwork and Coopertition. Encourage your team to not only cheer for their robot, but to cheer and encourage all the other robots at the tournament.

CARING ABOUT COMMUNITY

Project and Sharing

The greatness of a community is most accurately measured by the compassionate actions of its members
-Coretta Scott King

WHAT AND WHY? FLL PROJECT

Every year, the FIRST® organization releases a different challenge theme for FLL® Competitions. The Project is one of the most important and exciting parts of the FLL Tournament.
The **preliminary goals** of the project in FLL competitions are to

- Encourage kids to learn more about the technology and science behind the challenge theme.
- Brainstorm real world problems related to the challenge theme.
- Research and understand the programs and work related to the challenge theme by domain experts and professionals.
- Design innovative solutions

Examples of challenge topics in the past:

- Improve the way people use, transport, dispose, or find water.
- Think about the human/animal interactions problems and how to improve them
- Learn about Trash and Improve a way to reduce, recycle or reuse the trash
- Improve the way people learn different things

The **Key Components** of the FLL Project are:

- Learn about Challenge Topic
- Identify real world problems
- Create innovative solutions
- Share your research and solution

PROJECT JUDGING AND AWARDS

Judging Criteria:

- Team research
- Problem identification
- Design of Solution
- Sharing with the community
- The implementation of Core Values within the project
- Project poster
- Project presentation
- Question and Answer session

Project Awards:

There are 2 project awards presented at qualifying tournaments and 3 project awards presented at championship tournaments

- Best Project Award
- Global Innovation Award

PROJECT EXECUTION STEPS

1. Discuss and Brainstorm the Challenge theme:

Once the challenge topic is released, ask the team to think it over.

In the weekly FLL team meet, ask the team members what those challenge questions mean to them. Brainstorm the answers and create a thorough understanding of the challenge question after the brainstorming session.

2. Problem Identification

The team will have to narrow the general challenge theme to a specific problem. Ask the team members to do research about the challenge questions, and discuss possible resources for research. Sample resources we used in the past are

- Internet
- Books/eBooks
- Field trips to the library, Children Discovery Center, Tech Museum... (based on the challenge theme.)
- Formal/Informal discussions with field experts
- Conducting formal surveys

Ask each team member to come up with 5 problems related to the challenge questions that they came across during their research.

3. Solution Identification

Once the problem is identified, the team can start brainstorming about possible solutions. They can start by finding existing solutions and find out whether there are any shortcomings to it

If the team finds that there is no existing solution, then they can start thinking about designing a completely new one. If the team finds that there is an existing solution that has shortcomings, they can find a way to improve and change it.

Every team member can come up with 3-4 different designs for solutions. From my experience, the best project solution is one that is innovative, unique, and cost effective. These three pillars will provide you with the best chance to win the competition.

The team and coach should discuss all the designs that every team member comes up with. Factors to be considered while discussing the design

- Feasibility
- Cost effective solution
- Users of the solution (Organizations, professionals, kids, community)
- Sharing audience

Not all the designs that the team came up with will have the makings of a good solution. After the brainstorming session, combine multiple designs and come up with the one which will have most of the above properties.

4. Share Research and Solution

After creating the solution, the next important step is to share the solution with field experts, schools, libraries, nonprofit organizations and many others. Sharing the solution helps create awareness about the problem and allows you to hone your solution.

Poster Creation:

The Team should prepare a tri fold poster to present in the competition.

The poster should include the problem description, and the team name and number.

COMPETITION DAY PROJECT ACTIVITIES

The project judging happens in a separate room than the FLL Competition. Only team members are allowed into this judging session. Teams should take their poster, and any other additional presentation materials.

Once they enter the judging room they have 5 minutes to set up their poster, and their project prototype. Once set up, teams should introduce themselves and get permission from the judges to start their presentation.

During their presentation, teams should explain

- Research, resources used to in research.
- How the team decided on their specific problem
- What problems they faced?

- How they developed solution?
- Who did they share the solution and why?

Each team member should participate in the project presentation and in the Q and A Session.

PREPARING FOR THE PROJECT JUDGING SESSION

The most important component of a project presentation is that each team member should talk.

Judges will be looking for these specific points:

- Depth of information provided.
- All students participated in the research process, or understand the process and results of the team's research.
- Supporting printed materials provided to judges.
- Entire team participated in the discussion.
- How the team interacts with each other?
- Do they all talk, or only a few? If so, why?
- Does the team look to the coach often or are they focused on the presentation and judges?

I have included questions below to help prepare teams in all aspects of their projects

Project Questions:

Research Quality

1. What resources did you use to research your problem and why did you choose these?
2. Did you use any unusual methods to research your topic? If so what and why?
3. Did the information you used offer different ideas than what you expected to find? If so, what and how did your team use this information?
4. Did you consider any other design?
5. Did you speak to anyone whose work relates to the Challenge area? What did you learn
6. from them?
7. Can you tell us about a problem you discovered or something that you learned that surprised you while completing this project?
8. After working on this project, what is the most important thing that your team learned?

Innovative Solution

1. What makes your solution different from what is being used to solve this problem now,
2. and why do you think it is better?
3. How did you arrive at your solution and why?
4. Were there solutions that you thought of that you decided not to use? Why?

Project Sharing

1. With whom did you share your project? Why did you choose that individual or group?
2. How did you share the information? Did you present it in the same manner as you presented to us, or did you choose a different approach? Why?
3. What impact did your presentation have on them?

4. What changes have you or others made as a result of your research and presentation?

Creative Presentation

1. How did you decide on this presentation style that you used?
2. Why did you choose the presentation style that you chose? How does this style help your audience understand what you are telling them?
3. What do you think was the most creative aspect of your presentation or project and why?
4. One aspect of the project asked you to share your ideas with others. How did your team do this?

INTRODUCTION TO FTC

Using Android and Java

TOTALLY DIFFERENT BALLGAME

You can use any parts

In the beginning of Roomba, we all took turns answering the support line. Once, a woman called and explained that her robot had a defective motor. I said, 'Send it back. We'll send you a new one.' She said, 'No - I'm not sending you Rosie.'
—Colin Angle, Founder iRobot Corp.

IN the not so distant future you can expect to see the following passage in a newspaper 'The RCMR-6 Remote controlled mobile robot (or "MOROB" suit) is a distant descendant of the first military robotic exoskeletons used on Earth in the mid-21st century. **It finds its origin in the competition robots that were developed for the FTC competition.** The suit is used extensively on the Moon and Mars colonies (where they are powered by fuel cells and/or mc turbines). Its well-tested capabilities have proved invaluable in the harsh environment of Proxima b, the first ever exoplanet colonized by humans outside of the sun's solar system'. The same way that you will one day be able to control these exosuits, in FTC you can finally have full control over your robot. This feature and many others are very exciting for participants and my team and I have thoroughly enjoyed competing in the FTC competitions.

In this chapter and the next few chapters I am going to briefly describe the FTC competition, tools, methods, and resources you can use. The FTC section of this book is just an introduction and is not as extensive as the FLL section of this book.

THE FTC competition is a totally different ball game. You can use any raw materials or parts that you can buy in your local hardware stores, local grocery stores, basically almost anywhere. The only restriction is that it shouldn't be a finished assembly (like a finished camera assembly) or an off the shelf light sensor. Now instead of LEGO parts you will be using metal connections from kits such as Tetrix, Vex, and more. With all this freedom, safety is the most important requirement and you have to wear safety gear at all times (safety goggles and gloves). You will continue to have restrictions on how many motors you can use and restrictions on the types and powers of these motors.

Another amazing change is that you are allowed to attend MORE THAN ONE qualifier. Yes, more than one. You are allowed to go to 2-3 qualifiers for a chance to qualify to the regional competition.

The matches will now be played on 12 feet by 12 feet field. The match timing will be broken up into a 30 seconds autonomous period followed by a 2 minutes driver-operated period. To program you will use block programming (similar to MIT App inventor) or the Java Programming Language. The matches will involve 4 teams competing against each other in a 2 v 2 pattern. (2 teams will form an alliance and compete against the opposing alliance of 2 teams). The alliance is selected by the referees randomly at the beginning of the tournament.

SAFETY FIRST

1- Wear safety glasses at all times while building the robot.
2- Wear work gloves and ear protection while operating heavy noisy tools
3- Adult supervision is necessary during build sessions
4-All manufacturers' safety precautions must be followed while operating their tools
5-Emergency kits and communication means should be available in the build area
6-The filing of rough edges and metal shavings should be cleaned up immediately
7- Safety education should be provided to every new team member.

FIELD SETUP

You can buy or create the FTC field (12 by 12 feet) that will house the challenge for the entire season. It will also be used during build and programming team meetings.

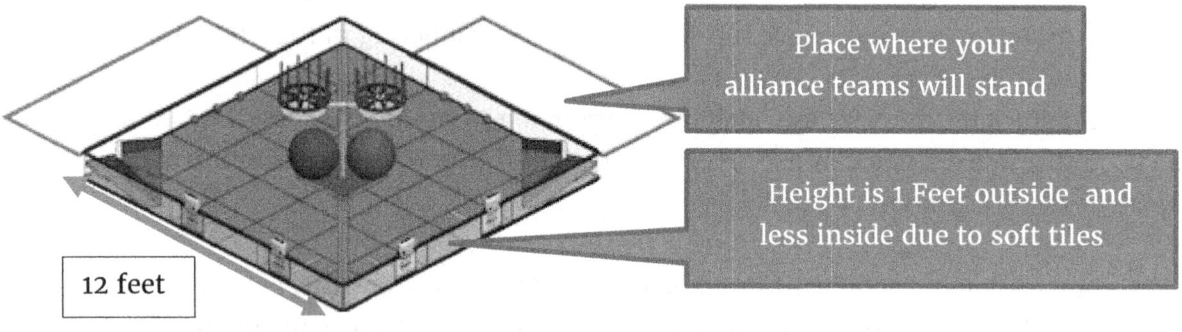

The first option is that you can buy the kit from Andy Mark at approximately $500 -$600, which also includes soft tiles for the floor. The second option is to create your own field. I would recommend buying the kit, as it is easier to dismantle and store during the off-season.

PARTS

The following pictures show the main parts you will be using in your FTC robot.

The next picture shows electrical and electronics parts that will be on the robot. This will include the android device (brain), battery (power), core power distribution module, actuator and sensor controllers, actuators, and sensors.

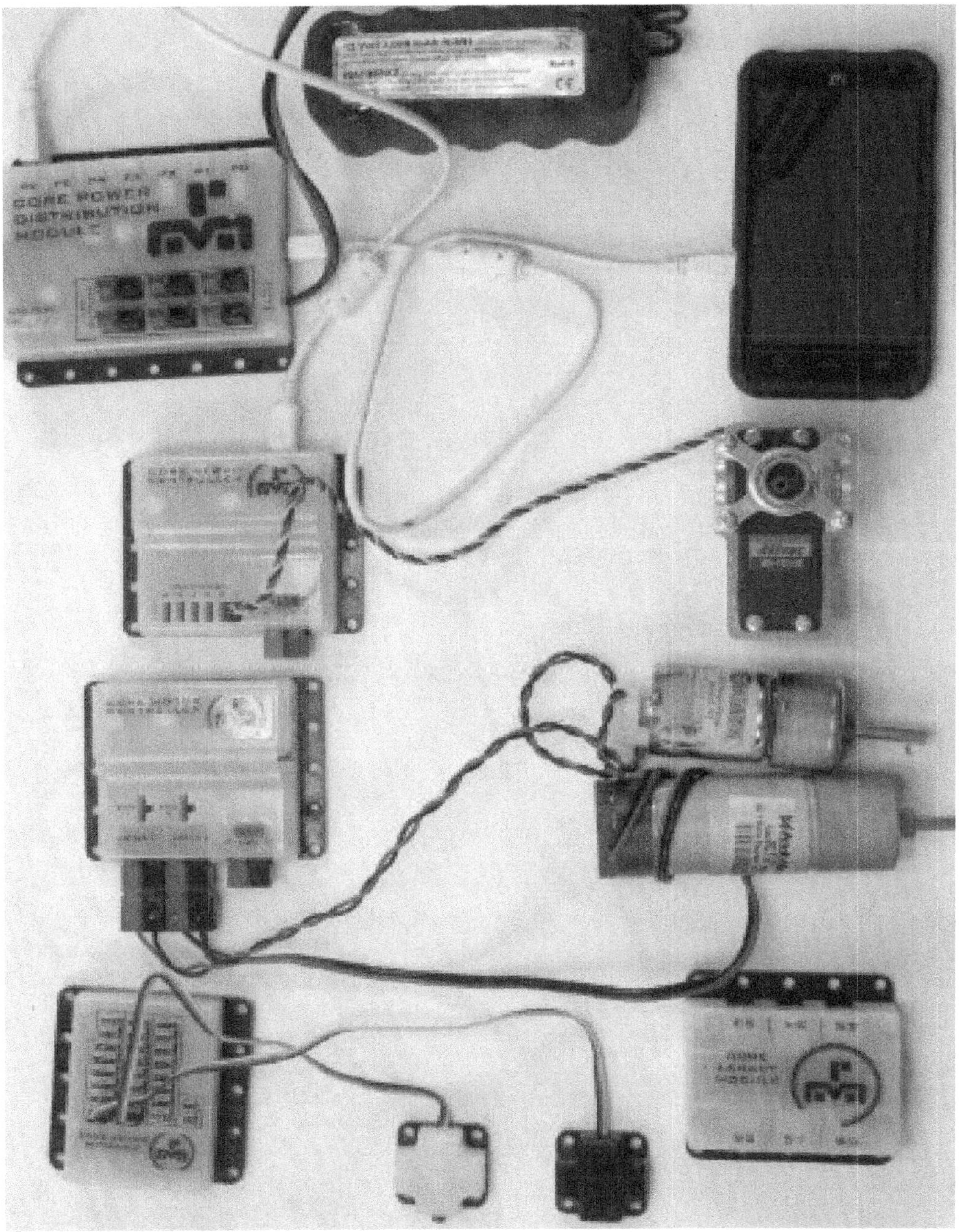

The parts in the next picture will be used for the driver side unless you are using a different device.

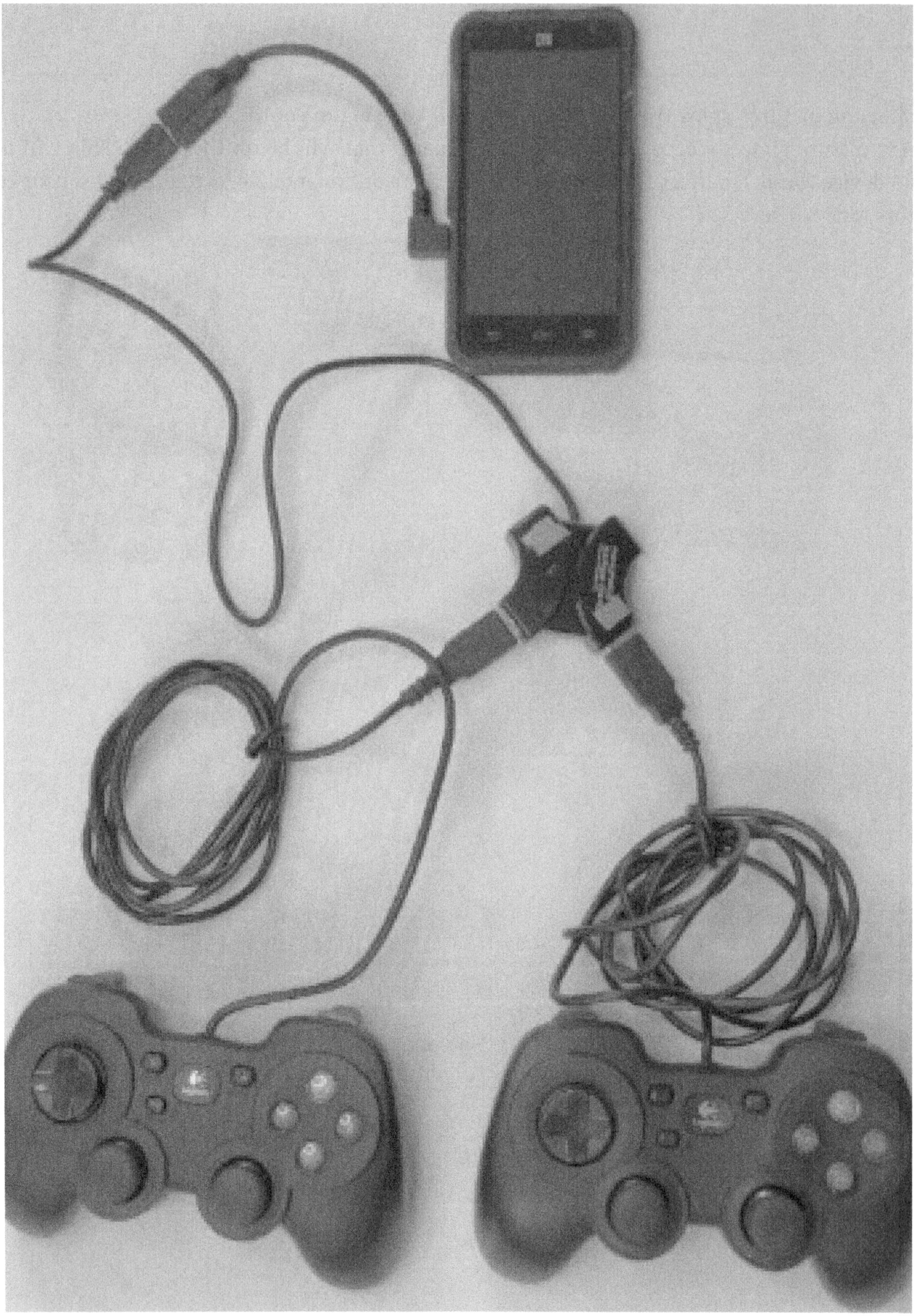

The next picture shows tools that you may use.

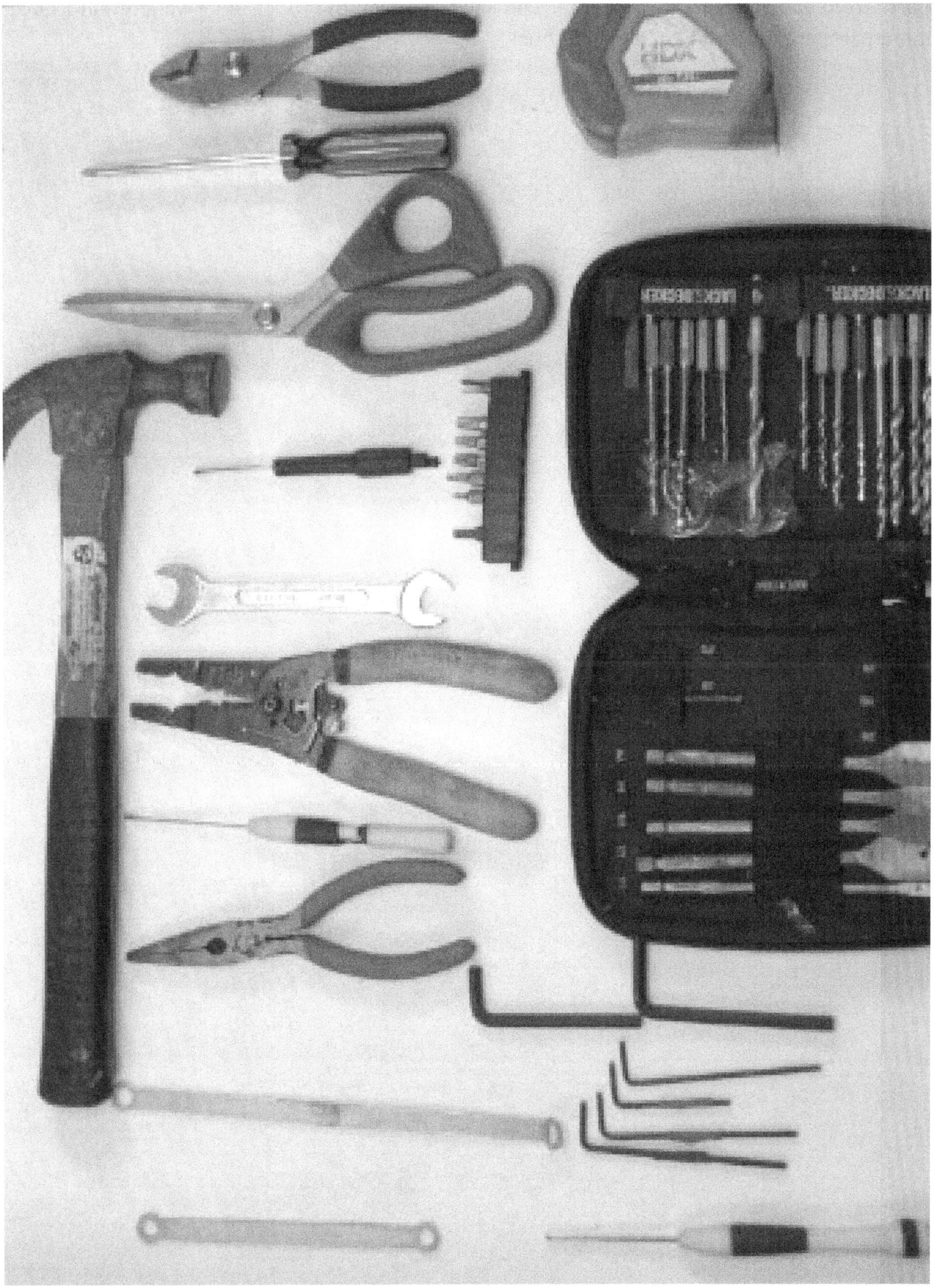

The next picture shows structural parts you may use from any Tetrix kit. You can always augment these with parts from your local hardware store. The key is to keep the robot light weight and I have found aluminum parts are the best bang for their buck.

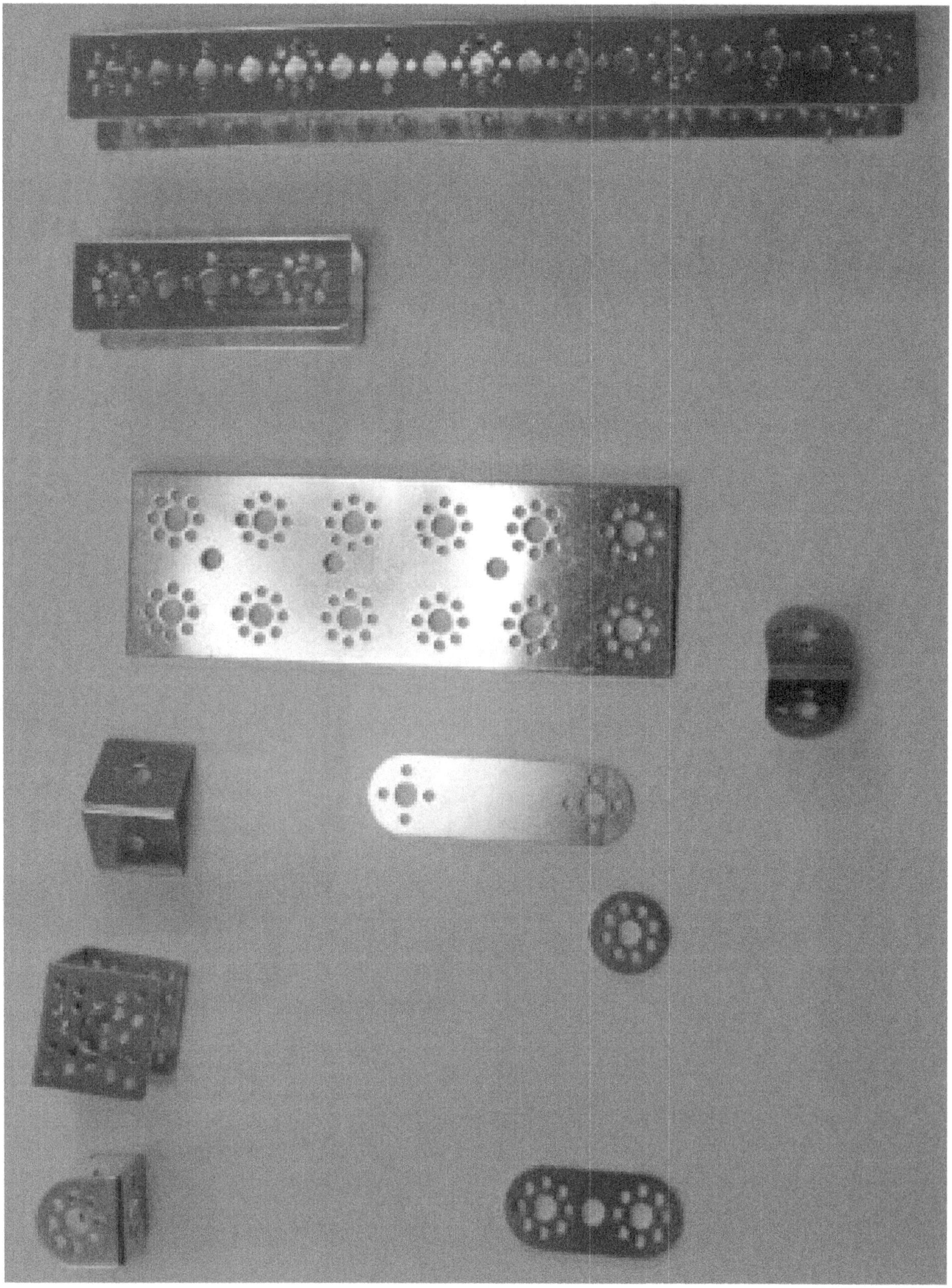

The next picture shows the drive train parts you may use. Omni wheels when placed in the proper 'X' configuration, allows the robot to move sideways.

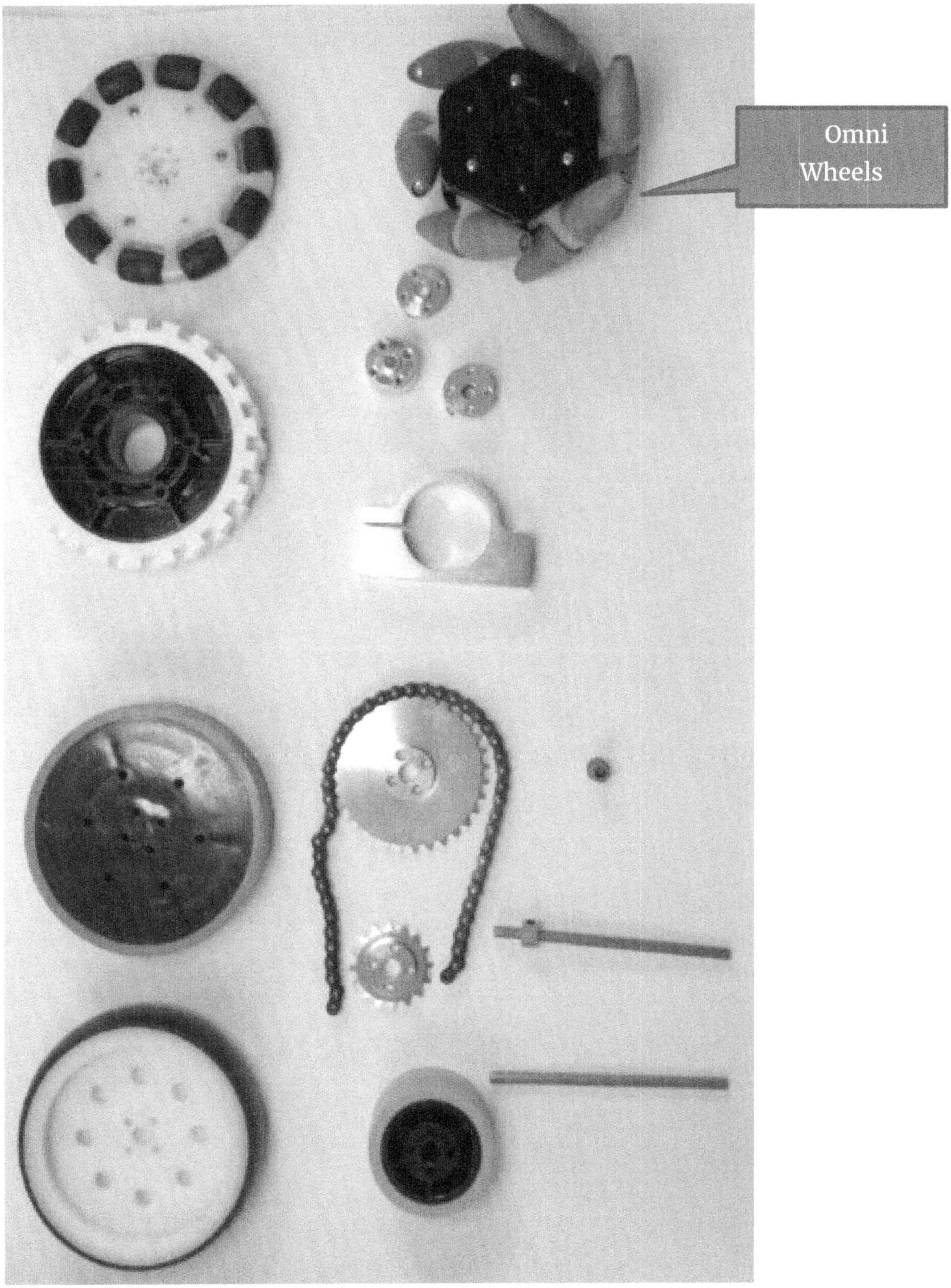

The next picture shows various gears and the rack/pinion mechanism you may use in building your robot.

The next picture shows fasteners (aluminum nuts and bolts) and other parts you may have in your stocked bins.

The next picture shows electrical parts you may have in your storage bins. Having a multimeter is highly recommended for testing out electronics.

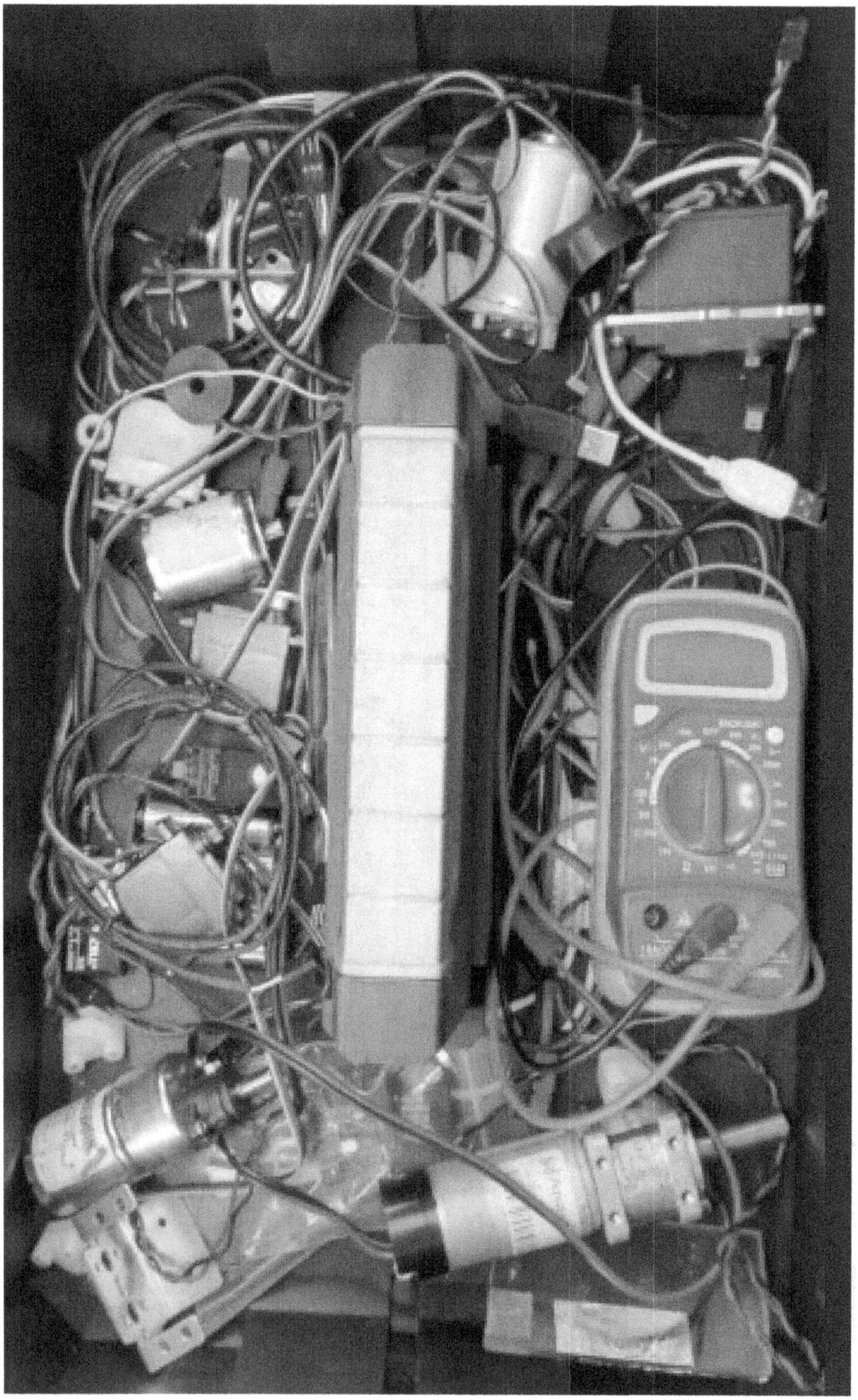

The next picture shows gears and a few other required parts you might need.

3D PRINTED PARTS

3D printed parts allow you to create a sturdy component out of your imagination.
It is very helpful in building parts without cutting, sawing, or milling and is much safer too. The following pictures are a few examples of 3D printed parts. 3D printed parts can be cost-savers if the parts you are ordering are extremely costly. Most of the time, 3D printed parts should be used for creating custom assemblies and parts, particularly those that are not available on the market.

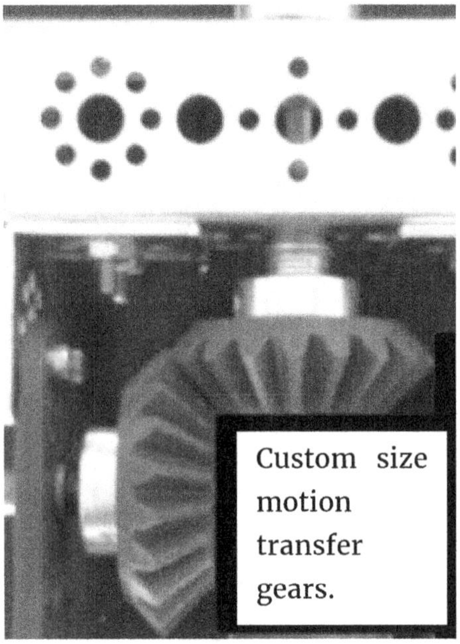
Custom size motion transfer gears.

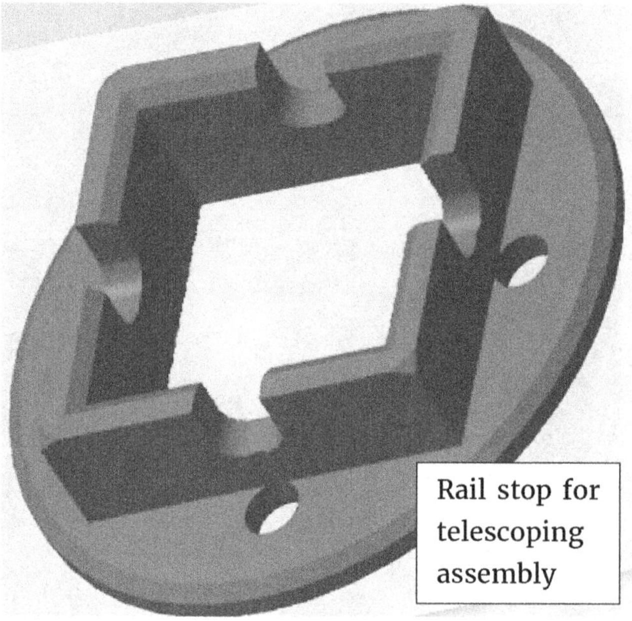
Rail stop for telescoping assembly

PROGRAMMING- JAVA OR BLOCK

To start programming you will first need to set up your devices. You will install the 'FTC Driver Station' App on one android phone and you will install the 'FTC Robot Controller' App on the second android phone. You will install either a block programming tool, the OnBot Java Programming Tool, or Android Studio on your laptop. The program will be developed on these tools and then the program (opmodes in case of java) or program and opmode in case of block programming will be stored in the 'FTC Robot Controller' App.
The 'FTC Driver station' App will communicate with the 'FTC Robot Controller' App and communicate the commands to the robot. The next picture shows the flow for running your programs. You have to learn Java or block programming and decide on which programming language you want to use. You can try out both before deciding. I programmed in both and liked them equally. Our team decided on Java programming due to our team members' prior experience in Java.

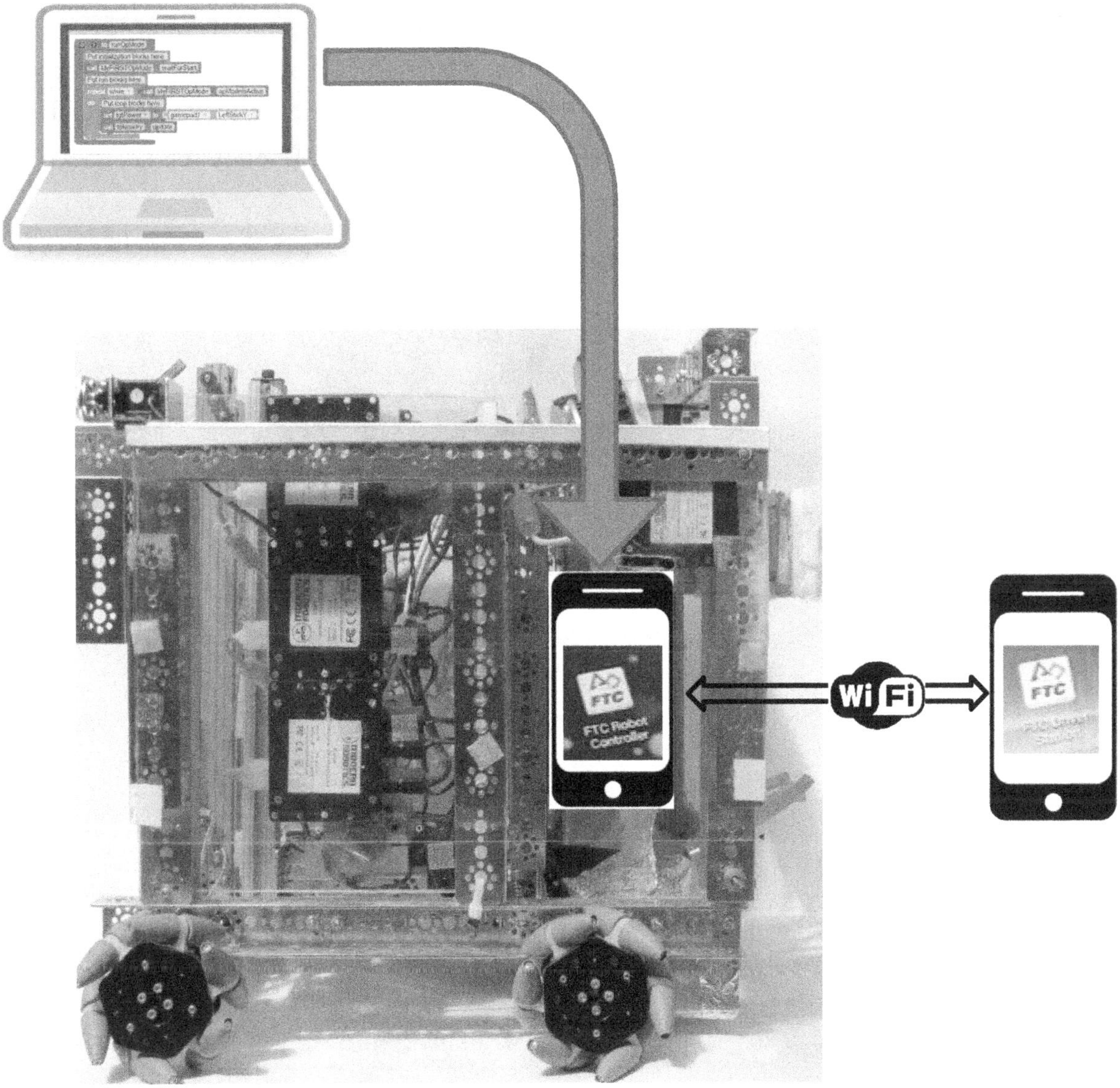

COMPUTER VISION

The 2017-2018 FIRST Tech Challenge® game includes special vision targets. These targets contain secret clues that can be used to score extra points during the autonomous portion of a match. These special vision targets are known as VuMarks®. The VuMarks use PTC's Vuforia® computer vision technology to encode hidden information within each picture. This information isn't easily noticeable to the casual human observer. However, the FIRST Tech Challenge software for the 2017-2018 season includes special functions that let a robot read the VuMarks using the Robot Controller's built-in camera.

Version 3.3 and higher of the FTC Robot Controller app includes a sample op mode that demonstrates how to check for VuMarks and extract the hidden information when a VuMark is identified.
The ability to use computer vision is extremely helpful and is useful for many real-world applications. I am currently working on using Computer Vision to help detect when students are engaged in learning environments. Next picture shows you how the program detects facial expressions.

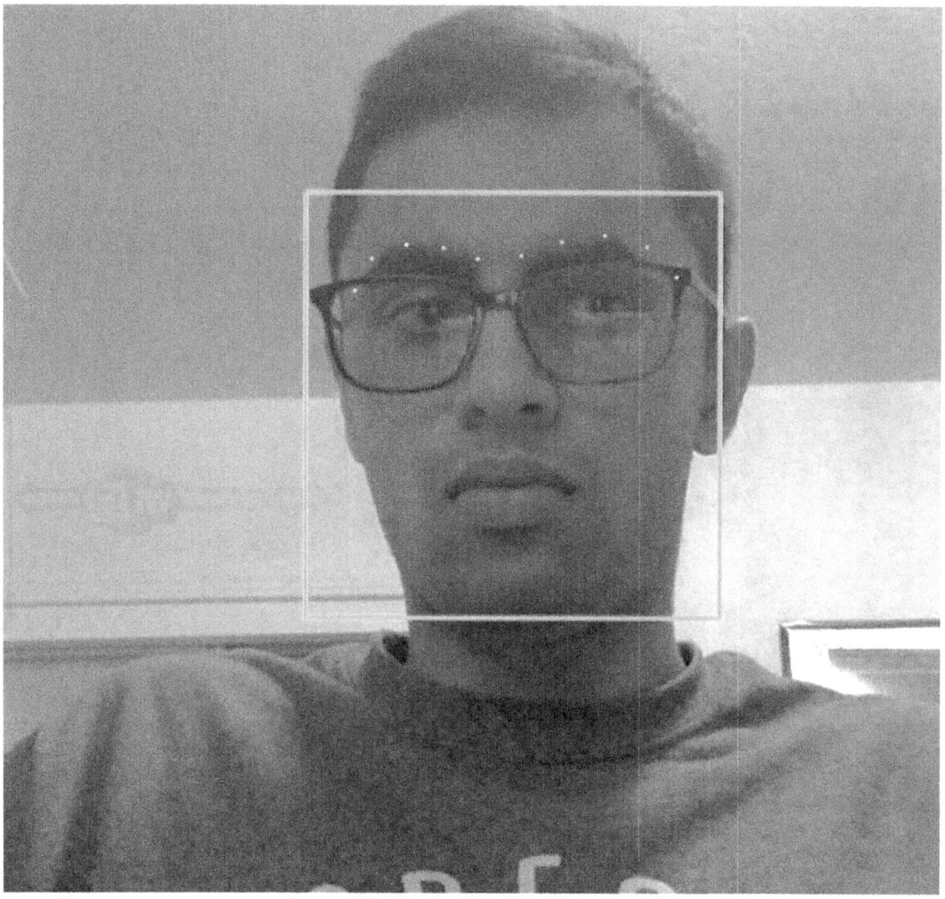

ENGINEERING NOTEBOOK

The Engineering Notebook is a key that judges use to decide team advancement. You should maintain a clear and concise history of all your experimentation, prototypes and observations in the engineering notebook. You should update it at every meeting and make sure you have sections for all aspects of the competition. This includes Outreach, Sponsors, and the Robot Game.

OUTREACH AND SPONSORS

Gracious professionalism, Community and Sponsors

Education is for improving the lives of others and for leaving your community and world better than you found it.
—Marian Wright Edelman

COre values are equally important in FTC competitions. Outreach and sponsors are equally important considerations along with the robot game in the full judging process.

Gracious Professionalism: You should always show Gracious Professionalism throughout the season and during the tournaments.

- Be strong competitors, but also treat one another with respect and kindness in the process.
- Avoid leaving anyone feeling as if they are left out or unappreciated
- Always blend knowledge, pride and empathy.

Outreach: Build the FIRST community by introducing more young people to the experience, and share STEM concepts with the world. Outreach events include activities to encourage students and mentors to join existing robotics teams or to start new teams, as well as to raise awareness of robotics in general.

Sponsors: The cost of the FTC season can be met through grants and contributions from parents but getting sponsors to help instills a business sense in teams. By marketing your team and its achievements, the team will be able to alleviate some of their costs and learn valuable life skills in the process. The costs of FTC are drastically higher than the costs to participate in FLL.

GAME TIME

Strategy

Strategy is about making choices, trade-offs; it's about deliberately choosing to be different.
-Michael Porter

Strategy is what will set you apart. Other teams will also have great robot designs, outreach events, and sponsors but whoever uses their skills and resources more efficiently will win. A strategy during robot games is necessary to win. On tournament day you will be randomly paired with other teams to form alliances. Your team and another team might be alliance partners for one match and compete with each other in another match. Knowing the strengths of the other team's robot, negotiating with others, and coming up with a game strategy for a particular match will win you the tournament.

TYPES OF TOURNAMENTS

1-Scrimmages
2-Qualifiers
3-Regionals
4-Super-Regional
5- World championship

TOURNAMENT DAY

On tournament day you will be given a schedule for your judging session as well as your matches for the day. This is shown in the next picture.

In your matches the red alliance will compete with the blue alliance. The score for every match will be summed to come up with the Qualifying points cumulative score and Ranking points cumulative score.

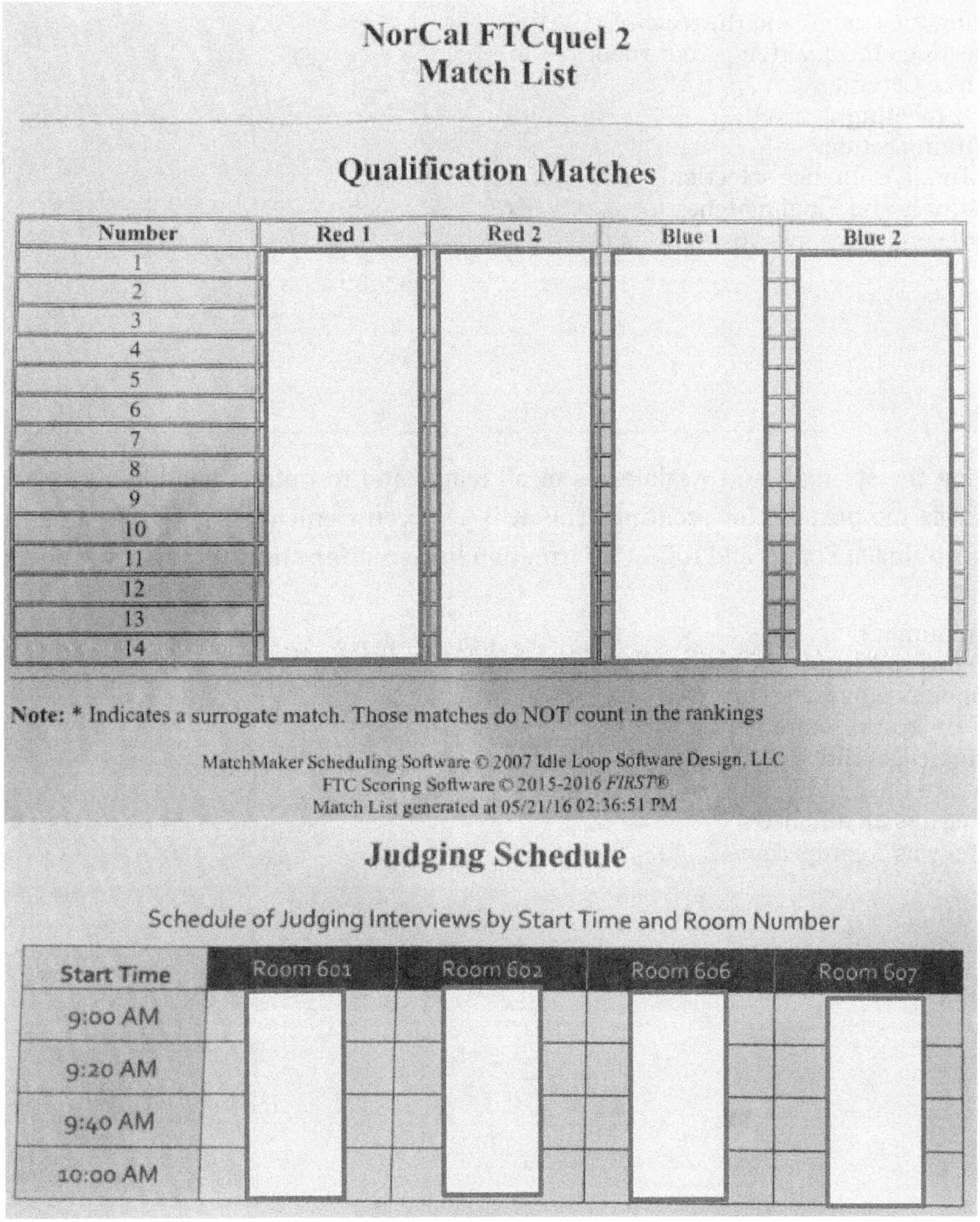

NorCal FTCquel 2
Match List

Qualification Matches

Number	Red 1	Red 2	Blue 1	Blue 2
1				
2				
3				
4				
5				
6				
7				
8				
9				
10				
11				
12				
13				
14				

Note: * Indicates a surrogate match. Those matches do NOT count in the rankings

MatchMaker Scheduling Software © 2007 Idle Loop Software Design, LLC
FTC Scoring Software © 2015-2016 *FIRST*®
Match List generated at 05/21/16 02:36:51 PM

Judging Schedule

Schedule of Judging Interviews by Start Time and Room Number

Start Time	Room 601	Room 602	Room 606	Room 607
9:00 AM				
9:20 AM				
9:40 AM				
10:00 AM				

(Definitions can be found on the FIRST website)

After the qualifying matches are over the semifinals and final matches will be held on same day. During semifinals and finals, the top few teams are allowed to select an alliance team from all other teams present. The team selecting the alliance team are designated as alliance captain. Having a good strategy and scouting significantly helps in making these decisions in the finals and semifinals.

The following are the activities that you will do during the tournament.

1. Registration to get qualification matches and judging schedule
2. Setup your robot at the designated table and display your 'Outreach' and 'Design' posters. Robot pits will allow you to service and charge your robot.
3. Judging for Design and Outreach.
4. Inspections for qualifying your robot.
5. Opening Ceremony.
6. Driver meeting.
7. Qualifying rounds.
8. Semifinalist Alliance selection.
9. Semifinals and Final matches.
10. Award ceremony and closing.

SCOUTING

Understanding the strength and weaknesses of all teams and forming a bond between your team and another team is the purpose for scouting. This will help you tremendously during alliance selections, semifinals, and finals. You should collect information in a scouting sheet that may include the following elements.

1. Team number
2. Team overall score
3. Autonomous overall score
4. Tele-op overall score
5. Scoring capability
6. What are the complimentary capabilities?
7. Strategy as an alliance
8. Strategy as a competitor.

INDEX

Made in the USA
Monee, IL
05 November 2026

67380872R00155